Basic Contract Law
for Paralegals

PARALEGAL SERIES

Basic Contract Law for Paralegals

Ninth Edition

Hon. Jeffrey A. Helewitz

Special Referee, New York State Supreme Court

Wolters Kluwer

Published by Wolters Kluwer in New York.

Wolters Kluwer Legal & Regulatory U.S. serves customers worldwide with CCH, Aspen Publishers, and Kluwer Law International products. (www.WKLegaledu.com)

To contact Customer Service, e-mail customer.service@wolterskluwer.com, call 1-800-234-1660, fax 1-800-901-9075, or mail correspondence to:

Wolters Kluwer
Attn: Order Department
PO Box 990
Frederick, MD 21705

Printed in the United States of America.

1 2 3 4 5 6 7 8 9 0

ISBN 978-1-4548-9628-9

Library of Congress Cataloging-in-Publication Data

Names: Helewitz, Jeffrey A., author.
Title: Basic contract law for paralegals / Hon. Jeffrey A. Helewitz, Special
    Referee, New York State Supreme Court.
Description: Ninth edition. | New York : Wolters Kluwer, [2018] | Series:
    Aspen college series | Includes index.
Identifiers: LCCN 2018024799 | ISBN 9781454896289
Subjects: LCSH: Contracts—United States. | Legal assistants—United
    States—Handbooks, manuals, etc.
Classification: LCC KF801.Z9 H36 2018 | DDC 346.7302—dc23
LC record available at https://lccn.loc.gov/2018024799

About Wolters Kluwer Legal & Regulatory U.S.

Wolters Kluwer Legal & Regulatory U.S. delivers expert content and solutions in the areas of law, corporate compliance, health compliance, reimbursement, and legal education. Its practical solutions help customers successfully navigate the demands of a changing environment to drive their daily activities, enhance decision quality and inspire confident outcomes.

Serving customers worldwide, its legal and regulatory portfolio includes products under the Aspen Publishers, CCH Incorporated, Kluwer Law International, ftwilliam.com, and MediRegs names. They are regarded as exceptional and trusted resources for general legal and practice-specific knowledge, compliance and risk management, dynamic workflow solutions, and expert commentary.

To Sarah—my first, and best, teacher

Summary of Contents

Contents	*xi*
Acknowledgments	*xxi*
Introduction	*xxiii*

Chapter 1	Overview of Contracts	1
Chapter 2	Offer	29
Chapter 3	Acceptance	59
Chapter 4	Consideration	83
Chapter 5	Legality of Subject Matter and Contractual Capacity	109
Chapter 6	Contractual Intent	127
Chapter 7	Contract Provisions	145
Chapter 8	The Uniform Commercial Code	171
Chapter 9	Third Party Contracts	211
Chapter 10	Discharge of Obligations	237
Chapter 11	Remedies	263
Chapter 12	Drafting Simple Contracts and Proving Their Terms in Court	295

Appendix A	Sample Contracts	325
	Antenuptial Agreement (Simple Form)	326
	Consulting Agreement	327
	Employment Contract (Simple Form)	329
	Employment Contract	331
	Equipment Lease Agreement	336
	General Partnership Agreement (Simple Form)	341
	Limited Partnership Agreement	343
	Real Estate Lease	362
	Retainer Agreement	363

Shareholders Agreement   370
Subscription Agreement (Limited Partnership)   378
Work for Hire Agreement   381

Appendix B   Supplemental Cases   383
    Don King Productions, Inc. v. Douglas   383
    Matter of Baby M   388
    Hong v. Marriott Corp.   398
    In re Peregrine Entertainment, Ltd.   402

Appendix C   Answers to the Quick Quizzes   413

Glossary   415
Index   423

Contents

Acknowledgments   *xxi*
Introduction   *xxiii*

Chapter 1
OVERVIEW OF CONTRACTS   1

Learning Objectives   1
Chapter Overview   1
Contract Defined   2
Basic Contract Requirements   2
    Offer   3
    Acceptance   3
    Consideration   4
    Legality of Subject Matter   4
    Contractual Capacity   5
    Contractual Intent   5
Classification of Contracts   6
    Type of Obligation: Bilateral or Unilateral   6
    Method of Creation: Express, Implied, or Quasi-Contracts   7
    Type of Form: Formal and Informal Contracts   9
    Timing: Executory and Executed Contracts   10
    Enforceability: Valid, Void, Voidable, and Unenforceable 11
Sample Clauses   12
Chapter Summary   14
Synopsis   15
Key Terms   15
Exercises   16
Cases for Analysis   16

         Casale v. Nationwide Children's Hosp.   17
         Questions   24
         McCabe v. ConAgra Foods, Inc.   25
         Questions   26
Suggested Case References   27
         Ethical Considerations   27

Chapter 2
OFFER   29

Learning Objectives   29
Chapter Overview   29
Offer Defined   30
         Present Contractual Intent   31
         Communication to the Offeree   32
         Certainty and Definiteness in the Terms of the Offer   33
Essential Terms of an Offer   34
         Price   34
         Subject Matter   36
         Parties   38
         Time of Performance   39
         Two Related Concepts   40
Sample Offers   42
Chapter Summary   43
Synopsis   43
Key Terms   44
Exercises   44
Cases for Analysis   44
         Lopez v. Charles Schwab & Co., Inc.   44
         Questions   51
         Phil Watkins, P.C. v. The Krist Law Firm, P.C.   52
         Questions   56
Suggested Case References   57
         Ethical Considerations   57

Chapter 3
ACCEPTANCE   59

Learning Objectives   59
Chapter Overview   59
Acceptance Defined   60
         Varying the Terms of the Offer   60
         Silence as Acceptance   62

Who May Accept   63
Method of Acceptance   64
    Acceptance of a Bilateral Contract   64
        Mailbox Rule   65
    Rejection of a Bilateral Contract   66
        Rejection and the Mailbox Rule   66
    Acceptance of a Unilateral Contract   67
Termination of the Ability to Accept   68
    Revocation of Bilateral Contracts   69
    Revocation of Unilateral Contracts   70
    Termination by Operation of Law   71
    Effect of Termination of Offer   72
Sample Clauses   72
Chapter Summary   72
Synopsis   73
Key Terms   74
Exercises   75
Cases for Analysis   75
    United States v. Lauckner   75
    Questions   77
    Monsour's, Inc. v. Menu Maker Foods, Inc.   78
    Questions   81
Suggested Case References   81
    Ethical Considerations   81

Chapter 4
CONSIDERATION   83

Learning Objectives   83
Chapter Overview   83
Consideration Defined   84
    Benefit Conferred   84
    Detriment Incurred   85
What Is Not Consideration   86
Sufficiency of the Consideration   89
Promissory Estoppel   91
Special Agreements   92
    Accord and Satisfaction   92
    Charitable Subscription   93
    Debtor's Promises   94
    Guarantees   94
    Formal Contracts   95
Sample Clauses   96
Chapter Summary   96
Synopsis   97
Key Terms   98

Exercises   98
Cases for Analysis   99
    Yerkovich v. AAA   *99*
    Questions   103
    Mass. Eye & Ear Infirmary v. Eugene B. Casey Found.   103
    Questions   107
Suggested Case References   107
    Ethical Considerations   107

Chapter 5
LEGALITY OF SUBJECT MATTER AND
CONTRACTUAL CAPACITY   109

Learning Objectives   109
Chapter Overview   109
Legality of the Subject Matter   110
    Malum in Se   *110*
    Malum Prohibitum   *111*
Contractual Capacity   114
    Age   114
    Mental Capacity   116
    Alcohol and Drugs   116
Chapter Summary   117
Synopsis   118
Key Terms   118
Exercises   118
Cases for Analysis   119
    First Colony Insurance Company v. Alfred Kreppein, et al.   *119*
    Questions   122
    Achee Holdings, LLC v. Silver Hill Financial, LLC   *122*
    Questions   124
Suggested Case References   124
    Ethical Considerations   124

Chapter 6
CONTRACTUAL INTENT   127

Learning Objectives   127
Chapter Overview   127
Contractual Intent Defined   128
Fraud and Misrepresentation   129
Duress   130
Mistake   133
Chapter Summary   135

Synopsis   136
Key Terms   136
Exercises   136
Cases for Analysis   137
       Schulte v. Harvey   *137*
       Questions   139
       Levey v. CitiMortgage, Inc.   *139*
       Questions   142
Suggested Case References   143
       Ethical Considerations   143

Chapter 7
CONTRACT PROVISIONS   145

Learning Objectives   145
Chapter Overview   146
The Statute of Frauds   146
    Contracts for an Interest in Real Estate   147
    Contracts in Consideration of Marriage   148
    Contracts Not to Be Performed Within One Year   149
    Guarantees   151
    Contracts for the Sale of Goods   151
    Executor's Promise to Pay Decedent's Debts   151
    What the Statute of Frauds Is Not   152
Covenants   152
Conditions   153
    Conditions Precedent   154
    Conditions Subsequent   154
    Conditions Concurrent   155
    Express Conditions   155
    Implied-in-Fact Conditions   156
    Implied-in-Law Conditions   156
Court Doctrines: Rules of Construction and the Parol Evidence Rule   157
Sample Clauses   159
Chapter Summary   160
Synopsis   161
Key Terms   161
Exercises   162
Cases for Analysis   162
       Estate of Church v. Tubbs   *163*
       Questions   167
       Eastern Baby Stores, Inc. v. Central Mutual Insurance
          Company   *167*
       Questions   169
Suggested Case References   169
       Ethical Considerations   170

Chapter 8
THE UNIFORM COMMERCIAL CODE   **171**

Learning Objectives   171
Chapter Overview   172
General Background   172
Article I, General Provisions   173
    Basic Guidelines   173
        Law of the State Applies   174
        Parties May Agree to Vary UCC Provisions   174
        UCC Provisions Are to Be Liberally Construed   174
    Obligations Imposed by Article I   175
Article II, Sales   176
    General Background   176
    Types of Contracts Covered by Article II   177
        Goods   177
        Leases   179
        Contracts for the Sale of Goods Between Merchants   179
    Contractual Provisions   181
        Warranties   181
    Risk of Loss   183
    Remedies   185
        Remedies Available to Seller   186
        Remedies Available to Buyer   187
        Written Assurances   188
        Summary   188
Article II-A, Leases   189
Article IX, Secured Transactions   190
    Secured Transaction Defined   190
    Requirements to Create a Security Interest   191
    Priorities   195
Sample Clauses   196
Chapter Summary   197
Synopsis   198
Key Terms   199
Exercises   200
Cases for Analysis   200
        Jacq Wilson et al. v. Brawn of California, Inc.   201
        Questions   206
        Demarco California Fabrics, Inc. v. Nygard
            International, Ltd.   206
        Questions   209
Suggested Case References   209
        Ethical Considerations   209

Chapter 9
THIRD PARTY CONTRACTS   **211**

Learning Objectives   211
Chapter Overview   211
Third Party Beneficiary Contracts: Generally   212
Third Party Creditor Beneficiary Contracts   215
Third Party Donee Beneficiary Contracts   218
Assignment   220
    Creating the Assignment   220
    Consent of the Promisor   222
    Effect of Assignment   223
    Multiple Assignees   225
Delegation   226
Sample Clauses   228
Chapter Summary   229
Synopsis   230
Key Terms   230
Exercises   231
Cases for Analysis   231
    Delta Mech., Inc. v. Garden City Grp., Inc.   231
    Questions   233
    Bay Corrugated Container, Incorporated v. Gould,
      Incorporated   233
    Questions   235
Suggested Case References   235
    Ethical Considerations   235

Chapter 10
DISCHARGE OF OBLIGATIONS   **237**

Learning Objectives   237
Chapter Overview   237
Methods of Discharge   238
    Excuse of Conditions   239
    Performance   242
    Breach of Contract   243
    Agreement of the Parties   245
    Impossibility of Performance/Impracticability of Performance   247
    Supervening Illegality   248
    Death of the Parties or Destruction of the Subject Matter   248
    Frustration of Purpose   249
Sample Clauses   250
Chapter Summary   251

Synopsis   251
Key Terms   252
Exercises   253
Cases for Analysis   253
      Felt v. McCarthy   253
      Questions   257
      Club Factorage, LLC v. Wood Duck Hiding, LLC   257
      Questions   261
Suggested Case References   261
      Ethical Considerations   262

Chapter 11
REMEDIES   263

Learning Objectives   263
Chapter Overview   263
Legal Remedies   264
    Compensatory Damages   265
    Punitive Damages   266
    Consequential Damages   267
    Liquidated Damages   268
Equitable Remedies   270
    Injunction   270
    Specific Performance   271
    Rescission and Restitution   271
    Reformation   272
    Quasi-Contractual Remedies   273
    Quantum Meruit   273
    Quantum Valebant   273
    Waivers and Their Effect   274
Arbitration Provisions   275
Sample Clauses   275
Chapter Summary   276
Synopsis   277
Key Terms   277
Exercises   278
Cases for Analysis   278
      Pioneer Exploration, Ltd. v. Rutherford   279
      Questions   285
      Fazio v. Cypress/GR Houston I, L.P.   285
      Questions   293
Suggested Case References   293
      Ethical Considerations   293

Chapter 12
DRAFTING SIMPLE CONTRACTS AND PROVING
THEIR TERMS IN COURT   295

Learning Objectives   295
Chapter Overview   295
Checklist of Clauses   297
    Description of the Parties   297
    Description of the Consideration   298
    Security Agreement   300
    Warranties   301
    Title   301
    Risk of Loss   302
    Waivers   302
    Assignments   303
    Delegation   303
    Terminology   303
    Special Provisions and Clauses   304
        Covenant Not to Compete   304
        Duties   304
        Pronouns   304
        Severability   305
        Successors   305
        Time of the Essence   305
        Trade Secrets   305
        Work Product   305
    Duration and Termination   305
    Notice of Default   306
    Remedies   306
    Choice of Law   307
    Arbitration   307
    Submission to Jurisdiction   308
    Signatures   308
Proving Contractual Terms   308
    Admitting a Contract into Evidence   309
    Determining the Validity of a Contract   312
    Analysis of a Contract's Terms   312
Chapter Summary   314
Key Terms   314
Exercises   315
Cases for Analysis   316
    Specialty Rental Tools & Supply, L.P. v. Shoemaker   317
    Questions   320
    American Express Travel Related Services, Inc. v. Weppler   320
    Questions   322
Suggested Case References   322
    Ethical Considerations   323

Appendix A
SAMPLE CONTRACTS   325

Antenuptial Agreement (Simple Form)   326
Consulting Agreement   327
Employment Contract (Simple Form)   329
Employment Contract   331
Equipment Lease Agreement   336
General Partnership Agreement (Simple Form)   341
Limited Partnership Agreement   343
Real Estate Lease   362
Retainer Agreement   363
Shareholders Agreement   370
Subscription Agreement (Limited Partnership)   378
Work for Hire Agreement   381

Appendix B
SUPPLEMENTAL CASES   383

Don King Productions, Inc. v. Douglas   383
Matter of Baby M   388
Hong v. Marriott Corp.   398
In re Peregrine Entertainment, Ltd.   402

Appendix C
ANSWERS TO THE QUICK QUIZZES   413

Glossary   415
Index   423

Acknowledgments

I wish to thank all of the people at Wolters Kluwer who worked on this edition, especially Nicholas T. Lasoff, Kelly Hussey, David Herzig, and Joe Terry. In addition, I would like to thank Susan McClung, Patrick Cline, and Nick Walther for their part in the production of this book.

Introduction

This book provides the paralegal student and practitioner with a quick, simple, and straightforward text on the law of contracts. It helps to clarify this very complex area of law using numerous practical examples of how to draft and interpret different types of contracts. This book is not intended to discuss every nuance of contract law, nor is it designed as a casebook for law students. *Basic Contract Law for Paralegals* is meant to be an easy-to-use, readable reference tool for the legal assistant.

The reader should be aware of the fact that there are two legal sources of law with respect to contract formation and interpretation. The first, and traditional source, is the common law, that law that has developed over the centuries based on judicial precedent (and sometimes codified by specific state statute). The second source of contract law is the Uniform Commercial Code (UCC), a form of which has been adopted by every jurisdiction in the country. The UCC regulates contracts for the sale of goods and contracts between merchants. Contracts for services or between nonmerchants are still governed by the common law. Throughout the text, the distinction between these two sources, whenever significant, will be specifically addressed.

The most important aspect of all laws is the relationship between the parties in dispute. The law is primarily concerned with relationships between and among individuals. In contract law, the value of the contract in monetary terms is of secondary importance; the relationship between the contracting parties is the most important determining factor. The simple contract for the sale of a morning newspaper and the multipage document for the development of a $20 million shopping center both involve identical legal principles. Because the law is concerned with principles and relationships, the logical starting point for the analysis of any legal problem is the legal relationship of the parties.

The most common problem encountered in analyzing a legal situation is that everyone immediately wants to jump to the end result—"What can I get?"—rather than discerning the actual rights and liabilities of the parties. It is more important to identify each element of the relationship to determine whether or not a legal dispute exists.

Contracts is only one area of law that defines particular relations between persons; it is not the exclusive area of law applicable to a given situation. To determine a person's rights and liabilities, first you must determine what area of law—for instance, contracts, torts, bankruptcy— best applies to the problem. Then you must determine that all of the requisite elements of the legal relationship, as defined by that area of the law, exist. You cannot bend the law to fit the facts; if the facts do not fit into a particular legal theory, that theory is incorrect and a new one must be found. Keeping this general principle in mind will help in your analysis of all legal problems.

The role of the paralegal with respect to contracts is multidimensional. A paralegal is often called on to draft the initial agreement for the client and, as negotiations develop, to see that all subsequent changes are incorporated into the document. If a problem arises, the paralegal is generally responsible for making the initial analysis of the contract in dispute to determine all potential rights and liabilities of the client. And finally, the legal assistant will work with the attorney to determine the appropriate remedies available to the client. To perform these tasks, the legal assistant must be conversant with all of the elements of basic contract law and drafting.

Basic Contract Law
for Paralegals

1 Overview of Contracts

Learning Objectives

After studying this chapter, you will be able to:

- Define a legally binding contract
- Identify the six basic requirements to forming a valid contract
- Explain the concept of offer and acceptance
- Define and exemplify "consideration"
- Classify contracts into bilateral or unilateral agreements
- Understand how a contract is created
- Explain the difference between executory and executed contracts
- Differentiate between valid, void, voidable, and unenforceable contracts
- Discuss various contractual provisions
- Know what is meant by the term "contractual capacity"

CHAPTER OVERVIEW

This chapter discusses the six basic requirements for every valid contract and then indicates the various classifications into which all contracts fall. The chapter is intended to give a general overview of, and introduction to, contract law. The specific details involved in analyzing contractual situations are covered in the following 11 chapters.

The law of contracts is one of the most complex and important areas of substantive law taught in law school. Every law school in the country teaches contracts as part of the first year of required courses because, more than any other course of law, contracts affect everyone's daily existence.

Think of everything that you do each day: You wake up in your home, brush your teeth, dress, eat breakfast, read the morning newspaper, and travel to work or to school. Each of these activities involves contract law. Rent or mortgage payments involve a contract with a landlord or lender; brushing your teeth requires the purchase of a toothbrush and toothpaste; getting dressed is accomplished only after buying the clothes worn; buying the newspaper is a simple sales transaction; and even taking public transportation involves a contract with the municipality. Every aspect of normal life is dominated by contractual principles, but few people realize the extent to which they are, in fact, contracting parties. To the nonlaw professional, a contract is a long and complicated legal document that is drafted by an attorney and involves huge sums of money. Yet, in reality, most contracts involve little, if any, written documentation, no lawyer, and only small amounts of money (if money is involved at all). It is this all-pervasive element of contracts that makes contract law both interesting and challenging.

Contract Defined

A **contract** is a legally enforceable agreement that meets certain specified legal requirements between two or more parties, in which each party agrees to give and receive something of legal value. It is distinguishable from a gift, in that each party gives and receives something. In a gift situation, only one party gives; the other one receives. Also, a contract is more than just an agreement. An agreement may not meet all of the specific requirements needed to create a contract; hence, it will not be legally enforceable under a contractual claim.

Basic Contract Requirements

To determine whether a contractual relationship exists between two persons, it is necessary to ascertain that all six of the requisite elements of a valid contract exist. If *all* of these elements are not present, the parties do not have a contractual relationship (although they may have a relationship described by some other theory of law, which, if true, then would have to be addressed). Even if all of the elements are present in the agreement, the contract may be unenforceable because of some other statutory reason, such as the Statute of Frauds or the Statute of Limitations.

The six requisite elements of every valid contract are:

1. offer;
2. acceptance;
3. consideration;
4. legality of subject matter;
5. contractual capacity; and
6. contractual intent.

Offer

An **offer** is a proposal by one party to another manifesting an intention to enter into a valid contract. Every valid contractual relationship starts with an offer.

 EXAMPLE:

One student asks another, "Will you buy my used Contracts book for $5?" The student has stated a proposal to sell a particular object (the used book) at a particular price ($5). Without this initial proposition, the two students could not possibly develop a contractual relationship.

The offer defines the boundaries of the potential relationship between the parties and empowers the other party to create the contract by accepting the proposition.

Acceptance

To create the contract, the party to whom the offer is made must **accept** the proposal. If she does not, then no contract comes into existence. The law will not force a person to fulfill an obligation to which she or he has not agreed.

 EXAMPLE:

The paralegal student in the example above says "OK, I'll take the book." In this case, a contract has been created because the student has agreed to the proposal of the seller.

The concepts of offer and acceptance go hand in hand in determining whether a contract exists. The offer and acceptance together form the **mutual assent** of the parties—the agreement that they do intend to be contractually bound to each other. Without this meeting of the minds, no matter what else may exist, there is no valid contract.

Consideration

Consideration is the subject matter of the contract; it is the thing for which the parties have bargained. Most people assume consideration to be the price, but that is not completely accurate. Although money may be part of the bargain, it is not always the complete bargain. Nor is money itself always necessary. The crucial aspect of consideration is that each party both gives and receives consideration. Each must give something of value.

EXAMPLE:

In the example given above, the consideration is both the $5 and the book itself. The seller is bargaining for the money; the buyer is bargaining for the book.

Consideration is deemed to be anything of legally significant value—monetary worth is not the ultimate determining factor of legal value.

EXAMPLE:

In the example above, instead of asking for $5, the student says "Will you exchange your used Torts book for my used Contracts book?" If the second student agrees, a contract is formed. In this instance, the books themselves are the consideration—no money changes hands.

These first three elements—offer, acceptance, and consideration—are the three most important aspects of every valid contract because they form the provisions of the contract itself. Without these three components, there can be no contract.

Legality of Subject Matter

To be valid, a contract can only be formed for a legal purpose and must fulfil any statutory regulations with respect to form.

EXAMPLE:

Acme, Inc., a major producer of automobile tires, enters into an agreement with Goodyear to run Dunlop out of business by fixing prices. Although this contract may meet all of the other contractual requirements, it is not enforceable because it violates U.S. antitrust laws. This contract is not formed for a legal purpose.

Contractual Capacity

Contractual capacity refers to the ability of a person to enter into a valid contract. The most typical examples of capacity (or rather, the lack of capacity) deal with the age of the party and the person's mental condition.

EXAMPLE:

John, a precocious 14-year-old, wants to buy some woodland for potential real estate development. Although it may be a good idea and may possibly bring in millions of dollars, the law considers a 14-year-old incapable of entering into a contract. His age and presumed lack of experience make him contractually incapable.

Contractual Intent

Contractual intent is the last of the requisite elements of a valid contract, but the one that is all-pervasive. Even if the contract meets all of the other requirements enumerated above, if it can be shown that the parties did not subjectively intend to form a contractual relationship, there will be no contract. Many times, this aspect of intent is not readily discernible by the words of the parties themselves, and surrounding circumstances must be analyzed to determine whether a contract exists.

EXAMPLES:

1. Kevin agrees to sell Bruce his house for $50,000. The contract is in writing, describes the house, and specifies the method and terms of payment. On the face of it, the contract appears valid. But what if it were shown that Kevin was forced to sign the contract at gunpoint? Under these circumstances, Kevin obviously did not willingly intend to enter into the contractual relationship with Bruce.

2. William agrees to pay Sally $500 a week to be his housekeeper. Once again, on its face, this appears to be a valid contract. However, what if William were 85 years old, and Sally had convinced him that none of his relations wanted anything to do with him? She also told him that if he didn't hire her, he'd be all alone and helpless. Under these circumstances, it would appear that William was the victim of mental coercion. Consequently, his intent to enter the contract of his own free will is suspect.

The abovementioned six elements must exist if there is to be a valid contract. Each of these elements will be discussed in detail in the following chapters. The foregoing is intended only as a general overview. However, it is necessary to keep all six of these elements in mind when discussing contracts because each one is necessarily intertwined, regardless of the type of contract created.

Classification of Contracts

All contracts fall into a certain number of classifications, or types. Generally, it is a good idea to classify the contract in question prior to analyzing its validity and provisions. This classification process is like making selections from a restaurant menu. Take one item from each category, and when completed, a meal (that is, a contract) is formed.

Type of Obligation: Bilateral or Unilateral

The type of obligation refers to the kind of duty imposed on the parties to the contract. This category defines every contract as belonging to one of two classifications.

All contracts are either **bilateral** or **unilateral.** A bilateral contract is a promise for a promise. A unilateral contract is a promise for an act. This division into bilateral or unilateral is important with respect to what performance is expected from the parties and at what point the contract comes into existence. With a bilateral contract, the parties are expecting a mutual exchange of promises, with the performance to be carried out only after the promises have been given. Most contracts are bilateral, even though it is rare that the parties actually use the word "promise" (except in the most formal of situations).

EXAMPLE:

In the situation discussed above, with respect to the sale of the used textbook, the actual words used were "Will you buy my used Contracts book for $5?" "OK." These words created a bilateral contract. What the parties legally said were: "Will you promise to pay me $5 if I promise to sell you my used Contracts book?" "I promise to pay you $5 if you promise to sell me your used Contracts book." The contract was created when the promises were given. The performance—the exchange of the book for the money—is intended to take place *after* the agreement has been made.

Conversely, in a unilateral contract, the contract is only created when one side has performed a requested act. Instead of an exchange of mutual promises, a unilateral contract is an exchange of a promise for an act.

EXAMPLE:

Allison promises to pay Tim $1,500 if Tim paints her apartment on Wednesday. In this instance, Allison is requesting a specific act: Tim's painting the apartment on Wednesday. Allison does not want Tim's promise that he will do the painting; she wants to see the job done. Until Wednesday arrives, and Tim actually paints the apartment, no contract exists. When Tim does the painting, Allison must fulfill her promise to pay him $1,500.

There tends to be a lot of confusion in identifying a contract as bilateral or unilateral, simply because most ordinary contracts are formed and completed simultaneously. Consequently, it is difficult to distinguish between the promise and the act. This determination is crucial, however, because it times the start of the contractual relationship. If the contract is bilateral, the relationship is formed at the exchange of promises. The parties are entitled to contractual remedies if one side does not fulfill his promise. (This is the "What can I get?" as discussed in the Introduction.) On the other hand, if the contract is unilateral, the contractual relationship is only formed when one side actually performs the requested act. Until that time, no contractual remedies are available to the parties. If, in the example above, Tim does not paint the apartment on Wednesday, Allison has no recourse to sue him because he is under no contractual obligation.

To determine whether a contract is bilateral or unilateral, it is necessary to determine the intent and the specified wishes of the parties involved. Courts will generally go along with what the parties could most reasonably expect under the circumstances because that would indicate the true meeting of the parties' minds with respect to the manner of acceptance sought. Note that the law is generally pro-contract; that is, it favors contractual relationships and consequently presumes contracts to be bilateral. This creates the contractual relationship sooner than in a unilateral contractual situation.

Method of Creation: Express, Implied, or Quasi-Contracts

How does a contract come into existence? A contract is formed either by the words or conduct of the parties and is classified accordingly.

An **express** contract is one in which the mutual assent of the parties is manifested in words, either orally or in writing. An **implied-in-fact** contract is one in which the promises of the parties are inferred from their actions or conduct as opposed to specific words being used.

EXAMPLES:

1. Eric leases a house from Lisa. The parties use a standardized written lease purchased at a stationery store. This is an express contract because the rights and obligations of the parties are described in written words.

2. In the previous example of the sale of the used Contracts book, the parties have entered into an express contract. Their promises are given orally.

3. Louise goes to a newsstand to buy her morning paper. She picks up the paper and gives the news agent 50 cents. Louise and the news agent have completed an implied-in-fact contract. The contract was entered into by their actions, and no words were used or necessary.

In addition to express and implied-in-fact contracts, the law has also created another category known as **implied-in-law**, or **quasi-contracts**. As the term "quasi" might indicate, these are situations that look like contracts, but, in truth, are not contracts because one of the requisite elements is missing. However, in the interest of fairness, the law has determined that a party should be entitled to some remedy if injured by such a situation.

Whenever the words ""quasi" or "estoppel" are used, terms that will be discussed in subsequent chapters, the court is using its equitable jurisdiction. The difference between law and equity is basically the difference between justice and mercy. There are times and situations in which the legal result might be "just" under the laws of society—that is, reasonable under the circumstances—but it would not be "fair"—a party would be injured without recourse. In these situations, the concept of **equity** takes over. Equity was designed to right wrongs, to prevent unfairness and unjust enrichment. Equity was created specifically for those situations in which the application of the law would result in an injured party still suffering. For a more complete discussion of the equity courts, see Chapter 11, "Remedies."

With respect to the classification of contracts, the courts have created the concept of quasi-contractual situations—situations in which the parties do not have a contractual relationship, but in which it would be most fair to treat them as though a contract did exist. For a quasi-contractual situation to arise, it must be shown that one party unjustly benefited from the other party under circumstances in which a mutual benefit had been expected.

 EXAMPLES:

1. Joan has just completed her paralegal training, but before she starts work, she receives a telephone call from her elderly aunt in the Midwest. Her aunt tells Joan that she is very ill, not long for this world, and needs someone to take care of her. The aunt promises Joan that if Joan comes to the Midwest and looks after her, she'll remember Joan in her will.

Based on the foregoing, Joan moves to the Midwest, and for the next ten years cooks, cleans, and takes care of her aunt. When her aunt finally dies, Joan is simply "remembered fondly" in the aunt's will. All the aunt's cash goes to her cat, Fluffy.

Can Joan sue the estate for breach of contract? No. Why? Because no contract existed—the aunt merely said she would remember Joan in the will—there was no mutual benefit, and no consideration given to Joan, despite what Joan might have hoped for.

In this instance, the court will probably apply the doctrine of quasi-contract and permit Joan to recover the value of the services she provided for the aunt. Because Joan never intended to make a gift of her services to her aunt, if the aunt received them without compensating Joan, the aunt would be unjustly enriched. This would be unfair to Joan.

2. Sal opens the door to his house one morning and discovers a newspaper on his doorstep. He picks it up and takes it to work with him. For the next week, every morning a newspaper appears at his door. At the end of the week, Sal receives a bill from the publisher for the newspapers.

Does Sal have a contract with the publisher? No. However, the court, applying the doctrine of quasi-contract, will permit the publisher to recover the cost of the papers. Sal accepted the benefit of the papers by taking them and reading them, and now must pay. If Sal did not want the papers, it was his responsibility to contact the publisher to stop delivery.

Note that there are laws that would make the outcome different if the U.S. mail were used to deliver the goods. Several years ago, a statute was enacted stating that if the mail is used to send unsolicited merchandise, the recipient may keep the merchandise as a gift. Also, many states have consumer protection laws prohibiting the delivery of unsolicited goods.

To apply the concept of quasi-contract, it must be shown that no contract exists because a requisite element is missing, and one party is unjustly enriched at the expense of the other.

Type of Form: Formal and Informal Contracts

A **formal** contract is a contract that, historically, was written and signed under seal. The concept derives from a time when few people could read or write, and the solemnity of a seal gave importance to a document. The seal was used as the consideration for the agreement. Nowadays, seals are no longer used, and this term refers to a limited group of contracts that different states have declared valid and enforceable if certain statutory requirements are met. Some examples of formal contracts are negotiable instruments (such as checks and certificates of deposit) and guarantees.

EXAMPLE:

Fidelity Bank issues printed checks to its customers, which the customers use to pay their bills. These checks do not contain the words and elements of a contract, but they are enforced as a formal contract because of statutory regulations. The contract is between the bank and its customers.

Informal contracts are, simply put, all nonformal contracts. Despite the terminology, informal contracts are agreements that meet all the requirements of valid contracts; they can be quite specific and stylized in and of themselves.

EXAMPLE:

The contract for the sale of the used Contracts book is an example of an informal contract. All the contractual requirements are present, and its form is not regulated by a statute.

Timing: Executory and Executed Contracts

One of the most crucial questions for the parties to a contract involves the timing: "*When* are the contractual obligations to be performed?" This timing element indicates when the parties have enforceable rights and obligations. Contracts are categorized by indicating whether or not the parties have uncompleted duties to carry out. An **executory** contract is a contract in which one or both of the parties still have obligations to perform. An **executed** contract is complete and final with respect to all of its terms and conditions.

EXAMPLE:

When the two paralegal students discussed above agree to the terms for the sale of the used Contracts book, the contract is formed, but it is still executory. Once the book and the money have changed hands, the contract is complete with respect to all of its terms, and is now completely executed. Note that the term "executed" is also used to indicate the signing of a document; in that context, the obligations are still executory even though the contract is executed (signed).

Enforceability: Valid, Void, Voidable, and Unenforceable

Finally, getting to the "What can I get?" element, the law classifies contracts in terms of their enforceability. Can a party to a contract have that agreement enforced in a court of law, and which party to the contract has that right of enforceability?

A **valid** contract is an enforceable contract that meets all of the six requirements discussed above: There is a proper offer and acceptance; legally valid consideration is given and received; the parties have the legal capacity to enter into a contract; the contract is for a legal purpose; and the parties genuinely intend to contract—it is complete under the law. Either party can bring suit for the enforcement of a valid contract.

A **void** contract is, in reality, a contradiction in terms because there is no contract, and therefore the law does not entitle the parties to any legal remedy. The agreement has not met the contractual requirements.

In a **voidable** contract, a party to the agreement has the option of avoiding his legal obligation without any negative consequences, but could, if he wished, affirm his obligation and thereby be contractually bound. A contract entered into by a minor is an example of a voidable contract. Legally, a minor does not have contractual capacity and can avoid fulfilling contracts into which he has entered. (There are exceptions for certain types of contracts. See Chapter 5.) However, if, upon reaching majority, the former minor affirms the contract, he will be contractually bound.

 EXAMPLE:

Seventeen-year-old Gene enters into a contract with Bob, an adult, to buy Bob's used car. If Gene changes his mind, he can avoid the contract. However, if, on Gene's 18th birthday, Gene affirms his promise to Bob by giving Bob a payment, the contract will be totally enforceable. The option of avoidance is with Gene, who is under the disability, not with Bob, who is not.

A voidable contract may become valid and enforceable if the party under the disability—a minor, or a person induced by fraud, duress, or like condition to enter the agreement—later affirms his obligation when the disability is removed. A void contract, on the other hand, can never be made enforceable, regardless of what the parties do; any addition to the agreement that the parties attempt in order to meet contractual requirements actually creates the contract at that time; it does not validate what was void.

An **unenforceable** contract is a valid contract for which the law offers no recourse or remedy if its obligations are not fulfilled. For instance, a contract may exist in which one party failed to meet her contractual obligation; by the time the aggrieved party decides to sue, the Statute of Limitations has run, meaning that the law has determined that the proponent has waited so long to bring the suit that the court will not hear the question. Or, parties agree to open a store at a particular location, but before the contract can be fulfilled, the town rezones the area for residential use only. Even though the contract is valid, it can no longer be enforced because of a subsequent change in the law that makes its purpose incapable of being legally performed.

In classifying any given contract, remember that it will consist of elements of each type discussed above. The following chart summarizes these five types:

Type of Obligation	Method of Creation	Form	Timing	Enforceability
Bilateral Unilateral	Express Implied in fact Implied in law (quasi)	Formal Informal	Executory Executed	Valid Void Voidable Unenforceable

Every contract will have one item from each of these five categories; the terms are not mutually exclusive.

SAMPLE CLAUSES

1

Dear Irene,
Pursuant to our telephone conversation yesterday, I hereby agree to buy the pearl necklace you inherited from your Grandmother Rose for $500. Come to my house for dinner next Monday, and I'll give you a check.

Love,
Jeannette

P.S. Don't forget to bring the necklace.

The above letter constitutes an example of a bilateral contract between Jeannette and Irene. Irene made an offer for the sale of her necklace, which Jeannette has acknowledged and accepted in writing. The consideration Irene is giving is the necklace; the consideration Jeannette is giving is the $500. In terms of classification, this is an informal bilateral express contract that is executory until the consideration changes hands. Remember that to be legally enforceable, a contract does not have to take any particular form or include words of overt legality. Even a handwritten note may constitute a valid contract.

2

This contract dated the _____ day of _____, 20 _____, is made between Samuel Smith, hereinafter Smith, whose address is _____, and Peter Jones, hereinafter Jones, whose address is _____.

Jones hereby agrees to paint the exterior of Smith's house, located at _____, on the _____ day of _____, 20 _____, in consideration for which Smith hereby agrees to pay Jones the sum of $2,500, inclusive of all expenses, upon the completion of said painting.

In Witness Whereof, the undersigned have executed this contract the date and year first above written.

_____
Samuel Smith

_____
Peter Jones

The preceding is a more formalized version of a simple bilateral contract, this time for services instead of for the sale of goods. Why is it bilateral instead of unilateral, since services are being requested? The answer is that both parties are making present promises to each other: Jones to paint the house, and Smith to pay for Jones's painting services. The contract is formed on the date indicated; performance is merely delayed until the date specified. Whenever there is a mutual exchange of promises, the contract is bilateral.

Note that Smith has included the cost of all of Jones's expenses in the contract price. This means that the $2,500 is all that Smith is liable for, and Jones is responsible for paying for all paints, brushes, and so forth, that are required to do the work. This is a written example of an informal express, executory, bilateral contract.

3

Dear Mr. Whitson:
This concerns the parcel of land I bought from you last month. On making a personal inspection of the property, I noticed that the drainage ditch was clogged. I will be out of state for the next two months and can't clear it myself. Please clear the ditch for me and send a bill to my office for $500.

Sincerely,
Alfred Brace

The following week, Mr. Whitson cleared the drain and sent Mr. Brace a bill for $500.

This is an example of an express unilateral contract. Mr. Brace has requested a service from Mr. Whitson and has agreed to pay Whitson upon completion of the requested task. Mr. Whitson accepted the offer by doing the act requested and now is waiting for payment. The contract is still executory because Mr. Whitson has not yet received Mr. Brace's check.

This example differs from Sample 2 in that here, the offering party has requested an act, not a promise, and the offer became a contract when the other party accepted by cleaning the ditch. Once again, the correspondence was more informal than a signed and printed document. This does not negate the fact that it is a binding contract between the parties.

In analyzing information that is presented, always go through the checklist of five contract classifications given above to determine the exact form of the documents you are handling. Do not be put off or swayed by the physical appearance of the materials. Handwritten letters, notes, and typed agreements all may be valid contracts, depending on the substance of the material itself. Remember, the classifications only help to organize the material; they do not determine the agreement's legal effect or the relationship created between the parties. That determination involves a minute examination of the six contractual requirements examined earlier in the chapter.

CHAPTER SUMMARY

The law of contracts is one of the most complex, yet most elemental, of all areas of the law. Contract law forms the basis of most people's daily existence, and therefore it is of paramount importance as a field of study.

To create a valid contract, the agreement must contain the following six elements: offer, acceptance, consideration, legality of the subject matter, contractual capacity of the parties, and the contractual intent of the parties. Without these elements, the parties are not in a contractual relationship and, if injured, must rely on a different legal relationship to resolve the dispute.

All contracts can be classified according to five different categories, and in analyzing a contractual situation, it is best to classify the agreement prior to determining the rights and liabilities of the parties. The five classifications are: type of obligation (bilateral or unilateral); method of creation (express, implied in fact, or quasi); type of form (formal or informal); timing of obligation (executory or executed); and enforceability (valid, void, voidable, or unenforceable). Once the situation has been appropriately classified, analysis of the specific provisions can begin.

SYNOPSIS

Six requirements of every valid contract
1. Offer
2. Acceptance
3. Consideration
4. Contractual capacity
5. Legality of subject matter
6. Contractual intent

Classifications of contracts
1. Type of obligation
   a. Bilateral
   b. Unilateral
2. Method of creation
   a. Express
   b. Implied
   c. Quasi
3. Type of form
   a. Formal
   b. Informal
4. Timing
   a. Executory
   b. Executed
5. Enforceability
   a. Valid
   b. Void
   c. Voidable
   d. Unenforceable

Key Terms

Acceptance: manifestation of assent to the offer proposed

Bilateral contract: a contract in which a promise is exchanged for a promise

Consideration: the bargain of the contract; a benefit conferred or detriment incurred at the request of the other party

Contract: a legally enforceable agreement between two or more parties in which each agrees to give and receive something of legal value

Contractual capacity: the legal ability of a person to enter into a contractual relationship

Contractual intent: the purposefulness of forming a contractual relationship

Equity: the branch of the law that deals with fairness and mercy to prevent unjust enrichment

Executed contract: a contract that is complete and final with respect to all of its terms and conditions

Executory contract: a contract in which one or both of the parties still have obligations to perform

Express contract: a contract manifested in words, oral or written

Formal contract: historically, a written contract under seal; currently, any contract so designated by a state statute

Implied-in-fact contract: a contract in which the promises of the parties are inferred from their actions, as opposed to specific words

Implied-in-law contract: see Quasi-contract

Informal contract: any nonformal contract

Mutual assent: agreeing to the same terms at the same time; the offer and acceptance combined

Offer: a proposal by one party to another manifesting an intent to enter into a valid contract

Quasi-contract: a legal relationship that the courts, in the interest of fairness and equity, treat in a manner similar to a contractual relationship, even though no contract exists

Unenforceable contract: a contract that is otherwise valid, but for a breach of which there is no remedy at law

Unilateral contract: a contract in which a promise is exchanged for an act

Valid contract: an agreement that meets all six contractual requirements

Void contract: a situation in which the parties have attempted to create a contract, but in which one or more of the requisite elements are missing, so no contract exists

Voidable contract: a contract that one party may avoid at his option without being in breach of contract

EXERCISES

1. Give three examples of bilateral contracts from your everyday life that are not mentioned in the text.
2. What elements would you look for to determine that an agreement is an enforceable contract?
3. Why would a valid contract be unenforceable? Give examples.
4. Create a bilateral contract for a situation that involves barter.
5. How would you attempt to prove the existence or nonexistence of contractual intent?

Cases for Analysis

To elucidate certain points discussed in Chapter 1, the following judicial decisions are included. The first case, *Casale v. Nationwide Children's Hospital*, discusses the differences between express and implied contracts and promissory estoppel. *McCabe v. ConAgra Foods, Inc.* highlights the difference between a bilateral and a unilateral contract.

Casale v. Nationwide Children's Hosp.
682 Fed. Appx. 359 (6th Cir. 2017)

Plaintiff Anthony Casale appeals the district court's order of summary judgment in favor of defendant Nationwide Children's Hospital (NCH) on his Ohio law contract and tort claims. Casale, a successful physician, alleges NCH persuaded him to leave a stable career in Kentucky for the promise of a prominent hospital leadership position, but "pulled the rug out from under him" and withdrew its offer before he started. Like the district court, however, we must acknowledge "the law does not provide redress for every act of unfairness." Finding no error requiring reversal, we affirm.

I.

In early 2010, with its Chief of Urology set to retire, NCH reached out to Dr. Anthony Casale to gauge his interest in running its urology program. Initially, Casale was a reluctant candidate. He already had "a pretty good job" as a tenured professor and acting Chair of the Department of Urology at the University of Louisville's School of Medicine, and he "intended to stay at the University of Louisville." Still, knowing his position as acting Chair remained "quite unsettled," plaintiff decided to pursue the offer. After two days of interviews, NCH's Chief Operating Officer, Dr. Rick Miller, informed Casale that NCH planned to make him an offer.

Defendant sent Casale a draft offer letter in late July. Miller emphasized the letter was just "the first offer." "[I]f it's something that's not adequate," he added, "I want you to come back and ask for it, and we'll probably meet it." Over the next few days, he and Casale discussed salary and bonuses. NCH proposed that Casale's annual bonus be tied to his productivity, including the number of patients he treated. Casale recognized it would take him time to build his practice as a doctor new to the Columbus area, and instead asked that NCH guarantee his bonus for the first two years of employment. NCH agreed. It also agreed to plaintiff's request for "academic support," including funding for educational conferences and research.

In its final form, the offer letter included no express durational term, or limit on defendant's ability to terminate Casale's employment—a topic plaintiff acknowledged he did not discuss with Miller. Casale was also free to terminate his employment under the agreement, provided he repay his signing bonus and relocation expenses "if for some reason [he] decided to leave NCH prior to eighteen months of service." Plaintiff signed the offer letter and faxed it to NCH on August 4, 2010.

Shortly after Casale's acceptance, NCH sent him an information packet regarding its medical staff credentialing procedure and instructions for obtaining an Ohio medical license. Casale's offer letter specified his employment was "contingent upon verifying [his] Ohio medical license and obtaining and maintaining medical staff privileges at NCH."

The packet warned that securing a license and staff credentialing was a "lengthy" process which could take 10 to 12 weeks to complete. Given his January 1, 2011, start date, Casale understood he had limited time to submit his application materials.

Yet by early December, plaintiff was neither licensed to practice in Ohio, nor credentialed as an NCH medical staff member. The parties "vigorously dispute[d]" the cause of the delay before the district court, and dispute it further on appeal. Defendant faults Casale for failing to submit complete application materials in a timely manner. Plaintiff maintains he did "everything within his power" to provide the necessary information, and instead pins the blame on Pam Edson—an NCH employee whose assistance with the process was "so inadequate" and "erroneous[]," it resulted in "[m]onths of licensing delay." Whatever the cause, defendant told Casale it could not "employ [him] until [his] licensure and credentialing is complete," and delayed his start date until February 1, 2011.

Meanwhile, plaintiff's former colleague Dr. Stephen Wright sent NCH a peer review reference to be considered as part of the credentialing process. Karen Allen, a member of NCH's medical staff services team, flagged the review as "very poor" and forwarded it to Drs. Brilli (NCH's Chief Medical Officer), Teich (NCH's Staff President), and Rothermel (Chair of NCH's credentials committee). Plaintiff contends the disclosure of this information outside the credentialing process violated Ohio's peer review confidentiality restrictions. *See Ohio Rev. Code § 2305.251-52.* He also suspects that NCH improperly relied on the reference in withdrawing its offer of employment, and suggests Allen's characterization of Dr. Wright's comments "poison[ed] the well" against him. "In my opinion," Allen wrote in an email to Rothermel, "there is no way we should hire this man!!"

Casale also attended two meetings at NCH in late 2010—one to assist with his licensing and credentialing applications, and another to meet with future NCH colleagues. At the first, plaintiff met with NCH employees Kelly Wheatley and Julie Zaremski. Both employees described the meeting as uncomfortable and unproductive; plaintiff appeared "visibly frustrated" and did not answer their questions concerning certain "holes" and "discrepanc[ies]" in his work history. Plaintiff agreed the meeting was "a negative experience for everyone," but attributed this to Wheatley and Zaremski, who "had no experience" with NCH's credentialing process. At the second meeting, plaintiff spoke with some of NCH's surgeons, including those "who might refer [patients] to him." Upon leaving, Casale purportedly told another NCH staff member "this is a waste of my time." Plaintiff admits he made this statement, but says NCH takes his remark out of context: "I told her it was a waste of what time we had at that point."

After the meetings, Miller had second thoughts about plaintiff. Casale had been "somewhat ambivalent" about joining NCH from the beginning. Plaintiff seemed more "focus[ed] on his issues in Louisville" than on his license and credential paperwork, which he took roughly three months to complete, resulting in a delayed start. Then, when he arrived for meetings at NCH, Casale had difficulty connecting with defendant's staff. One employee assigned to help with his credentials described their interaction "as the most difficult meeting she has ever had with a physician." "Any one of these [issues] we'd probably ignore," Miller observed, "but in aggregate, they are perhaps very concerning."

Ultimately, NCH asked plaintiff to withdraw his acceptance. Casale refused. Having "given up everything in Louisville in order to keep [his] commitment to NCH," he requested an in-person meeting with Miller to resolve NCH's concerns. NCH declined his request and formally withdrew its offer of employment. Thereafter, the University of Louisville accepted Casale back onto its faculty as acting Chair of Urology, but with a lower salary and no tenure.

II.

Casale filed suit against NCH in 2011, alleging its actions cost him significant damages and impaired his future employment prospects. After the district court granted its motion to dismiss two of plaintiff's claims, NCH moved for summary judgment on the remaining five: breach of express contract, breach of implied contract, anticipatory repudiation, promissory estoppel, and defamation. While it acknowledged defendant had treated plaintiff "quite shabbily," the district court granted the motion.

Casale timely appeals. He also moves to supplement the record on appeal, while NCH moves to strike "certain portions" of plaintiff's brief.

III.

We review the district court's grant of summary judgment de novo. *Keith v. Cty. of Oakland*, 703 F.3d 918, 923 (6th Cir. 2013). "Summary judgment is proper 'if the movant shows that there is no genuine dispute as to any material fact and the movant is entitled to judgment as a matter of law.'" *Id.* (quoting Fed. R. Civ. P. 56(a)). A dispute is "genuine" if the evidence permits a reasonable jury to return a verdict in favor of the nonmovant, and a fact "material" if it may affect the outcome of the suit. *Anderson v. Liberty Lobby, Inc.*, 477 U.S. 242, 248, 106 S. Ct. 2505, 91 L. Ed. 2d 202 (1986). Viewing the evidence in a light most favorable to the nonmoving party, our task is to determine "whether the evidence presents a sufficient disagreement to require submission to a jury or whether it is so one-sided that one party must prevail as a matter of law." *Id.* at 251-52.

A.

Ohio recognizes the doctrine of at-will employment, meaning the "relationship between employer and employee is terminable at the will of either" and "an employee is subject to discharge by an employer at any time, even without cause." *Wright v. Honda of Am. Mfg., Inc.*, 73 Ohio St. 3d 571, 1995 Ohio 114, 653 N.E.2d 381, 384 (Ohio 1995). It also recognizes two exceptions tempering the general at-will rule: (1) the existence of an express or implied contract altering the terms of discharge; and (2) promissory estoppel, where the employer makes representations or promises of continued employment. *Id.; see also Clark v. Collins Bus Corp.*, 136 Ohio App. 3d 448, 736 N.E.2d 970, 973 (Ohio Ct. App. 2000) (citing *Mers v. Dispatch Printing Co.*, 19 Ohio St. 3d 100, 19 Ohio B. 261, 483 N.E.2d 150, 154-55 (Ohio 1985)). Plaintiff here relies on both, asserting claims for breach of express or implied contract, anticipatory repudiation, and promissory estoppel. Neither party disputes the district court's finding that the offer letter between plaintiff and NCH is a "valid contract" for employment; the only question is whether it guarantees employment for a specific term.

For an individual hired under contract, "there is a strong presumption of at-will employment, unless the terms of the agreement clearly indicate otherwise." *Padula v. Wagner*, 2015-Ohio 2374, 37 N.E.3d 799, 808 (Ohio 2015). On its face, the offer letter does not rebut that presumption. It includes no express durational term and no limit on either party's ability to terminate the relationship. And "[w]here a contract of employment does not state the duration of employment, employment is considered to be at will." *Clark*, 736 N.E.2d at 973.

Still, Casale insists several of the letter's provisions demonstrate an express agreement for an initial term of three years' employment, renewable at his option thereafter. For instance, the letter lists Casale's salary for his initial three years of employment, and guarantees his bonus for the first two years, until he can "build clinical volumes" and earn a bonus based on productivity. Plaintiff is eligible for further salary increases after the first three years, and his pension does not fully vest until after five years. NCH also commits to a million dollar "research start up package" payable "over a three[-]year period," agrees to fund "two urology fellowships (one new fellow per year)," and pledges support for "three educational events per year." Yet, the district court was unconvinced; it concluded "[n]one of the contractual terms Plaintiff relies on raise a genuine issue of material fact as to the duration of the contract." We agree.

"In the absence of facts and circumstances which indicate that the agreement is for a specific term, an employment contract which provides for an annual rate of compensation, but makes no provision as to the duration of the employment, is not a contract for one year, but is terminable at will by either party." *Henkel v. Educ. Research Council of Am.*, 45 Ohio St. 2d 249, 344 N.E.2d 118, 118 (Syllabus by the Court) (Ohio 1976). Plaintiff agrees "[t]he simple statement of an annual rate, without more [i]s not enough . . . to constitute an express term of duration" under *Henkel*. "However," he continues, "it *was* enough" under the Ohio Supreme Court's decision in *Kelly*, "where the letter agreement also provided for a monthly amount, a settling up at year-end, and a guaranteed gross sum every year." Appellant's Br., at 33 (citing *Kelly v. Carthage Wheel Co.*, 62 Ohio St. 598, 57 N.E. 984 (Ohio 1900)). Casale argues the additional terms here—the guaranteed bonuses, potential future raises, and academic support—go further than the "settling up" in *Kelly* to prove NCH's intent to employ him for a specific term. He is incorrect. Ohio's Supreme Court rejected this same reading of *Kelly* in *Henkel*: "Our decision in *Kelly* does not resolve the issue . . . [of] whether a hiring at a specified sum per year constitutes a hiring for a year." 344 N.E.2d at 121. "The court merely held that because Kelly had initially been hired for one year, absent a new arrangement at the end of that year, he was rehired upon identical terms for a second year." *Id.*

Neither the statement of an annual rate of pay, *Henkel*, 344 N.E.2d at 118, nor the promise of "career advancement opportunities," *Daup v. Tower Cellular*, 136 Ohio App. 3d 555, 737 N.E.2d 128, 133 (Ohio Ct. App. 2000) (citation omitted), such as bonuses and academic funding, modify the presumed at-will relationship. *See id.* at 133-34 (promises to develop "many other ventures together" insufficient to alter at-will employment); *Clark*, 736 N.E.2d at 972-73 (employment contract specifying annual salary and bonus with no mention of duration is an at-will contract); *Shaw v. J. Pollock & Co.*, 82 Ohio App. 3d 656, 612 N.E.2d 1295, 1298 (Ohio Ct. App. 1992) ("The potential of future profitsharing is not a fact or circumstance which transforms a contract terminable at will into a contract for a term of years."). This is so because, as the district court explained, provisions concerning bonuses, raises, and research funding per year ultimately suffer from the same defect as provisions concerning annual compensation: they "refer to how much NCH will support *per year*; they say nothing to guarantee employment for a specific duration."

"The general rule in Ohio is that unless otherwise agreed to by the parties, an employment agreement purporting to be permanent or for life, or for no fixed time period is considered to be employment terminable at the will of either party." *Humphreys v. Bellaire Corp.*, 966 F.2d 1037, 1040 (6th Cir. 1992) (citing *Henkel*, 344 N.E.2d at 118). Because the offer letter does not "clearly indicate" a specific term of employment, plaintiff has failed to rebut the "strong presumption" in favor of an at-will relationship. *Padula*, 37 N.E.3d at 808. NCH's withdrawal of the employment offer was therefore not a breach of an express contract.

B.

While failure to specify duration in the offer letter may be fatal to a claim for breach of express contract, the same cannot be said of a claim for breach of implied contract. *See, e.g., Wright*, 653 N.E.2d at 384. Contractual limits on an employer's right to discharge an employee need not be in writing; they can also be implied from "the 'facts and circumstances' surrounding the employment-at-will relationship." *Id.* (quoting *Mers*, 483 N.E.2d at 154). "These facts and circumstances include the character of the employment, custom, the course of dealing between the parties, company policy," oral representations, and "any other fact which may illuminate the question." *Id.* (internal quotation marks omitted).

Plaintiff argues that even if NCH did not expressly promise him a specific term of employment, the facts and circumstances here nevertheless support the finding of an implied contract for a specific term of employment. In this regard, Casale compares his case to *Miller v. Lindsay-Green, Inc.*, 2005-Ohio-6366, 2005 WL 3220215 (Ohio Ct. App. 2005), and *Wright*, 73 Ohio St. 3d 571, 1995 Ohio 114, 653 N.E.2d 381. Neither comparison is apt.

Miller involved an employee who claimed his employer made an oral promise to employ him for a ten-year period. *Miller*, 2005-Ohio-6366, 2005 WL 3220215 at *1, *4. Plaintiff cites *Miller* for the proposition that parol evidence, such as oral promises of employment, can supplement a written agreement which is silent as to duration in order to establish an implied promise of a specific term of employment. But the oral promise in *Miller* did not support a breach-of-contract claim. It supported a promissory estoppel claim. 2005-Ohio-6366, [WL] at *4-6, *8. The distinction is significant, because "[p]romissory estoppel . . . is not a contractual theory but a quasi-contractual or equitable doctrine designed to prevent the harm resulting from [an employee's] reasonable and detrimental reliance . . . upon the false representations of his employer." *Karnes v. Doctors Hosp.*, 51 Ohio St. 3d 139, 555 N.E.2d 280, 283 (Ohio 1990) (per curiam); *see also Dunn v. Bruzzese*, 172 Ohio App. 3d 320, 2007 Ohio 3500, 874 N.E.2d 1221, 1228-29 (Ohio Ct. App. 2007) (distinguishing promissory estoppel as a "tool of equity" or contract implied-in-law, from a contract implied-in-fact). A claimant proceeding on a theory of promissory estoppel can, for instance, prevail without demonstrating a "meeting of the minds" between the parties. *Dunn*, 874 N.E.2d at 1228-29 (citation omitted).

But a claimant proceeding on a theory of an implied-in-fact contract cannot. *Id.* "On the contrary, the existence of . . . [an] implied-in-fact contract[] . . . hinge[s] upon proof of all the elements of a contract." *Id.* at 1228 (citation omitted). "To establish a contract implied in fact, a plaintiff must demonstrate that the circumstances surrounding the parties' transaction make it reasonably certain that an agreement was intended." *Id.* at 1228-29 (citation omitted).

The employee in *Wright*, who was hired without a written agreement, made that showing. Honda terminated Wright for violating its anti-nepotism policy, but she presented evidence demonstrating "that an implied employment agreement existed [under] which [she] could not be terminated unless she failed to perform her job adequately." 653 N.E.2d at 384. Honda's employee handbook, progress reports, and promotional letters emphasized the plaintiff's "continued growth" with the company, and her supervisor testified "that if an employee performs his . . . job in an acceptable manner," he can "expect to have continued employment with Honda." *Id.* "Once [Wright] became aware of [the anti-nepotism] policy," management at first informed her "that she had no reason to be concerned and that there were other employees who retained their positions under similar circumstances." *Id.* at 385. Despite these assurances, Wright's supervisor sent her home from work to "investigate" the policy violation, then invited Wright back "as if nothing had happened," only to terminate her a month later. *Id.* at 383, 385.

These "[p]articularly egregious" circumstances did not befall Casale. *Id.* at 385. Plaintiff acknowledged he and Miller had no discussions "regarding the circumstances under which [his] employment with [NCH] could be terminated." Unlike in *Wright*, plaintiff points to no handbook, progress reports, or statements by management suggesting "that if an employee performs his . . . job in an acceptable manner," he can "expect to have continued employment" at NCH. *See id.* at 384. Further, the circumstances plaintiff does identify are unrelated to duration. For instance, plaintiff notes that NCH introduced him in internal emails, letters to staff, and marketing materials as its "new Chief of Urology." He also complains that NCH required him to undergo extensive "pre-employment onboarding," such as attending meetings and obtaining his Ohio medical license and staff credentials. These circumstances prove only the undisputed fact that defendant hired plaintiff—not that it intended to limit its ability to terminate him.

Finally, plaintiff argues that to accept NCH's offer, he left a secure, lucrative position at the University of Louisville, one he would not have abandoned if he understood defendant was offering only at-will employment. Here again, Casale confuses facts that may support the finding of an equitable remedy, such as promissory estoppel, with facts necessary to demonstrate an implied-in-fact contract. *See Dunn,* 874 N.E.2d at 1228-29; *see also Clark,* 736 N.E.2d at 973 (no anticipatory repudiation where the at-will plaintiff "made [the] necessary arrangements to leave his former employer, move to the new employer's city, and pursue his job duties," and the defendant withdrew its employment offer before he started). As the district court put it, plaintiff's "citation to his own testimony that he would not have accepted an at-will offer or that another chief was given a contract with a term of five years does nothing to assist a trier of fact in determining whether *both parties to this agreement* mutually assented to a guaranteed period of employment of three years."

Because plaintiff has failed to demonstrate an express or implied contract for a specific term of employment, the district court did not err in granting defendant summary judgment on his claims for breach of contract and anticipatory repudiation.

C.

Invoking equitable remedies more directly, plaintiff also alleged a claim of promissory estoppel. To prevail on this claim, Casale must show: (1) a clear and unambiguous promise on the part of NCH; (2) his reliance on the promise; (3) that the reliance was reasonable and foreseeable; and (4) that he was injured as a result of his reliance. *Dunn,* 874 N.E.2d at 1227. Although plaintiff's willingness to "giv[e] up his . . . secure employment in reliance upon [NCH's] representations" may well establish the second element, *see Patrick v. Painesville Commercial Props., Inc.,* 99 Ohio App. 3d 360, 650 N.E.2d 927, 931 (Ohio Ct. App. 1994), the district court found Casale failed at the first, having cited no evidence "of any promise of employment for a specific term." Casale argues this decision was in error, because Ohio does not require that a promise for continued employment be "for a specific term."

Plaintiff misinterprets the district court's holding. As explained in its order denying plaintiff's motion to alter or amend the judgment, the court used the phrase "specific term of employment" merely to "repeat[] Plaintiff's theory of the case, not [to] stat[e] that Ohio law requires a promise of a specific term." "Elsewhere, the Court phrased the standard as whether there had been a detrimental reliance on a 'specific promise of job security,' and noted that Plaintiff failed to cite any evidence of a 'specific promise.'"

This was the reason the district court granted defendant summary judgment on Casale's promissory estoppel claim—because plaintiff failed to identify the "clear and unambiguous promise" upon which he relied. *Shaw*, 612 N.E.2d at 1298. And the court was right to require that the promise be specific." [V]ague, indefinite promises of future employment or mere representations of future conduct without more specificity do not form a valid basis for the application of the doctrine of promissory estoppel." *Daup*, 737 N.E.2d at 134 (internal quotation marks omitted). Likewise, "[i]n the absence of a specific promise of continued employment, a promise of future benefits or opportunities does not support a promissory estoppel exception to the employment-at-will doctrine." *Clark*, 736 N.E.2d at 974 (internal quotation marks omitted).

Plaintiff now argues he demonstrated a specific promise of employment for "a minimum three-year term, renewable by him, through age 70," based on the offer letter, and a discussion he had with Miller about working to age 70 before signing it. However, Casale did not press either point below, and "the failure to present an issue to the district court forfeits the right to have that argument addressed on appeal." *600 Marshall Entm't Concepts, LLC v. City of Memphis*, 705 F.3d 576, 585 (6th Cir. 2013) (citation omitted). "Our function is to review the case presented to the district court," not "a better case fashioned after a district court's unfavorable order." *Id.* (citation omitted). And the result in this case would be no different if we did. The offer letter includes no specific promise of employment for any term, and "promissory estoppel does not apply to oral statements made prior to the written contract where the contract covers the same subject matter." *Clark*, 736 N.E.2d at 974 (citation and brackets omitted). Accordingly, the district court did not err in granting summary judgment on plaintiff's promissory estoppel claim.

D. [OMITTED]

Questions

1. What are the exceptions to the "at-will" employment doctrine?
2. What is the difference between a breach of contract claim and one for promissory estoppel?
3. What is the significance of a contract that does not indicate a specific termination?

McCabe v. ConAgra Foods, Inc.
681 Fed. Appx. 82 *; 2017 U.S. App. LEXIS 3755

I. Background

ConAgra Foods, Inc. ("ConAgra") conducted an annual promotion to help end child hunger from 2011 to 2015. The company would donate a certain amount—up to a yearly maximum—to a non-profit organization called Feeding America for every code entered on its website from certain ConAgra products' packaging. Kevin McCabe filed suit in the Eastern District of New York, alleging that ConAgra's promotion created a contract. He brought claims for breach of contract and violation of the *District of Columbia Consumer Protection Procedures Act ("DCCPPA"), D.C. Code §§ 28-3901-3913.*

A. Contract Claim

Pursuant to New York law, on which both parties rely in connection with this contract claim, the elements of a cause of action for breach of contract are: the existence of an agreement, performance by the plaintiff, breach of contract by the defendant, and resulting damage. *Eternity Glob. Master Fund Ltd. v. Morgan Guar. Trust Co. of N.Y.*, 375 F.3d 168, 177 (2d Cir. 2004). An agreement stems from "a manifestation of mutual assent sufficiently definite to assure that the parties are truly in agreement with respect to all material terms." *Express Indus. and Terminal Corp. v. N.Y. State Dep't of Transp.*, 93 N.Y.2d 584, 715 N.E.2d 1050, 1053, 693 N.Y.S.2d 857 (N.Y. 1999); *see also Arbitron, Inc. v. Tralyn Broad., Inc.*, 400 F.3d 130, 137 (2d Cir. 2005). An agreement generally requires an offer and an acceptance. The general rule in New York is that a promotion or advertisement is not an offer. *Leonard v. Pepsico, Inc.*, 88 F. Supp. 2d 116, 122-23 (S.D.N.Y. 1999), aff'd, 210 F.3d 88 (2d Cir. 2000). An advertisement can constitute an offer when it is "clear, definite, and explicit, and leaves nothing open for negotiation." *Id.* at 123 (quoting *Lefkowitz v. Great Minneapolis Surplus Store, Inc.*, 251 Minn. 188, 86 N.W.2d 689, 691 (Minn. 1957)); *Amalfitano v. NBTY Inc.*, 128 A.D.3d 743, 744, 9 N.Y.S.3d 352 (N.Y. App. Div. 2d Dep't 2015), leave to appeal denied, 26 N.Y.3d 913, 22 N.Y.S.3d 165, 43 N.E.3d 375 (N.Y. 2015).

We agree with the district court that McCabe failed plausibly to allege the existence of a unilateral contract for each year from 2011 through 2014. A unilateral contract was not formed, *inter alia*, because the promotion was limited to a certain maximum donation per year. *See Amalfitano*, 128 A.D.3d at 744 (promotion was an invitation for offers, not an offer, because it expressly stated that supplies were limited). An individual entering a code would have no knowledge whether the maximum donation had been reached in 2011, 2012, 2013, or 2014. *Cf. Lefkowitz*, 86 N.W.2d at 691 (potential customer knew that he was the first one in line for a "first come, first served" opportunity). Thus, ConAgra's promotion was not an offer because McCabe and the other plaintiffs had no "power of acceptance." *See Leonard*, 88 F. Supp. 2d at 123 (quoting *Mesaros v. United States*, 845 F.2d 1576, 1580 (Fed. Cir. 1988)).

The district court also concluded that McCabe did not plausibly allege the existence of a bilateral contract for each year from 2011 through 2015, and we agree. Under McCabe's bilateral contract theory, the terms of participation constituted an invitation for an offer. The entry of a code by a promotion participant then was an offer which ConAgra supposedly accepted by acknowledging the code's receipt. ConAgra's supposed invitation for offers, however—made prior to any code entry—was insufficiently definite to set the terms of the "offer" supposedly made on entry of a code, and McCabe fails to allege facts suggesting that the code entry in any way clarified the terms on which an alleged bilateral contract was created.

McCabe alleges that, in 2015, an individual entering an online code would know whether the yearly maximum donation had been reached because of a counter used during that year's promotion on the promotion website. Thus, he claims, a unilateral contract was formed at least as to this year. But even assuming *arguendo* that the individual was aware of whether the yearly maximum donation had been reached and that the terms of the offer were sufficiently definite, McCabe fails to allege that ConAgra breached that contract. Nowhere does he state that ConAgra did not make the 10-cent or 20-cent monetary donation to Feeding America upon the entry of an online code—the only promotion term arguably definite enough to constitute an offer. He merely criticizes the methodology that Feeding America used to calculate the cost of providing a meal. Therefore, McCabe fails to state a claim for breach of contract even as to the 2015 promotion.

B.   DCCPPA Claim [OMITTED]

III.   Conclusion

We have considered McCabe's remaining arguments and find them to be without merit. Accordingly, we AFFIRM the judgment of the district court.

Questions

1. What are the requirements for maintaining a breach of contract claim?
2. What facts led to McCabe losing his claim?
3. What is the court's interpretation of ConAgra's advertisement?

Suggested Case References

1. For a discussion of express and implied contracts, as well as promissory estoppel, read *Tuttle v. ANR Freight System*, 797 P.2d 825 (Colo. App. 1990).
2. Can a unilateral contract become a bilateral contract? See *Cook v. Johnson*, 37 Wash. 2d 19, 221 P.2d 525 (1950).
3. To see how the federal court sitting in New York defines consideration, read *Banque Arabe et Internationale D'Investissement v. Bulk Oil (USA)*, 726 F. Supp. 1411 (S.D.N.Y. 1989).
4. *Allgood v. Procter & Gamble Co.*, 72 Ohio App. 3d 309, 594 N.E.2d 668 (1991), provides a brief discussion of the basic elements of a valid contract.
5. For a discussion of express and implied contracts, and their relation to employment law, see *Duplex Envelope Co., Inc. v. Baltimore Post Co.*, 163 Md. 596 (1933).

Ethical Considerations

According to Rule 2.1 of the American Bar Association (ABA)'s Rules of Professional Conduct, when rendering advice to a client, a lawyer, as well as the lawyer's legal assistant, may refer not only to law, but to other considerations such as moral, economic, social, and political factors that may be relevant to a client's situation. In other words, remember that the best objective advice may be the worst subjective advice for a particular client. Always be sure to take into account the educational, intellectual, physical, and emotional nature of the client, so that the advice that is proffered actually assists that client to resolve a problem in a manner most beneficial to that individual.

Quick Quiz

Answer TRUE or FALSE. (Answers can be found in Appendix C, on page 413.)

1. An enforceable agreement may be formed by means of a quasi-contract.
2. One can be bound by a contract even if he or she did not intend to enter into such a contract.
3. Informal contracts are not legally enforceable.
4. Voidable contracts may be enforceable.
5. Only bilateral contracts are enforceable.

2 Offer

Learning Objectives

After studying this chapter you will be able to:

- Define "offer"
- Identify the three conditions necessary to create a valid offer
- Explain the concept of "certainty and definiteness in the terms of an offer"
- List the four required terms in a valid offer
- Briefly define the "Universal Commercial Code" (UCC)
- Discuss the impact of the UCC on traditional legal principles of a contractual offer
- Know what is meant by an "output contract"
- Apply basic concepts of an offer to contractual clauses
- Draft a basic offer that would meet legal standards
- Indicate the difference between contracting with a member of the general public and contracting with a merchant

CHAPTER OVERVIEW

This chapter focuses on the creation of the contractual relationship. It describes the process and requirements of the first essential element of every valid contract: the offer. For a contract to be deemed valid, the parties to the contract must manifest to each other their mutual assent to the same bargain at the same time. A contract is the meeting of two minds for one purpose. Therefore, the law expects the parties to indicate to each other that they are of the same mind. Without this mutuality of purpose, the parties would have misplaced expectations.

This contractual process of agreement begins with the party known as the offeror, who first proposes the contractual relationship. It is the offeror's function to initiate the contract process and to determine the boundaries of that agreement under the common law. The terms of the contract are entirely determined by the words or actions of the offeror, except for contracts for the sale of goods between merchants pursuant to the provisions of the Uniform Commercial Code (UCC). See infra. It is the offeror who creates all the provisions of the contract.

In order to guarantee that there is, in fact, a meeting of the minds between the offeror and the person to whom the offer is made, the offeree, the common law requires that the offer be definite and certain in all of its relevant terms. The relevant terms are price, subject matter, parties to the contract, and the time of performance of the contractual provisions. The law will not countenance an offer that is so indefinite in its provisions that a reasonable person would be unable to recognize and understand the relevant terms of the contract.

Offer Defined

An offer is a proposal by one party, the offeror, to a second party, the offeree, manifesting an intention to enter into a valid contract. The offer creates a power in the offeree to establish a contract between the parties by making an appropriate acceptance.

The offeror, the one making the proposal, is the creator and the initiator of the contractual process under the common law. It is the offer itself that determines all of the relevant provisions of the contract. The terms of the offer are the terms of the contract. Once the offer has been made, the power or ability to create the contract rests with the offeree. This is the key element of all contractual relationships. The offeror proposes; the offeree disposes. Without the assent of the offeree, no contract can exist.

EXAMPLE:

Jessica proposes to sell her car to Elizabeth so that she can use the money for a vacation. Jessica's asking price is $1,200. Elizabeth, when she hears the price, thinks the price is too high, and declines. No contract exists. Elizabeth, the offeree, has refused to accept the terms of the contract that Jessica has proposed.

Not all proposals are considered to be legal offers. For instance, in the example above, if Jessica did not mention a price for the car, how could Elizabeth accept? Elizabeth would not know the terms of the contract she was accepting. Furthermore, what if Jessica simply said she would sell the car to Elizabeth for $1,200, but Elizabeth was not around to hear the proposal? How could someone accept a proposition of which she was unaware?

Consequently, the common law requires that the following three conditions be met for a proposal to qualify as a contractual offer:

1. the offeror must manifest a present contractual intent;
2. the offer must be communicated to the offeree; and
3. the offer must be certain and definite with respect to its terms.

Unless these requirements are met, the proposal may exist, but it will not be considered an offer to contract. It must be noted that contracts for the sale of goods between merchants are now governed by the Uniform Commercial Code, a statute that has made significant changes to the common law for contracts that come within its purview. Therefore, throughout the text, where appropriate, these differences will be addressed.

Present Contractual Intent

The element of intent is a basic requirement of all contractual relationships. Unlike other aspects of life and law, a contract cannot be thrust upon an unsuspecting person. For the offer to have legal validity, it must appear to an objective, reasonable person that the offeror actually intended to make an offer. How is this element of intent determined? Intent is shown by taking into consideration all of the circumstances surrounding the proposal. The more serious the words and expressions used, the more likely it is that the element of intent can be demonstrated. The court will always attempt to find the most reasonable interpretation of the facts based on the circumstances presented.

EXAMPLES:

1. Philip is showing a group of friends a valuable watch he inherited from his grandfather. While joking around about how old-fashioned the watch is, Philip laughingly offers to sell it for an inexpensive up-to-date plastic sports watch. If one of his friends attempts to accept by giving Philip a plastic watch, there would be no contract. Under these circumstances, reasonable persons would assume Philip was joking, not making a valid offer.

2. Darren, having constant trouble with his car, kicks the wheels and says out loud that for 2¢ he'd sell the car. John,

overhearing him, gives Darren two pennies and tries to drive off with the car. There is no contract. Under the circumstances, it is unreasonable to assume that Darren intended to offer his car for sale for 2¢. Words spoken in jest or frustration lack the requisite element of intent.

Communication to the Offeree

For an offer to be capable of acceptance, the offer must be communicated to the offeree. It is the offeree who has the power to create a valid contract by making the appropriate acceptance, but that acceptance can occur only if the offeree is aware of the offer.

The precise method of communication is left to the discretion of the offeror. The law supposes that the offeror will use effective means of communicating an offer to the offeree so that a contract can come into existence. Oral, written, telephonic, and mechanical means of communication are all considered legally sufficient methods of communication. The offeror is not limited to making the offer specifically to just one person. An offer can be made to a group, or class, of persons, any of whom is capable of accepting the offer.

The effect of a valid communication is to give the person to whom it was communicated the ability to accept. The method of acceptance is discussed in detail in Chapter 3, Acceptance.

 EXAMPLES:

1. Mildred leaves a message on Kate's answering machine offering to sell Kate a used Real Property textbook for $10. This offer has been validly communicated to Kate, even though the words were not spoken to her directly.

2. Upset at her grade in a Litigation course, Mildred screams out in her room that she'd sell her litigation text for $2. Walter, passing by Mildred's window, hears her scream, and tries to buy the book. There is no contract. Not only is it unlikely that Mildred intended an offer, but the proposal was not effectively communicated. Merely making a statement in the presumptive privacy and solitude of one's own room does not constitute communication of an offer.

3. In the school newspaper, Mildred inserts a notice offering to sell her used Torts book for $10. This is a valid offer that has been communicated to anyone who reads the paper.

Take careful note that although the above example illustrates a valid communication of an offer via the newspaper, not all newspaper advertisements are considered to be offers. Courts have determined that in many instances newspaper ads are merely "invitations" to the public to make an offer, or to patronize a particular establishment. The distinguishing factors between a valid offer and a mere invitation turn on intent of the advertisers and the certainty and definiteness of the terms employed. The more certain and definite the words used by the advertiser, the more likely it is that the ad will be considered an offer.

EXAMPLE:

An advertisement to sell a particular named product at 25 to 50 percent below the listed price is not an offer to the public, but is an invitation to the public to negotiate for the item. Why? Because the terms of the ad are not sufficiently definite. The presumed intent of the seller is not to make an offer but to invite the public to bid for the product in a range from 25 to 50 percent below the listed price.

Certainty and Definiteness in the Terms of the Offer

Because the offeror creates the terms of the contract by what is expressed in the offer, the court carefully scrutinizes the terms specified in the proposal. As previously discussed, the more certain and definite the proposal, the more likely it is that the court will construe the proposal as an offer to create a valid contract.

To determine that the terms are indeed definite and certain, the law looks for the presence of four essential elements:

1. the price of the contract;
2. the subject matter of the contract;
3. the parties to the contract; and,
4. the time of performance for fulfilling the contract.

The more certain and definite these elements, the more likely it is that the proposal will be considered an offer under the common law; conversely, the more indefinite or ambiguous these terms, the less likely it is that the proposal will be considered a valid offer. Because the parties are required to demonstrate mutual assent, it would be impossible to have assent if the parties did not know or were uncertain as to what they were agreeing.

To ascertain that these four elements exist, the court will examine all the circumstances surrounding the creation of the offer. It will consider all the statements made by the parties, all preliminary negotiations that may have existed, and any other documentation that can indicate the intent, certainty, and communications of the parties.

Essential Terms of an Offer

Contracts are a matter of private concern between the contracting parties themselves, and, unless the contract includes some aspect of life that is governmentally regulated, the law leaves the creation of the contract terms completely up to the parties.

Under the common law, when drafting the provisions of an offer, the offeror must be as specific as possible with respect to price, subject matter, parties, and timing of performance. The law requires that these terms be certain, definite, and capable of being readily understood by a reasonable person. If the offeror indicates terms that are not objectively definite but are vague and ambiguous, the offer will not be considered valid.

As a general rule, the courts will not correct vague terms mentioned in an offer in order to create a valid contract. To uphold contracts, however, and consequently the legal expectations of the parties, the court will, under certain circumstances, apply the concept of "reasonableness" with respect to a contract provision that the parties have neglected to include. On the other hand, the court will not insert "reasonable" terms if the parties themselves have attempted to specify a term but have done so badly. In sum, the court can sometimes correct omissions but can never change the terms the parties themselves have used.

How all this fits together will be analyzed in the following discussion of the four essential terms of an offer.

Price

The price stated in the contract is an example of contractual consideration. Consideration is the bargain of the contract; it is the benefit conferred or the detriment incurred. Both sides must give and receive something of legal value to make the contract valid. Price—that is, money—is the most typical example of consideration, but it is not the only one. For a detailed discussion of consideration, see Chapter 4, Consideration.

If the parties are intending the sale of a good or service, usually the good or service is exchanged for cash or a cash equivalent such as a check or money order. Because this forms part of the consideration, a requisite element of every valid contract (see Chapter 1), the law requires that the price be specified in the offer itself. If the parties indicate in the offer that the price will be left for future negotiations, no offer or contract exists, even if every other contractual requirement has been met. Why? Because without knowing an essential term, the parties cannot have mutual assent.

EXAMPLE:

Sam agrees to sell Hank three roasting chickens, to be delivered Friday morning, for a price to be determined at the time of delivery. There is no contract. Hank might have thought that the price would be 29¢ per pound, whereas Sam might have thought $3 per chicken was fair. There is no mutual assent to this offer despite what the parties might have thought.

Under certain circumstances, the price of a contract can be determined by a court inserting the element of reasonableness and thereby salvaging an otherwise void contractual agreement. If the parties completely neglect to mention a specific price, the court can interpret a "reasonable price" and then entertain evidence as to what the reasonable price would be. The court can only apply the reasonableness rule if the term has not been mentioned at all, or the parties state "reasonable price" themselves. On the other hand, if the parties attempt to state a price but indicate one that is vague or uncertain, as in the example given above, the court's hands are tied; the contract will fail on grounds of indefiniteness. The court cannot vary the terms the parties have stated.

Note that for contracts for the sale of goods covered by the Uniform Commercial Code (UCC), exceptions to the common law rule have been carved out. For contracts for the sale of goods between commercial traders, the UCC will permit contracts to be formed even if the price is not quoted, provided that the parties have a history of past dealings and some objective standard can be used to determine a price.

The parties do not have to specify a particular dollar amount to have a definite price. If the parties refer to some objective standard by which the price can be determined, then the offer will stand. Should the parties refer to some subjective measure, the offer will fail.

EXAMPLES:

1. After completing her paralegal program, Rosa starts looking for a job. Rosa remains unemployed for several months. Finally, the firm of Hacker & Slacker agrees to hire her. Nervously, Rosa asks what her salary is to be, and Hacker says they'll pay her what they think she's worth. There is no contract. The determination of "worth" has been left up to Hacker's subjective evaluation; therefore, the offer lacks the essential term of price.

2. In the situation above, when Rosa asks about her salary, Hacker says he'll pay her the average starting salary paid to new paralegals at mid-size law firms in their city. This is a valid offer. Hacker has specified an objective standard for determining price, and that price can be proven by analysis of salaries in the area.

Any attempt by the parties to create a situation in which one side has total discretion with respect to filling in the terms will fail because of vagueness and indefiniteness. What one person considers "fair" may be deemed unjust by the other party. Terms such as a "fair profit," "fair price," or "fair rate of interest" are too uncertain to be enforceable. "Fair" is a subjective term. The court can only interpret "reasonableness." It cannot cure defects created by the specific words of the parties themselves.

Subject Matter

The subject matter of a contract is another example of the consideration for the contract. If one side is providing the price, the other side is usually providing a good or service, such as a textbook or paralegal services, which is that party's consideration for the contract.

Under strict common law principles, if the offer is to be deemed valid, the subject matter of the contract must be specifically described, not only in terms of content but in terms of quantity as well. How many textbooks of which subject are offered for sale? How many hours per week is the paralegal expected to work, and what are her functions? Any description of the subject matter that is inconclusive, vague, or ambiguous will cause the contract to fail.

Some typical problems that are encountered regarding the subject matter are discussed below.

Ambiguity.   If the subject matter is described in terms that are capable of more than one interpretation, the offer is deemed ambiguous and will not stand.

 EXAMPLE:

Celeste offers to sell Bonnie her brooch for $100. Celeste has three brooches and fails to specify which brooch is meant in the offer. No contract exists. The subject matter has been ambiguously described.

As in the example given above, if the subject matter is described in words that are ambiguous, the offer will not stand. The offeror must be sufficiently descriptive in her choice of words so that any reasonable person should be able to determine the subject matter of the contract. Ambiguity destroys the certainty of the terms of the offer.

 **EXAMPLE:**

Andy offers to sell his house in Los Angeles to Jim for $500,000. Andy has two houses in L.A., one worth $450,000, the other worth $3 million. Which house is meant? Andy may mean the less valuable house; Jim may assume the more valuable one. The offer is too ambiguous to stand.

If neither party is aware that the language is ambiguous, and both intend the same object, the court will let the offer stand because there is a meeting of the minds. Both parties intend the same object. On the other hand, if only one party is aware of the ambiguity, the court may uphold the offer based on the intention of the innocent party. In other words, the court won't let one party "pull a fast one" on the other.

 EXAMPLES:

  1. Aaron offers to sell his house in Chicago to Brian for $500,000. Unknown to Aaron, Aaron's uncle has died and left him a house in Chicago worth $5 million. Brian hears of the uncle's death, agrees to the offer, and then sues Aaron to have Aaron convey the more expensive property. There is no contract. Because Aaron, at the time of making the offer, did not know the term was ambiguous (he thought he only owned one house in Chicago), the court will find the offer refers to the less expensive house.

  2. In the same situation described above, both Aaron and Brian intend the contract to be for the sale of the less expensive house. Because both parties intend the same subject matter, the offer is valid.

Alternate Offers.   The offeror may offer to the offeree alternative subject matter. Making alternative proposals does not necessarily mean that the offer is uncertain. Provided that each alternative is certain and definite, the offeror is considered to be making two offers. Acceptance of one cancels the other.

EXAMPLE:

Louise offers to sell Sophie her house in Maryland for $500,000 or her house in Delaware for $350,000. Assuming that Louise only owns one house in each state, the offer is definite in its terms, but gives Sophie a choice. Sophie can agree to buy either house, or neither. This constitutes a valid offer.

Note that in the example above, had either alternative been vague or ambiguous (for instance, if Louise owns two houses in Delaware), there would have been only one valid offer capable of acceptance.

Output Contracts.   Just as with the element of price discussed above, the offer will stand if the quantity or quality of the subject matter can be sufficiently determined by an objective standard to which the parties have agreed, both under the common law and the UCC.

The calculation of Rosa's salary by reference to average salaries in the area is a case in point. Another example of this type of agreement is known as an output contract. In an output contract, one party agrees to purchase all of the output of the other party for a specified price. If one party agrees to purchase from a supplier all supplies actually used during a given period, this is known as a requirements contract. Even though the exact amount of the product that is the subject of the contract is uncertain, the parties have specified an objective standard that can be used to fill in the uncertain term.

 EXAMPLES:

1. A juice manufacturer agrees to buy all of the oranges Farmer Brown grows in a given season at the price of $10 per bushel. This agreement is a valid contract because the amount of oranges can be determined by an objective standard: how many oranges are actually grown during the season.

2. Acme Inc., offers to buy all the coal it will need for its factory furnaces from Ace Mining Company for the next six months at a price of $10 per ton. This is a valid offer because the actual use of the factory furnaces can be mathematically determined.

Just as with the price discussed above, if one of the parties retains the absolute discretion to determine the standard for measuring the quantity or quality of the subject matter, the offer will fail for vagueness. The key is whether the standard used by the parties in the term of description is objective or subjective. Only an objective standard will create a valid offer.

EXAMPLE:

Bijoux Jewelers offers to buy from Beta Diamond Mines for $1,000 per carat all of the diamonds Beta cuts from its mines for the next six months that Bijoux finds of an acceptable grade for its customers. The offer is invalid. Bijoux has retained the right to determine which diamonds are acceptable to its customers; it is not purchasing all of Beta's output. The standard used is subjective.

Parties

The requirement that the parties be specifically described in the offer generally refers only to the offerees. Usually the identity of the offeror is readily ascertainable because he or she is making the proposal. In rare circumstances, a particular offeror may wish her identity to be unknown in order to have a better bargaining position, and this will usually not affect the validity of the offer. If the identity of the offeror is a prime concern of the offeree, as in the example of a contract for personal services, then identity must be revealed for the offer to be deemed valid. For example, Pavarotti might wish to accept an offer to sing at the New York Metropolitan Opera, but he might not want to accept an offer to sing at the National Opera of Costa Rica. Here the identity of the offeror is of great importance.

The offer creates a power of acceptance in the offeree. Therefore, it is important to determine who is capable of accepting the offer. Only the offeree may accept a valid offer, but the offeree does not have to be particularly identified in the offer, provided that his identity can be determined by an objective standard.

And, unless the offeror expressly identifies the intended offeree, any person or persons to whom the offer is communicated is an offeree. The intended offeree may be an individual or a group of persons known as a class, and any member of the class may accept the offer.

 ## EXAMPLES:

1. Sid offers to buy 100 shares of Gamma, Inc., stock for $3 a share from the first shareholder who accepts. He makes this offer to all Gamma shareholders. Gamma shareholders are the class, and the first shareholder to accept creates a valid contract.

2. Rhonda offers to sell her bicycle for $50. She makes the offer in front of three of her friends but specifies that the offer is made only to Sue. In this instance, only Sue is capable of accepting, even though several other people are aware of the offer.

Time of Performance

The fourth essential element of a valid offer is the aspect of the timing of the performance. Offers are not expected to last indefinitely, nor are contracts intended to be performed forever. Some words of limitation must be expressed by the offeror. Only in this manner can the parties know when the contract is to be fulfilled and, conversely, know if the parties have not lived up to their obligations.

Just as with a missing price term, if the parties neglect to mention time, the court will interpret "reasonable time" as the intent of the parties. On the other hand, if the parties attempt to designate a time period but do so imperfectly, the offer will fail.

EXAMPLE:

Farmer White offers to sell five bushels of apples for $10 a bushel to Anne, time of delivery to be determined later. Anne intends to use the apples to bake pies for a church sale. The offer is not valid. Since the delivery time may be too late for Anne's purposes, unless the time is specified in the offer there can be no meeting of the minds.

If time is an important element for the parties—for example, in a contract involving the sale of perishable goods or involving parties who need the goods for a specific purpose—the element of time must be made a specific term of the offer. Such provisions are known as time of the essence clauses. They create a specific enforceable duty on the part of the deliverer to convey the goods by the specified time or be in breach of contract. These clauses are used in circumstances in which "reasonable time" would be too late for one of the parties.

"Reasonable time" is one of those terms that is determined by general custom or usage, and may vary depending on the specific circumstances in a particular area, business, or transaction. The court will consider all the surrounding circumstances to determine what is reasonable for a given situation.

EXAMPLE:

Jim is having a house built and contracts with Richard to deliver piping so the builder can install it. The builder can only do the work on a specific day, and if the pipe isn't there at that time, Jim will have to wait another two weeks to have the pipe installed. This delay will incur additional expense for Jim. In this instance, delivery time of the pipe would be of the essence and should be specified in the contract as such.

Two Related Concepts

Two specific concepts must be mentioned at this point with respect to all of the foregoing. The first deals with the Uniform Commercial Code The UCC is a model law adopted in whole or in part by each state as a statutory enactment that, among other things, has codified certain contractual concepts with respect to the sale of goods. For the most part, contract law still remains an area of law ruled by common law, but the UCC has made several significant changes to the common law of contracts. A complete discussion of the UCC is found in Chapter 8, but at this point one UCC provision should be noted.

If the contract is a contract for the sale of goods between merchants, the contract must comply with the provisions of the UCC. The purpose of the UCC is to promote commerce. To achieve this end, the UCC states that the absence of one or more of the preceding elements of an offer will not render the offer invalid. This exception is based on the presumption that the merchants intend a contract and, as business professionals, are best able to determine the essential requirements of their contracts. But remember, this exception applies only to contracts for the sale of goods between merchants, not for service contracts or contracts between nonmerchants. (See Chapter 8.)

EXAMPLE:

Oscar, a fabric manufacturer, agrees to sell Barbara, a clothing designer, ten bolts of fabric. No mention is made of timing of delivery or price, but Oscar has sold fabric to Barbara in the past. There is a valid contract. Because they are both merchants, and the contract is for the sale of goods, the UCC will let the offer stand. It is assumed that the parties know how to transact business, and time and price can be determined by their past business practices or other UCC provisions.

The second concept worthy of mention is that, regardless of any defect in the terms of the offer, if the parties to the agreement have performed or have started to perform, any defect can be cured by their actual actions. The parties' acts will be construed as creating the specifics of the vague term.

EXAMPLE:

Return to the example given above involving Rosa and the law firm. If Rosa had gone to work for Hacker, even though the salary was left up to Hacker's discretion, and received a paycheck for $300 at the end of the week, the defect of the offer would have been cured by Hacker's actions. The contract would now be interpreted as providing Rosa a salary of $300 per week.

However, if the parties' performances cure one defect but leave other terms indefinite or vague, the offer will still fail.

SAMPLE OFFERS

1   **For Sale**

One blue 1956 Chevy convertible. Excellent condition. Only used by an elderly man to drive three blocks to church on Sundays. Price: $1,200. Non-negotiable. If interested, call Ray: 555–1234.

This simple notice for the sale of an automobile constitutes a valid offer. All of the essential terms for an offer have been met. Remember, it is the elements of an offer that are paramount, not the form that the offer takes. However, should the advertisement have requested offers or said the car would sell for the best price, the notice would not be an offer, but rather would be an invitation to bid or to make an offer. The person who answered that type of ad would, in fact, become the offeror.

2

To: William Smith
Acme, Inc., hereby offers to sell to William Smith 500 yards of decorative copper piping at the price of $.25 per inch, to be delivered by the 15th of next month. To be effective, acceptance of this offer must be sent via certified mail by _____, 20 _____.

Signature
President, Acme, Inc.

The above example constitutes a sample offer for the sale of goods in which the offeror, Acme, Inc., has specified the means of acceptance for William Smith. As indicated above, the offeror establishes the terms of the contract, while the offeree creates the contract by giving the appropriate acceptance. As will be discussed in the next chapter, the offeree must accept in the manner requested by the offeror in order to make a valid contract.

3   **Offer**

_____, hereinafter Offeror, hereby agrees to sell to _____, hereinafter Offeree, the following items for the price indicated next to each item so mentioned.

(FILL IN ITEMS AND PRICES)

The above constitutes a simple form offer, once again for the sale of goods. If the contract were for the sale of services, the services would be specified in the offer where the items and prices are now. As demonstrated, the wording of an offer may be quite simple, provided that the subject matter of the contract and its price are sufficiently described. Precision of wording, as opposed to any particular words, is the key to drafting a valid offer.

CHAPTER SUMMARY

The first requirement of every valid contract is that the parties manifest to each other their mutual assent to the same bargain at the same time. The process by which this assent is manifested starts with an offer. An offer is a proposal by one party (the offeror) to the other party (the offeree) manifesting an intent to enter into a valid contract and creating a power in the offeree to create a contract between the parties by making an appropriate acceptance.

It is the offer that establishes all of the terms of the contract. Consequently, the law requires that the offer manifest a present contractual intent, that it be communicated to the offeree, and that it be certain and definite in all of its essential terms. It is only by meeting these requirements that the offeree knows what he is agreeing to, thereby creating the contract between the parties.

There are four essential elements with respect to the terms of an offer: The offer must be certain and definite with respect to the contract price, subject matter, parties, and time of performance. If the offer's terms are indefinite or ambiguous, the offer cannot create a valid contract because the offeree would be uncertain as to what she was accepting. Generally, the courts will not fix terms inaccurately stated by the offeror; however, should the offer completely fail to mention time or price, the courts usually will infer a "reasonable" time and "reasonable" price in order to uphold the contract. Any defect in the terms of the offer can be cured by the actions of the parties themselves. If they begin to perform the contract, their performance creates the certainty of the indefinite term.

Finally, when dealing with contracts for the sale of goods between merchants, the UCC has provided exceptions to the foregoing, permitting the merchants to determine the terms in their own contracts in order to further and advance commercial transactions.

SYNOPSIS

Three requirements of an offer
1. Manifestation of present contractual intent
2. Communication to offeree
3. Certainty and definiteness as to terms

Four required terms
1. Price
2. Subject matter
3. Parties
4. Time of performance

UCC exception: Sale of goods between merchants

Key Terms

Class: group of persons identified as a group rather than as named individuals

Consideration: the bargain of the contract; a benefit conferred or a detriment incurred

Offer: proposition made by one party to another manifesting a present intention to enter into a valid contract and creating a power in the other person to create a valid contract by making an appropriate acceptance

Offeree: the person to whom an offer is made; the one who has the power to create a valid contract by making an appropriate acceptance

Offeror: the person who initiates a contract by proposing the offer

Output contract: an agreement whereby one person agrees to buy or sell the goods produced by the other party

Requirements contract: agreement whereby one person agrees to buy all his supplies during a given period from one supplier

Time of the essence clause: contractual clause in which a specified time for performance is made a key element of the contract

Uniform Commercial Code (UCC):   statutory enactment codifying certain areas of contract law, specifically with respect to sales contracts between merchants

EXERCISES

1. Take an advertisement from your local newspaper and argue that it is an offer.
2. Using the same ad as above, argue that it is an invitation to bid.
3. What is your opinion of the UCC exceptions to general contract law?
4. Write an offer to sell a piece of your own personal property.
5. Draft an offer that is capable of being accepted by a specified class.

Cases for Analysis

The following case, *Lopez v. Charles Schwab & Co, Inc.*, discusses the court's role in determining whether a valid offer has been communicated. In *Phil Watkins, P.C. v. The Krist Law Firm, P.C.*, the Texas court discusses problems with ambiguity in contracts.

Lopez v. Charles Schwab & Co, Inc.
118 Cal. App. 4th 1224 (1st App. Dist. 2004)

Plaintiff Cynthia M. Lopez appeals the judgment entered in this action after an arbitration award. We conclude the trial court erred in granting defendant Charles Schwab & Co., Inc.'s (Schwab) motion to compel arbitration. Accordingly, we reverse.

I. Background

Schwab is a securities broker, and as part of its business opens and maintains trading accounts for its clients and executes transfers of securities and buy and sell orders. On January 24, 2000, at Schwab's Albuquerque branch, Lopez applied to open an account by filling out two forms. The first was entitled "Open a Schwab Account Today." This application form included a section in which the applicant could select either a "Schwab Account" or a "Schwab One Account." The Schwab One Account had a higher minimum balance and offered features that the Schwab Account did not, such as a daily sweep of uninvested cash balances into a Schwab money fund, checks or a debit card, and automatic margin trading. Lopez checked only the box indicating she wanted a Schwab One Account. The third page of the application stated in bold print: "! Remember to sign the Account Agreement on the next page."

The following page contained the bold-print heading "Agree to Terms." Among those terms was an arbitration provision, which stated: "I agree to settle by arbitration any controversy between myself and Schwab and/or any Schwab officers, directors, employees or agents relating to the Account Agreement, my brokerage account or account transactions, or in any way arising from my relationship with Schwab as provided in Section 17, pages 11–13, of the Brokerage Account Agreement and Section 23, pages 29–31, of the Schwab One Account Agreement. The following disclosures are made pursuant to applicable self-regulatory organization rules: (1) arbitration is final and binding on all parties; (2) the parties are waiving their right to seek remedies in court, including the right to a jury trial; (3) pre-arbitration discovery is generally more limited than and different from court proceedings; (4) the arbitrators' award is not required to include factual findings or legal reasoning, and any party's right to appeal or seek modification of rulings by the arbitrators is strictly limited; and (5) the panel of arbitrators will typically include a minority of arbitrators who were or are affiliated with the securities industry." At the bottom of this form was a box for Schwab use only, labeled "Approved." This box was signed, apparently by a Schwab representative, and an account number was assigned.

On the same day, Lopez also completed and signed a form headed "Transfer Your Account to Schwab," on which she indicated she wanted Schwab to transfer all of her Intel shares from an account with another financial institution.

As noted above, the application's arbitration provision stated that the applicant agreed to settle controversies by arbitration "as provided in Section 17, pages 11–13, of the Brokerage Account Agreement and Section 23, pages 29–31, of the Schwab One Account Agreement." The referenced section of the Schwab One Account agreement contained similar language agreeing to arbitration, as well as disclosures similar to those in the application. In addition, it provided that the arbitration would be conducted by the rules of the National Association of Securities Dealers (NASD), the New York Stock Exchange, the Pacific Stock Exchange, or the Chicago Board Options Exchange; and that either party could initiate arbitration by filing a written claim with one of those organizations. It also provided that

arbitration would be binding, and included provisions that would be effective if the account holder was not a United States resident. The referenced
section of the Schwab Account agreement contained similar provisions.

The Schwab One Account agreement included several other provisions relevant to this dispute. It defined the Schwab One Account agreement as "[t]he agreement you make with us and the Bank when you
open a Schwab One Account, consisting of the Schwab One Application,
this Schwab One Account Agreement and any other written agreements between you and us concerning your Schwab One Account, all as
amended from time to time." A section entitled "Provision of Services"
stated: "To open a Schwab One® Account, you complete an account application. When we approve your application and subject to credit verification, we will open a Schwab One Account for you and act as your broker
to purchase and sell securities for your account and on your instructions."
In a section entitled "Approval of Application, Credit Verification and
Account Information," the agreement stated: "The Schwab One Account
Agreement is effective only after we approve your Schwab One Account
Application. We may decline your application for any reason."

In response to Lopez's application, Schwab directed a letter headed
"Account Verification" to Lopez on January 24, 2000. The letter began,
"Welcome to Schwab"; it included the account number, indicated the
account in question was a Schwab One Account, and included account
handling instructions.

The following day, however, Schwab sent a letter to Lopez denying
her request for a Schwab One Account. The letter stated in pertinent part:
"Thank you for your interest in establishing a Schwab One /Schwab One
International account. [¶] At this time we are unable to honor your request
for this account and are also unable to maintain a standard brokerage
account for you. This decision is based on a credit analysis that included
a consumer credit report . . . . [¶] . . . [¶] You will earn interest for one full
week after the date of this letter and then your account will be closed and
the assets mailed to you."

Lopez stated in a declaration that she went to Schwab's Albuquerque
office on January 28, 2000. A broker there told her an account had not
been opened for her, and she had not been approved for an account due
to her poor credit report. Lopez told the broker she was only interested in
a Schwab One Account and that she did not want the transfer of assets to
go forward. She had no further contact with Schwab until March 1, 2000.

According to Lopez's declaration, she contacted her broker at another
firm, Merrill Lynch, to place a trade of Intel securities on March 1, 2000. She
was informed that all of her Intel shares had been transferred to another
account on February 24, 2000. She contacted Schwab that day, and spoke with
broker Lee Lauderdale. He told her that when he learned her application had
been rejected, he reopened a Schwab account by "pulling a few strings"—
although not a Schwab One Account—and had transferred her Intel shares
from Merrill Lynch to Schwab. He admitted he had acted without Lopez's
permission. Lopez demanded that her stock be returned to Merrill Lynch.
Lauderdale agreed, but the stock was not returned until after April 1, 2000.

Lopez filed this action on June 26, 2000, alleging causes of action for conversion and intentional infliction of emotional distress. Schwab moved to compel arbitration and to stay proceedings, and the motion was granted on October 5, 2000. On January 28, 2003, the court dismissed the action, noting the matter had been resolved at a binding NASD arbitration that resulted in an award dated April 8, 2002. Judgment for Schwab was entered on April 3, 2003. This timely appeal ensued.

II. Discussion

Lopez contends the trial court erred in granting Schwab's motion to compel arbitration, arguing she never entered into an enforceable contract with Schwab. Where there is no factual dispute as to the language of the agreement or conflict in the extrinsic evidence, we determine the meaning of the contract de novo. (*Coast Plaza Doctors Hospital v. Blue Cross of California* (2000) 83 Cal.App.4th 677, 684 [99 Cal. Rptr. 2d 809]; *Valsan Partners Limited Partnership v. Calcor Space Facility, Inc.* (1994) 25 Cal.App.4th 809, 817 [30 Cal. Rptr. 2d 785]; *Titan Group, Inc. v. Sonoma Valley County Sanitation Dist.* (1985) 164 Cal. App. 3d 1122, 1127 [211 Cal. Rptr. 62].)

Schwab argues we should resolve any ambiguities in the contract in favor of arbitration, pointing out that there is a public policy in favor of arbitration under both federal and California law. (*McManus v. CIBC World Markets Corp.* (2003) 109 Cal.App.4th 76, 85 [134 Cal. Rptr. 2d 446], citing *Moses H. Cone Hospital v. Mercury Constr. Corp.* (1983) 460 U.S. 1, 24 [74 L. Ed. 2d 765, 103 S. Ct. 927] *(Moses H. Cone Hospital)* and *Armendariz v. Foundation Health Psychcare Services, Inc.* (2000) 24 Cal.4th 83, 97 [99 Cal. Rptr. 2d 745, 6 P.3d 669].) While it is true that under the FAA, "'any doubts concerning the scope of arbitrable issues should be resolved in favor of arbitration'" (*Rice v. Dean Witter Reynolds, Inc.* (1991) 235 Cal. App. 3d 1016, 1023 [1 Cal. Rptr. 2d 265], overruled on other grounds in *Rosenthal v. Great Western Fin. Securities Corp.*, supra, 14 Cal.4th at p. 407, quoting *Moses H. Cone Hospital*, supra, at pp. 24–25), that policy does not come into effect until a court has concluded that under state contract law, the parties entered into an agreement to arbitrate. As stated in *Cione v. Foresters Equity Services, Inc.* (1997) 58 Cal.App.4th 625, 634 [68 Cal. Rptr. 2d 167] *(Cione)*, "'The right to arbitration depends upon contract; a petition to compel arbitration is simply a suit in equity seeking specific performance of that contract. [Citations.] There is no public policy favoring arbitration of disputes that the parties have not agreed to arbitrate. [Citation.]' [Citation.] As noted, the FAA does not apply until the existence of an enforceable arbitration agreement is established under state law principles involving formation, revocation and enforcement of contracts generally. [Citations.]" (See also *NORCAL Mutual Ins. Co. v. Newton* (2000) 84 Cal.App.4th 64, 74, fn. 8 [100 Cal. Rptr. 2d 683] ["California's public policy favoring alternative dispute resolution does not come into play unless parties have entered an enforceable arbitration agreement"].)

   With these principles in mind, we consider whether Lopez and Schwab formed a contract that included an agreement to arbitrate the dispute at issue here. The essential elements of a contract are: parties capable of contracting; the parties' consent; a lawful object; and sufficient cause or consideration. (Civ. Code, §1550.) "An essential element of any contract is the consent of the parties, or mutual assent. (Civ. Code, §§1550, subd. 2, 1565, subd. 2.) Mutual assent usually is manifested by an offer communicated to the offeree and an acceptance communicated to the offeror. [Citation.] ' " 'An offer is the manifestation of willingness to enter into a bargain, so made as to justify another person in understanding that his assent to that bargain is invited and will conclude it.' " [Citations.]' [Citation.] The determination of whether a particular communication constitutes an operative offer, rather than an inoperative step in the preliminary negotiation of a contract, depends upon all the surrounding circumstances. [Citation.] The objective manifestation of the party's assent ordinarily controls, and the pertinent inquiry is whether the individual to whom the communication was made had reason to believe that it was intended as an offer. [Citations.]" (*Donovan v. RRL Corp.* (2001) 26 Cal.4th 261, 270–271 [109 Cal. Rptr. 2d 807, 27 P.3d 702].)

   Schwab takes the position that its application form, headed "Open a Schwab Account Today," constituted an offer to the public to submit the application and an agreement by Schwab to consider it. Schwab contends that Lopez accepted the offer by completing and signing the application. But the application does not support this interpretation. The signature page of the application was headed "Agree to Terms." This page began, "I hereby request that [Schwab] open a brokerage account as indicated above in the names listed as account holders on this Schwab Account Application. I agree to read and be bound by the terms of the applicable Account Agreement . . . . " This language, particularly the words, "I hereby request," indicates Lopez did not expect that filling out the application would conclude her bargain with Schwab; rather, it reflects an expectation that the application was a request for a bargain or, in other words, an offer to transfer assets to Schwab in exchange for brokerage services.

   Schwab argues that the application contained a present agreement to arbitrate. Again, we view the application differently. The arbitration provision stated Lopez will arbitrate controversies with Schwab "as provided in Section 17, pages 11–13, of the Brokerage Account Agreement and Section 23, pages 29–31, of the Schwab One Account Agreement." By its terms, the Schwab One Account agreement was effective only after Schwab approved the application. Schwab argues that the reference to the account agreements "serves only to incorporate by reference the specific forums that one uses to institute the arbitration detailed in those Account Agreements." In fact, the referenced sections do much more than establish forums: they describe the scope and nature of the arbitration agreement, make the legally required disclosures, and set forth numerous other provisions governing costs and fees, choice of law, enforceability, jurisdiction, and notices, to name a few. In our view, the application serves to ensure that the applicant is aware of the arbitration provision contained in the account agreement, and does not provide independent arbitrability of disputes that arise when no contract is formed between the applicant and Schwab.

Schwab contends, however, that a contract was formed based on its agreement to expend resources checking her credit and considering her application. We see no such agreement in the application. The application authorized Schwab "to make inquiries for the purpose of verifying my creditworthiness and the creditworthiness of my spouse if I am married and live in a community property state. Such inquiries may include verifying information I have given in my Account Application, contacting my employer and obtaining credit reports." It did not obligate Schwab to make any such inquiries. In fact, the Schwab One Account agreement provided that Schwab could deny the application for any reason.

Schwab relies on out-of-state and federal cases in the employment context indicating that an employer's agreement to consider an applicant may be consideration for an arbitration provision in an employment application. In *Martindale v. Sandvik, Inc.* (2002) 173 N.J. 76 [800 A.2d 872, 875], for example, the employee had signed an application stating that as a condition of her employment, she agreed to arbitration of claims related to her employment with the defendant. The court concluded that the employer's consideration of plaintiff's application, its extension of an offer, and its subsequent employment of the plaintiff constituted sufficient consideration of the arbitration agreement, and stated: "That agreement is binding, as would be any other contractual term not contrary to public policy contained in a signed employment application that led, as here, to employment." (Id. at p. 879, italics added.) Similarly, in *Sheller by Sheller v. Frank's Nursery & Crafts* (N.D.Ill. 1997) 957 F. Supp. 150, 154, the plaintiffs agreed in their employment applications that, if they were employed, all disputes would be submitted to arbitration. The defendant subsequently hired the plaintiffs, and the court concluded the arbitration agreements were enforceable. (Ibid.) Here, on the other hand, Schwab rejected Lopez's application.

Defendant draws our attention to only one case in which a prospective employee who was not hired was held bound by an arbitration provision in an employment application; but that case contains crucial differences from this one. The plaintiff in *Johnson v. Circuit City Stores* (4th Cir. 1998) 148 F.3d 373 applied for a job at Circuit City. The application contained a "Dispute Resolution Agreement," which stated in part: "This agreement requires you to arbitrate any legal dispute related to your application for employment or employment with Circuit City. Circuit City will not consider your application unless this agreement is signed . . . . [¶] . . . . [¶] . . . . I recognize that if I sign the Agreement and do not withdraw within three days of signing I will be required to arbitrate any and all employment-related claims I may have against Circuit City, whether or not I become employed by Circuit City. [¶] This Agreement will be enforceable throughout the application process, my employment, and thereafter with respect to any claims arising from or relating to my application or candidacy for employment . . . . [¶] . . . [¶] STOP! [¶] IF YOU HAVE NOT SIGNED THE

AGREEMENT . . . . [¶] If you have decided not to agree to the terms of the preceding DISPUTE RESOLUTION AGREEMENT then you do not need to complete the balance of this application. We appreciate your interest in the company." (Id. at pp. 374–375.) The language of this application indicated unambiguously that the dispute resolution agreement was binding on the applicant throughout the application process, whether or not she was hired, and that Circuit City would not consider her application unless she agreed to arbitration of application-related disputes. Here, in contrast, the arbitration provision in the application was limited to disputes related to the account agreement, the account, or the applicant's relationship with Schwab. It does not refer to disputes arising out of the application, and does not indicate it is binding even if the application is rejected.

As a fallback, Schwab contends that even if the arbitration provision was not effective unless an account was opened, Schwab did in fact open an account for Lopez. As evidence, Schwab points to Lopez's application. On the bottom of the first page of the application is a section for Schwab use only. One box in this section is labeled "Approved," and a Schwab representative signed this box. An account number was also assigned. The "Welcome to Schwab" letter dated January 24, 2000, also contains this account number. Finally, the January 25, 2000, letter telling Lopez that Schwab could not honor her request for an account indicated she would earn interest for a week and that her account would then be closed.

The problem with Schwab's position is that Lopez did not apply for the number of an unfunded account—she applied for an account that would include brokerage services. Schwab unequivocally declined to provide those services when it informed Lopez on January 25, 2000, the day after she applied for an account: "At this time we are unable to honor your request for this [Schwab One] account and are also unable to maintain a standard brokerage account for you." It is undisputed that Schwab did not fund the Schwab One Account Lopez requested, that it never provided the services included in a Schwab One Account, and that it did not transfer assets into any Schwab account in Lopez's name until approximately a month after it denied her request for a Schwab One Account. The Schwab One Account agreement provided that an account would be opened "subject to credit verification." Schwab then refused to enter into a brokerage agreement with Lopez when it sent the January 25, 2000, letter indicating it could not honor her request for an account due to a poor credit report. Schwab could not later unilaterally rescind that rejection. (See *Beverly Way Associates v. Barham* (1990) 226 Cal.App.3d 49, 55 [276 Cal.Rptr. 240] ["[i]t is hornbook law that an unequivocal rejection by an offeree, communicated to the offeror, terminates the offer; even if the offeror does no further act, the offeree cannot later purport to accept the offer and thereby create enforceable contractual rights against the offeror"].)

Thus, we conclude the parties did not enter into a contractual relationship, or indeed, any other kind of relationship. In the absence of such a relationship, we must necessarily reject Schwab's argument that the claims fall within the scope of the arbitration provision. First, as noted above, no obligation to arbitrate exists unless the parties have entered into a contract to arbitrate. (*Cione*, supra, 58 Cal.App.4th at p. 634.) Second, the arbitration provision applies to controversies "in any way arising from my [the applicant's] relationship with Schwab as provided in [the account agreements]." Here, we see no relationship to serve as the basis for the obligation to arbitrate. The cases Schwab cites to argue that this dispute is within the scope of the arbitration provision all presuppose an enforceable agreement to arbitrate, something that does not exist here. (See, e.g., *Izzi v. Mesquite Country Club* (1986) 186 Cal.App.3d 1309, 1314–1316 [231 Cal.Rptr. 315] [arbitration provision in condominium purchase agreement applied to tort claims]; *Pacific Inv. Co. v. Townsend* (1976) 58 Cal.App.3d 1, 9–10 [129 Cal.Rptr. 489] [bound parties participated in limited partnership agreement]; *Bos Material Handling, Inc. v. Crown Controls Corp.* (1982) 137 Cal.App.3d 99, 104–106 [186 Cal.Rptr. 740] [arbitration provision in dealer agreement applied to tort claims]; *Berman v. Dean Witter & Co., Inc.* (1975) 44 Cal.App.3d 999, 1005 [119 Cal. Rptr. 130] [arbitration clause applied to "disputes arising out of transactions based upon the client-broker relationship which the [customer agreement] established"]; *Lewsadder v. Mitchum, Jones & Templeton, Inc.* (1973) 36 Cal.App.3d 255, 257–259 [111 Cal.Rptr. 405] [agreement to arbitrate any controversy arising out of employment broad enough to include tort liability].) Furthermore "[c]ontract formation is governed by objective manifestations, not subjective intent of any individual involved. [Citations.] The test is 'what the outward manifestations of consent would lead a reasonable person to believe.' [Citation.]" (*Roth v. Malson* (1998) 67 Cal.App.4th 552, 557 [79 Cal.Rptr.2d 226].) Here, even if Schwab briefly opened an account for Lopez, her application was immediately rejected and the account she applied for was never funded. A reasonable person standing in Lopez's shoes would not have understood any relationship, contractual or otherwise, was formed with Schwab.

III. Disposition

The judgment is reversed. The matter is remanded to the superior court for further proceedings consistent with this opinion.

Questions

1. Under what circumstances may an appellate court determine the meaning of a contract?
2. What standard does the court articulate to determine whether a communication is an offer?
3. What does the court say is the major problem with the defendant's position?

Phil Watkins, P.C. v. The Krist Law Firm, P.C.
2003 Tex. App. LEXIS 6693

This is a breach-of-contract case in which appellant Phil Watkins, P.C. challenges a summary judgment based on the trial court's determination that a one-page letter agreement between Phil Watkins, P.C. and appellee The Krist Law Firm, P.C. was supported by consideration and is unambiguous. Although we find the agreement was supported by consideration, we hold that it is ambiguous and so reverse the trial court's judgment, and remand this case for further proceedings consistent with this opinion.

I.   Factual and Procedural Background

At issue in this breach-of-contract dispute is the extent, if any, to which Krist can recover attorneys' fees and expenses based on its representation of two former clients subsequently represented by Watkins. Krist represented Kinley Sorrells, Sides, Inc., and other plaintiffs in a lawsuit filed against E.I. DuPont de Nemours & Company, alleging damages to their pecan orchards caused by the Benlate 50 DF (R) fungicide manufactured by DuPont (hereafter, the "DuPont Suit"). Krist claims that, while acting on behalf of these clients, it reached a settlement agreement with DuPont under which each plaintiff would receive $200 per affected acre owned by the clients plus an amount to be calculated under a "most-favored-nations provision." Krist asserts that, under this most-favored-nations provision, Kinley Sorrells and Sides, Inc. (collectively, the "Clients") would have received an additional amount equal to the difference, if any, between the $200 paid and the average per acre value paid by DuPont in the highest 25% of pre-verdict settlements that DuPont paid between the date on which the Clients signed their releases and December 31, 2000, in pecan cases in Texas alleging damage from Benlate (R).

Krist claims that the Clients initially consented to this settlement but then discharged Krist without just cause and without Krist relinquishing its right to reimbursement of expenses plus a 40% fee interest in the Clients' claims. Watkins asserts that the Clients discharged Krist for just cause and that the Clients never consented to any proposed settlement negotiated by Krist. Watkins claims that the Clients assured Watkins they did not owe any obligation to Krist and that Krist had told them to get another lawyer if they did not like the settlement proposed by Krist. In any event, after the Clients approached Watkins about representing them in their claims against DuPont, Watkins asked Krist if the Clients had any financial obligation to Krist. After communications with Kevin Krist, a lawyer employed by the Krist firm, Watkins received the letter dated November 22, 1999, which forms the entire basis for the contract claim in this case. The body of this letter reads in its entirety:

> Thank you for your correspondence of October 12, 1999 relative to Kinley Sorrells and the Sides. [sic] We certainly don't have any problem with you assuming representation of these parties since they

have discharged us. Nevertheless, they did discharge us in the context of us having reached a settlement agreement with DuPont to which they initially consented. Our suggestion is as follows: if the cases are resolved by your firm in such a fashion as to allow for a recovery on their behalf when none would have existed under the terms of our proposed agreement, then we will forfeit all of our fees and expenses. On the other hand, if circumstances are such that our proposed settlement agreement would have resulted in the same or greater recovery than you eventually achieve, then we would insist upon a full fee and reimbursement of expenses.

Please let me have your thoughts on this as soon as possible as the judge is pressing for substitution of new counsel in order to keep the matter from stagnating on his docket.

Kevin Krist testified that Phil Watkins expressed agreement to these terms during a telephone conversation. Furthermore, Phil Watkins later wrote to the Krist firm, "I will not forget the agreement in your letter of November 22, 1999." Watkins substituted in the DuPont Suit as new counsel for the Clients and arranged for these claims to be litigated in the counties where the respective orchards are located. Watkins eventually obtained settlements for the Clients in an amount greater than the Clients would have obtained under the settlement proposed by Krist. When Watkins refused to pay Krist its fees and expenses, Krist sued Watkins and the Clients.

Krist alleged a variety of claims against Watkins and the Clients, and all defendants filed motions to transfer venue. Watkins did not set its venue motion for hearing or obtain a ruling on it. Meanwhile, Krist moved for partial summary judgment alleging that the one-page letter agreement was unambiguous and that, under its terms, Krist was entitled to recover from Watkins $544,411 plus attorneys' fees. The trial court granted summary judgment as to liability and damages on Krist's contract claim but denied the motion as to attorneys' fees. After Krist nonsuited its other claims against Watkins and all its claims against the Clients, and after Krist asked for a final judgment that awarded no attorneys' fees, the trial court signed a final judgment awarding Krist $544,411 plus postjudgment interest.

II.   Issues and Analysis

A.   Did the Trial Court Err by Not Ruling on the Motions to Transfer Venue Before Granting Summary Judgment? [Omitted]

B.   Was There Consideration for the Contract?

In the sixth issue, Watkins asserts the trial court erred in granting summary judgment because there was no consideration for the contract. Watkins argues there was no detriment to Krist in entering into the agreement, and thus no consideration to support it. We disagree. Watkins states that the Clients told him they had no obligation to Krist and that he called Krist to confirm this representation. The contract resulted from the ensuing communications between Krist and Watkins. Although Watkins and the Clients contend the Clients owed Krist nothing after they discharged that firm, the language of the agreement itself shows that Krist was still asserting its rights to recover attorneys' fees and expenses out of any settlement the Clients obtained from resolution of the DuPont Suit. By compromising and limiting its rights to seek attorneys' fees, for example, its right to claim a full 40% fee interest in any settlement reached by Watkins on the Clients' behalf, Krist suffered a detriment, and so the contract was supported by sufficient consideration. See *Northern Nat. Gas Co. v. Conoco, Inc.*, 986 S.W.2d 603, 607, 42 Tex. Sup. Ct. J. 75 (Tex. 1998); *Leonard v. Texaco, Inc.*, 422 S.W.2d 160, 165, 10 Tex. Sup. Ct. J. 462 (Tex. 1967). Accordingly, we overrule the sixth issue.

C.   Is the Contract Ambiguous?

Under its fourth issue, Watkins argues that the contract unambiguously requires Krist to forfeit all of its claims to fees and reimbursement of expenses if, as turned out to be the case, Watkins obtained a better settlement for the Clients than the settlement allegedly proposed by Krist. Watkins also urges that, if we disagree with this contention, we should find the contract to be ambiguous. Krist responds by arguing that the contract unambiguously requires Krist to forfeit only its claims to fees in any recovery that the Clients realize in excess of the settlement allegedly proposed by Krist. Krist also asserts that Watkins has waived its right to assert ambiguity on appeal by agreeing in the trial court that the contract is unambiguous.

As a preliminary matter, any agreement in the trial court by Watkins and Krist that the contract is unambiguous does not prevent this court from concluding that the contract is ambiguous. See *City of Bunker Hill Village v. Memorial Villages Water Auth.*, 809 S.W.2d 309, 310–11 (Tex. App.—Houston [14th Dist.] 1991, no writ) (reversing summary judgment because the contracts in question were ambiguous and holding that agreement of parties that a contract is unambiguous does not prevent an appellate court from finding ambiguity under the ordinary rules of contract construction). Therefore, in evaluating the fourth issue, we must first determine if the contract is ambiguous.

If a written instrument is so worded that it can be given a certain or definite legal meaning or interpretation, then it is not ambiguous and it can be construed as a matter of law. *Lenape Resources Corp. v. Tennessee Gas Pipeline Co.*, 925 S.W.2d 565, 574, 39 Tex. Sup. Ct. J. 496 (Tex. 1996). If its meaning is uncertain and doubtful or it is reasonably susceptible to more than one meaning, taking into consideration circumstances present when the particular writing was executed, then it is ambiguous and its meaning must be resolved by a finder of fact. See id. In construing a written contract, our primary concern is to ascertain the true intentions of the parties as expressed in the written instrument. See id. This court need not embrace strained rules of construction that would avoid ambiguity at all costs. See id. If the contract is ambiguous, then the trial court erred in granting summary judgment because the interpretation of an ambiguous contract is a question for the finder of fact. See *Coker v. Coker*, 650 S.W.2d 391, 394–95, 26 Tex. Sup. Ct. J. 368 (Tex. 1983).

The contract, addressing the issue of Krist's rights against any future settlement by the Clients, states:

> If the cases are resolved by [Watkins] in such a fashion as to allow for a recovery on [the Clients'] behalf when none would have existed under the terms of [Krist's] proposed agreement, then [Krist] will forfeit all of [its] fees and expenses. On the other hand, if circumstances are such that [Krist's] proposed settlement agreement would have resulted in the same or greater recovery than [Watkins] eventually achieves, then [Krist] would insist upon a full fee and reimbursement of expenses.

It is undisputed that the settlement Watkins achieved for the Clients resulted in a recovery for the Clients that was greater than the recovery the Clients would have realized under Krist's proposed settlement agreement. Therefore, the second sentence above cannot apply. Under the circumstances present when the contract was made, the meaning of the first sentence is uncertain and doubtful. The trial court apparently accepted Krist's argument that the contract unambiguously forfeits Krist's fees only to the extent that Watkins's settlement for the Clients exceeds Krist's proposed settlement. This construction is problematic because it conflicts with the ordinary meaning of "[Krist] will forfeit all of [its] fees and expenses." On the other hand, it does not seem likely that Krist would agree to forfeit a claim of more than half a million dollars because Watkins achieved a better settlement than the Clients would have received under Krist's proposed settlement. Though there is a dispute as to whether the Clients discharged Krist with just cause, even if it were determined that they did, Krist still would have a claim against the Clients based on quantum meruit. See *Rocha v. Ahmad*, 676 S.W.2d 149, 156 (Tex. App.—San Antonio 1984, writ dism'd). It would be unusual for Krist to have agreed to waive its entire claim simply because Watkins achieved a better settlement. Though we may not rewrite the contract to insert provisions the parties could have included, we must construe the contract from a utilitarian standpoint, bearing in mind the particular business activity sought to be served. See *Lenape Resources Corp.*, 925 S.W.2d at 574; *Tenneco, Inc. v. Enter. Prods. Co.*, 952 S.W.2d 640, 646, 39 Tex. Sup. Ct. J. 907 (Tex. 1996).

If the first sentence required Krist, under certain circumstances, to completely waive its claim to more than $500,000 in fees and cost reimbursement, then it would be important to know under what circumstances this drastic result would occur. However, the language of the first sentence is opaque in this regard, stating that it is triggered "if the cases are resolved by [Watkins] in such a fashion as to allow for a recovery on [the Clients'] behalf when none would have existed under the terms of [Krist's] proposed agreement." It is undisputed that the "terms of [Krist's] proposed agreement" included an unconditional recovery of $200 per affected acre owned by the settling party. Therefore, there could have been no circumstances under which "[no recovery] would have existed under the terms of [Krist's] proposed agreement."

Watkins asserts that the first sentence is triggered if Watkins obtains a settlement for more money than the Clients would have received under Krist's proposed settlement. Krist asserts that it waived its right only as to any recovery in excess of what the Clients would have recovered under Krist's proposed settlement. We presume that the parties did not intend an impossible condition. See *Page v. Superior Stone Prods., Inc.*, 412 S.W.2d 660, 663 (Tex. Civ. App.—Austin 1967, *writ ref'd n.r.e.*). If we construe the condition in the first sentence to mean "to the extent the Clients recover more than they would have under Krist's proposed settlement," then this language, combined with the phrase "full fee and reimbursement of expenses" in the second sentence (emphasis added) might favor Krist's construction. On the other hand, if we construe the condition to mean "if the Clients recover more when represented by Watkins than they would have under Krist's proposed settlement," then Watkins's construction might be favored. Given the uncertain and doubtful meaning of the contract, we hold that it is ambiguous. See *Lenape Resources Corp.* 925 S.W.2d at 574 (holding contract provision to be ambiguous); *Coker*, 650 S.W.2d at 393–94 (holding that contract language was unclear and ambiguous); *A.W. Wright & Associates, P.C. v. Glover, Anderson, Chandler & Uzick, LLP* 993 S.W.2d 466, 470 (Tex. App.—Houston [14th Dist.] 1999, pet. denied) (holding that language in referral contracts between attorneys was uncertain and doubtful and therefore ambiguous); *Gibson v. Bentley*, 605 S.W.2d 337, 338–39 (Tex. Civ. App.—Houston [14th Dist.] 1980, *writ ref'd n.r.e.*) (holding that condition triggering provision for sharing amounts to be recovered in lawsuit was susceptible of two irreconcilable interpretations and was ambiguous). Accordingly, we sustain the fourth issue to this extent, overrule the remainder of the fourth issue, reverse the trial court's judgment, and remand this case to the trial court so that the trier of fact may determine the true intent of the parties. See *Coker*, 650 S.W.2d at 394–95.

III. Conclusion

Watkins waived its motion to transfer venue by failing to set it for hearing before the trial court's ruling on Krist's motion for summary judgment. The contract, though supported by sufficient consideration, is ambiguous. Therefore, we reverse the trial court's judgment and remand this case to the trial court so that the trier of fact may determine the true intent of the parties.

Questions

1. What is the ambiguity in the contract that the court discusses?
2. According to the court, what is the primary concern of the courts in interpreting contracts?
3. How was the alleged contract accepted?

Suggested Case References

1. In a newspaper advertisement, a department store advertised mink coats for sale for $150. The ad is a misprint; the store meant to say $1,500. A customer came into the store and agreed to buy the coat for $150. Is there a valid offer and acceptance? Read the Georgia court's opinion in *Georgian Co. v. Bloom*, 27 Ga. App. 468 (1921).
2. A judicial interpretation of the concept of good faith in making a valid offer is discussed by the court in *Phoenix Mut. Life Ins. Co. v. Shady Grove Plaza, Ltd.*, 734 F. Supp. 1181 (D. Md. 1990).
3. For an analysis of the terms necessary to create a valid offer read *Patton v. Mid-Continent Systems*, 841 F.2d 742 (7th Cir. 1988).
4. In *Rogus v. Lords*, 804 P.2d 133 (Ariz. App. 1991), the Arizona court discusses how membership in a professional association might be considered as creating a contractual relationship.
5. To see how a court would construe contract terminology, read *Sheridan v. Crown Capital Corp.*, 251 Ga. App. 314, 550 S.E.2d 296 (2001).

Ethical Considerations

Rule 7.3 of the ABA Rules of Professional Conduct prohibits a lawyer, or his or her staff, from soliciting professional employment from a prospective client, by any manner of communication. This means that, whereas a law office may advertise, it may not directly solicit offers from the public. Remember, a retainer agreement between a law office and a client is a contract, and the offer to retain the lawyer, or the offer to represent the client, may not be the result of direct solicitation. Example: ambulance chasing!

Quick Quiz

Answer TRUE or FALSE. (Answers can be found in Appendix C on page 413.)

1. Failure to agree on the time of performance of a contract renders it unenforceable.
2. Consideration is a benefit conferred or a detriment incurred at the request of the other party.
3. Today, all contracts are subject to the Uniform Commercial Code.
4. Under contract law, a class is a group of people individually defined.
5. To be valid, the terms of an offer must be communicated to the offeree.

3 Acceptance

Learning Objectives

After studying this chapter you will be able to:

- Define "acceptance"
- Differentiate between an acceptance and a counteroffer
- Discuss the mirror image rule
- Indicate the effect of silence on an offer
- Explain who is capable of accepting an offer
- Discuss the methods of accepting a bilateral offer and a unilateral offer
- Discuss the impact of the mailbox rule on the acceptance of a contract
- Explain the effect of the rejection of an offer
- Define "revocation"
- Discuss the effect of the termination of an offer on the parties' ability to create a valid contract

CHAPTER OVERVIEW

As discussed in the preceding chapter, the offeror creates a power in the offeree to establish a valid contract by giving the appropriate acceptance. The acceptance is the second major component of every valid contract, and the offer and acceptance together are what constitute the mutual assent.

This chapter discusses the actual formation of the contract when the offeree gives the appropriate assent. To be valid under the common law the acceptance must correspond exactly to the terms established by the offeror in the offer; any variance in these terms may prevent the creation of a contract between the parties. For contracts covered by the Uniform Commercial Code, different legal rules apply.

The manner of the acceptance is dependent on the nature of the contract contemplated: bilateral or unilateral. For bilateral contracts, the offeree must manifest a promise to perform; for unilateral contracts, the offeree must actually perform the requested act.

However, the offeree cannot wait indefinitely to accept or reject the offer. Each offer must be either accepted or rejected in a reasonable time or before circumstances make fulfillment of the contract unlikely or impossible. Unless the offeror has accepted something of value to keep the offer open, the offeror may terminate the offeree's power of acceptance by revoking the offer.

Acceptance Defined

The law is concerned with relationships between persons, and the threshold question in analyzing every legal problem is to determine the exact legal relationship between the parties. Therefore, if a party is attempting to assert a contractual claim, one must be certain that a contract does in fact exist. By giving an appropriate acceptance, the offeree not only creates the contract, but also establishes the moment at which the parties to the contract have enforceable rights and obligations, provided all other elements of a valid contract exist. This element of the acceptance cannot be stressed too strongly; it determines whether the parties have a contract claim against each other, or whether the injured party must seek remedies under a different legal concept.

What is an **acceptance**? Legally defined, acceptance is the manifestation of assent in the manner requested or authorized by the offeror. In making the offer, the offeror may specify exactly how he or she wishes to receive a response. Acceptance requires the offeree to make some affirmative gesture, either by words or actions, depending on the nature of the prospective contract. For the acceptance to be valid, the acceptance must be both unequivocal and unqualified. In other words, the offeree must respond to the *exact* terms stated by the offeror.

Varying the Terms of the Offer

The typical method used to accept an offer is to restate the exact words of the offer or merely to say "I accept." Any change in the terms of the offer or any conditioning of the acceptance on another event ("I accept, provided that I have enough money by the date of the sale") will be interpreted as a **counteroffer** (or **cross-offer**). A counteroffer is a response by an offeree that so significantly changes the terms of the original offer that the roles of the parties are reversed; the offeree becomes the offeror of the new terms. A counteroffer, in effect, rejects the original offer and terminates the original offeree's power of acceptance. A new power of acceptance is created in the original offeror to agree to the terms of the offeree's counteroffer.

EXAMPLES:

1.   Peter offers to sell Rob his home in downtown Los Angeles for $350,000, and Rob attempts to accept by saying "I agree to buy your home in Los Angeles for $325,000." Rob has not accepted the original offer but has made his own offer for the house at a lower price.

2.   In the situation above, if Rob says to the homeowner, "I will think about your offer, but do you think you might be willing to accept less than $350,000?" Rob has not made a counteroffer but has merely inquired as to whether the offeror would consider changing the terms while still keeping the original offer open.

3.   In the same situation, if Rob had responded by saying "I accept your offer to sell me your house in Los Angeles for $350,000, provided that you have a title sufficient to transfer to me a good title to the property," once again this is not deemed to be a counteroffer, because having title sufficient to transfer the property is an implicit condition of the homeowner's ability to make the offer.

What can be gleaned from the foregoing? *First*, to be valid, the acceptance must parrot exactly the terms of the offer. This is known as the **mirror image rule**. *Second*, any variance in the terms of the offer creates a counteroffer, which rejects and therefore terminates the original offer. On the other hand, a mere inquiry, couched in terms of a hypothetical proposal, does not create a counteroffer. *Third*, if the variance is merely a term that is implicit in the original offer, that variance will not constitute a cross-offer.

An exception is made under the Uniform Commercial Code for contracts for the sale of goods between merchants. Because the purpose of the UCC is to promote commerce, the Code permits merchants to vary the terms of the offer in their response without falling into the category of counteroffer. Under the UCC, if the merchant offeror wishes to have the offer accepted exactly as stated, he or she must state that it is an "**iron-clad offer**, take it or leave it." Under these circumstances, the common law rules apply. Absent such a restriction on the part of the offeror, the offeree may vary the terms and that variance will form a part of the contract unless its provisions materially change the offer. If the offeror does not wish to have the new terms made part of the contract, he or she must object within ten days. What constitutes a "material" alteration is determined on a case-by-case basis. The terms that appear in the last communication between the merchant traders become the contractual provisions. The situation is sometimes referred to as the battle of the forms (see infra). For a complete discussion of the UCC provisions, see Chapter 8.

Although the preceding section involved bilateral contracts (a promise for a promise), the same rules apply to unilateral contracts. If the offeree attempts a performance that varies from the requested act, no contract is formed.

EXAMPLE:

Jack offers Jill $2 if she will bring him a cup of coffee. Jill brings tea. Jill has not accepted this unilateral offer.

Silence as Acceptance

If making changes in the terms of the offer constitutes a counteroffer (except under the UCC, as noted above), what is the effect of silence on the part of the offeree? The basic rule is that silence is not an acceptance, even if the offeror says that silence will constitute acceptance.

EXAMPLE:

Jeff writes to Brittany offering to sell his used answering machine for $30. In the letter, Jeff says that if he does not hear from Brittany to the contrary within two weeks, he will send the machine. Jeff cannot assume acceptance by Brittany's silence. As the recipient of an offer, Brittany has the right to speak but not the obligation. However, silence may constitute an acceptance in two situations:

1.   if the offer was solicited by the offeree; or

2.   the contract is implied in fact (see Chapter 1).

Also note that under the UCC a merchant trader may accept simply by shipping the goods ordered. No actual words of acceptance are required.

EXAMPLES:

1.   Imogene admires Jane's antique ring and says, "Will you offer to sell me that ring for $100?" In this example, the offeree has

asked Jane to make her an offer she couldn't refuse. Response becomes superfluous, and the contract is created. This is an example of a solicited offer.

2. Sal goes into the grocery store to buy a can of peas. He places the can on the counter, and the clerk rings up the sale. No words were spoken by either party, but their actions created an offer and acceptance. The contract is implied in fact.

Who May Accept

While at first glance it may appear that only the person to whom the offer is made, the offeree, may accept the offer, this is not always the case. The offer need not specifically identify an individual as the offeree. It may refer just as easily to a class or group of persons, any of whom is capable of accepting the offer. The most typical example of this type of offer is a catalog sale. The "person" who is capable of accepting is anyone who is cognizant of the catalog, subject to any limitations the offeror might have made (for example, offer available only to the first 100 customers).

 EXAMPLE:

Howard sees a J. Crew catalog on the lobby floor of his apartment building. He looks through the catalog and decides to order a shirt. Even though the catalog was addressed to Howard's neighbor, Howard is capable of accepting because J. Crew is making an offer to anyone who sees the catalog, not only to the specified addressee.

There are two exceptions to this rule. The first exception relates to options. An **option** is a situation in which, for consideration, an offeror agrees to hold the offer open exclusively for the option holder, or his transferee, for a specified period of time.

 EXAMPLE:

Rashid wants to buy Clio's house and gives her $1,000 as a binder for one month. During this time period, Clio is prohibited from selling her house to any other person. However, Rashid, as the option holder, can transfer his right to purchase to someone else. The option only binds the person who has received the tangible consideration.

The second exception to the general rule that only the person to whom the offer is made may accept the offer is the case of the **undisclosed principal**.

To understand the undisclosed principal, first you must understand the **principal-agent** relationship. Briefly, an *agent* is one who acts for and in the place of another, known as the *principal*, in order to enter into contracts with third persons on the principal's behalf. The consequence of these contracts is to bind the principal to the third person. The agent is merely the conduit for the negotiation and completion of the contract. Consequently, when a third person makes an offer to an agent, it is in fact the principal who has the power to accept. Even when an agent does not disclose to the offeror who the principal is, it is still only the principal who has the ability to create the contract.

EXAMPLE:

A famous actress wants to buy a Van Dyke painting; however, she knows that the price will go up if the current owner finds out that she is the buyer. She has her sister Lee go to the owner as her agent to negotiate the sale. Lee tells the owner she represents someone who doesn't want her identity known. When the owner makes an offer to Lee as the agent, the actress is actually the purchaser. Only the actress has the power to accept the offer.

Method of Acceptance

The appropriate method of acceptance depends on the type of contract contemplated: bilateral or unilateral. As stated in Chapter 1, a **bilateral** contract exchanges a promise for a promise, and a **unilateral** contract exchanges a promise for an act. To accept a bilateral contract, the offeree must make the promise requested. In contrast, the only way that a unilateral contract can be accepted is by performing the act requested.

The preceding idea may seem quite simple, yet it is extremely important because it is the acceptance that creates the contract. All contract rights and obligations flow from and are dependent on the existence of a valid contract. Consequently, the timing of the acceptance is crucial to the determination of the rights of the parties.

Acceptance of a Bilateral Contract

Whenever the offeree gives the promise requested, the bilateral contract comes into existence (assuming all other contractual requirements are met). As long as the offeree outwardly manifests intent to accept the offer, the contract is formed, regardless of the offeree's subjective intent. Even if the offeree is not serious in her intent, as long as her outward appearance gives no indication to a reasonable person that she does not intend to accept, she will be bound by the contract. If all the circumstances lead the offeror to reasonably believe that the offeree was manifesting contractual intent, then the offeror's expectation that a contract exists is usually given full weight. Of course, the "reasonableness" of the situation is crucial to this determination and can only be ascertained by particular facts in a given circumstance.

Not only may a bilateral offer be accepted by giving the requested promise, it may also be accepted impliedly by *doing* the act promised. Action, as well as words, may be used to create a binding contract. See the above reference to the UCC.

EXAMPLE:

A customer sends an order for buying goods. The seller may respond either by promising to sell the goods at the offered price or by shipping the goods, thereby implying his promise by fulfilling his obligation. In either instance, it is a bilateral contract that is formed.

To give the appropriate acceptance, the offeree must be conversant with all of the terms of the offer. The offeree's incomplete knowledge of the terms of the offer would preclude his ability to give a valid acceptance. How can he accept what he doesn't know? There would be no mutual assent in this situation.

As indicated above, the timing of this manifestation of assent is imperative in determining whether a contract has come into existence. Obviously, if the offer and acceptance are made verbally by each party to the other, there would be no question whether the contract was formed; the parties were face-to-face at that moment. However, what if another method of communication is used? How are the parties to know at what precise moment in time the contract was created?

Mailbox Rule

Back in the days before the telephone, telegram, fax machines, email, and other electronic devices, the postal service was the typical method of communication used by persons living some distance from each other. From those times, a rule was formulated to help determine the moment of the creation of a contract. The **mailbox rule** states that the acceptance of an offer of a bilateral contract is effective when properly dispatched by an authorized means of communication. The moment the acceptance is dropped in the mailbox, the contract is formed.

The mailbox rule requires that the letter be "properly dispatched" and that the means of communication be "authorized." If the letter is incorrectly addressed or does not contain sufficient postage, it would not be "properly dispatched." Also, if the offeror specifies an answer by letter only, an attempt to answer by telegram would not be an authorized means of communication. In these instances, the acceptance would only be effective when actually received by the offeror, and only if he agreed to the variance.

 EXAMPLE:

On Monday Janet offers to sell Brenda her Ming vase for $10,000, provided that Brenda accepts in writing by Friday. At 11:00 on Friday morning, Brenda mails a letter to Janet accepting her offer. On Saturday, Janet agrees to sell the vase to someone else. Does Brenda have a contract with Janet? Can Brenda force Janet to convey the vase to her? The answer to both questions is yes. Even though Brenda's letter didn't reach Janet until Monday, because she dispatched the acceptance on Friday, according to the terms of the offer a contract was formed.

There is an exception to the mailbox rule for option contracts. Acceptance of an option is only effective on receipt. This exception exists because of the nature of an option—a contract to limit the offeror's ability to sell the item to someone else, even though the offeree has not yet accepted the sale itself. Because of the limiting nature of the option, the offeror must actually receive the acceptance to be bound.

Rejection of a Bilateral Contract

If a person is not interested in accepting a specific offer, the offeree has the ability to reject. Be aware, however, that the offeree's rejection terminates the offeree's ability to accept, thus ending that particular offer.

 EXAMPLE:

Jaime offers to sell his used Contracts book to Mitch for $10. Mitch thinks he can get a better price at the bookstore and turns Jaime down. Later, realizing that Jaime's offer was a bargain, Mitch attempts to accept. He cannot. Once rejected, the offer cannot be revived. Mitch's attempted acceptance to Jaime constitutes a counteroffer.

The general rule with respect to the rejection of bilateral contracts is that rejection is effective only when actually received. The offeror does not actually have to have read the rejection for it to be effective. Only receipt is required.

Rejection and the Mailbox Rule

Historically, the mailbox rule and the rule of rejection under contract law have created certain conflicting situations.

EXAMPLE:

In the example posited above with Brenda, Janet, and the Ming vase, what if Brenda decides that she really didn't need a Ming vase? On Friday morning at 9:00 a.m. she writes to Janet rejecting her offer. However, at 10:00 a.m. her neighbor mentions to Brenda that he is in the market for a Ming vase and will pay $15,000 for one. Immediately, Brenda writes to Janet accepting the offer, mailing the acceptance at 11:00 a.m. The rejection arrives at Janet's on Monday morning; Monday afternoon she sells the vase. Tuesday morning Brenda's acceptance arrives. Does Brenda have a contract right against Janet?

Under the historical interpretation, Janet would be in breach of contract because the contract was formed on Friday at 11:00 a.m. when Brenda dispatched the acceptance. The rejection is effective only on receipt—Monday—so clearly the acceptance occurred first. Therefore, Janet and Brenda have a contract, which Janet breached by selling the vase on Monday afternoon.

By modern standards, however, this solution does not seem fair to Janet. Consequently, the modern approach to the problem is to determine the reasonable expectations of the offeror. In this situation, it is reasonable that Janet would have assumed that Brenda rejected her offer, and so the rejection would take precedence over the mailbox rule.

What if Janet still had the vase on Tuesday, not having agreed to sell it to anyone else? Would Brenda then have a contract with Janet? Probably, because Janet had not changed her position in reliance on Brenda's rejection.

Acceptance of a Unilateral Contract

Unlike bilateral contracts, where the contract is formed before either side has performed any of the promised acts, a unilateral contract may only be accepted by the offeree by actually performing the act requested. Only when the requested act has been performed is the contract accepted.

EXAMPLES:

1. Hillary promises to pay Lorraine $75 if Lorraine types Hillary's term paper this afternoon. If Lorraine does not do the typing, Hillary has no legal recourse. She requested an act, not a promise, and until the act is performed no contract exists.

2. Jeanne's mother promises to give Jeanne $1,000 if Jeanne quits smoking for two years. Until Jeanne completes two smoke-free years, no enforceable contract exists.

Usually, the law imposes no duty on the offeree to notify the offeror that the act has been performed. However, there are three exceptions to this general rule with respect to notification.

1. The offeree must notify the offeror if the offeror has requested such notification as part of the offer.
2. The offeree must notify the offeror of the performance if the offeror would have no other way of knowing that the act has been performed.

 EXAMPLE:

Sara, who lives in Illinois, offers Frank $1,500 to paint her summer house in Vermont. If she weren't told that the house had been painted, she wouldn't know the contracted had been accepted.

3. The offeree must notify the offeror in a reverse unilateral contract. In a reverse unilateral contract, the performer makes the offer rather than the promisor.

 EXAMPLE:

Eric says to Jeff, "I will paint your house if you promise to pay me $1,500." The offer proposes that an act be exchanged for a promise, and the offeree must accept by giving the promise (the giving of the promise constitutes the "notice"). This is an unusual situation, but it is interesting to note.

Because unilateral contract offers are only accepted by performance of the act, they are much easier to analyze than bilateral contract offers. One must merely pinpoint the moment at which the act was completed to determine the moment the contract is formed.

Termination of the Ability to Accept

The ability of the offeree to accept the offer exists only for as long as the offer remains open. The law does not anticipate that offerors will keep their offers open indefinitely. Therefore, either by an act of the parties or by operation of law, every offer will have a finite period during which it is capable of acceptance. After that period, the offer is viewed as terminated, and any attempt on the part of the offeree to accept constitutes a counteroffer. A terminated offer cannot be revived unless *both* parties agree to the revival.

To terminate an offer by an act of the parties, either the offeree must reject the proposal or the offeror must **revoke** the offer. An offeror may revoke an offer any time prior to acceptance by the offeree. Once the offeree has accepted, a contract is formed, and any attempt by the offeror to revoke could be construed as a breach of his contractual obligations (see Chapter 10).

Revocation of Bilateral Contracts

For bilateral contracts, the offeror may revoke at any time prior to the offeree giving her promise, the acceptance. However, there are four situations in which the offeror may not revoke an offer prior to acceptance by the offeree.

First, an offeror may not revoke an offer prior to acceptance in the case of an option contract. As discussed previously, one of the peculiar elements of an option is the obligation of the offeror to keep the offer open for a specified period of time. Because the offeror has received consideration for this promise, he is automatically bound to fulfill it.

Second, an offeror may not revoke an offer prior to acceptance if the offeree has detrimentally relied on the offer, even though he has not yet accepted.

EXAMPLE:

Lil offers to sell her house to Isobel and gives her two weeks in which to accept. During this time, Isobel receives an offer for her own house, and sells it based on Lil's offer. If Lil were to revoke her offer within this two week period, Isobel would be homeless, and consequently, the court would not permit Lil to revoke.

Third, an offeror may not revoke an offer prior to acceptance in an auction without reserve. An **auction without reserve** is a situation in which the property owner agrees to auction her property and specifically to accept as selling price whatever is the highest bid. Because of the specific promise on the part of the property owner and the expectations of the auction dealer and the bidders, the parties are precluded from revoking. Note that this is not the case if the property is put up at an **auction with reserve**, which gives the parties the right to revoke at any time before the gavel finally comes down.

Fourth, under the UCC a merchant offeror may not revoke a **firm offer** for a period of 90 days, even if such offer is not supported by consideration.

Revocation of Unilateral Contracts

The general rule true for bilateral contracts—that the offeror has the power to revoke an offer any time prior to acceptance by the offeree—is just as true for unilateral contracts. However, the time element is different with a unilateral contract because an act must be completed rather than a promise given. Only when the offeree completes the act is the offer considered accepted and a contract created.

EXAMPLE:

On Monday, Steven offers to pay Cal $2,000 if Cal will paint his house on Friday. Steven is to supply all the paints and brushes. On Wednesday, Steven revokes the offer. No contract exists between Cal and Steven because the requested act has not yet been performed, and neither party has suffered any damages. But what if Steven revokes on Friday afternoon, after Cal has already painted half the house? What if Cal were supposed to buy the paints and brushes, which he did on Monday afternoon, and Steven revokes on Wednesday? In these instances, would Cal have a cause of action against Steven?

To resolve the questions in the above example, it would help to know about a case decided many years ago that addressed similar problems: the case of Jimmy the Human Fly.

EXAMPLE:

As an advertising gimmick, a store owner put an ad in the newspaper offering "Jimmy the Human Fly" $10,000 if he would climb to the very top of the Washington Monument on a particular day and time. Jimmy was a performer for the circus who claimed he could climb any surface.

On the day in question, a large crowd gathered, and the store owner handed out circulars about a sale at his store. At the appropriate moment, Jimmy arrived and started up the edifice. Just before he reached the very top of the monument, the store owner screamed, "I revoke!"

Jimmy sued the store owner for the $10,000 and won. The court held that because Jimmy had made a *substantial beginning* on the performance, the offeror no longer had the ability to revoke. Although Jimmy hadn't completely accepted at that point (because he had not reached the very top), it would be unfair to him if the offeror could terminate the offer at that point.

Back to Cal and Steven. Based on the foregoing, it would appear that after Cal had painted half of Steven's house, Steven would no longer be able to revoke his offer. If he revoked after Cal bought the paints and brushes, but before he started painting, the purchase of the equipment would probably not be considered a "substantial beginning," and therefore there would not be a contract. Would Cal lose the money he spent on the paint and brushes? Probably not, because he only made these purchases in reliance on the offer. Steven would most probably have to reimburse Cal for the purchases. If Cal could prove that the paints and brushes could only be used for Steven's project, and that he had no other need for the materials, it would be unjust to Cal not to have Steven reimburse the money Cal had expended in reliance of the proposed contract with Steven.

Termination by Operation of Law

An offer may also be terminated by **operation of law**. Operation of law is a legal term for the circumstance in which one event has a legal effect on a second, unconnected event. With respect to the law of contracts, there are four circumstances, or events, that terminate offers by operation of law:

1. *Lapse of time.* If the offeree takes an unreasonable length of time to respond, the offer is considered terminated by operation of law. The courts do not expect offers to be kept open indefinitely, and the offeree's attempt to accept after a long delay constitutes a new offer to the original offeror.
2. *The death or destruction of the subject matter.* For example, it is impossible to sell a horse to stud if the horse has died, and substitution in this instance is not possible.
3. *The death or insanity of the offeror or offeree.* Death would appear to be self-explanatory, and insanity falls under the capacity of the parties to enter into a valid contractual relationship (see Chapter 5).
4. *Supervening illegality.* **Supervening illegality** means that the contract was legal at the time of the offer, but prior to acceptance a statute or court decision makes the subject matter illegal.

EXAMPLE:

Dot is offered a contract to operate a gambling casino in Atlantic City, New Jersey. Prior to acceptance, the town officials of Atlantic City decide that having gambling on the boardwalk is not a good idea and rescind the ordinance permitting gambling in the city. Dot would no longer be able to accept such an offer because the subject matter of the contract, managing a gambling casino, is now illegal.

Effect of Termination of Offer

Once an offer has been terminated, either by act of the parties or by operation of law, it can no longer be accepted. Any attempt on the part of the offeree to accept after that point constitutes a new offer to the original offeror. The roles of the parties are then reversed, and all of the rules with respect to offers and acceptance apply in reverse. The original offeree is now the offeror and must make her offer according to the dictates of the law with respect to offers. The power of acceptance now rests with the erstwhile offeror, who must follow the guidelines of this chapter. This is an important concept because it relates to the issue of whether, and when, a contractual relationship has been created between the parties.

The entire series of events must now be analyzed. Was the original offer valid? Was it terminated before acceptance? Does the acceptance, after termination, convey sufficient precision so as to constitute a valid offer? How can the new offer be accepted? Always remember that every action and word of the parties in a contractual situation has specific legal meaning and ramifications. Never assume a result until a full analysis has been made.

SAMPLE CLAUSES

Unlike other sections of contractual negotiations, there are no specific clauses that one can point to and say, "That is an acceptance!" As a general rule, the offer and acceptance merge into the basic terms of the contract. The offeror creates the contract terms; the offeree merely agrees to those terms. This agreement can take the form of signing the completed contract, agreeing to the terms orally, or, for a unilateral contract, performing the act. No words other than the ones used by the offeror can be used to accept. Any variance in the offeror's stated terms may constitute an offer to the offeror and thus do not form an acceptance, except for contracts between merchants for the sale of goods covered by the UCC.

CHAPTER SUMMARY

Acceptance is the manifestation of assent in the manner requested or authorized by the offeror under the common law. To be effective, the acceptance must be unequivocal and unqualified; any variance in the terms, except those implicit in the offer, may constitute a counteroffer (or cross-offer). This common law rule has been changed significantly for contracts for the sale of goods between merchant traders where changes in the offeree's terms, except for an ironclad offer, act to modify the original offer. Acceptance requires an affirmative act, either in words or deeds. Silence, except in solicited offers or implied-in-fact contracts, is never deemed to be assent. The offer and acceptance together constitute the requisite mutual assent to form a contract.

An offer may be accepted only by the person or group to whom it has been made, and the offeree must know all the material terms of the offer to make a valid acceptance. A bilateral contract is accepted by giving a promise or by implying the promise by performing the promised act. A unilateral contract is accepted by performing an act. At the moment acceptance is validly given, the contract is formed, and the parties are thereby obligated to its terms.

Bilateral contracts are accepted when the acceptance is properly dispatched by an authorized means of communication (the mailbox rule). Rejection of a bilateral contract is only effective when actually received by the offeror. But, in any event, the court will uphold the reasonable expectations of the parties as determined by the particular factual situation.

Unilateral contracts are accepted whenever the offeree performs the act requested. The offeree of a unilateral contract, except in special circumstances, has no duty to communicate with or notify the offeror of his performance of the requested act. The act itself is sufficient acceptance.

An offer may no longer be accepted if it is terminated by the parties. An offeree terminates his ability to accept by rejecting the offer. An offeror terminates the offer by revoking the offer prior to the acceptance. In unilateral contracts, the offeror may not revoke once the offeree has made a substantial beginning on the requested performance.

An offer may also terminate, not by act of the parties, but by operation of law (lapse of time, destruction of the subject matter, death or insanity of the parties, or supervening illegality). Any attempt to accept an offer after it has terminated does not revive the offer but creates a new offer extending from the original offeree to the original offeror.

The key questions with respect to acceptance are:

1. Is the acceptance timely and valid?
2. At what point does the contract come into existence?
3. Has the offer terminated?
4. What are the reasonable expectations of the parties?
5. Is the contract covered by the UCC?

SYNOPSIS

Acceptance
1. Must be unequivocal and unqualified
2. Must be in the exact manner and form indicated by the offeror
3. Any variance in terms of the offer is a counteroffer
4. Silence is not an acceptance

Method of acceptance
1. Bilateral
   a. Give promise
   b. Mailbox rule

    2. Unilateral
       a. Do act
       b. Substantial beginning
Termination of offers
    1. Rejection
    2. Revocation
    3. Varying terms
    4. Operation of law

Key Terms

Acceptance: manifestation of assent in the manner requested or authorized by the offeror

Auction with reserve: parties have the right to revoke any time before gavel comes down

Auction without reserve: property owner relinquishes the right to revoke

Bilateral contract: a contract that exchanges a promise for a promise

Counteroffer: a variance in the terms of the offer that constitutes a rejection of the original offer and a creation of a new offer

Cross-offer: see Counteroffer

Firm offer: offer made under the UCC that remains open for a reasonable period of time but in no event more than 90 days

Ironclad offer: under the UCC, an offer whose terms may not be altered by the offeree

Mailbox rule: rule stating that the acceptance of a bilateral contract is effective when properly dispatched by an authorized means of communication: formulated to help determine the moment of creation of a contract

Mirror image rule: to be valid, the acceptance must correspond exactly to the terms of the offer

Operation of law: the manner in which one event has a legal effect on a second, unconnected event

Option: a contract to keep an offer open for a specified time that is secured by consideration

Principal-agent: an agent is one who acts for and on behalf of another, the principal, for the purpose of entering into contracts with third persons

Rejection: to refuse an offer

Reverse unilateral contract: a contract in which the performer, rather than the promisor, makes the offer

Revocation: to recall an offer

Supervening illegality: a law that renders a once-legal activity illegal

Undisclosed principal: a person, represented by an agent, who is party to a contract but has not revealed his or her identity to the other party

Unilateral contract: a contract that exchanges a promise for an act

EXERCISES

1. What elements make an attempted acceptance a counteroffer?
2. Give two examples in which the actions of the offeree reject a written offer.
3. Compose an offer that specifically limits the offeree's ability to accept.
4. Using the example of Jimmy the Human Fly, argue the case for the store owner.
5. Discuss the circumstances that would terminate a person's ability to accept a valid offer.

Cases for Analysis

The first case summary that follows, *United States v. Lauckner*, highlights the manner in which a contractual offer may be accepted. The second, *Monsour's Inc. v. Menu Maker Foods, Inc.*, discusses the difference between an acceptance and a counteroffer.

United States v. Lauckner
101 Fed. Appx. 870 (3d Cir 2004)

We will recount only those facts essential to our determination. Lauckner was employed as the Vice President of Finance of AAA in December 1989, at a time when the company was experiencing financial difficulties. A few months later, in February 1990, AAA filed for relief under *chapter 11 of the Bankruptcy Code*, and the federal employment taxes withheld on account of wages of the employees of AAA remained unpaid for a number of quarters, including the quarter ended December 31, 1989 ("Fourth Quarter Taxes").

As a person required to collect, account for, or pay over withholding taxes, who has "willfully" failed to do so, Lauckner was assessed a penalty under *section 6672 of the Internal Revenue Code* in an amount equal to the total amount of the Fourth Quarter Taxes. This amount, originally in excess of $ 2.9 million, was assessed against Lauckner in March of 1991, and later reduced to $919,208.17.

Lauckner challenged his liability for this amount in a refund suit, and the parties moved for summary judgment ("Lauckner I"). The District Court for the District of New Jersey held that Lauckner was a "responsible person" under the Internal Revenue Code but concluded that the question of "willfulness" was not ripe for summary judgment because there was a factual issue as to whether there were unencumbered funds from which AAA could have paid the taxes.

Thereafter, Lauckner and the IRS exchanged correspondence regarding a possible resolution of his liability and, ultimately, the government contends, entered into a settlement that entitled the IRS to enter a consent judgment against Lauckner in the amount of $919,208.17, if he defaulted under their agreement. To the contrary, Lauckner argues either that his agreed liability under their settlement agreement was zero or $7,000, or, in the alternative, there was no agreement to settle the liability in the first place because the government's "acceptance" of the offer by Lauckner contained an additional term, namely, a provision regarding attorneys' fees that had not previously been a part of the negotiations. We need not decide the amount of the consent judgment purportedly agreed upon, because we find that there was no mutual agreement on the terms of the settlement as a matter of law.

The settlement arose from a series of letters between Lauckner's counsel and the government. On May 1, 1996, Lauckner's counsel wrote to the IRS offering a settlement whereby Lauckner would make payments of $7,000 to the government in addition to the payments made over time as contained in an attached "Collateral Agreement," and Lauckner would agree further that the government would keep any income tax-related refunds that would otherwise be due to him.

Lauckner's counsel followed up with a further letter, dated the same date, attaching a revised Collateral Agreement calling for Lauckner to pay thirty percent of his annual income in excess of $65,000 to the government. In addition, Lauckner's counsel indicated that he "will agree to the entry of a consent judgment against him, to take effect only upon his default under the terms of the Settlement Offer. The other terms of the offer remain the sam. . . . " The Collateral Agreement was a ten-page, single-spaced document containing several provisions not specifically referenced in any correspondence.

Thereafter, Lauckner's counsel sent a letter dated May 6, 1996, clarifying "our understanding" that the consent to the entry of judgment against him would be "for his fourth quarter liability relative to AAA Tcking Corporation." The letter also noted that this judgment would only be entered should Lauckner default under the terms of the Collateral Agreement and the terms of the Settlement Offer.

Thereafter, in a letter dated July 31, 1996, Lauckner's counsel confirmed that a $7,000 cash portion of the Settlement Offer would be paid within fifteen days of the United States' acceptance of the offer.

Several months later, in December 1996, the government responded to the Settlement Offer, indicating, "This is to advise you that the offer has been accepted on behalf of the Attorney General with the understanding that each party will bear its own costs, including any attorneys' fees." The correspondence from the government set forth the salient terms that had been referenced in the correspondence, including the fact that Lauckner would execute the Collateral Agreement, and that judgment would be entered against Lauckner but would only be enforced if Lauckner were to default. The government enclosed five copies of the Collateral Agreement to be executed by Mr. Lauckner and eight copies of the Statement of Annual Income to be completed by Mr. Lauckner each year, and noted that upon receipt of the total amount due under the "settlement agreement," including amounts due under the Collateral Agreement, the government would file a satisfaction of judgment.

This is the last activity which occurred before the government brought suit in the United States District Court for the District of New Jersey to enforce the "settlement agreement" or, in the alternative, to collect the Fourth Quarter Taxes from Lauckner ("Lauckner II"). The District Court held that the settlement agreement was enforceable and that the government had the right to entry of judgment for the $919,208.17 amount. The District Court believed that, since Lauckner did not have a right to fees as a matter of law, the last-minute insertion of this issue should not prevent the formation of a contract.

We will reverse, as we have great difficulty enforcing a "settlement agreement" where the "acceptance" violates the "mirror image" rule. *Step-Saver Data Systems, Inc. v. Wyse Technology*, 939 F.2d 91, 99 (3d Cir. 1991). At common law, "if the purported acceptance attempts to restate the terms of the offer, such restatement must be accurate in every material respect. . . . A variation on the substance of the offered terms is material, even though the variation is slight. . . . " 1 Joseph M. Perillo, *Corbin on Contracts* § 3.32, at 478-80 (1993). Similarly, under the *Restatement (Second) of Contracts* § 59 (1979), "[a] reply to an offer which purports to accept but is conditional on the offeror's assent to terms additional to or different from those offered is not an acceptance but is a counteroffer." *Id.*

Here, as Lauckner points out, the issue of attorneys' fees was not even referenced until the last correspondence from the government that "accepted" Lauckner's offer "with the understanding that each party will bear its own costs, including any attorneys' fees." Although the law would appear to deny Lauckner the right to such fees, had he sought them in litigation, we cannot say categorically that such an understanding, whereby the government would pay all or a portion of the fees, could not have been agreed upon as part of a settlement. Also, as Lauckner points out, he believed that the government's initially overstated assessment, and the efforts he had to go through to have that assessment reduced, created litigation, the costs of which he should not have to bear. Accordingly, we do not think it as clear as the District Court apparently did, that the raising of the term was immaterial. Because the government's purported acceptance restated the terms of Lauckner's offer while adding an additional material term to the offer, it was, as a matter of law, not an acceptance, but a rejection and a counter-offer. Therefore, the parties never formed an agreement.

Accordingly, we will REVERSE and REMAND to the District Court for further proceedings.

Questions

1. Why does the court say that the mirror image rule was violated?
2. Based on this decision, what would you look for to make sure any settlement that you reach is legally enforceable as a contract?
3. How would you describe, legally, the correspondence between the parties?

Monsour's, Inc. v. Menu Maker Foods, Inc.
2007 U.S. Dist. LEXIS 39870 (D. Kan. 2007)

This is a breach of contract action. The matter is currently before the court on the plaintiff Monsour's motion to enforce an alleged settlement agreement. For the reasons stated herein, the plaintiff's motion is denied.

Findings of Fact

On March 14, 2007, Monsour's presented Menu Maker with a written settlement offer of $420,000 by email. Counsel discussed the matter two days later by telephone, and defendant's counsel offered settlement in the amount of $250,000. In a second telephone conference held later the same day, plaintiff's counsel rejected defendant's offer and counter-offered to settle the case for $400,000. Later the same day, Menu Maker's counsel sent an email, reciting the negotiations during the day and stating, with respect to the earlier, rejected offer, "I was authorized by Mr. Graves to offer $250,000 in settlement." Dick Graves is the president and sole shareholder of Menu Maker Foods, Inc.

On the morning of March 26, Monsour's counsel telephoned counsel for Menu Maker and sought to get defendant to raise its settlement offer. Menu Maker's counsel stated that his client would not pay $400,000 to settle, but had again authorized an offer of $250,000. Defendant's counsel expressed doubt that his client would pay more than $300,000, and would not accept any offer that increased the settlement amount by between $50,000 and $75,000.

Later that morning, plaintiff's counsel sent an email stating that "if Menu Maker Foods offers $300,000, this firm will recommend the same to the Monsours."

Creighton Cox, the General Manager of Menu Maker, told Graves that plaintiff's counsel had stated he would recommend his client accept an award of $300,000, if such an offer was advanced by the defendant. Cox told Graves that plaintiff's counsel had been told it was unlikely Menu Maker would agree to a $300,000 settlement, but that the information would be presented to the company.

Graves has stated by affidavit that he believed the $300,000 figure was a rejection of the $250,000 settlement offer. He told Cox to inform defense counsel that the company would not accept a $300,000 offer. He also told Cox that he was reconsidering whether to settle at all.

At 3:51 p.m., on March 26, 2007, defendant's counsel responded that the response of Dick Graves is that he will not pay $300,000 in settlement of this case. In truth, Dick indicated that he was getting 'iffy' about his $250,000 offer.

According to Cox's affidavit, the term "iffy" was his rather than Graves's.

Plaintiff's counsel responded with an email at 4:55 p.m.:

> I just spoke with my clients. They accept Menu Maker's settle-
> ment offer of $250,000. The PACA lien has been negotiated down to
> $50,000 and we will pay it directly from our trust account. You can con-
> firm that with Larry in Florida.

On the next day, counsel for the PACA trust beneficiaries confirmed to both plaintiff and defense counsel that it accepted $50,000
in settlement to release their judgment. The same day, plaintiff's counsel emailed counsel for defendant congratulating them on a well-de-
fended case, requesting defense counsel prepare a journal entry of
dismissal and a release, and stating that the court had been notified of
the settlement.

At 10:09 a.m. the same day, defense counsel sent an email stating: I
have been unable to communicate with Mr. Graves regarding your email
'accepting' our $250,000 settlement offer. Given my inability to speak with
Mr. Graves I cannot speak for Menu Maker and confirm that the offer was
still outstanding.

> What?
> Val, when you and I spoke yesterday I specifically asked you if
> the $250 was still on the table early yesterday morning and you said it
> was. My notes from the conversation reference the same. That is why
> my 9:18 a.m. email from yesterday did not reject the 250, but advised
> we would recommend 300 if Dick would go to that.
> Your 3:51 p.m. email from yesterday indicated that Dick would
> not go to 300 and was starting to get "iffy" about the 250 settlement
> offer. That is when my clients accepted the same. Your 3:51 email never
> indicated the 250 was off the table.
> I do not remember saying that the offer was still on the table. I
> recall saying that I believed that it was. I would have no authority from
> Graves regarding whether or not the offer still lived. If I did in fact say
> that the offer was still on the table, I was speaking out of turn and with-
> out having first spoken with Mr. Graves.
> With regard to the statement 'iffy,' I was simply reporting what
> Mr. Cox had reported to me.

Between March 27th and March 30th, counsel for the parties continued to have conversations regarding settlement. On March 30th, defendant rejected what it viewed as an offer to settle the case for $250,000.

Conclusions of Law

The court finds that no binding contract of settlement exists between
the parties. First, the power of Monsour's to bind Menu Maker was terminated when it failed to accept the latter's $250,000 settlement offer,
and instead substituted its own offers to settle the case for $400,000 or,
later, for $300,000. Monsour's responses were counter-offers, which are
traditionally understood to represent a revocation of an offer. Kansas has

generally adhered to the modern view of contracts as stated in the Second Restatement of Contracts. The Restatement observes:

> An offeree's power of acceptance is terminated by his making of a counter-offer, unless the offeror has manifested a contrary intention or unless the counter-offer manifests a contrary intention of the offeree.

In the present case, there is no evidence that Monsour's counter-offer was explicitly accompanied by a manifestation of intent to preserve the original, $250,000 offer, and no evidence of a manifestation of intent by Menu Maker to preserve its $250,000 offer even in the face of counter-offers or rejection by Monsour's.

Further, the court finds that, even if Menu Maker's offer was not extinguished by the counter-offer responses by Monsour's, the offer was in any event revoked by the explicit indication, conveyed to Monsour's prior to its putative acceptance, that Menu Maker's adherence to the offer was doubtful, or to use the term conveyed to Monsour's, "iffy." Not wishing to force parties into contractual relations against their own clear manifestations of consent, courts have recognized that an offer may be revoked by an expression that the offeror has become equivocal in adherence to the offer. Thus, in the leading case of *Hoover Motor Express Co. v. Clements Paper Co.*, 193 Tenn. 6, 241 S.W. 2d 551 (1951), the court held that an offeror's expression that "we might not want to got through with it," was sufficient to revoke the offer. The decision in *Hoover Motor* underlies Illustration 5 to Restatement §42:

> A makes an offer to B, and later says to B, 'Well, I don't know if we are ready. We have not decided, we might not want to go through with it.' The offer is revoked.

Having previously consistently rejected Menu Maker's offers to settle the case for $250,000 and then being informed that Menu Maker was "iffy" about adhering to those earlier offers, the court holds that Monsour's no longer had the power to bind Menu Maker to that settlement offer. Any such offer was revoked by the 3:51 p.m. email of March 26, 2007.

Nor is the result any different in light of the plaintiff's additional argument that defense counsel had apparent as well as actual authority to bind Menu Maker. Monsour's initiated the counter-offer which revoked Menu Maker's offers. The communication that Menu Maker was "iffy" about agreeing even to a $250,000 settlement was also conveyed to Monsour's. The plaintiff's reliance on *Sawtelle v. Cosden Oil & Gas Co.*, 128 Kan. 220, 277 P. 45 (1929), which dealt with the general apparent authority of attorneys, is inapposite. *Sawtelle* involved no issues of counter-offer or revocation, and thus cannot stand for the proposition that apparent authority can bind Menu Maker, even in the face of Monsour's own actions (counter-offering) and knowledge (that the offer had in any event become equivocal), both of which as a matter of law terminated any offer which had been extended.

IT IS ACCORDINGLY ORDERED that the plaintiff's Motion to Enforce Settlement is hereby denied.

Questions

1. What does the court say was the effect of Monsour's substitution of its own offer instead of accepting Menu Maker's offer?
2. Would the result have been different if Monsour's manifested intent to preserve Menu Maker's offer?
3. Why do you think the court spent so much time going through the timing of all of the parties' emails?

Suggested Case References

1. The case that established the mailbox rule is *Adams v. Lindsell*, 1 B & Ald. 681 (1818). Read and analyze the case. Do you agree with the court's decision? What factors did the court consider determinative to its final conclusion?

2. You are staying at a hotel and, while unpacking your clothes, you find a diamond brooch in the closet. Being honest, you inform the front desk and discover that a reward was offered by the guest who lost the brooch to anyone who found it. Are you entitled to the reward? Is this an example of a unilateral contract? Can you accept terms of which you are unaware? Read *Vitty v. Eley*, 51 A.D. 44, 64 N.Y.S. 397 (1900).

3. To see how a New York court interpreted silence as acceptance (or not), read *Joseph Schultz & Co. v. Camden Fire Ins. Co.*, 304 N.Y. 143 (1952).

4. For an additional discussion of the ability to revoke a unilateral contract, read *Marchiondo v. Scheck*, 78 N.M. 440, 432 P.2d 405 (1967).

5. *University Emergency Medicine Foundation v. Rapier Investments, Ltd. et al.*, 197 F.3d 18 (1st Cir. 1999), poses an intriguing variation on the mailbox rule.

Ethical Considerations

ABA Rule of Professional Conduct 5.3 mandates that a lawyer is held responsible for all acts of his or her legal assistant, which include both ethical violations as well as contractual agreements that the legal assistant may enter into on behalf of the law office. An attorney will be bound, ethically and contractually, for any action taken by the paralegal that the attorney ratifies.

Quick Quiz

Answer TRUE or FALSE. (Answers can be found in Appendix C on page 413.)

1. An offeree varying the terms of the offer creates a counteroffer.
2. The mailbox rule is a legal theory designed to determine the timing of the acceptance of an offer.
3. A supervening illegality terminates a person's ability to accept an offer.
4. A cross-offer differs from a counteroffer.
5. An option need not be supported by consideration to be valid.

4 Consideration

Learning Objectives

After studying this chapter you will be able to:

- Define "contractual consideration"
- Discuss the concept of mutuality of consideration
- Differentiate between a benefit conferred and a detriment incurred
- Exemplify what is not considered to be legally sufficient consideration
- Explain the "preexisting duty rule"
- Discuss the impact of the UCC on traditional concepts of consideration
- Explain what is meant by the "sufficiency of the consideration"
- Define "promissory estoppel"
- Discuss "accord and satisfaction"
- Indicate how one becomes a guarantor

CHAPTER OVERVIEW

Consideration is the third essential element of every valid contract. It is the bargain that supports the entire contractual relationship. Without consideration, no contract can exist. An agreement unsupported by consideration may legally bind the parties to each other, but the parties' legal relationship is not a contractual one.

What is "consideration"? Consideration is the subject matter of the agreement over which the parties have negotiated. It is the used textbook the student wants to sell, the paralegal services the attorney wants to employ, the land the developer wants to buy. For a contract to be valid, both parties to the contract must give *and* receive consideration. If consideration flows only to one person, then it most probably is intended as a gift. The basic premise of a contractual relationship is a bargain, an element lacking if both sides do not receive something of value.

The monetary value of the object of the contract is, for the most part, irrelevant to the law. A 5 cent piece of gum may have as much legal significance as a $5 million piece of real estate, whereas, under certain circumstances, a $1 million diamond necklace may not be considered sufficient to support a contract. (The adequacy of the consideration may involve questions of capacity. See Chapter 5.) The law is looking for proof of the bargain: It must be evidenced that the parties truly wanted and bargained for the object or service in question.

Consideration Defined

Consideration is something that has legal value. It is generally defined as a benefit conferred or a detriment incurred at the behest of the other party. Because consideration is the subject matter of a bargain, there must be **mutuality of consideration**—each side must give and receive something of legal value (the **quid pro quo**).

In bilateral contracts, the mutuality of the consideration is evidenced by the promise each side makes to the other. Mutuality of consideration in unilateral contracts is evidenced by giving the promise and performing the act. The act is consideration, and its performance creates a duty to perform on the part of the promisor.

The monetary value of the consideration is of little importance. Because the law is looking for the bargain, the only requirements are that the consideration have legal value (benefit or detriment) and be valuable to the person requesting it.

Benefit Conferred

The benefit-conferred concept of consideration is the easier of the two to understand. Simply stated, it is the exchange of the exact object or service described in the contract. Usually it is a good or service that one side is selling, and the other side is purchasing. The exchange of goods or services is the most typical type of consideration encountered in everyday contracts.

EXAMPLES:

1. Ted offers to sell, and William agrees to buy, a used textbook for $10. The consideration is both the book and the money. Ted gives the book and receives the $10. William gives the $10 and receives the book. There is a mutuality of consideration.

2. Irene offers to exchange her gold earrings for Denise's pearl earrings, and Denise agrees. Each side gives and receives something of value. Each party has conferred "benefit" (earrings) on the other. The consideration is valid.

3. Leroy is employed as a legal assistant by the law firm of Smith & Jones, P.C., for a salary of $300 per week. Leroy is conferring on the firm his paralegal services, and the firm is conferring on Leroy a salary. There is mutuality of consideration.

Detriment Incurred

Conceptualizing consideration as a detriment incurred at the request of the other party is generally more difficult to comprehend. Most people look for objects, services, or money as consideration because these things are tangible and easily identified as having value. But of what value is a detriment?

For a "detriment" to qualify as consideration, the person incurring the detriment must:

1. give up a legal right,
2. at the request of the other party,
3. in exchange for something of legal value.

All three elements must coexist for the detriment to qualify as consideration.

EXAMPLES:

1. Maria's mother is worried about Maria's smoking. Mom offers Maria $1,000 if Maria quits smoking for a year, and Maria agrees. There is a contract. This is an example of a detriment incurred. Maria is giving up her legal right to smoke at her mother's request in exchange for $1,000. On the other hand, if Maria quits smoking for her own health concerns or simply

to please her mother, there would be no contract because she would bargain nothing of legal value for her forbearance.

2. Lisa's mother is worried about Lisa smoking marijuana. Mom offers Lisa $1,000 if she quits smoking marijuana for a year. Lisa agrees. There is no contract. This is not an example of a detriment incurred because Lisa has no legal right to smoke marijuana. Consequently, Lisa is not giving up a right at the request of the other party in exchange for something of value. Because no legal right exists, it cannot be offered as contractual consideration.

Usually consideration is specifically noted in the contract. The important factors to ascertain are that the consideration mentioned has legal value, and that both parties give and receive consideration.

What Is Not Consideration

Far more difficult than determining what is consideration is determining what it is *not*. In making this determination, the court uses the following rules and guidelines.

"Past consideration is no consideration." Even if the object or service mentioned by the parties has legal value, it must be shown that it was meant to be exchanged as part of the present contract. Former gifts or consideration given in prior contracts cannot be consideration for a current contract simply because the parties wish it. It must satisfy legal principles as well. In some jurisdictions, past consideration may be deemed sufficient consideration if that fact is put in writing by the party to be charged. Each state's law must be analyzed to determine whether this situation is available for a given contract.

EXAMPLES:

Three years ago John gave Dorothy a mink coat. Two years ago, he gave her a trip around the world. Last year he gave her a diamond watch. Now he wants to use these items as consideration for Dorothy's current domestic services as his housekeeper. The law says no. John must offer new, current consideration.

"Moral consideration is no consideration." Simply because someone feels morally obligated to another person, it does not follow that the moral obligation is sufficient to form the consideration of a contract. The parties must demonstrate that they bargained with each other, not simply that one felt indebted to the other.

EXAMPLES:

1. Hassan's parents pay for his school tuition. When he graduates, Hassan says he will repay his parents with interest. There is no contract. Hassan's parents did not intend to loan the money to Hassan, and the fact that he feels morally obligated to promise to repay them does not mean that they have a contractual relationship. They did not bargain with each other.

2. Leslie cannot afford school tuition and so gets a job to save money, thereby delaying her schooling. Leslie's parents offer to loan Leslie the tuition, with repayment to be made after graduation at 5 percent interest. This is a contract. Even though Leslie may feel morally obligated to repay her parents, more importantly she is legally obligated to them because the tuition was bargained for, and Leslie's parents expect its return with interest.

"A gift can never be legal consideration." Just because the parties use words that, on their face, would appear to represent consideration, no contract will be formed if it can be shown that under the circumstances the true intent of the parties was to confer a gift. The courts will review all the surrounding circumstances to ascertain that the element and intent of a bargain exist.

EXAMPLES:

Mr. and Mrs. Jones offer to sell their four-bedroom house to Mr. and Mrs. Smith for $10,000, and the Smiths agree. Is there a contract? That would depend on the surrounding circumstances. Consider two different scenarios:

1. The Joneses are the parents of Mrs. Smith. The house has a market value of $450,000.

2. The Joneses have to move to another state for job reasons. They have to sell the house as quickly as possible, and their employers have agreed to compensate them for any loss they incur on the sale. The Joneses have never met the Smiths prior to the sale.

In the first example there would be no contract. It would appear that Mrs. Smith's parents intended to make a gift of the house but used words of consideration to make it appear like a contract (probably for tax advantages).

In the second example, although it may appear the Joneses have made a bad deal, a mutual exchange of bargains has occurred. A contract has been created.

"Illusory promises are never consideration." Recall Chapter 2, Offer, in which the concept of the certainty and definiteness of the terms of an offer was discussed. If a party to the contract retains the discretionary right to

determine the subject matter of the contract, the offer will fail. This is an example of an illusory promise. Even if words of consideration are used, the "consideration" is legally inadequate because it cannot be objectively determined what is to be given.

EXAMPLE:

The law firm of Smith & Jones, P.C. agrees to pay Emmet what they think he's worth in consideration for his employment as a paralegal. The firm's promise is illusory. There is no determinable consideration, and so there is no valid offer or contract.

To prove an illusory promise, it must be shown that one party has subjective control over its terms. If the term can be objectively determined, like an output contract discussed previously, and can be objectively quantified, it is not illusory.

"Promises to do that which one is already bound to do are not consideration." If one is under a preexisting duty to perform, either because of a contractual or other obligation, a promise to fulfill that obligation is insufficient consideration. The other party has received nothing of value. This is known as the **preexisting duty rule.** However, under certain circumstances, a preexisting duty may be consideration for a new agreement if:

1. new or different consideration is given;
2. the purpose is to ratify a voidable obligation;
3. the duty is owed to a third person, not the promisee;
4. unforeseen circumstances make the duty more difficult to fulfill.

EXAMPLES:

1. Officer Green promises to catch the burglar who robbed Mr. White's house in exchange for Mr. White's promise to give her $300. There is no contract. The police officer is already obligated by virtue of her job to find the thief and has given nothing of additional value to induce Mr. White's promise. She has a preexisting duty to assist Mr. White.

2. Chris owes Fred $200. Chris asks Fred to accept $100 in full payment of the debt. There is no consideration for Fred to take less than what he is already owed. However, if Chris asks Fred to accept $100 now and $110 at a later date, the compromised agreement would be valid because Fred received something of value in addition to what he was previously entitled.

3. Phyllis and Lupe have a contract for the sale of Lupe's computer for $300. After the contract is signed, Phyllis tries to change

the contract to include Lupe's computer programs for the same price. The second agreement is invalid. Lupe received no new or additional consideration for giving Phyllis the programs. Every contract must be individually supported by consideration, and any modification to an existing contract must be supported by additional consideration.

Under the UCC, merchant traders may modify their prior contractual obligations without new or different consideration provided that the modification is made "in good faith." This rule substantially changed the common law concepts for contracts for the sale of goods between merchants.

Sufficiency of the Consideration

The concept of the **sufficiency of the consideration** concerns itself, once again, with the element of the bargain. The law is only interested in the legal value of the bargain, not its monetary worth. For this reason, not only must the object, service, or detriment itself be analyzed, but it is also necessary to analyze all of the circumstances surrounding the making of the agreement to determine that a bargain, not a gift, was intended. So, although the value of the consideration per se is not important, it remains a factor in determining whether a bargained-for exchange has occurred.

Does it matter that a party to a contract makes a "bad" bargain—that she does not receive consideration monetarily equivalent to what was given? No. The law does not concern itself with ensuring the fairness of every contractual relationship. Obviously, persons only enter into a contract because each thinks he is making a good deal. Unless some other factors exist that would make the contract invalid (see Chapter 6), the law applies the doctrines of **caveat emptor** and **caveat venditor**—"Let the buyer beware" and "Let the seller beware." The only factors that the law looks at are the legal value of the consideration, the mutuality of the consideration, and the element of the bargain.

EXAMPLE:

Horace offers to sell an old trunk for $25. The trunk has been around for years, Horace doesn't like it, and he wants the space it takes up in the attic. Joanne agrees to buy the trunk, which she needs for storage. Later, Joanne finds out the trunk is an antique worth $1,000. The contract is valid, and Joanne has made an exceptionally good purchase. Both Horace and Joanne received what they wanted for the contract; Joanne just made a better deal.

Nominal consideration, consideration that has such an obviously small monetary value relative to the consideration for which it is exchanged, is always immediately suspect by the law. Even though the monetary value is never a primary concern of the law, and the courts usually leave the parties to their own devices when it comes to bargaining powers, the law wants to make sure that a bargain does exist. Consequently, the courts will usually inquire into the surrounding circumstances if the bargain, on its face, appears to be overly one-sided. If a bargain can be proved, however, the contract will stand.

EXAMPLE:

An advertisement in the newspaper offers one mint condition Rolls Royce for $1 to the first person who presents the cash to the seller at a given day and time. Is the $1 legally sufficient consideration for a Rolls Royce?

The background of the notice is this: A wealthy man dies, and his will names his wife as executrix. All of the deceased's property is left to his wife, except for the proceeds of the sale of his Rolls Royce, which was to go to his mistress. In this instance, the consideration is sufficient. The widow truly wants the least amount of money possible for the car. She may have violated a fiduciary obligation to the mistress, but the person who bought the car has a valid contract.

Sham consideration is consideration that, on its face, appears to have no true value at all. The concept typically applies to gifts. One party intends to make a gift to the other but phrases the exchange in words of contract for some private purpose. For example, a statement such as "In consideration of $1 plus other good and valuable consideration" represents sham consideration. Terms such as "good and valuable consideration," without being specifically defined, are legally insignificant and tend to indicate lack, rather than presence, of consideration. The circumstances surrounding the contract, not just the words used, may also indicate sham consideration.

Conditional promises are not necessarily insufficient simply because they involve an element of doubt. A conditional promise is dependent on the happening, or nonhappening, of some event that would trigger the obligation. (See Chapter 7.) Provided that the consideration promised has legal sufficiency, the contract will be valid.

EXAMPLE:

Shirley agrees to buy Pam's house for $250,000, provided that she can get financing within 30 days. This is a valid contract. Both the house and the money are legally sufficient; simply because Shirley's obligation to pay is conditioned on her getting a mortgage does not mean the consideration is not sufficient, only that the right to receive the money may not come to Pam.

Promissory Estoppel

Promissory estoppel is a doctrine originally established by the courts of equity. Equity courts, as opposed to law courts, were designed to remedy situations in which the "legal" result might be just but was unfair or unduly hard on one of the parties. Equity provides "mercy" to persons when the legal result appears unfair. (See Chapter 11, Remedies.)

The doctrine of promissory estoppel arises in certain situations in which a person reasonably believes that he has entered into a contract, even though no contract exists. Relying on this reasonable belief that there is a contract, the promisee materially changes his position. This circumstance arises when the promise made by the presumptive offeror is illusory—what has been promised cannot be objectively defined or is left to the discretion of the promisor. These are not contractual relationships, even though at first glance it might appear that a contract was intended. If it can be shown that the promisee has materially changed his position in reasonable reliance on the promise, the law will not allow him to suffer. The promisor will be obligated to compensate the promisee. The promisor is barred, or estopped, from avoiding a promise because to do so would be unjust to the promisee.

The concepts of promissory estoppel and gifts are very closely related; however, with promissory estoppel the element of donative intent is lacking. For a gift to exist, it must be shown that a gift was intended. For promissory estoppel to exist, it must be shown that the promisee detrimentally relied on the promise, and that the promisor never intended to give the promisee a gift.

 EXAMPLES:

1. Simone promises to give Loretta $100,000, so that she will not have to work anymore. Based on this promise, Loretta quits her job. Here there is no mutuality of consideration because Simone did not promise the money in exchange for Loretta's promise not to work; she simply promised the money so that Loretta would not have to work. But because Loretta quit her job based on Simone's promise, she can sue Simone under the doctrine of promissory estoppel to recover her lost wages. The court will not give her the full $100,000, but it will compensate her for her actual loss based on Simone's promise.

2. Simone promises to pay for Loretta's college education. Based on this promise, Loretta enrolls in school. There is no contract. Simone didn't exchange her promise for Loretta's promise to go to college, but based on her promise Loretta has incurred the expense of tuition. The court will permit Loretta to recover her tuition from Simone because she acted in reliance on Simone's promise.

3. Simone promises to convey her farm in Vermont to Loretta so that Loretta won't have to live in the city anymore. Based on this promise, Loretta sells her house in the city, packs her belongings, and moves to Vermont. The court will enforce Simone's promise. Even though there was no mutuality of consideration, and thus no contract, Loretta has detrimentally relied on Simone's promise by changing her entire living condition. It would be unjust to let her suffer.

In each of the foregoing situations, Loretta has changed her position based on her reasonable belief that Simone would adhere to her promise. There is no specific indication that Simone intended a gift, and in no example did Simone receive anything of legal value, so there is no contract. However, under the court's equitable jurisdiction, these types of promises will be enforced to prevent injustice. Be aware, though, that under the doctrine of promissory estoppel, even though the promise is enforced, it is only enforced to the extent the promisee relied on the promise. Take note of the fact that if the promise is not relied on by the promisee to her detriment, the doctrine of promissory estoppel will not apply. It is an equitable doctrine designed to prevent injustice. If the promisee cannot prove detrimental reliance on the promise, it would be unfair to the promisor to force him to fulfill his promise when no injury was sustained.

To determine whether contract law or promissory estoppel exists, look for the mutuality of consideration, the intent of the offeror, and the possible illusory nature of the promise. If mutuality or legally sufficient consideration and contractual intent can be shown, a contract exists. It is not a situation to which the theory of promissory estoppel applies.

Special Agreements

There are several other types of agreements that ordinarily would fail as valid contracts for lack of consideration but that, because of the formality of the circumstances and the dictates of public policy, stand as enforceable obligations.

Accord and Satisfaction

An **accord and satisfaction** is a very particular type of agreement that results from a disagreement between the parties to an existing contract. One (or both) of the parties disputes that he has received the consideration promised in the contract; however, rather than litigating to have the court decide the parties' respective rights, they agree to modify their original agreement. Ordinarily, there would be no consideration for the parties to rewrite an existing obligation; however, both sides have agreed to forgo their legal right to sue in court. This mutual detriment (forbearance of the right to sue) constitutes sufficient consideration for the new agreement.

 EXAMPLE:

Farmer Green has a contract to sell 1,000 bushels of Grade A oranges to Ace Supermarkets for $10 a bushel. On delivery day, Ace claims the oranges are Grade B, and is unwilling to pay more than $8 a bushel. Rather than sue, Green and Ace enter into an accord and satisfaction, and agree to a price of $9 per bushel, making no comment about the grade of the oranges.

In the example above, each side could have sued under the original contract, and, presumably, the accord and satisfaction gives each party less than he was promised under the original contract. But because each has forborne the lawsuit and has saved the expense of litigation, the accord and satisfaction will stand.

The requirements for a valid accord and satisfaction are:

1. a valid contract;
2. a dispute between the parties with respect to that contract; and
3. an agreement to compromise the dispute rather than sue.

Accord and satisfactions are typically titled as such on the top of the agreement.

Charitable Subscription

A **charitable subscription** is a pledge made to a charitable organization. Under most theories of law, it should be identified as a gift. However, as a matter of public policy, the law has mandated that these pledges are enforceable by the charities. Unlike the promisee in promissory estoppel, who is limited to his actual loss, the charity will get the full pledge, not just what it lost in reliance on the promise.

 EXAMPLE:

Every year the Muscular Dystrophy Foundation has a telethon to raise money. In the heat of the moment, Vivica calls in a pledge of $250. When the charity moves to collect the money, Vivica says she has changed her mind. The foundation can sue Vivica to redeem her pledge because it is a charitable subscription.

Debtor's Promises

A debtor who has been discharged of his obligation by the legal system is under no further duty to repay his creditors. A person can be legally discharged from his debt by going through bankruptcy or because the statute of limitations on the claim has expired.

If a debtor, under the above circumstances, voluntarily agrees to repay the debt, this gratuitous promise is enforceable against her, even though the promise is not supported by consideration. Again, the law has determined that, as a matter of public policy, it is beneficial to encourage people to repay their debts. Therefore, even though the consideration is only moral consideration, the law will hold the debtor to her promise.

If the debt has been deemed unenforceable due to bankruptcy, the Bankruptcy Act imposes certain additional requirements to make the promise enforceable. The act requires the debtor to reaffirm the promise prior to final discharge by the court and to receive the court's consent. On the other hand, if the debt is barred only by the statute of limitations, the promise itself is generally considered sufficient to make the contract enforceable.

 EXAMPLE:

Floyd has been judicially declared bankrupt, and his creditors are being paid 50 cents on the dollar. Feeling very guilty about his creditors' losses, Floyd promises Jennifer, one of his creditors, that he will pay her back all he owes her within six months. He gets the court's approval. Jennifer now has a legally enforceable claim against Floyd for the amount.

Guarantees

A **guarantee** is a written promise to answer for the debts of another that is enforceable against the **guarantor**. The guarantee is given at the same time the debtor receives the subject consideration.

Under general contract law principles, it would appear that the guarantor is not legally bound because she has not received any benefit from the promise. However, this is an example of a statutorily created *formal contract* designed to promote business and industry.

For the guarantee to be valid, the following requirements must be met:

1. a valid contract is entered into between two or more parties;
2. the guarantor creates the guarantee at the time the contract is executed; and
3. the guarantee is in writing.

EXAMPLE:

Joanne wants to buy a house, but her credit record is poor. The bank agrees to give her a mortgage if her parents guarantee the loan. When Joanne takes out the loan, her parents sign the mortgage contract as Joanne's guarantors. This is a valid guarantee.

Note that in the example given above, Joanne's parents are merely agreeing to answer for Joanne's payments *if* Joanne does not pay. This is to be contrasted with **co-signers.** Co-signers are persons who agree to be *equally* bound with the obligor, and the creditor can go after a co-signer *instead* of the actual obligor because each is equally liable. With co-signers, a joint and several liability is incurred: The mortgage can sue either Joanne, or her parents, or all three of them together.

For the guarantee to be valid, the obligor must receive consideration at the time the guarantee is given.

EXAMPLE:

In the circumstances given above, assume Joanne has an excellent credit history, and the bank loans her the money on her own signature. Two years later, Joanne loses her job, and the bank, worried about the mortgage payments, asks Joanne to have her parents come in to guarantee the loan. Joanne's parents agree to sign the mortgage. However, because Joanne already received the consideration and became obligated prior to the guarantee, the guarantee is not enforceable against her parents.

For the above guarantee to be enforceable against Joanne's parents, the bank must give Joanne some additional consideration at the time the guarantee is given, such as extending the time for payments, reducing the interest rate, or giving her additional money to increase the overall mortgage. Unless the guarantee is given at the time the obligation is incurred, the guarantee will not be enforceable.

Formal Contracts

A **formal** contract is a contract that meets special statutory requirements and as such is valid even though no consideration is mentioned. The statutory formality of these agreements gives them special status under the law and creates a special situation with respect to consideration. (See Chapter 1.) Each state's statutes indicate what is to be deemed a formal contract.

SAMPLE CLAUSES

1   Accord and Satisfaction

In Accord and Satisfaction of all claims arising out of the contract between Farmer Green and Ace Supermarkets dated _____, 20 _____ (Copy affixed hereto), the parties agree that the price for the oranges shall be $9 per bushel, payable in 30 days from this date.

2   Bill of Sale

Know all men by these presents that I, _____, of _____, in consideration of One Hundred Dollars ($100.00) to me paid by _____ of _____, have bargained and sold to said _____ the following goods and chattels, to wit:

(Specify goods and chattels)

Witness by hand and seal this _____ day of _____, 20 _____.

(Signatures)

_____

In drafting any contract, always be sure to specify all consideration.

3   Guarantee

In consideration of the mortgage entered into this _____ day of _____, 20 _____, between _____ of _____, and _____ bank, we, the undersigned, do hereby guarantee all payments due under said mortgage should said mortgagor be found in default.

(Signatures)

_____

CHAPTER SUMMARY

Consideration is the third major element of every valid contract. It is the subject matter of the contract for which the parties have bargained. Consideration is generally defined as a benefit conferred or a detriment incurred at the request of the other party. For the contract to be enforceable, each party to the contract must give and receive consideration. This is known as mutuality of consideration.

The actual market value of the consideration is not important; it simply must be something legally sufficient to support the contract. The law is not concerned with the market value of the good, service, or forbearance described in the contract; it is only concerned with whether the consideration is actually bargained for and is not intended to mask a gift.

Past consideration, moral consideration, gifts, and illusory promises are never sufficient to support a contractual agreement. However, there are certain situations in which the law has determined that in the interests of public policy, a contract will be found even though consideration is lacking. These situations are accord and satisfaction agreements, charitable subscriptions, debtors' gratuitous promises to pay otherwise unenforceable debts, written guarantees, and statutorily defined formal contracts.

Closely associated with the concept of contractual consideration is the doctrine of promissory estoppel, which the court uses to enforce a promise for reasons other than lack of consideration, even though no contract exists. This occurs when the promises made are unsupported by consideration, but the promisee has materially changed his position in reasonable reliance on those promises. In this instance, the court will permit the promisee to recover what he has lost based on the promise.

For a contract to be enforceable, the consideration must always be definite, certain, and specifically described.

SYNOPSIS

Consideration
1. Benefit conferred
2. Detriment incurred
3. Each side must give and receive bargained-for consideration

What is not consideration
1. Past consideration
2. Moral obligations
3. Gifts
4. Illusory promises
5. Legal duties

Sufficiency of consideration
    Must be sufficient to support the contract

Promissory estoppel
    Illusory promises enforced by the court if detrimentally relied on

Special agreements
1. Accord and satisfaction
2. Charitable subscription
3. Debtor's promises
4. Guarantees
5. Formal contracts

Key Terms

Accord and satisfaction: a special agreement in which the parties to a
    disputed contract agree to new terms in exchange for forbearing to
    sue under the original contract
Caveat emptor: Latin phrase meaning "Let the buyer beware"
Caveat venditor: Latin phrase meaning "Let the seller beware"
Charitable subscription: pledge or promise to donate money to a charity;
    given the enforceability of a contract under law
Conditional promise: a promise dependent on the happening or
    nonhappening of a future event
Consideration: a benefit conferred or a detriment incurred; a basic
    requirement of every valid contract
Co-signer: person who agrees to be equally liable with a promisor under a
    contract
Formal contract: written contract under seal specifically enforced by statute
Guarantee: an enforceable written promise to answer for the debts of another
Guarantor: person who agrees to be responsible to answer for the debts of
    another should the debtor default
Mutuality of consideration: the bargain element of a contract that requires
    each side to give and receive something of legal value
Nominal consideration: consideration of insufficient legal value to support
    a contract
Preexisting duty rule: promises to do what one is already bound to do is
    not consideration
Promissory estoppel: doctrine in which promises not supported
    by consideration are given enforceability if the promisee had
    detrimentally relied on the promises
Quid pro quo: Latin phrase meaning "this for that"; the mutuality of
    consideration
Sham consideration: legally insufficient consideration used to mask a gift
    in words of contract
Sufficiency of the consideration: doctrine that each party to a contract
    must contribute something of legal value for which he has bargained

EXERCISES

1. Give two examples of consideration as a detriment incurred not
   discussed in the chapter.
2. Discuss mutuality of consideration with respect to your contract
   with your school.
3. Under what circumstances would a person argue the doctrine of
   promissory estoppel?
4. Find out what contracts are considered formal contracts in your
   jurisdiction.
5. Find and analyze a contract that requires a co-signer.

Cases for Analysis

The concept of consideration is generally one of the most confusing in contract law. To expand the previous discussion, the cases of *Yerkovich v. AAA* and *Mass. Eye & Ear Infirmary v. Eugene B. Casey Fdn.* are included.

Yerkovich v. AAA
461 Mich. 732 (2000)

The issues presented are: (1) whether the subrogation agreement between defendant fund and plaintiff Yerkovich entitled the fund to reimbursement from plaintiff for medical expenses and, if so, (2) whether plaintiff's no-fault insurer, defendant AAA, must refund plaintiff for that reimbursement. We hold that the subrogation clause did not confer upon the fund the right to be reimbursed out of plaintiff's third-party recovery from tortfeasors. Because we hold that the fund was not entitled to reimbursement, we do not reach the second question.

Facts

Plaintiff's minor daughter was injured in an automobile accident when the driver of the vehicle in which she was riding negligently collided with another vehicle. At the time of the accident, plaintiff was a participant in the Michigan United Food and Commercial Workers Unions and Food Employers Health and Welfare Fund. The fund is a self-funded employee welfare benefit plan created and administered pursuant to the Employee Retirement Income Security Act (ERISA), 29 USC 1001 et seq. Plaintiff also had a no-fault policy issued by defendant AAA.

Plaintiff filed this action on behalf of her daughter against both defendants, seeking payment of medical expenses. The fund had initially denied coverage, claiming plaintiff had failed to execute a subrogation agreement. The fund claimed this was required by the plan's subrogation clause. Plaintiff eventually signed the "Subrogation Agreement and Assignment" form, and the fund paid $6,832 in medical expense benefits. The AAA also denied coverage, claiming that plaintiff's policy contained a coordination of benefits clause that made the fund primarily responsible for medical expenses from the accident. Plaintiff also filed a negligence claim seeking noneconomic damages against the driver of the vehicle in which her daughter was riding. That case was settled for $20,000.

Plaintiff and the fund each filed motions for summary disposition in the trial court, essentially advancing the same position. The fund argued that, pursuant to the plan, plaintiff was required to reimburse the fund the $6,832 it had paid for medical expenses out of her third-party tort recovery. Plaintiff and the fund agreed that if such reimbursement were required, it would result in plaintiff paying her own medical expenses, contrary to the provisions of the no-fault act. Plaintiff and the fund argued that the AAA should be responsible for paying for the medical expenses. The AAA argued that the language of the subrogation agreement between plaintiff and the fund did not support a right to reimbursement and limited reimbursement to situations where plaintiff recovered medical expenses from a third-party suit. The trial court granted the motions for summary disposition and ordered the AAA to repay plaintiff any sums she paid to reimburse the fund. The Court of Appeals affirmed. *Yerkovich v. AAA a/k/a ACIA*, 231 Mich. App. 54; 585 N.W.2d 318 (1998).

The Subrogation Agreement

At issue in this case is the interpretation of the plan agreement between the fund and plaintiff. Specifically, we must answer whether the fund was entitled to a refund from plaintiff for medical expenses. The fund provided plaintiff with a plan booklet that laid out the rights, benefits, and duties of the parties. Under the "General Provisions" section, the plan provided a subsection entitled "Third Party Subrogation." The fund argues that, under this section, plaintiff was required to sign further documents ensuring its rights to subrogation, reimbursement, repayment, and assignment. It provides in pertinent part:

This Plan will take advantage of its *right to subrogation* if you or an eligible dependent are paid benefits by the Plan due to accidental injuries for which someone else may be liable.

Subrogation means that the Plan can recover *from the person who caused the injury*, or that person's insurance company, the benefits paid on your behalf by the Plan for that injury, including but not limited to . . . tortious conduct by a third party.

* * *

You or your dependents will have certain responsibilities to the Plan. When you or your eligible dependent submit a claim to this Plan for injuries, the Fund Office will have you complete a form requesting information as to how the injuries occurred and the identity of any potentially responsible third parties. At the request of the Fund Office, *you must also sign any other documents* and do whatever else is reasonably necessary *to secure this Plan's right of subrogation*. You must not do anything to impair or negate this Plan's right of subrogation; *if* any of your acts or omissions to act compromise this Plan's right of subrogation, this Plan will seek *reimbursement* of all appropriate benefits paid directly to you . . . .

If you recover lost wage benefits from another source, e.g. from an individual who caused the injury which resulted in your receiving Time Loss Weekly Benefits, the Plan has the *right to seek repayment* from *you* . . . . [Emphasis added.]

Under this plan, the fund declared "subrogation" rights in order to recover from a third party medical expense benefits it paid. In contrast, it declared the right to "repayment" from plaintiff for lost wage benefits it paid in the event that plaintiff recovered the lost wages "from any other source."

Traditional subrogation is defined by Black's Law Dictionary (4th ed); p 1595, as "the substitution of one person in the place of another with

reference to a lawful claim, demand or right, . . . so that he who is substituted succeeds to the rights of the other in relation to the debt or claim, and
its rights, remedies, or securities." As a subrogee, one stands in the shoes
of the subrogor and acquires no greater rights than those possessed by the
subrogor. *Shermer v. Merrill*, 33 Mich. 284, 287 (1876). In this case, the fund
provided its own definition for "subrogation" in the second paragraph of
that subsection. It explains that subrogation means the fund may "recover
from the person who caused the injury, or that person's insurance company . . . ." This is consistent with the traditional definition.

   Although the agreement provides that the fund may "recover *from
the person who caused the injury*," the fund seeks to recover instead from
plaintiff. It has done so by arguing that the second agreement signed by
plaintiff required plaintiff to repay, reimburse, subrogate, and assign sums
and rights to the fund. It is agreed that plaintiff signed the second agreement—that greatly expanded her duties under the plan agreement—only
after the fund conditioned the payment of medical expenses on her signing the second agreement.

   Under the plan agreement, the fund was entitled to seek recovery
from the negligent driver for the medical expenses it paid. Plaintiff, in
return, was required to sign documents necessary to secure the fund's
right of subrogation. Plaintiff was also required to provide any information requested regarding the injuries and the identity of the tortfeasor. *If* plaintiff impaired that right of "subrogation," the fund could *then*
seek reimbursement. Plaintiff has done nothing to hinder or obstruct the
fund's rights of subrogation. Plaintiff did not sue the tortfeasor for medical expenses or any economic damages. Instead, plaintiff recovered from
the tortfeasor purely noneconomic damages for pain and suffering. The
fund does not claim that it has paid noneconomic damages. It does not
claim that it had a right of subrogation for noneconomic damages, only
for benefits it paid. It paid only medical expense benefits. Nor does the
plan agreement provide that it may seek reimbursement from plaintiff for
medical expenses from plaintiff's noneconomic damage recovery. Under
the language of the plan agreement, the fund's right of reimbursement is
triggered only if the plaintiff impairs or negates the fund's right of subrogation. This was not triggered. In fact, the fund may step into plaintiff's
shoes and sue the negligent driver for medical expenses incurred, because
plaintiff has yet to seek them.

   Moreover, the fund might have, but did not, place language in the
plan agreement requiring reimbursement of medical expenses from plaintiff. Instead, it sought only subrogation as defined in the second paragraph.
Therefore, it has no right to reimbursement from plaintiff for medical
expenses. This view is strengthened by examining the final paragraph
quoted from the plan agreement where the fund demanded "repayment"
from the *plaintiff* for lost wage benefits, in contrast to the "subrogation"
clause, which allows recovery from the *person who caused the injury* for
medical expense benefits.

   The fund argues that subrogation *and* reimbursement rights are triggered whenever a plan participant recovers monies for the same injury or

accident from a third party. It also urges that we should apply an "arbitrary and capricious" standard of review to the fund's interpretation of the plan agreement, citing *Firestone Tire & Rubber Co v. Bruch*, 489 U.S. 101; 109 S. Ct. 948; 103 L. Ed. 2d 80 (1989). Even under such a standard, we cannot read into the plan agreement that which does not exist. The fund had the opportunity to write into its agreement repayment or reimbursement rights. It did not.

Whether the second agreement entitled the fund to reimbursement is irrelevant to our analysis because the fund was under a preexisting duty to pay plaintiff's medical expenses and could not require her to take on additional duties absent additional consideration.

Preexisting Duty Rule

An essential element of a contract is legal consideration. *Detroit Trust Co v. Struggles*, 289 Mich. 595, 599; 286 N.W. 844 (1939). Under the preexisting duty rule, it is well settled that doing what one is legally bound to do is not consideration for a new promise. *Puett v. Walker*, 332 Mich. 117, 122; 50 N.W.2d 740 (1952). This rule bars the modification of an existing contractual relationship when the purported consideration for the modification consists of the performance or promise to perform that which one party was already required to do under the terms of the existing agreement. *Borg-Warner Acceptance Corp v. Dep't of State*, 433 Mich. 16, 22, n. 3; 444 N.W.2d 786 (1989).

In this case, the plan agreement provided that the fund had a preexisting duty to pay plaintiff's medical expenses. This promise was conditioned upon the fund's right of subrogation being protected. As stated, these rights were protected.

Although the parties focus on the second agreement, we find it is void for lack of consideration. Plaintiff was required only to sign documents ensuring the fund's right of subrogation as defined by the fund. The second agreement instead attempted to add to plaintiff's duties and burdens. The second agreement added an obligation to "repay" sums paid by the fund out of "any judgment or settlement" she received. The next paragraph required her to "reimburse" the fund out of any recovery she received. Although the third paragraph included subrogation rights, we will not interpret the language to allow greater rights or duties than those in the original plan agreement. The final paragraphs added assignments of plaintiff's claims and rights to the fund. The result is that plaintiff took on additional obligations, without consideration, in order to be paid that which she was already owed. All such additional obligations are unenforceable.

Conclusion

The original plan agreement between plaintiff and the fund required the fund to pay plaintiff's medical expenses as long as its right of subrogation was protected. Absent a breach by plaintiff, the fund had no rights of reimbursement for medical expense benefits from plaintiff. We hold that the preexisting duty rule barred the fund from requiring plaintiff to take on additional burdens, without consideration, in order to get paid that which she was owed. Because the second contract was invalid for lack of consideration, we hold that the fund was not entitled to a reimbursement from plaintiff. We, therefore, reverse the Court of Appeals affirmance of the trial court's grant of summary disposition and order defendant fund to repay to the plaintiff any sums plaintiff paid to reimburse the fund.

Questions

1. How is "subrogation" defined?
2. What does the court say about the preexisting duty rule?
3. What is your opinion of this decision?

Mass. Eye & Ear Infirmary v. Eugene B. Casey Found.
47 F. Supp. 2d 192 (D. Mass 2006)

The plaintiff, Massachusetts Eye & Ear Infirmary ("MEEI"), brings an action against the Eugene B. Casey Foundation ("the Foundation") and Thomas F. Reilly ("Reilly"), the Attorney General of Massachusetts, seeking a declaratory judgment and damages arising out of an alleged contract dispute with the Foundation. The Foundation moves to dismiss pursuant to *Fed. R. Civ. P. 12(b)(6)* for failure to state a claim. Having reviewed the memoranda in support of and opposition to the motion, the Court resolves it as follows.

* * *

II. Factual Background

According to the complaint, on or about November 27, 2002, the Foundation and MEEI entered into a contract whereby the Foundation promised to make a substantial gift to MEEI in seven installments totaling $ 2 million to be used in connection with MEEI's Voice Restoration Research Program. MEEI understood the agreement to be that the gifts were to be used solely in support of voice restoration research. At the time of the donation, MEEI's voice restoration program was under the direction of Dr. Steven Zeitels, one of the nation's leading laryngologists, but MEEI insists that the gift was not conditioned on Dr. Zeitels's continued employment.

On May 12, 2004, Dr. Zeitels informed MEEI that he would resign effective June 30, 2004. On June 8, 2004, the Foundation informed MEEI that it would no longer support MEEI's voice restoration program in the absence of Dr. Zeitels. MEEI alleges that the Foundation 1) demanded the return of the portion of its gift previously submitted but not already expended (approximately $1 million) and 2) refused to make the gifts promised in the remaining installments (an additional $1 million). MEEI insists that its voice restoration studies will continue with a different research team.

MEEI seeks 1) a declaratory judgment that MEEI may retain the money it has already received and 2) damages for breach of contract for the Foundation's failure to pay the remainder of the promised gift.

The Foundation denies all material elements of the claims and offers 11 affirmative defenses, including an assertion that the gift is unenforceable for failure of consideration and because MEEI has not performed as promised. The Foundation also asserts that MEEI has failed to state a claim upon which relief can be granted.

The Foundation has filed counterclaims against MEEI, alleging that it is entitled to the return of the portion of the prior donations not yet expended by MEEI on the Voice Restoration Research Program. The Foundation alleges that 1) the gift was directly tied to the Voice Restoration Research Program and, more specifically, to Dr. Zeitels's direction of the Program and 2) when Dr. Zeitels left MEEI, the Voice Restoration Research Program ceased to exist and the "trust" in which the monies were held by MEEI, failed. As a result of that failure, the Foundation contends that it is entitled to a refund of the money not yet expended on voice restoration research and to a release from any further obligation to make additional gifts.

The Foundation counterclaims for 1) a return of the unexpended funds on the theory that when Dr. Zeitels resigned, the purpose of the donation failed and a resulting trust was created, 2) an accounting of the funds already donated, 3) imposition of a constructive trust on interest earned on the money held by MEEI and 4) conversion. MEEI's answer to the counterclaims denies all material elements and asserts six affirmative defenses, including failure to state a claim.

* * *

1. Contract Damages Claim

The Foundation faces a significant challenge in its effort to persuade this Court to dismiss MEEI's contract damages claim. The Foundation's principle argument is that the document in question is not a contract but is rather merely a schedule of payments. The most compelling piece of evidence confronting the Foundation is, however, the fact that the document in dispute is entitled "CONTRACT". Although the parties dispute whether the Foundation drafted the document, that inference can certainly be drawn from the statement at Paragraph 23 of its counterclaims which states that it "sent to MEEI a schedule of payments, to be made for the Voice Restoration Research Program." Moreover, in subsequent correspondence, the Foundation referred to the disputed document as "our contractual agreement of November 27, 2002."

The Foundation is quick to point out that "the legal effect given an agreement is not determined by the label attached to the agreement, but by the presence of consideration or detrimental reliance." See *Doyle v.*

Hasbro, Inc., 103 F.3d 186, 194-95 (1st Cir. 1996). MEEI responds that consideration and reliance exist with respect to the disputed document and, thus, there is a contract. The Court examines those contentions in order.

a. Standard for Reviewing Consideration and Reliance in the Context of Charitable Pledges

As a threshold matter, the parties disagree on the standard by which courts are to review consideration and reliance questions in the context of charitable pledges (also called subscriptions). MEEI asserts that courts may relax their standards and require a lesser showing of consideration or reliance in such cases while the Foundation argues that courts have adopted no such relaxation. The dispute revolves principally around the seminal case of *King v. Trustees of Boston University*, 420 Mass. 52, 647 N.E.2d 1196 (1995). The critical passage from that decision is:

> While we have been unwilling to abandon fundamental principles of contract law in determining the enforceability of charitable subscriptions, we do recognize that the "meeting of minds" between a donor and a charitable institution differs from the understanding we require in the context of enforceable arm's-length commercial agreements. Charities depend on donations for their existence, whereas their donors may give personal property on conditions they choose, with or without imposing conditions or demanding consideration.

Id. at 61 (internal citations omitted). As this Court understands the *King* decision, MEEI's contention for a lower standard for evaluating consideration and reliance in the context of charitable pledges is overblown. Rather, the *King* decision teaches that a *different* (rather than lower) standard should be applied, acknowledging the unique circumstances presented by charitable subscriptions versus traditional contracts and analyzing consideration and reliance issues in light of those circumstances.

b. Consideration

With that matter resolved, the Court addresses MEEI's contention that the agreement in question was supported by consideration. MEEI makes a colorable argument to support that position. First, it demonstrates that it made a promise to the Foundation to use the gift for an express purpose and not for any other purpose. In fact, in Paragraph 29 of the Foundation's counterclaims, it acknowledges that:

> In accepting the Foundation's gift of a projected $2,000,000.00, MEEI understood that the clear language of the schedule of payments required that it use those funds only "to do the Voice Restoration Research Program. . . ."

Moreover, the terms of the disputed agreement require that MEEI "shall send written reports" of the work every six months to the Foundation as well as a final report upon completion of the project. Even if this Court were to apply the traditional standard for evaluating consideration, those facts tend to demonstrate that consideration was given for the gift.

c. Reliance

Were this Court disinclined to find consideration, the complaint alleges, nevertheless, at least one kind of reliance Under Massachusetts case law:

> When a promise is enforceable in whole or in part by virtue of reliance, it is a "contract," and it is enforceable pursuant to a "traditional contract theory" antedating the modern doctrine of consideration.

Loranger Const. Corp. v. E.F. Hauserman Co., 376 Mass. 757, 761, 384 N.E.2d 176 (1978). In Paragraph 35 of the complaint, MEEI asserts that

> gifts have been solicited by MEEI from donors other than the Foundation in reliance upon the understanding that the Foundation had agreed to contribute $ 2,000,000 to MEEI for voice restoration research.

MEEI alleges in its opposition that it took other steps in reliance on the size and certainty of the Foundation's installment gifts, including: 1) entering into and extending Collaborative Research Agreements with Massachusetts General Hospital and Massachusetts Institute of Technology and 2) providing space and other support for Dr. Zeitels to perform voice restoration research.

For purposes of a motion to dismiss, this Court may depend upon MEEI's single allegation of reliance in the complaint. However, the case law in Massachusetts is neither clear nor particularly developed with respect to what constitutes reliance in the context of a charitable contribution. The Foundation argues that Massachusetts law expressly repudiates the suggestion that merely collecting other donations or subscriptions interdependent on the original donation creates sufficient detrimental reliance but the cases cited are unpersuasive. See *Congregation Kadimah Toras-Moshe v. DeLeo*, 405 Mass. 365, 540 N.E.2d 691 (1989); *Ladies' Collegiate Inst. v. French*, 82 Mass. 196, 16 Gray 196 (1860). This Court rejects the Foundation's contention that it should not have reasonably expected MEEI to solicit other donations in support of the Voice Restoration Research Program based on its contribution.

* * *

Declaratory judgment allowed; otherwise dismissed.

Questions

1. What does the court say about consideration and a charitable pledge?
2. How does the court deal with the concept of reliance to decide the issue?
3. Why does the court deny the damages request?

Suggested Case References

1. Does having a contract under seal negate the necessity of having consideration? Read what the Massachusetts court said in *Thomas v. Kiendzior*, 27 Mass. App. Ct. 370, 538 N.E.2d 66 (1989).
2. Can forbearance of right to assert a valid and mature claim be consideration for a promise? *First Texas Sav. Ass'n v. Comprop Inv. Properties, Ltd.*, 752 F. Supp. 1568 (M.D. Fla. 1990).
3. For a definition of consideration by an Arkansas court, read *Bass v. Service Supply Co., Inc.*, 25 Ark. App. 273, 757 S.W.2d 189 (1988).
4. For a detailed discussion of the preexisting duty rule, read *Rosati Masonry Co. v. Jonna Constr. Co.*, 1998 Mich. App. LEXIS 2418.
5. Is a reporter's promise of anonymity contractual consideration? Read *Cohen v. Cowles Media Co.*, 44 N.W.2d 248 (Minn. App. 1990).

Ethical Considerations

ABA Rule of Professional Conduct 1.5 establishes a guideline for assessing the reasonableness of the consideration an attorney requires from a client. Some of the items include (1) time and labor required; (2) likelihood that acceptance of the client's case will preclude other employment opportunities for the lawyer; (3) fees customarily charged for similar services by other attorneys in the area; (4) the amount of damages sought and the actual results obtained; (5) time limitations imposed by the client; (6) the nature and length of the professional relationship between the lawyer and the client; and (7) whether the fee is fixed or contingent.

Quick Quiz

Answer TRUE or FALSE. (Answers can be found in Appendix C on page 413.)

1. A gift can never be consideration for a contract.
2. To be valid, the consideration to support a contract must be legally sufficient.
3. Under certain circumstances, a preexisting duty may still be consideration for a new contract.
4. *Caveat emptor* means let the seller beware.
5. Promissory estoppel is a contractual remedy.

5 Legality of Subject Matter and Contractual Capacity

Learning Objectives

After studying this chapter you will be able to:

- Discuss the concept of the legality of the subject matter
- Define *"malum in se"*
- Define *"malum prohibitum"*
- List the six types of contracts that come under the Statute of Frauds
- Discuss what is meant by "usury"
- Explain the concept of "contractual capacity"
- Differentiate between infants and minors
- Know which types of contracts a minor cannot avoid
- Discuss the effect of alcohol and drugs on a person's contractual capacity
- Apply the concepts of legality and capacity to your everyday life

CHAPTER OVERVIEW

The first three elements of a valid contract—offer, acceptance, and consideration—discussed in the preceding chapters focus on the actual terms of the agreement itself. The last three requisite elements of a valid contract are concerned with the circumstances surrounding the agreement—the legality of the subject matter, the ability of the parties to enter into enforceable contractual agreements, and the intent of the parties. This chapter examines the fourth and fifth requirements: legality and capacity.

For a contract to be valid and enforceable, the contract must be formed for a legal purpose. If the subject matter of the agreement violates statutory law or public policy, the court would be unable and unwilling to permit its provisions to be carried out. Consequently, even though all the other elements of a valid contract may be present, if the subject matter of the contract is illegal, no enforceable agreement can exist.

In addition to the legality of the subject matter, the law is also concerned with the legal ability of the parties to create a valid contract. The law has decided that under certain circumstances and conditions a person is legally incapable of forming a valid contract. These standards of contractual capacity are based on the person's age and mental condition at the moment the contract is entered into.

Legality of the Subject Matter

Contracts that are entered into for an illegal purpose are not enforceable. The reason is obvious. How can a court, designated to uphold the law, enforce an agreement that purports to break the law?

However, not all laws involve heinous actions, and the law has divided "illegality" into two broad categories. The first category contains laws that support the very nature and fabric of society. Violation of these rules go against all public policy, and contracts violating them are completely void and unenforceable. The second category includes minor illegalities, those laws created by statute that bar actions which are not, in and of themselves, morally reprehensible. Contracts that violate this second category may still permit the injured party some form of **quasi-contractual** relief.

Malum in Se

The first category of illegality, those contracts that violate public policy, are deemed *malum in se*—bad in and of themselves. The actions prohibited by these laws are considered to be morally reprehensible, and contracts formed for purposes *malum in se* are entirely unenforceable. Typical examples of these types of laws are felonies, contracts in restraint of trade, contracts found to discriminate against a protected category of citizen (race, age, sex, national origin, and so forth), and contracts that are deemed unconscionable.

EXAMPLES:

1. Wally enters into a contract with Eddie, promising Eddie $10,000 if Eddie can find a hit man to kill Wally's business partner. Although all the other requisite elements of a valid contract may exist, in this instance the contract is still unenforceable because murder is considered *malum in se*.

2. Gamma, Inc. and Beta Corp. enter into a contract to fix their prices, thus driving all other competition out of their market. This contract is unenforceable because its purpose is to restrain trade, which is *malum in se*.

3. Violet needs a new secretary and hires an employment agency to find her a suitable employee. Violet makes it a condition of her agreement with the agency that they find her only white male secretaries. This contract is unenforceable. The provisions are meant to discriminate against persons based on race and sex, which is *malum in se*.

Malum Prohibitum

The second category of illegal subject matter encompasses actions that are not morally reprehensible or against public policy but are still minor violations of the law. This category is known as *malum prohibitum*—a prohibited wrong, or something prohibited by statutory regulation. Although contracts that are *malum prohibitum* are unenforceable, some quasi-contractual relief may be available if the aggrieved party can demonstrate that to deny recovery would unjustly enrich the other party to the agreement. The following is a sample list of contracts that are viewed as *malum prohibitum*. Every state code has its own statutory prohibitions, and you should review each state's laws independently.

Contracts That Violate the Statute of Frauds   The **Statute of Frauds** is a law that requires certain types of contracts to be in writing in order to be enforceable. Typically, six types of contracts come within the provisions of the Statute of Frauds:

1. contracts for an interest in realty;
2. contracts that are not to be performed within one year;
3. contracts in consideration of marriage;
4. guarantees;
5. sale of goods valued at over $500; and
6. executors' promises to pay the decedent's debts.

A complete discussion of the Statute of Frauds appears in Chapter 7, Contract Provisions.

Although the statute requires these types of contracts to be in writing, if the parties actually perform under the oral agreement, their performances will take the contract out of the Statute of Frauds and make it enforceable.

EXAMPLES:

1. In consideration of her promise to marry him, Donald promises to give $5 million to Marla. For this contract to be enforceable in a court of law, Marla had better get the promise in writing. Otherwise, it violates the Statute of Frauds and is *malum prohibitum.*

2. Cathy and LaWanda enter into an oral agreement whereby LaWanda agrees to buy Cathy's summer home for $25,000. Because the agreement is for the sale of an interest in real estate, the Statute of Frauds applies, and the parties can avoid the agreement because it is *malum prohibitum.*

3. Cathy and LaWanda enter into an oral agreement whereby La-Wanda agrees to buy Cathy's summer home for $25,000. Two weeks after the agreement was reached, LaWanda gives Cathy a check for the purchase price. The next day Cathy changes her mind and tries to avoid the agreement by saying it violates the Statute of Frauds. Because LaWanda has already performed, the court would most probably decide that LaWanda's performance has taken the contract out of the category of *malum prohibitum.*

Usury   Usury laws regulate the legal rate of interest that can be charged for extending credit. A contract for the loan of money that indicates a rate of interest above the legal limit is *malum prohibitum* because it is usurious and therefore unenforceable. If the lender has already performed, some courts will permit him to receive the legal rate of interest; to do otherwise would mean the borrower received the money interest-free, which would be unfair to the lender. (In some states, the usurer cannot even collect the principal. Each state statute must be specifically checked.)

EXAMPLE:

Rhonda agrees to lend Lennie $2,000 at an annual rate of interest of 50 percent. The contract is unenforceable as being *malum prohibitum.* However, if Rhonda actually gave the money to Lenny, Lenny may be required to repay the loan at the legal rate of interest.

Gambling   Gambling, except in certain locations and under certain prescribed situations, is illegal. Consequently, a contract entered into for the purpose of betting is *malum prohibitum.*

EXAMPLE:

Saul leases a building to operate a gambling casino in downtown St. Louis. Gambling is not permitted in Missouri, and so the contract is *malum prohibitum.* The lease may still be operative if the building can be used for a legal purpose.

Licensing Statutes   State and local communities have various licensing statutes, laws that require certain types of occupations or enterprises to receive governmental permission to operate. Any contract that would violate the government licensing statute is *malum prohibitum.*

EXAMPLE:

Sherree and Latoya enter into an agreement to open and operate a beauty and hair salon. Beauticians and hairdressers are required to be licensed by the state. If neither Sherree nor Latoya is licensed, the contract is *malum prohibitum.*

Laws that impose licensing requirements are created either to protect the public or to provide the government with income from the licensing fees. If the agreement violates a licensing law designed to protect the public, no recovery at all is possible. If the purpose of the licensing statute is merely to raise revenue, some quasi-contractual remedy may be available.

EXAMPLES:

1. Ernie goes to Veronica for medical assistance. Although Veronica holds herself out to be a doctor, she, in fact, is not a doctor. Therefore, Veronica's agreement with Ernie for a fee is *malum prohibitum.* In this instance, Veronica cannot recover the value of her services to Ernie. To do so would potentially endanger the public.

2. La Dolce Vita, an Italian restaurant, serves alcohol and wine to its customers. The restaurant does not have a liquor license. In this instance, even though the contract for the sale of liquor is *malum prohibitum,* the restaurant may be allowed to recover the

cost of the alcohol it sold. This statute is designed to raise revenue for the government.

As indicated above, contracts that are *malum prohibitum* are not considered as seriously wrong as those that are *malum in se*, although neither category creates a valid contract. But because the law generally favors contractual relationships, it does sometimes permit an agreement that has both legal and illegal provisions to be **severed:** that is, the legal portion of the contract, if possible, is separated from the illegal portion and upheld, whereas the illegal portion remains unenforceable. This concept was exemplified in the examples above when portions of the agreement were permitted to stand, such as the lease of the building in St. Louis and the loan of the money.

Contractual Capacity

Contractual capacity, the fifth requisite element of every valid contract, refers to the parties' legal ability to enter into a binding contractual relationship. In reality, the concept of contractual capacity is concerned more with defining contractual incapacity than it is with defining contractual capacity. There are four major areas of contractual capacity, which are discussed below.

Age

Age is the most common capacity issue to arise. The law divides a person's age into two major categories: *adulthood* (or **majority**) and **minority**.

An *adult* is anyone over the *age of consent*, which most states designate to begin at age 18. (Some statutes, however, may establish younger limits for the age of consent.) Adults are considered contractually capable with respect to age.

A minor is anyone under the age of consent pursuant to state statute. Minors are further subdivided into **natural infants** and **children of tender years**. A natural infant, a child younger than 7, is considered totally incapable of entering into any contract because of extreme youth. A child of tender years, a minor between the ages of 7 and 14, is usually considered too young to form a valid contract, but that decision is based on the particulars of the contract in question.

Those persons between puberty and the age of consent, the group in between the above-mentioned categories, are deemed to be minors. As mentioned in Chapter 1, minors are generally considered to lack contractual capacity. It is this age group that causes the most concern with respect to the capacity of a person to enter into a valid contract. Minors may avoid contracts they enter into at any point up to reaching their majority without being in breach of contract. The contracts entered into by minors are considered **voidable** at the option of the minor, which is why most people who contract with minors require that an adult, usually the minor's parent, guarantee the contract. Be aware of age distinctions in different states with respect to the types of contracts that persons may validly enter into based on age; for example, purchasing alcoholic beverages.

 EXAMPLE:

Floyd, a 17-year-old, has just received several CDs as a holiday present. Floyd doesn't own a CD player, but he sees one advertised at a price he can afford. If he enters into a contract with the store owner to buy the CD player, Floyd can rescind his acceptance anytime prior to reaching age 18 without being in breach of contract. However, Floyd may be charged for the use of the CD player until his disavowal of the agreement.

There are certain categories of contracts that the law has determined that minors cannot avoid. These contracts are contracts to provide the minor with **necessaries**—items deemed essential to support life such as food, clothing, shelter, and medical aid. Be aware, though, that some states require only **emancipated** minors to be bound to contracts for necessaries. Emancipated minors are those no longer under the legal care of an adult; they are responsible for all their own actions. These situations are usually treated as quasi-contracts; that is, the reasonable value of the item, not necessarily the contract price, may be recovered.

In addition, many states prohibit a minor from avoiding contracts for education or marriage, and the federal government has determined that minors cannot avoid their voluntary military enlistment simply because of age.

EXAMPLE:

Nick graduates high school at age 17 and decides to enlist in the army to fulfill a lifelong dream of becoming a soldier. After eight days of boot camp, Nick regrets his decision and tells his sergeant he wants out. Too late. A minor may not avoid his contract for enlistment with Uncle Sam.

Mental Capacity

A mentally deficient person lacks contractual capacity. If the person is in a mental institution, this lack of capacity exists until such time as he is adjudged mentally competent by an appropriate authority. If, on the other hand, the person merely suffers occasional mental lapses and is not confined, his mental capacity is determined by the nature of the contract and whether or not he understands the nature of what he is undertaking. Any question dealing with a person's mental capacity is always determined on the facts and circumstances of each individual situation.

 EXAMPLE:

Marvin hears voices that tell him what clothes to wear and what horses to bet on. After placing a bet with his bookie, Charlotte, Marvin gets hungry and goes to a fast food restaurant for a hamburger and fries. The contract with the restaurant is valid. Marvin's mental state has no effect on, or relationship to, this particular contract.

Alcohol and Drugs

A person who is under the influence of alcohol or drugs is incapable of entering into a valid contract. The incapacity is only temporary, however. When the effect of the alcohol or drug wears off, provided no other problems exist, the person is considered to be contractually capable once again. Any contract entered into during the period of incapacity may be reaffirmed and made valid once the temporary incapacity is removed. As with mental incapacity, the determination as to the person's mental state at the moment of contract is determined on a case-by-case basis. Be aware of age distinctions in different states with respect to the types of contracts that persons may validly enter into based on age—for example, purchasing alcoholic beverages.

 EXAMPLE:

Bess is 80 years old and takes medication whenever she has a heart palpitation. As a side effect of the drug, Bess becomes dizzy and disoriented. During the period of disorientation, an encyclopedia salesperson rings Bess's doorbell and convinces her to buy a set of encyclopedias. The next day, when the effect of the medicine wears off, Bess realizes what she has signed but feels the books would be a good gift for her son. Bess can either avoid the contract, because of her drug-induced mental state at the time of the signing, or affirm the contract now that the medicine has worn off.

CHAPTER SUMMARY

Even if an agreement possesses the elements of a valid offer and acceptance and is supported by legally sufficient consideration, the contract will still fail if it is formed for a legally proscribed purpose, or if one of the parties lacks contractual capacity.

A contract is considered formed for an illegal purpose if the subject matter is either *malum in se* or *malum prohibitum*. Agreements that are *malum in se* are those formed for purposes that go against the moral grain of society. Such contracts are unenforceable as a matter of public policy. Some examples of *malum in se* agreements are agreements to commit crimes, to discriminate, or to restrain trade.

By comparison, a contract is considered *malum prohibitum* if its subject matter violates some less serious prohibition. This type of illegality is not considered morally reprehensible, and, consequently, if injury can be shown, the court will permit the injured party some remedy based on a quasi-contractual claim. Some examples of *malum prohibitum* agreements are those that violate the Statute of Frauds, usury or licensing laws, or gambling statutes.

Each state has determined the legal age of contractual consent for its citizens. If a contract is entered into by someone considered a minor under the appropriate state statute, that contract is voidable by the minor any time until the minor reaches majority. Although the contract is voidable, on reaching majority the minor may choose to affirm the contract, thereby making it enforceable. Note that exceptions to this rule are made for contracts entered into by minors for necessaries, marriage, and enlistment in the armed services.

In addition to the age of the party to a contract, the law also looks to the person's mental state at the time of contracting. Persons who are mentally incapable lack contractual capacity. Persons who are under the influence of drugs or alcohol are considered to be temporarily incapable, but they may affirm the contract once the temporary infirmity is removed.

In any instance, anytime a person has performed his contractual obligation, except for contracts *malum in se* or when the person is totally incapable, that performance will usually entitle him to some form of legal recovery so as to avoid injury and to prevent unjust enrichment.

SYNOPSIS

Legality of subject matter
1.   *Malum in se*: Unenforceable
2.   *Malum prohibitum*: Quasi-contractual recovery may be permitted
Contractual capacity
1.   Age
2.   Mental condition
3.   Alcohol
4.   Drugs

Contracts formed when a party is incapable may be affirmed once the incapacity is removed.

Key Terms

Children of tender years: children between the ages of 7 and 14
Contractual capacity: the statutory ability of a person to enter into a valid contract
Emancipation: a minor no longer under the legal care of an adult
Majority: adulthood; above legal age of consent
*Malum in se***:**   bad in and of itself; against public morals
*Malum prohibitum***:**   regulatory wrong; violates statute
Minority: person under the legal age of consent
Natural infant: a child under the age of seven
Necessaries: food, clothing, shelter, medical aid
Quasi-contract: implied-in-law contract (see Chapter 1)
Severability: ability to separate a contract into its legal and illegal portions
Statute of Frauds: statute requiring certain types of contracts to be in writing (see Chapter 7)
Usury: rate of interest higher than the rate allowed by law
Voidable contract: a contract capable of being avoided without being in breach of contract (see Chapter 1)

EXERCISES

1.   Check your own state statutes for the age of consent and contracts that are deemed to be *malum in se* and *malum prohibitum*.
2.   Why can a person receive some remedy even if the contract is *malum prohibitum*?
3.   What factors would determine a person's lack of mental capacity?
4.   Are there circumstances in which a person's physical, not mental, state can cause her to lack contractual capacity? Why?
5.   Dr. Doe firmly believes in the terminally ill's right to die. He has contracts to assist Richard Roe, an 80-year-old man dying of

cancer, in committing suicide. The fee agreed on is $1,000. After Mr. Roe's death, Dr. Doe requests the fee from the Roe estate, which refuses to pay him. Argue for and against the legality of the contract.

Cases for Analysis

It is often difficult for a court to determine whether a party to a contract has sufficient capacity to contract. The first case, *First Colony Insurance Company v. Kreppein*, grapples with a person's mental capacity to change the beneficiary of a life insurance policy, and the second case, *Achee Holdings, LLC v. Silver Hill Financial, LLC* discusses usury.

First Colony Insurance Company v. Alfred Kreppein, et al.
2007 U.S. Dist. LEXIS 62770 (E.D. La. 2007)

[The court was called upon to decide the following issues: of: 1) effect of the temporary restraining order on the change of beneficiary of the life insurance policy [omitted], 2) the mental capacity of the deceased and 3) breach of contract in changing the listed beneficiary.]

I. Background

This case surrounds a dispute over decedent Stephanie Boyter Kreppein's insurance proceeds between the decedent's ex-husband, Alfred Kreppein ("Mr. Kreppein"), and the decedent's children, Ryan Brice Crane and Laurel Crane Luquette ("Crane" and "Luquette").

The decedent and Mr. Kreppein were married in November, 2000. Subsequently, each of them purchased a life insurance policy naming the other as the sole beneficiary. Mrs. Kreppein named Crane and Luquette as Contingent Beneficiaries of her policy. On July 28, 2005, the decedent moved out of her home with Mr. Kreppein to Baton Rouge with members of her family. On August 2, 2005, Mr. Kreppein filed a petition for divorce from the decedent. Subsequently, on August 29, 2005, First Colony received a Policy Change Form, signed by Mrs. Kreppein, revoking all prior beneficiary designations and designating Crane and Luquette as the Primary Beneficiaries under the Policy. Mrs. Kreppein died on October 11, 2005.

Under the applicable policy, upon the death of the insured, First Colony became obligated to pay the sum of $500,000, plus applicable interest, to the person/s rightfully entitled to the death benefit. On December 27, 2005, Plaintiff First Colony Life Insurance Company ("First Colony") filed a Complaint for Interpleader to determine the rightful beneficiary/beneficiaries of the insurance proceeds.

* * *

II. Contractual Capacity

Mr. Kreppein suggests that the decedent lacked the required contractual capacity at the time that she changed the beneficiary of her life insurance policy. His affidavit states that "she was unable to perform routine tasks," "she began to lose her ability to think," and "she could not remember people she had known for long periods of time." The affidavit of the insurance agent who procured the policies for the Kreppeins states that on July 29, 2005, the decedent, her mother and another woman came to see him about changing the beneficiary on the insurance policy. The agent, Terry Sullivan states "[a]t the time, it was clear that Stephanie was not able to understand or comprehend what was going on. . . . She smiled sweetly but did not recognize me or seem to comprehend anything that I said."

However, the decedent was not interdicted by law at the time of her death, and it is well settled that the law presumes contractual capacity. Exceptions to the presumption of capacity to contract must be shown quite convincingly and by the great weight of the evidence. Therefore, to determine whether the change of beneficiary should be nullified due to lack of contractual capacity, the Court looks to Louisiana Civil Code Article 1926:

> A contract made by a noninterdicted person deprived of reason at the time of contracting may be attacked after his death, on the ground of incapacity, only when the contract is gratuitous, or it evidences lack of understanding, or was made within thirty days of his death, or when application for interdiction was filed before his death.

The changing of a beneficiary under a life insurance policy is not a gratuitous contract; there was no application for interdiction filed before the decedent's death; and the Change of Beneficiary Form signed by the deceased was executed on August 22, 2005, more than thirty days before the decedent's death.

Therefore, the only way that the decedent's Change of Beneficiary Form can be challenged for lack of capacity is if it "evidences a lack of understanding." There is no evidence that the contract itself "evidences a lack of understanding." The Policy Change Form bears the decedent's signature and clearly sets forth a change of beneficiary from Mr. Kreppein to a 50% interest in Ryan Crane and a 50% interest in Laurel Crane Luquette. Furthermore, the sworn affidavit of Mary Elizabeth Perry, who witnessed the signing of the document notes that the decedent "made it clear it was something she wanted to do. She expressed understanding concerning the implications of signing the Change of Beneficiary Designation Form." As such, there is insufficient evidence to overcome the presumption that the decedent had contractual capacity at the time she executed the Policy Change Form document.

* * *

III. Reciprocal Insurance Obligation

Mr. Kreppein argues that even if the decedent did not lack contractual capacity to change the insurance policy beneficiary, she was precluded from doing so because she and Mr. Kreppein had mutually contracted away their rights to change the beneficiary of their respective policies. Mr. Kreppein states in his affidavit: "Stephanie and I had specifically agreed to secure two insurance policies on each other's lives to enable us to pay debts which we were continuing to incur as a result of business and other property we purchased during our marriage." The two allegedly agreed that the proceeds of the respective policies would reciprocally ensure each other and there would be "no change regarding the insurance policies or beneficiaries."

The only evidence that Mr. Kreppein has to attest to this seemingly oral agreement to reciprocally insure was Mr. Kreppein's own affidavit and that of Terry Sullivan, the agent who helped the Kreppeins procure their policies. Terry Sullivan states in his depositions: "He was aware that I had an insurance license and he indicated that he and Stephanie wanted to discuss obtaining life insurance policies that would protect each of them in the event of the death of the other."

The decedent's insurance policy states that the "Owner may change the designations of Owner, Contingent Owner, and Beneficiary during the insured's lifetime. Any change is subject to the consent of an irrevocable beneficiary." There is no indication in the policy nor any argument made by either party that Mr. Kreppein was made an "irrevocable beneficiary" under the policy. Without a designation of an irrevocable beneficiary, the decedent would be free to change the beneficiary under the policy at any time before his or her death. If the Kreppeins had truly intended to contract out of their right to change the designation of beneficiary, each should have designated the other as "irrevocable beneficiary" under the policy. If they had done so, any change to the policy beneficiary could only be made with the irrevocable beneficiary's consent.

It is well settled in Louisiana law that the owner of an insurance policy, usually also the insured, has the right to change the designation of the beneficiary of his or her policy under the terms of the policy without the consent of the original beneficiary. This is because absent a conventional agreement, "no one has the vested right to the status of a beneficiary under a life insurance contract, if the contingent event which vests such right, the death of the insured, has not occurred; until then, the parties to the insurance contract are free to change the beneficiary, if such a change is permitted by its terms."

Such a case is present here. Mr. Kreppein has adduced no evidence that the deceased sought to designate him as an irrevocable beneficiary. Furthermore, he has failed to introduce any evidence, other than his own testimony and the generalized testimony of his insurance agent, Terry Sullivan, that the deceased intended to enter into a binding conventional obligation to maintain Mr. Kreppein as the beneficiary of her policy.

* * *

[The court ruled in favor of the children.]

Questions

1. What does the court mean when it says that the decedent was not interdicted?
2. What evidence would you try to present to indicate a person's contractual capacity?
3. What would be the consideration for a reciprocal insurance obligation?

Achee Holdings, LLC v. Silver Hill Financial, LLC
2009 U.S. App. LEXIS 19231 (5th Cir. 2009)

In this usury case under Texas law, Plaintiff-Appellant Achee Holdings, LLC ("Achee") appeals the district court's order granting the Federal Rules of Civil Procedure 12(b)(6) motion to dismiss filed by Defendants-Appellees Silver Hill Financial, LLC ("Silver Hill") and Bayview Loan Servicing, LLC ("Bayview"). For the following reasons, we affirm.

In June 2007, Achee executed an adjustable rate promissory note ("the Note") with Silver Hill. Under the terms of the Note, Silver Hill lent to Achee the principal sum of $280,000.00. The Note provided for two prepayment penalties in the event that Achee sought to repay the principal during the initial thirty-six months of the loan period (the "Lockout Period"): (1) an amount equal to the interest which would have accrued on the unpaid principal balance during the Lockout Period (labeled the "Lockout Fee"); and (2) an amount equal to five percent of the then-outstanding unpaid principal balance (labeled the "Prepayment Consideration"). During the Lockout Period, Achee sought to prepay the principal amount. Bayview, as Silver Hill's loan servicer, notified Achee that it owed a payoff amount of $389,355.85, comprised of the following: the principal and interest then presently due under the Note ($282,969.19); the Lockout Fee $92,083.81); and the Prepayment Consideration ($13,993.32).

Achee refused to pay the Lockout Fee, and instead filed this lawsuit alleging that the Lockout Fee is disguised interest that exceeded the allowable amount under the Texas Finance Code. After consideration of Defendants-Appellees' Rule 12(b)(6) motion, the district court dismissed the complaint for failure to state a claim. Achee appealed.

We review *de novo* a district court's order granting a motion to dismiss under Rule 12(b)(6). *Lovick v. Ritemoney Ltd.*, 378 F.3d 433, 437 (5th Cir. 2004). All well-pleaded factual allegations are accepted as true, and all reasonable inferences are drawn in the plaintiff's favor. Id. Recently, the Supreme Court held that "[t]o survive a motion to dismiss, a complaint must contain sufficient factual matter, accepted as true, to 'state a claim for relief that is plausible on its face.'" *Ashcroft v. Iqbal*, 129 S. Ct. 1937, 1949 (2009) (citation omitted).

The single issue in this case is whether the Lockout Fee constitutes interest, such that it violates Texas usury laws. The essential elements of a usurious transaction are "(1) a loan of money; (2) an absolute obligation that the principal be repaid; and (3) the exaction from the borrower of a greater compensation than the amount allowed by law for the use of money by the borrower." *Najarro v. SASI Int'l, Ltd.*, 904 F.2d 1002, 1005 (5th Cir. 1990) (citation omitted). Unless otherwise provided by law, an interest rate greater than ten percent a year is usurious. Tex. Fin. Code Ann. §302.001(b) (Vernon 2006). Interest is defined under Texas law as "compensation for the use, forbearance, or detention of money . . . [but] does not include compensation or other amounts that . . . are permitted to be contracted for, charged, or received in addition to interest[.]" TEX. FIN. CODE ANN. §301.002(a)(4) (Vernon 2006).

Where a contract grants the borrower the right to prepay, Texas courts hold that a prepayment penalty is not interest because it is not compensation for the use, forbearance, or detention of money; rather, it is "a charge for the option or privilege of prepayment." *Parker Plaza W. Partners v. Unum Pension & Ins. Co.*, 941 F.2d 349, 352 (5th Cir. 1991) (citations omitted). This principle is codified at Tex. Fin. Code Ann. §306.005, which states that "a creditor and an obligor may agree to a prepayment premium . . . whether payable in the event of voluntary prepayment . . . or other cause that involves premature termination of the loan, and those amounts do not constitute interest." However, lenders can violate usury laws by charging fees that constitute "disguised interest." *Lovick*, 378 F.3d at 439. Whether a particular fee is disguised interest depends on the substance of the transaction, not how the parties label the fee. See *In re CPDC, Inc.*, 337 F.3d 436, 444 (5th Cir. 2003). Specifically, a fee will not be considered interest if it is not for the use, forbearance, or detention of money. Id. at 445. A fee may be considered interest, though, if it is not supported by separate and additional consideration. *Lovick*, 378 F.3d at 439.

Achee argues that the Lockout Fee is usurious because it is disguised interest. However, Achee has shown no set of facts indicating that it is plausible that the Lockout Fee is interest disguised as a prepayment penalty. Though the interest rate on the loan was used as part of the formula for calculating the Lockout Fee, the substance of the transaction shows that it is clearly a prepayment penalty. The Note granted Achee the option of paying the loan early and also paying the Lockout Fee, in exchange for avoiding the twenty-seven years of interest that would accrue over the remaining term of the loan. In other words, the Lockout Fee acted as consideration in exchange for the privilege of paying the loan in the first three years and avoiding further interest. See *Bearden v. Tarrant Sav. Ass'n*, 643 S.W.2d 247, 249 (Tex. App.—Ft. Worth 1982, *writ ref'd n.r.e.*). The fact that the parties contracted for two types of prepayment penalties, one of which only applied in the event of a payment within the first three years of the loan, does not change the fact that the Lockout Fee operated, in substance, as a penalty for very early prepayment. Moreover, Achee could avoid paying the Lockout Fee altogether by waiting until after the thirty-six month period expired to pay off the loan, a fact which we have recognized as the rationale for the rule that prepayment penalties are not interest. See *Parker Plaza*, 941 F.2d at 353. Accordingly, since the Lockout Fee is not compensation for the use, forbearance, or detention of money and is rather a charge for the option or privilege of prepayment, under Texas law the Lockout Fee is not interest and the usury laws are not violated.1[1] For the foregoing reasons, we AFFIRM the district court's order dismissing the complaint for failure to state a claim.

Questions

1. What does the court say are the essential elements of a usurious transaction?

2. How does the court view the prepayment penalty?

3. Research and indicate what is considered the usurious rate of interest in your state.

Suggested Case References

1. May a person who is suffering from a progressive mental disease still be mentally competent to contract? Read *Butler v. Harrison*, 578 A.2d 1098 (D.C. App. 1990).

2. May an elderly person suffering from great mental lapses still have capacity to contract? Read *Brown v. Resort Developments*, 238 Va. 527, 385 S.E.2d 575 (1989).

3. Contracts for the sale of sexual favors are *malum in se*, at least in Oregon. *State v. Grimes*, 85 Or. App. 159, 735 P.2d 1277 (1987).

4. Does marital status affect contractual capacity? See what the court said in *United States v. Yazell*, 334 F.2d 454 (5th Cir. 1964).

5. May one spouse exert undue influence over the other? See *Butler v. Harrison*, 578 A.2d 1098 (D.C. App. 1990).

Ethical Considerations

Occasionally, an attorney may represent a client under a disability. According to ABA Rule of Professional Conduct 1.14, in those circumstances, when a client's ability to make adequately considered decisions in connection with the representation is impaired, whether because of minority, mental disability, or for some other reason, the lawyer, and the legal assistant, shall, as far as reasonably possible, maintain a normal client-lawyer relationship with the client. Further, the lawyer may seek to have a guardian appointed, if the lawyer reasonably believes that the client cannot adequately act in his or her own best interests.

---

1 We have also observed that a prepayment premium may be usurious if it exceeds "the legal rate calculated to the stipulated maturity date." See Parker Plaza, 941 F.2d at 353. Though Achee does not raise this argument, we note that the prepayment penalties in this case do not exceed the legal interest rate calculated over the thirty-year term of the loan.

Quick Quiz

Answer TRUE or FALSE. (Answers can be found in Appendix C on page 413.)

1. *Malum in se* contracts may be enforceable.
2. A person's age is a factor in determining contractual capacity.
3. It is possible to sever a contract into its legal and illegal portions.
4. A guarantee need not be in writing to be valid.
5. Violating a licensing statute is an example of *malum prohibitum*.

6 Contractual Intent

Learning Objectives

After studying this chapter you will be able to:

- Define what is meant by "contractual intent"
- Define "fraud"
- Differentiate fraud from misrepresentation
- Explain the concept of duress
- List the three types of duress that may be encountered in contract law
- Discuss what is meant by undue influence
- Define a contract of adhesion
- Discuss the effect of a mistake on contract formation
- Discuss the enforceability of contract entered into with a unilateral mistake
- Understand how the concept of contractual intent may be applied to void contracts

CHAPTER OVERVIEW

The sixth, and final, requisite element of every valid contract is the contractual intent of the parties. For the contract to be enforceable, the parties to the agreement must intend to enter into a binding contractual relationship. Even if all of the other requirements are satisfied, if the parties do not objectively intend to contract, there is no binding agreement.

The intent of the parties relates back to the concept of mutual assent. If a person does not freely and voluntarily agree to the terms of a contract, regardless of how clear and specific those terms appear, there is no valid consent. Generally, the genuineness of a person's assent to a contract may be suspect in three situations: 1) if the person is induced to enter the relationship by fraud; 2) if the person is coerced or forced into agreeing to the terms of the contract; or 3) if the parties are in some way mistaken about the terms of the agreement.

A contract is fraudulently entered into if the innocent party is purposely misled or lied to in order to induce his contractual promise. The law will not enforce a contract that is induced by fraud.

If the person is forced to agree to a contractual relationship by threats of physical, emotional, or economic duress, the person obviously lacks voluntary contractual intent.

Finally, if the parties to the contract are mistaken as to the subject matter of the contract, no contract exists because there is no meeting of the minds. This is true even though the mistake is an innocent one. As long as the parties to the agreement do not contemplate the same subject matter, no contract can be formed.

Just as with the requirements of contractual capacity and legality of subject matter, this final requirement of intent concerns the circumstances surrounding the agreement, not the terms of the agreement itself. On its face, an agreement may appear to meet all of the formalities of contract law, but if the parties do not truly intend to contract, the agreement will fail.

Contractual Intent Defined

As introduced in Chapter 1, there must be a meeting of the minds before an agreement can be deemed an enforceable contract. The parties to the contract must actually intend to enter into a contract for the same bargain at the same time. If it can be demonstrated that a contract was not intended by one, or both, of the parties, no contract can exist because there is no mutual assent.

EXAMPLE:

Susan and Jon have been friends since childhood. Susan has to turn in a book report for school tomorrow, and asks Jon to come to her house to help her. To induce his promise, Susan offers him $10,000 for his help, and Jon laughingly accepts. There is no contract. The parties did not intend a contractual relationship; as friends they were merely agreeing to help one another.

The example given above is a situation in which the parties are joking with each other, based on a long-standing relationship. The intent to contract is obviously missing. As in most cases when contractual intent is called into question, it is the circumstances surrounding the transaction that determine intent.

Generally, when determining the contractual intent of an agreement, there are three areas of possible concern: fraud, duress, and mistake. Each of these situations will be discussed below.

Fraud and Misrepresentation

In **fraud**, one party to an agreement tricks a second party into entering the agreement. Only if all five of the elements of fraud are shown will a contract fail. The five elements of contractual fraud are

1. the misrepresentation
2. of a material fact,
3. made with the intent to deceive and
4. relied on by the other party
5. to his or her detriment.

If an agreement is induced by fraud, the innocent party has the option either to avoid the contract, because she lacked the requisite intent, or to fulfill the contract.

What, however, would be the result if the deception is innocent—that is, the person making the statements does not intend to deceive the other party? In this instance, there is no fraud, but there is a **misrepresentation**. If a material fact (a fact that goes to the heart of the transaction) is misrepresented, the injured party is entitled to the same relief she would be granted if she had been defrauded.

 EXAMPLES:

1. Paul is walking down the street when he sees a man selling watches. The man tells Paul the watches are Cartiers and offers to sell one to Paul for $50. Paul buys the watch, but two days later it breaks down. He brings the watch to a licensed Cartier dealer for repairs and discovers the watch is not a Cartier, but a cheap imitation. If Paul can ever find that man on the street again, he can get his money back. The contract was induced by fraud. The man lied about the subject matter to Paul to induce Paul's assent to the contract, and Paul was economically injured.

2. Lola is in the market for a Van Gogh painting. Charles is an art dealer selling a painting said to be a Van Gogh, although he

has not bothered to check its origins. Charles sells the painting to Lola, who discovers that the painting is a forgery. This is an example of misrepresentation. Charles was negligent in not establishing the genuineness of the painting, but he did not intend to deceive Lola. There is no mistake, because the genuineness of the painting could have been checked had Charles not been careless. Lola can get her money back.

3. In a recent trial decision, a man sued his ex-wife for fraud. After many years of marriage, the wife admitted to the husband that she never loved him. After the divorce, the former husband sued the wife for fraud in the marriage contract and won. The wife purposely misled the husband by saying that she loved him in order to induce the marriage. This constitutes a fraud, because marriage is a contract. The detriment the husband suffered was the property the wife acquired from him during the marriage.

A contract that is induced by fraud or misrepresentation is **voidable** by the innocent party. This means that even though the innocent party was misled into entering the contract, if he wishes to complete the agreement, he may do so. The innocent party may also avoid the obligation because of the other party's fraudulent actions. Fraud and misrepresentation are determined by the facts of each individual situation.

Duress

Duress connotes some form of force or coercion exercised over one party to the contract in order to induce that party's promise to contract. Because the innocent party is forced to enter into the agreement, there is no contract. The party did not freely intend to contract.

Duress can take several forms. The most obvious example of duress would be **physical duress**. Physical duress occurs when one party forces the other to enter into the contract by threatening physical harm.

EXAMPLE:

Bill holds a gun to Morris' head and tells him to sign a contract deeding over Blackacre to Bill for a stated price. There is no contract. Morris was forced to sign the contract at gun point, and so he did not freely intend to contract. Note that on its face the contract itself would appear to be valid; it is the surrounding circumstances that invalidate the agreement.

Another form of duress is **economic duress**, wherein, a person is induced to contract for fear of losing some monetary benefit. At the turn of the century, before unionism, this concept was exemplified by the saying, "If you don't come in Sunday, don't come in Monday." Workers were forced to work a seven-day week or lose their jobs. They did not agree to work seven days of their own free will but were forced to come in for fear of losing their livelihoods entirely. Any form of economic force used to induce agreement to a contract is economic duress.

EXAMPLE:

Iris receives a letter from her state tax department stating that she has underpaid her taxes and ordering an audit of her returns. Under the state law, the tax department can only audit returns for the previous three years. When Iris goes to the audit, the agent tells her that if she doesn't sign a waiver to permit an audit of all of her previous returns, he will order all of her assets frozen until a final determination of her tax liability is made. Iris agrees to the waiver. This is an example of economic duress, and the waiver is invalid.

A third type of duress is **mental duress**, wherein a person is coerced to enter into a contract by psychological threats. As with all forms of duress, the ability of a particular threat to induce a party to contract is determined on a case-by-case basis. It is the impact on the particular party that is conclusive of the duress.

One important factor that goes into this determination is the relationship of the threatening party to the innocent party. The greater the degree of psychological control the threatening person exercises, the more likely it is to be found that the contract was induced by mental duress. When the mental duress is exercised by someone who is in a close relationship with the innocent party, it is known as **undue influence**.

EXAMPLES:

1. Maxwell is 92 years old and lives in a nursing home. The owner of the home convinces Maxwell to sign over all of his property to the home in consideration of all of the loving care the home gives him. This contract is invalid because it was induced by the undue influence the owner of the home exercised over Maxwell.

2. Mary and David are getting divorced. David convinces Mary to sign a joint custody agreement for their three children by threatening to take the children out of the country if she refuses. The contract is unenforceable. Mary was coerced into signing the agreement because of the fear of never seeing her children again. This is mental duress.

   3. Hilda is 80 years old and frail. A real estate developer convinces
   her to sell her house by telling her that, because of her frail
   health, the state is going to take her house away and put her in
   a home. There is no contract. This is an example of both mental
   duress and fraud.

A type of contract known as a **contract of adhesion** also falls under
the category of duress. A contract of adhesion is a contract in which one
side has an unfair bargaining position, a position that is so unequal that
the other party's assent is suspect. Even though no actual duress exists,
because of the inequality of the parties the contract is called into question.
These types of contracts are voidable by the innocent party because of the
unconscionable aspect of the other side's bargaining position.

Generally, if a contract of adhesion can be shown, the party with the
weaker bargaining position can avoid his obligation. The unequal bargaining position can come about because of lack of competition in the area,
forceful salesmanship, or because the innocent party perceives the other
person as having special knowledge or expertise and is relying on that
person's greater experience.

 EXAMPLES:

   1. Leo lives in a small town, and there is only one car dealership
   within a 100-mile radius. When Leo is talked into buying a car
   for several thousand dollars more than he wanted to spend, the
   contract may be deemed a contract of adhesion because, if Leo
   wants a car, he really has no other choice. The dealer is in an
   unfair bargaining position.

   2. Sylvio, having put on a few pounds over the last several years,
   walks into a health club to inquire about joining. The club salesman, a powerfully built young man, walks Sylvio around the
   facility, takes him into his office, and tells him about a "special
   deal" only available for that day. If he signs up right now, he
   saves $300; if he doesn't sign immediately, he loses the oppor-
   tunity. The salesman also tells Sylvio that he is not getting any
   younger, and the longer he waits the harder it will be to take
   off the weight. Sylvio signs up for a three-year membership and
   immediately regrets it. This is a contract of adhesion. Because of
   aggressive salesmanship, Sylvio was put in a position of signing
   an agreement without having a chance to consider the possi-
   bilities. He can avoid this contract. Be aware that many states
   have special consumer protection laws specifically dealing with
   health club memberships because of the clubs' sales techniques.

   3. Wanda, the wistful widow of Winnetka, wants to put more fun
   in her life, and so she signs up for dance lessons. Her instruc-
   tor is young and handsome Raoul. After the initial ten sessions

are over, Raoul convinces Wanda to sign up for the advanced course because of her great dance potential. Halfway through the advanced course, Wanda attends a community dance where all of her partners comment on how badly she dances. Wanda sues to get her money back from the dance school. Wanda will prevail. Because of his perceived expertise, Raoul was able to convince Wanda to spend money on dance lessons. This is a contract of adhesion.

When dealing with any form of duress or with contracts of adhesion, it is the perception of the party involved that determines intent. If, under the circumstances, the innocent party reasonably believed that she was threatened, no contract will exist, even if the fear seems unfounded. Also, a contract of adhesion may be enforceable if the injured party wishes to fulfill the contract. It is voidable or enforceable at the election of the innocent party.

Mistake

The third situation that brings into question the parties' intent to contract is **mistake**. Mistake occurs when one (or both) of the parties is under a misconception as to the subject matter of the contract. Mistake is distinguishable from contractual fraud in that, with mistake, there is no intent to deceive or misrepresent; the mistake is due to the honest and innocent belief of the parties.

Contractual mistakes are divided into two broad categories: **mutual mistake** and **unilateral mistake**. A mutual mistake concerns the underlying consideration of the contract itself.

 EXAMPLES:

1. Sheila and Kathleen enter into a contract for the sale of Sheila's summer house, but unknown to both parties, the house is destroyed by a hurricane. There is no contract because the basic assumption of the contract, that the house exists, is mistaken.

2. Edward agrees to lease some property to Eve so that Eve can operate a retail store at that location. Unknown to both Edward and Eve, the town council passes a zoning ordinance restricting the use of the area in question to residential use only. There is no contract. Both parties are mistaken with respect to a basic assumption underlying the agreement, that is, that the property could be used for commercial purposes. This is an example of mutual mistake.

A mutual mistake is a defense to contract formation if the mistake goes to a basic assumption of the agreement, the mistake has a material adverse effect on the parties, and the mistake was of the type that could not be foreseen.

A unilateral mistake usually concerns a situation in which only one party to the contract is mistaken because of some typewritten or computation error. In this instance, the contract may still be enforceable by the innocent party, the one who neither caused nor knew that there was in fact a mistake.

 EXAMPLE:

Arnold submits a contracting bid to Ace, Inc., for the construction of a warehouse. Arnold makes a mistake in computing his expenses, and the bid is $2,000 lower than it should be. Ace accepts. There is a contract. This is an example of a unilateral mistake in which Ace, the innocent party, has no way of knowing that Arnold has miscalculated his bid, and so a valid contract exists. Note, however, that if Arnold's bid had itemized all his expenses and only the total was incorrect, there would be no contract at the low bid because Ace could see the mistake simply by doing the totals itself. Also, if Arnold realized his error before Ace accepted and he notified Ace, Ace could not accept the low bid because it would then be aware of the error.

A similarity exists between the concept of mistake and the concept of the ambiguity of the terms discussed in Chapter 2, Offer. There are circumstances in which the ambiguity of the language used by the parties can create mistaken impressions. In those instances, the law will go with the most reasonable and most legally fair interpretation of the parties' intent. Generally, ambiguities are held against the party who drafted the contract.

Take careful note of the fact that the concept of mistake does not concern itself with the risk of contracting, that is, the risk that one or both of the parties may not get the bargain for which he or she had hoped. As discussed previously in Chapter 4, Consideration, the law is not the insurer of every contractual agreement. It cannot and will not guarantee that every contract will be as economically beneficial as the parties had hoped. However, the law will guarantee that the parties do receive the object or service for which they bargained.

EXAMPLES:

1. Sophie offers to sell Lindsay a blue stone she has in her possession for $100. Sophie thinks the stone is a blue quartz; Lindsay thinks the stone is a sapphire. Lindsay agrees to the contract. Later, Lindsay discovers the stone is a blue quartz and wants

her money back, claiming she was mistaken as to the object of the contract. The contract is valid. Because the parties only contracted for the sale of a "blue stone," the fact that a party was mistaken as to its value is irrelevant. Sophie received exactly what she bargained for. Let the buyer beware!

2. Sophie offers to sell Lindsay a blue stone designated as a blue quartz she has in her possession for $100. Sophie and Lindsay both think the stone is a blue quartz. Lindsay agrees to the contract for the sale of a blue quartz. Later, Lindsay finds out the stone is a sapphire worth $10,000. The contract is not valid. Sophie sold a blue quartz, but Lindsay received a sapphire. In these circumstances, since the contract specified the blue quartz, the contract is not enforceable.

As indicated above, when dealing with a contractual mistake, it is important to differentiate between a mutual mistake and a unilateral mistake. With a mutual mistake, both parties are intending different subject matter, and so no contract exists because there is no meeting of the minds. With a unilateral mistake, only one party to the contract is mistaken, and the contract can be enforced by the innocent party (the one who did not cause the error).

CHAPTER SUMMARY

For a contract to be deemed enforceable, it must be shown that both parties actually intended to enter into a contractual relationship. If it can be demonstrated that this requisite element of contractual intent is missing, then no contract is formed.

Just as with the legality of the subject matter and contractual capacity, the contractual intent is concerned with the circumstances surrounding the formation of the agreement, not the provisions of the agreement itself. Even if the contract meets all of the other five requirements to create a valid contract, if the intent to contract is lacking, there is no contract.

Contractual intent is a concept that is always determined by the facts and circumstances of each individual situation. If it can be shown that the particular party lacked contractual intent, even though such a situation would seem unreasonable, there is no contract.

There are three major legal concepts associated with intent: fraud, duress, and mistake. If a party to an agreement is defrauded into entering the agreement, no contract exists. If the party is coerced into entering the agreement, no contract exists. And finally, if the parties are mistaken as to the subject matter of the contract, no contract exists.

SYNOPSIS

No contract exists if the contract is induced by fraud, duress, or mistake
Fraud
1.   A misrepresentation
2.   of a material fact,
3.   made with the intent to deceive and
4.   relied on by the other party
5.   to his or her detriment
Duress
1.   Physical
2.   Economic
3.   Mental (undue influence)
4.   Contracts of adhesion: Unfair bargaining position
Mistake
1.   Mutual mistake: No contract
2.   Unilateral mistake: May be enforced

Key Terms

Contract of adhesion: contract entered into where one party has an unfair
        bargaining position; voidable
Duress: force or coercion used to induce agreement to contract
Economic duress: threatening loss of economic benefit to induce a person
        to contract
Fraud: a misrepresentation of a material fact made with the intent to
        deceive; relied on by the other party to his or her detriment
Mental duress: psychological threats used to induce a person to contract
Misrepresentation: misstatement of a material fact relied on by the other
        party to his or her detriment; no intent to defraud
Mistake: misconception of the subject matter of a contract
Mutual mistake: misconception of the subject matter of a contract by both
        parties; unenforceable
Physical duress: threatening physical harm to force a person to contract
Undue influence: mental duress by a person in a close and particular
        relationship to the innocent party
Unilateral mistake: misconception of the subject matter of a contract by
        only one party to the contract; may be enforceable
Voidable contract: a contract that one party may void at his option without
        being in breach of contract

EXERCISES

1.   A salesman tells you that the diamond ring you want to purchase
     is "the best quality diamond he has in the entire store and, in fact,
     is the best diamond he has ever seen." After you buy the dia-

mond, you discover that the diamond is a very low grade. Have you been defrauded? Why?

2. Give two examples of contracts of adhesion not discussed in the chapter.
3. Explain the difference between a mutual mistake and ambiguity.
4. Explain the difference between misrepresentation and fraud.
5. Give an example of a contract induced by economic duress not discussed in the chapter.

Cases for Analysis

To highlight the concepts of mutual mistake and contracts of adhesion, the following case summaries are presented for analysis. *Schulte v. Harvey* concerns mutual mistakes in a contract and *Levey v. CitiMortgage, Inc.* discusses unconscionability and breach of fiduciary duties.

Schulte v. Harvey
2009 Iowa App. LEXIS 1632

Brian and Linda Harvey appeal from the district court order denying their claims arising from a real estate transaction. They claim the court erred in refusing to reform the contract and find a breach, in failing to consider the doctrine of merger, in finding Gary and Linda Schulte breached their warranty of title, and in calculating the damages award.

I. Background Facts and Proceedings

The Harveys entered into a contract to purchase a parcel of real estate from the Schultes, intending to move a house onto the lot. When the parties entered into the contract, they were under the belief that sewer and water lines were close to the lot being purchased. Sometime after the real estate purchase contract signed by the parties, they orally agreed to share the cost of installing a water line.

The Harveys' house was moved onto the site, and the water line installation began. It was during this time the parties learned the water main was not located where they had originally thought. Following extensive negotiations, the parties signed an "Agreement Relating to Water and Sewer" at the real estate closing. The agreement provides the Schultes pay one-half of the cost of extending the waterline through their adjoining property, and the Harveys "be responsible for the installation of the waterline from the City of Dyersville's nearest connection to the new line installed . . . at their sole cost." Ultimately, the Harveys drilled a well on their lot.

Various disputes arose between the parties as a result of the real estate transaction. The Schultes filed various claims against the Harveys and the Harveys counterclaimed. After trial, the court dismissed all claims and counterclaims and ruled the Harveys owed the Schultes $1,912.50 on a promissory note. At issue here is the district court's denial of the Harveys' breach of contract and breach of warranty claims.

II. Analysis

The Harveys contend the real estate contract was induced by a mutual mistake of fact as to the locations of the water main. They argue this mistake of fact warrants reformation of the contract. Once the contract is reformed, the Harveys contend the facts show the Schultes breached the contract. Because this matter was tried in equity, our review is de novo. Iowa R. App. P. 6.907 (2009).

The proper relief for a mutual mistake of a material fact in a written instrument is reformation of the instrument to reflect the true intent of the contracting parties. *Wilden Clinic, Inc. v. City of Des Moines*, 229 N.W.2d 286, 289 (Iowa 1975). The Harveys have the burden of establishing a mutual mistake of fact by clear, satisfactory and convincing proof. See *id.*

Mistakes involving contracts "can be made in the formation, integration, or performance of a contract." Mistake in expression, or integration, occurs when the parties reach an agreement but fail to accurately express it in writing. Mistakes in the formation of contracts include mistakes in an underlying assumption concerning matters relevant to the decision to enter into a contract. In this category of mistake, the agreement was reached and expressed correctly, yet based on a false assumption.

State ex rel. Palmer v. Unisys Corp., 637 N.W.2d 142, 151 (Iowa 2001) (citations omitted). When the mistake is in the expression of the contract, the proper remedy is reformation. *Nichols v. City of Evansdale*, 687 N.W.2d 562, 570 (Iowa 2004). When the mistake is in the formation of the contract, on the other hand, avoidance is the proper remedy. *Id.* at 571.

Specifically, when a mistake of both parties at the time a contract was made as to a basic assumption upon which the contract was made has a material effect on the agreed exchange of performances, the contract is voidable by the adversely affected party unless he bears the risk of the mistake. *Id.*

The Harveys are alleging a mistake in the formation of the contract— the belief that water was available near the property. Such mutual mistake makes the contract voidable by both parties. See *id.* "However, a mutual mistake in the formation of a contract does not render it void; it merely renders it *voidable.*" *Id.* In the case of a voidable contract, if neither party seeks avoidance, the court cannot void the contract, and the contract remains valid.

Although a mutual mistake of fact existed regarding the location of the nearest water main, neither party voided the contract upon discovery of the mistake. Rather, they sought to modify their purchase agreement to assign responsibility for the cost of extending the water line from the nearest water main. Their agreement is valid. Having found no basis to reform the contract, we likewise find no breach of contract and the denial of the Harveys' breach of contract claim is affirmed.

The Harveys also contend the Schultes breached their warranty of title by failing to deliver a deed without encumbrances. In its ruling, the district court found the agreement to deliver the real estate with clear title was modified by further negotiations between the parties. However, in the deed signed by the parties, it warrants the property is "free and clear of all liens and encumbrances." Absent any showing to the contrary, a contract for conveyance of real estate is deemed to have merged in a subsequent deed. *Lovlie v. Plumb*, 250 N.W.2d 56, 62 (Iowa 1977). This is true even though the terms and conditions of the deed are not identical to those of the contract. *Id.* In spite of the clear language in the deed to the contrary, the property was delivered subject to a mortgage in favor of Community Savings Bank. Accordingly, the district court erred in finding there was no breach of warranty of title and we reverse this portion of the ruling. As requested by the Harveys, the Schultes shall remove any liens or encumbrances on the property as soon as possible.

Finally, the Harveys contend the district court made a mathematical error in the amount of $200 in calculating the award of damages on the Schultes' breach of contract claim. We modify the award of damages made to the Schultes on their breach of contract claim, finding the remaining due is $1,712.50.

AFFIRMED IN PART, REVERSED IN PART, AND MODIFIED.

Questions

1. How does the court define a contractual mistake?
2. What does the court say is the proper remedy for a mutual mistake in a contract?
3. What would the result be if the mistake was a unilateral mistake?

Levey v. CitiMortgage, Inc.
2009 U.S. Dist. LEXIS 70210 (N.D. Ill. 2009)

I. Background

Defendant CitiMortgage has filed a motion to dismiss Dorothy Levey and Moses Hyles' Fourth Amended Complaint (the "Complaint"), which alleges violations of the Fair Housing Act ("FHA"), 42 U.S.C. §3601-19, and the Equal Credit Opportunity Act ("ECOA"), 15 U.S.C. §§1691-91f. Compl. ¶1. Plaintiffs additionally bring a statutory claim under the Illinois Consumer Fraud and Deceptive Business Practices Act ("ICFA"), and Illinois common law claims of unconscionability and breach of fiduciary duty under the court's supplemental jurisdiction. See Compl. Hyles' claims are brought against Mark Diamond, the individual who allegedly perpetrated the fraud against him, and CitiMortgage, Inc., the assignee of the loan brokered by Diamond and originally funded at closing by

Delta Funding Corporation ("Delta"). Levey's claims are brought against CitiMortgage, the reputed assignee of a loan originated by BNC Mortgage (the "BNC Loan"). *Id.*

In the Complaint Hyles specifically alleges that after entering into a series of loans over several years to pay various expenses he received a number of telephone calls from a representative of Diamond's firm inquiring whether Hyles wished to refinance his existing loan in order to have "extra money" to "re-do [his] bathroom and . . . kitchen." Compl. ¶¶27, 28. Subsequently, Diamond introduced Hyles and his wife to the mortgage lender Delta. Compl. ¶32. Hyles and his wife entered into a mortgage agreement (the "Mortgage") with Delta, the proceeds of which Hyles claims he never received. Compl. ¶¶30, 35. At an unspecified time the Mortgage was assigned to CitiMortgage, which is currently collecting on it. Compl. ¶¶5, 47, 83.

Levey avers that on February 20, 2002 she and her husband Dan Levey unknowingly signed papers for a mortgage loan from BNC Mortgage for $73,950 which they believed to be a debt-consolidation loan ("BNC Loan"). Compl. ¶¶9-10. At the closing, Levey paid a variety of fees including a "yield-spread premium" which she allegedly did not agree to. Compl. ¶¶12-16. Levey further states that BNC Mortgage "granted, bargained, sold, assigned, transferred or set over the Levey Mortgage to" CitiMortgage. Compl. ¶17.

CitiMortgage attaches various documents to its motion to dismiss which it maintains are properly before the court, and which show that Levey and her husband entered into a separate and succeeding mortgage loan in January 2003 with First National Bank of Arizona ("First National Loan"). Mot. 2, Ex. B. CitiMortgage asserts that it is the assignee of the First National Loan, not the BNC Loan that is the focus of Levey's allegations. Mot. 3, Ex. C, D.

II.   Analysis

A.   FHA Claim (Count V) [Omitted]

B.   ECOA Claim (Count VI) [Omitted]

C.   Illinois Common Law Unconscionability (Count I)

CitiMortgage argues that Hyles' common law unconscionability claim should be dismissed because Hyles has not alleged facts sufficient to establish that the Mortgage (1) was "so one-sided that only one under delusion would make [it] and only one unfair and dishonest would accept [it]," or (2) that "some impropriety during the formation of the contract . . . deprived one party of meaningful choice." Mot. 4. The court disagrees and denies CitiMortgage's motion to dismiss Count I of the Complaint, finding that Hyles has pled facts sufficient to support a finding of unconscionability.

In Illinois, a finding that an agreement is unconscionable "may be based on either procedural or substantive unconscionability, or a combination of both." *Kinkel v. Cingular Wireless LLC*, 857 N.E.2d 250, 263 (Ill. 2006). Substantive unconscionability "concerns the actual terms of the contract and examines the relative fairness of the obligations assumed." *Kinkel*, 857

N.E.2d at 267. "Procedural unconscionability consists of some impropriety during the process of forming the contract depriving a party of a meaningful choice." Id.

A finding of procedural unconscionability requires a court to consider "the circumstances surrounding the transaction including the manner in which the contract was entered into, [and] whether each party had a reasonable opportunity to understand the terms of the contract." *Keefe v. Allied Home Mortg. Corp.*, No. 5-07-0463, 2009 WL 2027244 (Ill. App. Ct. 2009) (citing *Frank's Maint. v. Eng'g, Inc.*, 408 N.E.2d 403, 409-10 (Ill. App. Ct. 1980)). Moreover, a finding of unconscionability may turn on a showing of acts of bad faith "such as concealments, misrepresentations, [or] undue influence." *Taylor v. Bob O'Connor Ford, Inc.*, No. 97-C0720, 2000 WL 876920, at *3 (N.D. Ill. 2000); see also *Mitchem v. Am. Loan Co., Inc.*, No. 99-C1868, 2000 WL 290276 at *4 (N.D. Ill. 2000) (unconscionability doctrine is "closely allied . . . to fraud and duress, [and] is designed to prevent overreaching at the contract-formation stage") (citing *Orig. Great Am. Choc. Chip Cookie v. River Valley*, 970 F.2d 273, 281 (7th Cir. 1992)). Here, Hyles has alleged that he is illiterate, and so did not and could not read the documents that he signed, and, furthermore, that neither Diamond nor the agent for Delta explained the contents of any of the documents he signed at the closing of the Mortgage. Additionally, Hyles has attached evidence to the Complaint showing that at least one of the closing documents was missing required information. Compl. ¶¶4, 33, Ex. 13. And, finally, Hyles avers that he never received the $23,208.29 that the closing documents state that he was paid in cash at closing. All of these statements if true are sufficient to sustain a cause of action for unconscionability in Illinois because they allege concealments and misrepresentations and show that Hyles may not have "had a reasonable opportunity to understand the terms of the contract." *Keefe*, 2009 WL 2027244 at *4.

Because the court finds that Hyles has made allegations sufficient to show procedural unconscionability, and such a showing is sufficient to plead that a contract is unconscionable in Illinois, the court declines to opine as to whether Hyles has adequately pled that the Mortgage was substantively unconscionable.

Levey's allegations of procedural unconscionability, however, are inadequate. Levey elliptically argues that her unconscionability claim is well pled because the Complaint states that she has difficulty reading documents because of her health issues and that her husband was very sick when he entered into the BNC Loan. Levey additionally alleges that she never "received the proceeds of the approximately $100,000 loan." Resp. Br. 10; Compl. ¶¶3, 19.

Levey cites no authority for the proposition that general averments of sickness or difficulty reading documents sufficiently state a claim that a contract was procedurally unconscionable. Moreover, Levey's allegation that she never received "approximately $100,000" from the proceeds of the BNC loan is flatly contradicted by the BNC Loan HUD-1 Statement (which Levey has attached to the Complaint as Exhibit 7), which shows that Levey was to be paid only $54.85 of the nearly $74,000 loan issued by BNC; the majority of the proceeds were distributed to pay off Levey's

142   Chapter 6 Contractual Intent

previous mortgages. See Compl., Ex. 7, Lns. 104-05, 303. The closing document that Levey submitted with the Complaint, then, contradict her assertion of fraud. See *Ogden Martin Sys. of Indianapolis, Inc. v. Whiting Corp.*, 179 F.3d 523, 529 (7th Cir. 1999) ("A plaintiff may plead [herself] out of court by attaching documents to the complaint that indicate . . . she is not entitled to judgment."). The court, therefore, cannot construe her claim to allege the bad faith or fraud which would bear on an unconscionability analysis. Cf. *Mitchem v. Am. Loan Co., Inc.*, No. 99-C1868, 2000 WL 290276 at *4 (unconscionability is closely related to fraud).

Count I of the Complaint is dismissed only as to Levey.

D. ICFA Claim (Count II)

To hold an assignee liable under the ICFA Plaintiffs must allege that CitiMortgage "actively and directly participated in the fraud" alleged in the Complaint. *Jackson v. South Holland Dodge, Inc.*, 726 N.E.2d 1146, 1155 (Ill. App. Ct. 2000). Unambiguous Illinois precedent limits ICFA claims to "conduct that defrauds or deceives consumers or others" and "does not provide a cause of action against those who knowingly receive benefits from the person committing the violation." *Zekman v. Direct Am. Mktrs., Inc.*, 692 N.E.2d 853, 859 (Ill. 1998) (emphasis added); see also *Costa v. Mauro Chevrolet, Inc.*, 390 F. Supp. 2d 720, 735 (N.D. Ill. 2005) (citing *Zeckman*, 692 N.E.2d); *Mfrs. & Traders Trust v. Hughes*, No. 99-C5849, 2003 WL 21780956, at *2 (N.D. Ill. 2003).

Hyles and Levey have averred that CitiMortgage was not present at the closing of the Mortgage or the BNC Loan and have alleged no facts which may be construed to allege that CitiMortgage was involved in the alleged fraud at the origination of either contract. Compl. ¶¶45(a), 46(a). Consequently, Plaintiffs have not pled that CitiMortgage "actively and directly" participated in the alleged fraud and Count II of the Complaint is therefore dismissed. *Jackson*, 726 N.E.2d at 1155.

E. Inducement to Breach Fiduciary Duty (Count III and IV) [Omitted]

Counts III and IV are dismissed.

III. Conclusion

CitiMortgage's Motion to Dismiss is granted in part and denied in part; Counts I-III and V-VI of the Fourth Amended Complaint are dismissed as to Plaintiff Dorothy Levey and Counts II and IV-VI are dismissed as to Moses Hyles. Count one of the Complaint remains against CitiMortgage, but only as to Moses Hyles.

Questions

1. According to the defendant, what must be alleged to constitute a claim of unconscionability?

2. Differentiate between procedural and substantive unconscionability.

3. How does this relate to mortgage fraud claims?

Suggested Case References

1. Contracting for the sale of leases that the seller knows, or has reason to know, have expired is not a mistake, but fraud. Read what the federal court sitting in Texas said in *Matter of Topco*, 894 F.2d 727, *reh'g denied*, 902 F.2d 955 (5th Cir. 1990).

2. A manufacturer attempts to avoid its collective bargaining agreement with a union. Under the contract, the manufacturer agreed to offer its employees the same insurance plan the employees had with a separate manufacturer, a copy of which was shown to the company. The company now asserts it was mistaken with respect to the clauses of the insurance plan. Is this a mistake permitting avoidance of the contract? Read what the federal court sitting in California had to say in *Libby, McNeil & Libby v. United Steelworkers*, 809 F.2d 1432 (9th Cir. 1987).

3. Even if both parties to a contract are mistaken as to the value or usefulness of the goods sold, as long as the goods are properly identified, the mistake does not invalidate the contract because it only pertains to the value of the subject matter. *Fernandez v. Western Ash Builders, Inc.*, 112 Idaho App. 907, 736 P.2d 1361 (1987).

4. If a party seeks to avoid a contract induced by duress, must he return the consideration he has received pursuant to that agreement? *Read Solomon v. FloWARR Management, Inc.*, 777 S.W.2d 701 (Tenn. App. 1989).

5. To read what the Delaware court says about the effects of disclaimers see *Alabi v. DHL Airways, Inc.*, 583 A.2d 1358 (Del. Super. 1990).

Ethical Considerations

"A lawyer shall not counsel a client to engage, or assist a client, in conduct that the lawyer knows is criminal or fraudulent, but a lawyer may discuss the legal consequences of any proposed course of conduct with a client and may counsel or assist a client to make a good faith effort to determine the validity, scope, meaning and application of the law." ABA Rules of Professional Conduct 1.2 (d).

Quick Quiz

Answer TRUE or FALSE. (Answers can be found in Appendix C on page 143.)

1. Fraud and misrepresentation are legally the same.
2. Contracts that are formed by means of a mutual mistake are enforceable.

3. A person may disclaim a voidable contract without being in breach.
4. To be found to have exerted undue influence, the person exerting that influence must be in a close relationship to the innocent party.
5. A contract of adhesion is an example of a contract entered into under duress.

7 Contract Provisions

Learning Objectives

After studying this chapter you will be able to:

- Distinguish between a covenant and a condition
- List the most generally encountered contractual rules of construction
- Apply general contract rules of construction to analysis of contract provisions
- List the types of contracts that are governed by the Statute of Frauds
- Define an "antenuptial agreement"
- Categorize conditions by when they create or extinguish a contractual duty
- Categorize conditions by the method whereby they have been created
- Define a "condition subsequent," a "condition precedent," and a "condition concurrent"
- Explain the parol evidence rule
- Analyze contractual clauses to determine the parties' rights and obligations

CHAPTER OVERVIEW

The preceding six chapters have discussed the general law of contracts that must be kept in mind when analyzing the validity of a contractual agreement. The time has now come to look at the actual provisions of a contract itself.

As indicated in the first chapter, contracts may be valid whether or not they are in writing. However, there is a small group of contracts that the law mandates must be in writing to be enforceable. This requirement exists for agreements that are described in the Statute of Frauds. However, regardless of the form, written or oral, all contract terms are given similar weight and interpretation.

Contracts are composed of various clauses, or paragraphs, that indicate the promises each party has made to the other. These specific promises form the consideration of the contract and are the parties' contractual obligations. Once there has been a meeting of the minds over the subject matter, these promises form the basis of the parties' enforceable rights. Such provisions are known as **covenants**.

The mere promise to perform is not totally indicative of the moment that the promise becomes enforceable in a court of law. Incident to every covenant is an element of timing: At what point is the promisor obligated to perform, and at what point does the promisee have an enforceable right? Although many everyday contracts lack this timing element, since the promise and the performance occur simultaneously, many contractual situations exist in which the contractual obligation is conditioned on some event that is not a specific part of the contract itself. This timing element, which forms its own clause in the contract, is known as a **condition**. A condition specifies the moment at which the covenant becomes legally enforceable.

Consequently, when analyzing any contract, these two separate elements must be specifically determined: 1) what has been promised in the contract; and 2) at what point does that promise become enforceable in a court of law. If a disputed provision winds up in court, the court has adopted several rules or guidelines to interpret and prove contract provisions. These guidelines are called **rules of construction** and will be discussed below.

The Statute of Frauds

The law generally makes no distinction between contracts that are written and contracts that are oral; each is given legal validity. The primary distinction between them deals not with contract law, but with the law of evidence. It is simply easier to demonstrate a contractual promise if the trier of fact can read the contract itself. If the terms of the contract have to be proven by oral testimony, there can be a conflict between what the parties to the agreement remember about the terms, and so an extra burden is placed on the trier of fact. Before he can determine what the parties' contractual rights are, he must first determine what the contract says.

Despite the preceding, the overwhelming majority of contracts entered into on a daily basis are either oral or implied, not written. Buying a newspaper, taking a bus, buying a cup of coffee, or purchasing clothing are usually effectuated without any written agreement. At most, a person might receive a receipt, which merely memorializes the transaction without meeting any of the requirements of a written contract. However, for historical reasons that will be discussed below, there are six situations in which the law has determined that, to be enforceable, the agreement must be in writing.

The law that requires certain contracts to be in writing is known as the **Statute of Frauds**. Every state has adopted a version of the Statute of Frauds, either legislatively or judicially. The origin of the Statute of Frauds lies in feudal England and is worth some mention.

In feudal times, travel and communication were extremely difficult, and the life expectancy of most people was very short. The major contractual relationships of the day dealt with land ownership and land rights. Consequently, to protect persons over geographic and time spans, the Statute of Frauds was enacted. The Statute of Frauds provided some assurance that the contract in question did, in fact, exist. The "fraud" in the Statute of Frauds was not the contractual concept of fraud discussed previously, but concerned preventing perjury and fraud with respect to proving contractual clauses. The Statute of Frauds required that, to be enforceable, the following six types of contracts had to be in writing:

1. contracts for an interest in real estate;
2. contracts in consideration of marriage;
3. contracts that are not to be performed within one year;
4. guarantees;
5. contracts for the sale of goods valued at over $500; and
6. executor's promises to pay a decedent's debts.

Contracts for an Interest in Real Estate

Because the entire concept of a feudal society was based on land ownerships, the Statute of Frauds required that any contract for an interest in real estate be in writing. In medieval times, requiring that deeds be in writing assured persons that ownership could be specifically traced without recourse to faulty memories. Also, contractual terms could be proved even if persons involved in the agreement had died and therefore could not testify about the contract. Land rights were too important to be left to such vagaries, and consequently the statute was enacted.

This provision is still in force today. To be enforceable, every contract for an interest in real estate must be in writing. Contracts for the sale of land are also permanently recorded in governmental offices in the county where the property is located. This insures that the title to the property can be traced and determined.

EXAMPLE:

Joseph agrees to sell the house he inherited in Florida to Mindy. They enter into a written contract for the sale of the house. When each side has performed under the contract—Mindy paying for the house and Joseph conveying the deed—the sale is recorded in the county Recorder's Office in the county where the house is located so that title to the property will read from Joseph to Mindy by contract of sale.

This provision of the Statute of Frauds is only concerned with the land itself. Anything that may be considered the "fruits of the land" (crops, minerals, and so on) are not within the provisions of the statute. Contracts for the sale of crops may be enforceable, even if they are oral.

EXAMPLES:

1. Gary agrees to buy all of the potatoes Bob grows on this farm this year for a set price per pound. The agreement between Gary and Bob is not in writing. The contract is enforceable because the subject matter of the agreement is crops, not the land itself. The Statute of Frauds does not apply.

2. The Greens have just bought a house next to the Richards. To get to the nearest shopping center, it is most convenient for the Greens to pass over a portion of the Richards' property. The Richards orally agree to assign this right over their property (called an easement) to the Greens for a nominal fee. This agreement may not be enforceable. An easement deals directly with an interest in the land and so comes within the Statute of Frauds. Generally, easements must be in writing.

The determining factor of whether the contract must be in writing is whether the agreement directly concerns the land itself or whether it concerns something that can be removed from the land. If the latter, it is not within the Statute of Frauds.

Contracts in Consideration of Marriage

In feudal times, marriage was more a matter of property transfer than of love and affection. The medieval husband was entitled to a dowry from his intended wife's family, and the law required this dowry to be written down. If the wife's family did not deliver the goods specified in the contract, the groom could sue to have the property transferred or, in certain countries, could return the wife.

Although nowadays dowries are exceedingly rare in the United States, the concept that any promise given in consideration of marriage must be in writing still exists. This usually takes the form of an **antenuptial**, or **prenuptial**, **agreement**. An antenuptial agreement is a contract between the intended bride and groom specifying each one's property rights in case of death or divorce. It is not unusual for wealthy, well-known persons to have prenuptial agreements, but even persons who are neither wealthy nor famous enter into such contracts.

EXAMPLES:

1. Gussie and Izzy are about to be married. The bride and groom are each in their 70s, it is a second marriage for both of them, and they each have children and grandchildren. Gussie wants to make sure that the money she inherited from her late husband goes to her children on her death, and Izzy feels the same way about his money and family. Consequently, they draw up a written prenuptial agreement specifying that each relinquishes claims to the other's estate in case of death or divorce. The agreement is valid and enforceable. The consideration is the impending marriage.

2. Hedda has agreed to marry Osbert, the unattractive son of a wealthy industrialist. To induce Hedda's promise, Osbert's father has promised to give $100,000 to her after the ceremony. Hedda gets this promise in writing and, after the ceremony, places the written agreement before her father-in-law. This agreement is enforceable, and he must now give Hedda the cash.

Do not get confused between contracts in consideration of marriage and what has become known as **palimony**. Palimony is an invented term used to enforce promises made between persons who are not legally married at the time of their break-up. The theory of law used to enforce these agreements is a contractual one, but it is specifically not based on a promise in consideration of marriage.

Contracts Not to Be Performed Within One Year

In feudal times, human life expectancies were so short that it could not be guaranteed that parties to a contract, or people who knew of the contract, would live long enough to testify about its provisions should a problem arise. Therefore, if the contract in question contemplated that the performance would take more than one year, it was required that the contract be in writing so that its provisions could be analyzed should there be a breach.

Today, this provision of the Statute of Frauds still exists. However, be aware that even though the statute requires the contract to be in writing, if the parties actually perform or make a substantial beginning on the performance, those actions will make the contract enforceable under equitable concepts previously discussed. Also note that for determining the applicability of the statute, the period starts from the day of the agreement, not the date on which the performance is to start.

EXAMPLES:

1. Maud agrees to buy Stacey's mink coat, which she's always admired. However, Stacey is asking $1,500, and Maud doesn't have that much cash on hand. Maud and Stacey enter into an agreement whereby Maud agrees to pay Stacey $100 per month until the coat is paid for. To be valid, the contract must be in writing because the performance will take more than one year.

2. Mark agrees to work as a paralegal on a temporary basis for the firm of Blacke & Blewe, P.C. on February 1. The job that Mark is assigned to do will take eight months and is to start on September 1. This contract does have to be in writing because performance will not be completed in less than one year from the date on which the agreement was made.

3. Kenny agrees to buy Jose's car for $1,800. They orally agree on a payment schedule whereby Kenny pays Jose $100 per month until the car is paid for, at which point Jose will transfer the registration. After Kenny makes five payments, Jose changes his mind and tells Kenny the deal is off. Because they have no written agreement, Jose claims there is no contractual obligation. Kenny sues. In court, because Kenny has already made a substantial performance, the contract would most likely be upheld because to do otherwise would be unfair to Kenny.

This provision of the Statute of Frauds is concerned with situations in which it is impossible for the performance to be completed within just one year. If, under *any* conceivable circumstance, the performance could be completed within 12 months, the contract does not come within the statute.

Regardless of the statute, if the parties have fully performed, partially performed, or made a substantial beginning on performance, the contract is taken out of the statute. Be aware that the issue of whether the partial performance or substantial beginning is sufficient to avoid the statute is a question of fact for the trier of fact. Also, because any uncertain event *may* occur in less than one year, the statute does not apply. The statute will apply if the performance of only one party to the contract will take more than one year.

EXAMPLE:

Arthur is terminally ill, and Danielle agrees to nurse him for a specified salary as long as he lives. This contract is not within the Statute of Frauds. Arthur could live one month or ten years. Because life expectancy is uncertain, performance of the contract could be performed within one year.

Guarantees

As discussed in an earlier chapter, a **guarantee** is a promise to answer for the debts of another. A guarantee is also a type of formal contract. The concept of a guarantee comes from the Statute of Frauds. Because there is, in fact, no consideration for this promise, it must be in writing to be enforceable. This provision of the statute is still in force today.

Contracts for the Sale of Goods

Historically, contracts for the sale of goods valued above a specified amount (the amount has increased over the years) had to be in writing to be enforceable. The concept evolved from the idea that personal property was not as valuable as real property until a certain value was reached. At that monetary point, the property became sufficiently important for the law to require a writing to protect parties.

Today, this provision of the Statute of Frauds has been absorbed by the **Uniform Commercial Code (UCC)** for most commercial contracts. The UCC, a version of which has been adopted in every jurisdiction, provides that any contract for the sale of goods valued at over $500 must be in writing to be enforceable. The UCC will be fully discussed in Chapter 8; for the moment simply realize that this type of contract is now governed by the UCC, not the Statute of Frauds.

Executor's Promise to Pay Decedent's Debts

Under the Statute of Frauds, an executor's agreement to pay the debts of the deceased out of the executor's own pocket must be in writing. This provision evolved in a manner similar to that of guarantees, and the same theories hold true for both.

This section of the Statute of Frauds concerns estate administration, not contracts, and is most appropriately discussed in a work dealing with that area of law. It is noted here only to complete our discussion of the Statute of Frauds.

What the Statute of Frauds Is Not

Bear in mind that the Statute of Frauds is concerned with the *enforceability* of a contractual agreement, not with the *validity of its terms*. The validity of any contract is determined by its meeting the six requirements mentioned in the earlier chapters. Enforceability is concerned with whether the contract can be given force in a court of competent jurisdiction.

Nor does the Statute of Frauds change the interpretation of the contract clauses. It merely places an additional requirement on the formation of those clauses for certain categories of contracts—the requirement that those contracts be in writing. Aside from that one point, the interpretation given to the clauses is identical, whether written or oral. The clauses will represent either the enforceable promises of the parties or the timing element with respect to when those promises must be performed.

Regardless of the statute, if the parties have performed or made a substantial beginning on the performance, the contract is taken out of the statute. Also, if the entire contract is not in writing but the parties have made a written memorandum that sufficiently details the provisions of their agreement, that memo will take the contract out of the statute. (Note that a memo will not be sufficient if the contract is for an interest in realty; that must still be a complete written contract.) Be aware that the issue of whether the partial performance or substantial beginning is sufficient to avoid the statute is a question for the trier of fact.

Covenants

A **covenant** is defined as an unconditional, absolute promise to perform. It is the contractual promise to which no conditions are attached. If a party fails to fulfill his contractual covenant, it is deemed to be a breach, or violation, of the entire contract per se (in and of itself).

What is an unconditional, absolute promise to perform? It is consideration that the party has promised to give to induce the other side's promise. It is the promise to convey the textbook in a contract for the sale of a book; it is the promise to perform paralegal duties in an employment contract; it is the promise to pay for a mink coat in a sales contract. If a person fails to perform on her covenant, the contract is breached, and she can be sued. Furthermore, the other party is relieved of all other performance promised under the contract.

EXAMPLE:

Suzanne agrees to work as a paralegal for the firm of White & Lace, P.C. The agreed-on salary is $300 per week, payable every two weeks. At the end of her first two weeks, Suzanne expects a paycheck. When the firm's partner apologizes and says the firm cannot afford to pay her, the firm has breached the contract. Suzanne is no longer obligated to work for the firm, and she can sue them for back wages. In this contract, Suzanne's covenant is to perform paralegal services, and the firm's covenant is to pay Suzanne a salary of $300 per week.

Not every clause in a contract is considered to be a covenant. The covenants are only the specific contractual promises. Consequently, if there are any terms that a party wants to make determinative of contractual rights, they should be phrased as unconditional promises and thus as covenants. Any clause that would otherwise be a condition can be made a covenant by the intent and wording of the parties.

Conditions

The covenant is the specific promise made by the parties to the contract. It is the basis of the contractual agreement. However, as incident to every contractual covenant, the parties must come to some agreement with respect to when the promises are to be performed. This timing element for performance of the covenant is known as a condition.

A **condition** is a fact or event, the happening or nonhappening of which creates or extinguishes an absolute duty to perform. Simply stated, the covenant is what must be performed, and the condition indicates when it is to be performed. In the example given above, with the paralegal Suzanne and the law firm, the covenants were the promises to perform paralegal duties and to pay a salary; the condition was Suzanne's performing for two weeks *before* the firm was to pay her. In other words, Suzanne's performance created the timing element of the contract. If she didn't perform, the law firm would not be obligated to pay her. Conversely, once she had performed for two weeks, the condition or timing element of the contract had been met, and the firm was obligated to pay. Any words modifying a provision contingent on an uncertain event create a condition.

How do you know that a particular contract contains conditions as well as covenants? The answer lies in what the parties themselves have either specifically agreed to, what can be inferred from their actions, or what has been imposed by the law.

Conditions are categorized by *when* they create, or extinguish, the duty to perform the covenant. There are three such categories of conditions:

1. conditions precedent;
2. conditions subsequent; and
3. conditions concurrent.

Conditions are categorized not only by their timing element, as indicated above, but also by *how* the parties have arrived at them. Once again, there are three categories to indicate how the conditions were created:

1. express conditions;
2. implied-in-fact conditions; and
3. implied-in-law conditions.

Each of the six categories of covenants is examined more carefully below.

Conditions Precedent

A **condition precedent** is a condition that must occur before the contractual promise becomes operative and enforceable. The example above, of Suzanne and the law firm, is an example of a condition precedent: Suzanne must perform for two weeks *before* the firm becomes obligated. If Suzanne decides not to work for the firm, the firm is under no contractual obligation.

 EXAMPLE:

Karen and Bertram enter into a contract for the sale of Bertram's house. Bertram promises to sell, and Karen promises to buy, the house for $95,000. However, Karen inserts a clause in the contract conditioning the sale on her ability to arrange financing within 30 days of the date of signing the agreement. This is a condition precedent. For the parties to be contractually obligated, Karen must arrange financing. The financing is an external event that gives rise to her enforceable promise to purchase. Should she not be able to arrange financing, the contract for the sale of the house would not come into existence.

Conditions Subsequent

A **condition subsequent** is a condition that extinguishes a previous absolute duty to perform. This type of condition relieves the parties of their contractual obligations without being in breach of contract.

 EXAMPLES:

1. Helen buys a blouse on credit at Macy's. When she gets home she decides she doesn't like the blouse, and the next day she goes back to Macy's to return it. Macy's has a return policy that says if an item is returned within seven days of the purchase, with all tags and receipts attached, Macy's will accept the return. Helen has met all of the store's conditions, and the store credits her charge account. This is an example of a condition subsequent. At the time of purchase, Macy's was obligated to give Helen the blouse, and Helen was obligated to pay for it. Because of Macy's return policy, Helen has the option of returning the blouse for a full refund; in other words, her returning the item extinguishes her previous duty to pay for the blouse.

2. Dorothy and Jack are getting divorced. As part of the divorce settlement, they agree to alimony payments for Dorothy. The alimony payments are to be paid monthly until Dorothy or Jack dies, or Dorothy remarries. Dorothy's remarriage is an example of a condition subsequent. Jack is obligated to make these payments until the condition (Dorothy's remarriage) extinguishes his absolute duty to perform.

Conditions Concurrent

A **condition concurrent** is the most typical type of condition encountered in everyday contracts. A condition concurrent occurs when the mutual performances of the parties are capable of simultaneous execution, and the parties expect the promise and the performance to occur at the same time. Most contracts are formed and executed at the same time.

 EXAMPLES:

1. Hazel agrees to sell, and Olivia agrees to buy, Hazel's textbook for $10. When Olivia gives the money, she expects to receive the book; when Hazel gives the book, she expects to receive the money. This is an example of a condition concurrent.

2. Raymond goes to his neighborhood grocery store to buy his weekly food supplies. At the checkout counter, Raymond pays for the goods as the checker bags and gives him the items. Once again, the promise and the performance occur simultaneously.

Express Conditions

An **express condition** is a condition that has been specifically manifested in so many words by the parties themselves. This manifestation can either be written or oral, depending on the nature of the contractual agreement.

EXAMPLE:

Leah agrees to purchase Phyllis' used car for $900; however, Phyllis still has $200 outstanding on the loan she took out when she first bought the car. The parties condition the sale on Phyllis' paying off the loan before the sale goes through, so that Leah won't have to worry about a problem of title to the automobile. This is an example of an express condition, specifically agreed to by the parties. It is also a condition precedent, because the contract for the sale will not obligate the parties until and unless the prior loan is paid off.

Implied-in-Fact Conditions

An **implied-in-fact condition** comes about out of necessity; it is what the parties would, in good faith, expect from each other. As contrasted with an express condition, in which the parties have specifically manifested some timing element, an implied-in-fact condition comes about because of what the parties could reasonably expect under the circumstances; no words are used at all.

 EXAMPLE:

Felix agrees in writing to buy Oscar's house for a certain sum of money. Although nothing is specifically stated, it is reasonable that Felix would assume that Oscar has a transferable title to the house. Although this is not specifically stated by the parties, it is implied in the transaction and, consequently, is deemed an implied-in-fact condition. If Oscar does not have a transferable interest, there is no contractual obligation on Felix's part to buy the house.

Implied-in-Law Conditions

An **implied-in-law condition**, also known as a **constructive condition**, is a condition that the law imposes in the interest of fairness. This category of conditions arises in situations where the parties have not specifically agreed to any definite time element. Its purpose is to give each party to the agreement the same amount of time in which to perform. There are three general rules with respect to constructive conditions.

1. When one party's performance requires time to complete, the other side may take the same amount of time.
2. When a date is set for one party's performance, the other party is expected to perform on that date as well.
3. When the performances can be simultaneous, they will be simultaneous.

As can be seen, implied-in-law conditions impose an element of fairness with respect to the timing of the performances. Of course, the parties themselves are totally free to establish any particular conditions they wish, but if none are expressed or implied in fact, the law gives each side an equivalent amount of time to perform.

Court Doctrines: Rules of Construction and the Parol Evidence Rule

The courts have fashioned several principles to assist them in interpreting and enforcing contract provisions. These rules should always be kept in mind when drafting contracts. Knowing how the court will interpret clauses and what kind of evidence will be permitted to prove clauses is critical for the practitioner in drafting these provisions.

Rules of construction are the guidelines that the courts use to interpret all contractual provisions. The rules of construction attempt, if possible, to uphold contracts as valid and to give proper interpretation to the presumptive intent of the contracting parties. There are four primary rules of construction with respect to analyzing the validity of contractual provisions.

1. *Lengthy communications are viewed as a whole, and any inconsistent words are discarded*. Many contracts form only after a lengthy negotiation process. In the course of this extended negotiation period, the parties may create inconsistent clauses. Because the prime objective of the court is to salvage the contract, the court will examine the entire negotiation and discard any provisions that are inconsistent with the existence of a valid contract.

2. *Contracts are to be interpreted according to business custom and usage*. People in business or business situations contract with certain expectations based on the nature, history, and customs of a particular industry. The court refers to industrywide standards, as well as to the history between the parties, in interpreting the meanings of a contract's provisions.

3. *Words are to be construed according to their ordinary meaning*. Unless the parties stipulate otherwise, the words used in an offer or completed contract are given their ordinary dictionary interpretation. However, the parties are always free to define any words they wish to in the contract itself, and the parties' specific definition will prevail. Consequently, in drafting a contract, it is essential to define specifically any words to which the parties want to give a specialized meaning or that may create definitional problems at a later time.

4. *If there is an inconsistency with words that are printed, typed, or handwritten, handwriting prevails over typing, and typing prevails over mechanical printing*. The purpose behind this rule of construction is to ascertain the exact intent of the parties at the moment of signing the contract.

Handwriting presumably would be done at the last moment, and therefore it most clearly reflects the intent at the time of contracting. Typing may be inserted on a preprinted form to make changes or insertions and so, again, indicates intent close to the moment of contracting.

All of these rules exist to help uphold existing contracts, but be careful not to convolute the rules and argue for the existence of a contract where one does not legally exist. These rules are intended to facilitate interpretation, not creation, of contractual clauses.

Another principle adopted by the courts deals with written contracts and how disputes over the terms of those contracts are to be handled. The **parol evidence rule** was created to prevent parties from attempting to change the provisions of a written agreement by offering oral evidence to dispute the terms of a contract. The basic rule states that once a contract is reduced to writing, the writing itself prevails. Oral testimony will not be admitted to vary the terms of a written instrument. It is assumed that the writing will speak for itself.

There are four exceptions to the parol evidence rule that permit a court to accept oral testimony in interpreting a written contract. Although these four instances are called "exceptions" to the rule, in fact they are not. Exceptions would indicate instances in which oral testimony is permitted to vary the written terms. In the following instances, the oral evidence is not being used to vary the terms of the writing but to show something outside the writing that changes the meaning of the contract.

The first exception involves showing a failure of consideration. Here the contract provision is not being questioned, but the fact that the consideration was not what was promised in the writing.

EXAMPLE:

A contract says that the buyer paid for the object of the sale by check. Oral testimony shows that the check bounced. Note that the written contract provision isn't being changed at all. It is the failed consideration that the oral testimony addresses.

The second exception permits a party to show that the contract was induced by fraud, duress, or mistake, and therefore the party to the contract lacked the requisite intent to enter into the contractual relationship. If the intent is there, the contract as written will still stand unquestioned.

EXAMPLE:

Lee holds a gun to Ingrid's head and tells her to sign a contract for the sale of her house. Ingrid's testimony is not used to change the written provision, but to show that she was forced to sign the contract and lacked the intent to contract.

The third exception permits oral testimony to prove the existence of a collateral oral agreement. Again, the written contract isn't being questioned, but the existence of a second, oral contract is being proved. The purpose of this exception is to permit *both* contracts to be considered.

EXAMPLE:

Connie has a written contract with Bill to sell him her gold bracelet for $100. After the contract is signed, Connie agrees to sell Bill her gold ring as well for a price of $150 for both pieces of jewelry. Oral testimony may be used to show the existence of both these contracts.

Finally, the fourth exception to the parol evidence rule permits oral testimony to explain ambiguities in a written contract. A writing on its face may appear unambiguous, but there may in fact be ambiguities. Consider the offer mentioned about the sale of a house in Los Angeles. On the face of the writing, it would appear to indicate only one house, but in fact two could fit the description given. Oral testimony can be used to show this ambiguity.

The preceding rules are rules of the court. They are used when problems arise between the parties to a questionable contract, but they should always be kept in mind when drafting offers and contracts. Knowing how the court will most probably interpret clauses and prove their intent suggests how these clauses should be created.

SAMPLE CLAUSES

1

In an antenuptial agreement:

All monies or property hereinafter acquired by the above-mentioned parties, or either of them, shall be held in joint or equal ownership.

In the case of the death of one of the above-mentioned parties, all of said property shall, subject to the claims of creditors, vest absolutely in the survivor.

The above two clauses are examples of covenants. Each of the parties has specifically promised that all property acquired during the marriage shall be owned equally and shall go to the survivor upon the death of the other. In this case, the consequence of death is not a condition but is made part of the covenant to which the parties have agreed.

2

In a construction contract:

Said building shall be completed according to all of the above-mentioned specification by _____, 20 _____, time is of the essence.

In this instance, the date of completion of performance has been made a specific covenant of the contract. It is not merely a condition. How? By the insertion of the term **time is of the essence**. The term "time is of the essence" makes a covenant of a timing element. Whenever there is a specific need that performance be completed by a certain date, these words should be inserted so as to give the parties greater protection. See Chapters 10 and 11.

| 3 |

In a promissory note:

Thirty (30) days after the date of this instrument I hereby promise to pay to the order of _____ the sum of Five Hundred Dollars ($500), in consideration of value received.

This **promissory note** is an example of both a covenant and a condition. The covenant is to repay the loan of $500. The condition is the timing element: 30 days after the date of the note. The promise to perform is only absolute at the end of the 30-day period.

CHAPTER SUMMARY

Contracts are deemed to be valid regardless of whether they are in writing or come about by the oral representations of the parties, provided that they meet the six requirements of all contractual agreements. The only exception to this general statement comes under the Statute of Frauds. The Statute of Frauds states that certain types of contracts, to be enforceable, must be in writing. However, even if the contract should be in writing because of the statute, if the parties actually perform their oral agreement, that performance may make the contract enforceable in a court of law. In other words, the Statute of Frauds generally makes contracts voidable, not necessarily void.

Regardless of how the contract comes into existence, all contractual provisions are classified either as covenants or conditions. A covenant is an absolute, unconditional promise to perform. It is the basis of the contractual agreement, and a party's failure to perform a covenant is deemed to be a breach of contract.

On the other hand, a condition is the timing element of the contract. A condition specifies when, if ever, the parties must perform. With conditions precedent, if the condition does not happen, no covenant comes into existence. With conditions subsequent, when the conditional event occurs, the parties are no longer obligated to perform. With conditions concurrent, the promise and the performance of the contract occur simultaneously.

Conditions are created either by the express words of the parties, by implication of what would be reasonable under the particular circumstances, or are imposed by law in the interest of fairness.

If possible, the court attempts to uphold contracts. To this end, the court has established certain guidelines, referred to as rules of construction. It uses these rules to interpret contractual clauses. The four main rules of construction with respect to contracts state: (1) lengthy communications are viewed as a whole, and inconsistent words are discarded; (2) contracts are to be interpreted according to business use and custom; (3) words are construed according to their ordinary meanings; and (4) handwritten words prevail over typewritten ones, and typewritten words prevail over printed ones in construing the final terms of a contract.

In addition to the rules of construction, the court has adopted the parol evidence rule, which states that oral testimony cannot be used to vary the terms of a writing. The written offer, or contract, must stand or fall on its own.

SYNOPSIS

Statute of Frauds: Requires certain types of contracts to be in writing
1. Contracts for an interest in realty
2. Contracts in consideration of marriage
3. Contracts not to be performed within one year
4. Guarantees
5. Contracts for the sale of goods over $500 (UCC)
6. Executor's promise to pay a decedent's debts

Contractual clauses
1. Covenant: Unconditional promise to perform
2. Condition
   a. Timing element
      i. Precedent
      ii. Subsequent
      iii. Concurrent
   b. Created
      i. Express
      ii. Implied in fact
      iii. Implied in law

Court doctrines
1. Rules of construction
2. Parol evidence rule

Key Terms

Antenuptial agreement: contract entered into prior to marriage determining parties' rights on dissolution of the marriage; must be in writing

Condition: fact or event, the happening or nonhappening of which creates or extinguishes an absolute duty to perform

Condition concurrent: promise to perform and performance occur
    simultaneously
Condition precedent: fact or event that must occur before an absolute duty
    to perform is created
Condition subsequent: fact or event that extinguishes an absolute duty to
    perform; no breach of contract
Constructive condition: same as implied-in-fact condition
Covenant: an absolute, unconditional promise to perform
Express condition: condition created by words of the parties
Guarantee: promise to answer for the debts of another; must be in writing
Implied-in-fact condition: condition created by the reasonable expectations
    of the parties
Implied-in-law condition: condition imposed by law in the interest of
    fairness
Palimony: payment made to a person under certain circumstances
    pursuant to the break-up of a nonmarital relationship
Parol evidence rule: oral testimony may not be used to vary the terms of a
    contract in writing
Prenuptial agreement: same as antenuptial agreement
Promissory note: written promise to pay money in repayment of a loan
Rules of construction: court guidelines used to interpret contractual
    provisions
Statute of Frauds: law requiring certain types of contracts to be in writing
    to be enforceable
Time of the essence clause: contractual clause that makes a covenant of a
    timing element
Uniform Commercial Code: statutory enactment that covers the sale of
    goods valued at over $500, among other things (see Chapter 8)

EXERCISES

1. Find and analyze your own state's Statute of Frauds.
2. How can a condition precedent become a condition subsequent?
Draft an example.
3. Must a lease for an apartment be in writing to be enforceable?
Why?
4. Give two examples of implied-in-fact conditions not discussed in
the chapter.
5. How can a condition become a covenant? Draft an example.

Cases for Analysis

The following two cases highlight implied-in-fact conditions to contract formation and the importance of a condition precedent: *Estate of
Church v. Tubbs* and *Eastern Baby Store, Inc.. v Central Mutual Insurance Co.*

Estate of Church v. Tubbs

72006 U.S. Dist. Lexis 15446 (E.D. Mich 2006)

I. Background

The underlying circumstances of this lawsuit are set forth in a December 6, 2005 Order denying defendant Jacqueline Tubbs' motion for summary judgment. Plaintiff Estate alleges its decedent Keith George Church, a citizen of the United Kingdom, and defendant Tubbs, a citizen of Michigan, developed an Internet relationship, with Church later visiting Tubbs in Michigan. Church and Tubbs allegedly became engaged in February 2000, and agreed to be married in July 2000. Estate alleges Church paid off Tubbs' $4,100.00 credit card debts in return for Tubbs' promise to repay the loan with money she expected to receive in a workers' compensation settlement. Estate also alleges Church gave Tubbs a $7,274.40 engagement ring and deposited $194,852.56 into a bank account for the purpose of purchasing a marital home in Michigan. Following Church's instructions, Tubbs purchased a Michigan home on April 7, 2000 using the bank account proceeds, titling the real property in both their names as unmarried joint tenants. Church allegedly delivered personal belongings to the Michigan home, including a $4,560.00 family-heirloom diamond ring.

Tubbs allegedly informed Church by e-mail on June 5, 2000, without explanation, that their relationship was over. Two days later, on June 7, 2000, Church executed a will in England. Tubbs thereafter allegedly refused to repay the $4,100.00 credit card loan, to return the engagement ring, to return Church's personal property, or to convey her interest in the Michigan home to Church. Church died on July 24, 2000. His Estate filed suit in federal court on December 29, 2004 pursuant to the court's diversity jurisdiction seeking recovery of the alleged $4,100.00 loan, return of the engagement ring, return of Church's personal property, and full ownership of the Michigan home under theories of breach of an implied in law contract of marriage, unjust enrichment, and conditional gifts vesting only upon marriage.

* * *

B. Conditional Gift Implied In Law Contract, Quantum Meruit

As a federal district court exercising diversity jurisdiction in Michigan, this court must construe Michigan law in the absence of Michigan Supreme Court precedent by reviewing the decisions of Michigan appellate courts, other federal courts construing Michigan law, restatements of law, law review commentaries, and/or the decisions from other jurisdictions as to the "majority" rule. See *Meridian Mutual Ins. Co. v. Kellman*, 197 F.3d 1178, 1181 (6th Cir. 1999). This court must predict how the Michigan Supreme Court would rule if faced with the issue. Id.

Engagement Ring

The Michigan Court of Appeals has expressly ruled that an engagement ring is a conditional gift, and if the engagement is called off for any reason, the ring is incapable of becoming a completed gift and must be returned to the donor. *Meyer v. Mitnick*, 244 Mich. App. 697, 703-704, 625 N.W.2d 136 (2001). Tubbs does not dispute that she received an engagement ring from Church on February 16, 2000, and that its price was $7,274.42. Tubbs Tr. at 29-31. Tubbs also testified that she no longer has the ring because she threw it into the Elk Creek River. Tubbs Tr. at 32. Tubbs' unsupported argument that Church intended to marry her to acquire a green card, even if true, is irrelevant with respect to the conditional gift nature of the ring. Based on Tubbs' own testimony, Estate is entitled to recover the engagement ring or its $7,274.42 value from Tubbs as a matter of Michigan law. *Meyer*, 244 Mich. App. at 703-704; *Redding*, 241 F.3d at 532; E.E.O.C., 996 F.Supp. at 713.

Michigan Home

Estate cites *Meyer* and decisions from Pennsylvania, New Jersey, and South Dakota for the legal proposition that, like an engagement ring, a gift of real property made in contemplation of marriage is likewise a conditional gift that must be returned to the donor if the engagement is called off. The Michigan Court of Appeals decision in Meyer is limited to engagement rings which, "by their very nature [are] conditional gifts given in contemplation of marriage." *Meyer*, 244 Mich. App. at 702. Michigan courts have generally limited recovery on an agreement reached between an unmarried couple to theories of express contract or implied in fact contract, reasoning that to allow recovery based on contracts implied in law or quantum meruit would essentially resurrect common-law marriage in Michigan. See *Featherston v. Steinhoff*, 226 Mich. App. 584, 588, 575 N.W.2d 6 (1998). Yet, with respect to an engagement ring, it is "the inherent symbolism of this gift" that permits the conditional nature of the gift to "be implied in fact or imposed by law in order to prevent unjust enrichment." *Meyer*, 244 Mich. App. at 701-702 (quoting *Brown v. Thomas*, 127 Wis.2d 318, 326-327, 379 N.W.2d 868 (Wis.App. 1985)).

As advanced by Estate, other state jurisdictions have applied the principle of a conditional gift in contemplation of marriage to real property. See *Nicholson v. Johnston*, 2004 PA Super 279, 855 A.2d 97 (Sup.Ct.Pa. July 19, 2004) (awarding entire down payment to joint tenant who had made payment in contemplation of marriage and had made all mortgage, tax, insurance and sewer payments); *Fanning v. Iversen*, 535 N.W.2d 770 (Sup.Ct.S.D. Aug. 9 1995) (awarding entire real estate to tenant in common who had made entire down payment in contemplation of marriage and had paid all taxes, insurance, and maintenance costs); *Aronow v. Silver*, 223 N.J.Super 344, 538 A.2d 851 (Sup.Ct. Nov. 17 1987) (awarding entire condominium interest to tenant in common who had made entire down payment in contemplation of marriage and had lived by himself there before and after the engagement was broken). No Michigan court has apparently ruled on the precise issue of whether the principle of a conditional gift in contemplation applies to real estate.

The Michigan Court of Appeals instructs that, just because a couple is unmarried, that does not preclude them from entering enforceable agreements. *Tyranski v. Piggins*, 44 Mich. App. 570, 573, 205 N.W.2d 595 (1973). As explained in Featherston:

> Michigan does not recognize common-law marriages arising after January 1, 1957. M.C.L. § 551.2; M.S.A. § 25.2. Those engaged in meretricious relationships do not enjoy property rights afforded a legally married couple. *Carnes v. Sheldon*, 109 Mich.App. 204, 211, 311 N.W.2d 747 (1981). This Court will, however, enforce an agreement made during the relationship upon proof of additional independent consideration. Id.; *Tyranski v. Piggins*, 44 Mich.App. 570, 573-574, 205 N.W.2d 595 (1973). The agreement must be either express or implied in fact.

Featherston, 226 Mich. App. at 588. Such is the case with engagement rings, where the gift vesting condition of marriage may be "implied in fact or imposed by law" by the very nature and symbolism of the ring itself. *Meyer*, 244 Mich. App. at 701-702. Proof that a gifted ring was in fact an engagement ring is enough to show that the couple reached an enforceable agreement that the ring would be returned to the donor if the engagement ended without marriage. Id.

Consistent with *Meyer, Tyranski*, and *Featherston*, as well as the out-of-state cases cited by Estate, this court finds that, if faced with the issue, the Michigan Supreme Court would hold that a gift of real property made in contemplation of marriage to the anticipated donee spouse may be enforced as a conditional gift that must be returned to the donor upon proof of an express or implied in fact contract. *Carnes*, relied upon by Tubbs as disfavoring for the proposition that Michigan disfavors granting mutually enforceable property interests to knowingly unmarried couples under principles of an *implied in law* contract, is consistent with this court's holding. See *Featherston*, 226 Mich. App. at 588. Unlike an engagement ring which, by its very nature and symbolism creates an implied in fact condition of marriage before the gift vests, a gift of real property during an engagement period does not share the same symbolism, and does not alone raise a presumption of a conditional gift in contemplation of marriage. Rather, as in *Nicholson, Fanning*, and *Aronow*, supra, the donor must come forward with factual evidence beyond proof that the real property was gifted during the engagement period to prove an implied in fact condition that the gift of real property was to vest only upon marriage i.e. proof that the donor paid the entire price for the property in contemplation of marriage. *Jones v. Green*, 126 Mich. App. 412, 337 N.W.2d 85 (1983), cited by Tubbs as holding that property conveyed to joint tenants with rights of survivorship may not be partitioned as a matter of law, is inapplicable as the Warranty Deed proffered by the parties shows that the Michigan home was conveyed to "Keith G. Church, a single man and Jacqulyn J. Tubbs as single woman as joint tenants," with no express rights of survivorship,

Estate's Exhibit 12 attached to Complaint. See *Albro v. Allen*, 434 Mich. 271, 275, 454 N.W.2d 85 (1990) (recognizing that "rights of survivorship" are created by express words in the granting instrument). "All persons holding lands as joint tenants or as tenants in common may have those lands partitioned." M.C.L. § 600.3304.

Tubbs admitted during her deposition testimony that Church paid the entire $194,852.56 purchase price for the Michigan home. Tubbs Tr. at 43. Tubbs also testified that, before purchasing the house, she and Church discussed that "when we got married, you know, that this was our house and I was going to keep it." Tubbs Tr. at 44. Clearly, Estate has presented sufficient facts to support a finding that Church's purchase of the Michigan home for Tubbs as a joint tenant was a gift of real property made in contemplation of marriage which is enforceable as an express or implied contract. The issue that remains, however, is a proper partition of the Michigan property in that Tubbs has resided in the home since April 2000, and presumably made certain tax, insurance, and upkeep payments while residing in the home. An appropriate partition of the home cannot be accomplished based on the record now before the court. Consistent with the analysis herein, Estate is entitled to have the Michigan property partitioned as a matter of law. *Redding*, 241 F.3d at 532; E.E.O.C., 996 F.Supp. at 713.

$4,100.00 Credit Card Payment

As previously determined, the court lacks federal subject matter jurisdiction to decide whether the alleged $4,100.00 debt was released under Church's will. Tubbs has testified that the $4,100.00 was a gift from Church. Whether the $4,100.00 was a gift in contemplation of marriage that Tubbs must return pursuant to an express or implied in fact condition that the gift would vest only upon marriage remains subject to further factual development at trial. *Redding*, 241 F.3d at 532; *E.E.O.C.*, 996 F.Supp. at 713.

C. Church's Personal Property

Estate has alleged that Tubbs has wrongfully refused to return Church's personal property stored within the Michigan home, including a $4,560.00 Church family-heirloom diamond ring. Tubbs testified that she threw "rings" into the Elk River, but it is unclear from her testimony whether the ring in addition to the engagement ring was the alleged Church family-heirloom. See Tubbs Tr. at 64. Tubbs has generally denied failing to return Church's personal property. Whether Tubbs is liable for the return of Church's personal property awaits factual development at trial. *Redding*, 241 F.3d at 532; E.E.O.C., 996 F.Supp. at 713.

III. Conclusion

Summary judgment is hereby GRANTED, IN PART, in favor of plaintiff Estate of Keith George Church as to: (1) Estate's claim for return of a $7,274.40 engagement ring or payment of its value; and (2) Estate's claim for partition of a Michigan home as to liability ONLY. Judgment will enter in favor of Estate accordingly, and these issues will not be further addressed at trial. Summary judgment is hereby GRANTED, IN PART, in favor of defendant Tubbs, to the extent Church seeks recovery of $4,100.00 as a debt-loan ONLY. Estate's claim for repayment of a $4,100.00 debt is hereby DISMISSED without prejudice for lack of subject matter jurisdiction. This matter will proceed to a bench trial with respect to the remaining issue of an appropriate partition of the Michigan home, and Estate's remaining claims for recovery of $4,100.00 as a conditional gift and a return of decedent Church's personal property including a $4,560.00 family heirloom diamond ring. A bench trial schedule will enter under separate order.

SO ORDERED.

Questions

1. How does the court treat the engagement ring, in terms of contract law?

2. How does the court distinguish between the engagement ring and the realty?

3. Why does the court avoid deciding the issue of the credit card payment?

Eastern Baby Stores, Inc. v. Central Mutual Insurance Company
2009 U.S. App. LEXIS 15190 (2d Cir. 2009)

Eastern Baby Stores, Inc., d/b/a USA Baby ("EBS") appeals from a June 3, 2008 judgment entered in the United States District Court for the Southern District of New York (Preska, J.) in favor of the Central Mutual Insurance Company ("Central Mutual"). EBS seeks a declaratory judgment that Central Mutual has a duty to defend and indemnify EBS in a third-party action brought by Silver Lake Realty Corp. ("Silver Lake") against EBS for indemnification and contribution. The district court held that EBS is not entitled to coverage because it failed to provide timely notice and that its omission was not excused by a good faith belief in nonliability. We assume the parties' familiarity with the underlying facts, the procedural history, and the issues presented for review.

We review de novo the district court's decision granting Central Mutual's motion for judgment on the pleadings and denying EBS's motion for summary judgment. See *In re World Trade Ctr. Disaster Site Litig.*, 521 F.3d 169, 178 n. 5 (2d Cir. 2008); *Paneccasio v. Unisource Worldwide, Inc.*, 532 F.3d 101, 107 (2d Cir. 2008).

"Under New York law, compliance with a notice-of-occurrence provision in an insurance policy is a condition precedent to an insurer's liability under the policy." *Commercial Union Ins. Co. v. Int'l Flavors & Fragrances, Inc.*, 822 F.2d 267, 271 (2d Cir. 1987); see also *Great Canal Realty*

Corp. v. Seneca Ins. Co. (Great Canal), 5 N.Y.3d 742, 743 (2005). An insured's failure to provide timely notice of an occurrence vitiates an insurance contract and permits the insurer to disclaim coverage regardless of whether it was prejudiced. See *Olin Corp. v. Certain Underwriters at Lloyd's London,* 468 F.3d 120, 132 (2d Cir. 2006); *Great Canal,* 5 N.Y.3d at 744. "Where a policy of liability insurance requires that notice of an occurrence be given 'as soon as practicable,' such notice must be accorded the carrier within a reasonable period of time." *Great Canal,* 5 N.Y.3d at 744 (internal citation omitted).

Notwithstanding the notice requirement, "New York courts have held that an insured's good faith belief in nonliability may excuse delay in notifying its insurer of the occurrence." *State of N.Y. v. Blank,* 27 F.3d 783, 795 (2d Cir. 1994); see also *Great Canal,* 5 N.Y.3d at 744. "The test for determining whether the notice provision has been triggered is whether the circumstances known to the insured at that time would have suggested to a reasonable person the possibility of a claim." *Commercial Union Ins.,* 822 F.2d at 272. It is relevant to this analysis "whether and to what extent, the insured has inquired into the circumstances of the accident or occurrence." *Great Canal,* 5 N.Y.3d at 744 (internal quotation marks and citations omitted). The insured bears the burden of establishing that its belief in nonliability was reasonable. Id.

It is undisputed that EBS learned of Dennis Guariglia's accident in its store on August 20, 2003, and that it did not inform Central Mutual until June 2006. The Central Mutual Businessowners Policy required EBS to provide notice "as soon as practicable of an 'occurrence' . . . which may result in a claim." Under New York law, a delay of three years is not reasonable. See *Blank,* 27 F.3d at 796 (ten-month delay unreasonable); *Am. Home Assurance Co. v. Republic Ins. Co.,* 984 F.2d 76, 78 (2d Cir. 1993) (finding 36-day delay unreasonable under circumstances and citing New York cases holding delays of ten to 53 days unreasonable).

EBS argues that it reasonably believed that its workers' compensation policy would cover any liability. But EBS has failed to come forward with any evidence of that reason. The only affidavit submitted to the district court (by former EBS owner and principal Dean Alpert) says only that EBS provided notice when it learned of the lawsuit. Accordingly, EBS has not met its burden.

Moreover, EBS's belief that Guariglia was entitled to workers' compensation was not a reasonable basis for concluding that the accident was not "an 'occurrence' ... which may result in a claim." EBS's lease with Silver Lake required that it purchase liability insurance to indemnify Silver Lake for claims such as Guariglia's. At the very least, EBS should have conducted an inquiry into the circumstances of the accident, the extent of Guariglia's injury, and its potential liability under its lease. See *Macro Enters., Ltd. v. QBE Ins. Corp.,* 841 N.Y.S.2d 447, 447 (1st Dep't 2007) ("Plaintiff's claimed belief of nonliability, on the basis that its injured employee's exclusive remedy was under the Workers' Compensation Law, was not reasonable under the circumstances." (internal citation omitted)); *Heydt Contracting Corp. v. Am. Home Assurance Co.,* 146 A.D.2d 497, 499 (1st Dep't 1989) ("[P]laintiff's assumption that other parties would bear ultimate responsibility for its property loss is insufficient as a matter of law to excuse the more than four-month delay in giving notice.").

EBS also argues that it did not provide notice of the accident because it believed that coverage was unavailable based on an exclusion for "'bodily injury' to: 1) An 'employee' of the insured arising out of and in the course of: a) Employment by the insured; or b) Performing duties related to the conduct of the insured's business." See *Reynolds Metal Co. v. Aetna Cas. & Sur. Co.*, 259 A.D.2d 195, 199-200 (3d Dep't 1999) (stating that "an insured's good-faith belief in nonliability [or noncoverage], when reasonable under the circumstances, may excuse a delay in notifying an insurer of an occurrence or potential claim" (internal quotation marks and citations omitted)). However, a letter to Central Mutual from EBS's former president argued that the exclusion should not apply because Central Mutual was "incorrect" about Guariglia being an EBS employee.

We have considered EBS's remaining arguments and find them to be without merit. Because we agree with the district court's conclusion that EBS failed to provide timely notice of Guariglia's accident, we do not reach Central Mutual's alternative grounds for disclaiming coverage. The judgment of the district court is AFFIRMED.

Questions

1. How does a good faith belief that coverage doesn't apply vitiate the condition precedent of the insurance policy?

2. What facts does ESB argue to excuse its delay in notification?

3. How many days delay may be considered an unreasonable delay?

Suggested Case References

1. A man is home recuperating from an illness when he is approached by a contractor about installing aluminum siding. The salesperson is very persuasive, but because of his health, the customer is able to insert a clause stating that the contract for the siding will be null and void if he cannot obtain disability insurance. The contractor starts the work, but the customer cannot get the insurance because his health is so poor. The customer tells the contractor that he could not get the insurance. The customer shortly thereafter dies. Is his estate liable for the siding? If not, why not? Read *Cambria Savings & Loan Association v. Estate of Gross*, 294 Pa. Super. 351 (1982).

2. For a discussion of time of the essence clauses, read *Carter v. Sherburne Corp.*, 132 Vt. 88 (1974).

3. If a person fails to meet a condition of her contract, does she thereby lose all rights due to her under the agreement? Read *Brauer v. Freccia*, 159 Conn. 289 (1970).

4. For a discussion of restrictive covenants in an employment contract, see *Nestle Food Co. v. Miller*, 836 F. Supp. 69 (D. R.I. 1993).

5. In *Loyal Erectors, Inc. v. Hamilton & Son*, Inc., 312 A.2d 748 (Me. 1973), the court discusses the difference between a condition and a covenant.

Ethical Considerations

Ethical considerations even affect the nature of particular clauses that an attorney may wish to insert in his or her contract with a client. For example, Rule 1.8 (h) of the ABA Rules of Professional Conduct states:

"A lawyer shall not make an agreement prospectively limiting the lawyer's liability to a client for malpractice unless permitted by law and the client is independently represented in making the agreement, or settle a claim for which such liability with an unrepresented client or former client without first advising that person in writing that independent representation is appropriate in connection therewith."

Quick Quiz

Answer TRUE or FALSE. (Answers can be found in Appendix C on page 413.)

1. Contracts are often interpreted by means of legal rules of construction.

2. The Uniform Commercial Code is a statute that governs contracts for goods and services between merchants.

3. A covenant is an unconditional promise to perform.

4. The parol evidence rule permits oral testimony to vary the terms of an agreement.

5. Antenuptial agreements entered intro orally are given legal effect.

8 The Uniform Commercial Code

Learning Objectives

After studying this chapter you will be able to:

- Explain the background of the Uniform Commercial Code
- Discuss the basic guidelines to be used when applying the UCC
- Indicate the obligations imposed by Article I of the UCC
- Discuss the concept of "custom and usage" as it applies to contracts
- Distinguish between contracts for goods and contracts for services
- Define the UCC concept of "merchant"
- Discuss the UCC express and implied warranties
- List and discuss conditional sales contracts
- List and discuss shipment contracts
- Discuss the various remedies afforded parties under the UCC
- Define a "secured transaction"
- Indicate the requirements to create a security interest
- Define a "financing statement"

CHAPTER OVERVIEW

The Uniform Commercial Code (UCC) is the major statutory basis of several important areas of contract law. Although it is not a universally applied federal statute, every state, plus the District of Columbia, has enacted some version of all or part of the Code. To fully understand American contract law, it is necessary to discuss several sections of the UCC.

Three of the Code's articles are directly concerned with contract law: Article I, General Provisions; Article II, Sales; and Article IX, Secured Transactions.

Article I establishes the general outline, purpose, and objectives of the Code. Primarily, the UCC was created to promote commerce and to establish certain basic guidelines for those parties involved in commercial transactions. The UCC requires every party whose actions it governs to act in good faith, to perform in a timely manner, and to heed the dictates of the custom and usage prevalent in the industry.

Article II forms the primary modern statutory basis for contracts involving the sale of goods. This article regulates the sale of goods valued at over $500 and sales between merchants. It imposes certain warranties, or guarantees, that are passed by the manufacturer and/or seller of the goods to the ultimate consumer of those products. Additionally, this article provides certain remedies that differ from the general contractual remedies usually available to injured parties in a contractual dispute. (See Chapter 11, Remedies.)

Article IX creates the basis for creditors to secure their debtors' obligations with specific items of property that may be attached by the creditors in case the debtors default. Article IX sets out the specific procedures that a creditor must follow to create and establish a security interest against all other creditors of the debtor.

Before detailing each of the specifics of the articles, it would be helpful to understand some of the history and general background of the Code.

General Background

In 1952, after many years of work, The American Law Institute and the National Conference of Commissioners on Uniform State Laws promulgated a model act known as the Uniform Commercial Code (UCC). The objective of the codification was to clarify and modernize laws governing commercial transactions and to attempt to make mercantile law uniform among all of the states. This model statute represented the first major attempt to codify general contract law; unlike many other areas of law, contract law still rested firmly on its common law base.

Being a model (or proposed) act, the UCC had to be adopted by each state individually; it is not a federal law. Eventually, every jurisdiction adopted some version of the UCC, either in whole or in part (some states have only adopted a few of the provisions of the Code). It is necessary to research each jurisdiction specifically to determine whether its version differs from that of any other state that is involved in the transaction.

The UCC is important to all mercantile practices and transactions. The purpose of the Code is to promote interstate commerce and to facilitate the furthering of business interests. Consequently, the UCC forms a basic part of almost all business law and operations. However, it is important to bear in mind that, except where specifically noted, the Code generally only codifies the common law of contracts. The UCC was not intended or designed to create a radically new concept of contractual arrangements. Rather, it was intended to unify conflicting common law doctrines and to regularize existing commercial practices.

The Code is divided into thirteen articles, the articles are subdivided into parts, and the parts are further divided into sections and subsections. The UCC covers a wide spectrum of law, from sales to banking, to letters of credit and bulk transfers. For the purpose of contract law, three of the articles assume primary importance: Article I, General Provisions; Article II, Sales; and Article IX, Secured Transactions. Each of these articles will be discussed individually, emphasizing concepts not otherwise covered in previous and succeeding chapters.

Article I, General Provisions

Article I of the UCC establishes the form and operation of the entire statute. Not only does it affirmatively state the purpose and intent of the conference members in promulgating the Code, but it also establishes several basic guidelines for applying and interpreting the provisions of the Code. It imposes certain obligations on all parties to transactions that fall within the Code's province.

Basic Guidelines

Article I establishes three basic guidelines to be used in applying the provisions of the Code:

1. The law of the state applies unless otherwise superseded by the UCC.
2. The parties to a contract may, by their agreement, vary the provisions of the Code.
3. The UCC is to be liberally construed.

Law of the State Applies

Unless expressly superseded by the state's adopted version of the UCC, under §1-103 the general law of the site where the transaction occurs applies.

When the states' legislatures adopted their own versions of the Code, if they intended the UCC to be the prevailing law in a given subject, that intent was specifically stated in the statute. For example, in New York, when the UCC Article on Commercial Paper was adopted, it was affirmatively stated that this article was to revise the preexisting New York Negotiable Instrument Law, thereby superseding preexisting state law. Hence, when drafting a commercial agreement, you must determine exactly what the law of a given state is and whether the UCC supersedes it. You cannot assume that a UCC provision of one state is applicable in another state.

Parties May Agree to Vary UCC Provisions

The UCC was intended to help facilitate commerce; its rules were not intended, by their application, to hinder business. Therefore, §1-102 permits parties whose transaction comes within the UCC to vary the UCC terms by their own agreement in order to further their commercial interests. However, there must be evidence of the parties' agreement on the matter; if the parties are silent on a particular subject, the UCC provisions will prevail. Article I permits and encourages freedom of contract between the parties but supplies the legal standard should the parties be silent with respect to a given provision.

EXAMPLE:

Delta, Inc., a Michigan corporation, is contracting with TGI, Inc., a New York corporation, for the purchase of cement, bricks, and other building materials for the construction of a Delta warehouse in New Jersey. Although the contract is signed in New York, and delivery is to be made in New Jersey, Delta wants the law of Michigan to apply because it is a Michigan corporation and is more familiar with that state's law. Although this would be contrary to general UCC provisions, Article I §1-105 permits the parties to agree that the law of Michigan determines the interpretation of the contract.

UCC Provisions Are to Be Liberally Construed

Most importantly, §1-102 of the UCC states that its provisions are to be liberally construed. It may seem a simple statement, but it is fairly unique for statutory law. Most statutes and codes are created as regulatory devices to be strictly complied with. The UCC is different. Because it is meant to promote, not hinder, commerce, the UCC is to be applied in a manner that helps business along, which may mean a liberal interpretation. Of course, this liberal construction must be reasonably formed; the interpretation must still be consistent with the Code as a whole.

Obligations Imposed by Article I

Article I §1-102 imposes three obligations on all parties who come within the purview of its provisions. These obligations are

1. to perform in "good faith"—honesty in fact;
2. to perform in a "reasonable time," "reasonableness" to be determined by the facts and circumstances of each situation; and
3. to perform according to past business dealings and practices (custom and usage).

EXAMPLES:

1. Hiram agrees to sell 10,000 cardboard boxes to the Bon-Ton Department Store, delivery to be within two weeks. Hiram knows that he cannot possibly meet that time limit but is willing to pay some damages for delays in delivery. Hiram is violating the UCC by not acting in good faith. He is contracting for promises he *knows* he cannot meet. Even though he may be willing to pay for the delay, he is knowingly injuring Bon-Ton, which violates the intent of the Code to promote commerce.

2. Sylvester agrees to sell and deliver 10,000 nuts and bolts to the Mitchell Construction Company for a specific building project. Delivery is delayed, and Mitchell Construction must find a substitute supplier. Mitchell claims that Sylvester has failed to make delivery in a reasonable time. Sylvester's promise to deliver was conditioned, however, upon receipt of Mitchell's check, which was delayed in the mail. Under these facts, Sylvester's delivery was made within a reasonable time, and he is not in breach of contract or in violation of the UCC.

The most intriguing of these obligations is the codification of the concept of custom and usage. By establishing as law the past practices of the parties, the Code, in effect, is customizing the law to each particular industry and businessperson. In contracting under the UCC, it is necessary to determine the practices and terms peculiar to each industry and between the particular merchants, and make these customs a part of the contract itself. Consequently, contracts will vary with respect to the definitions of particular terms, dependent upon how each industry and the parties define those terms. There will be no one standard contract that can be used for all categories of business situation. Questions of proof also arise, i.e., what is the custom between these parties?

EXAMPLES:

1. Azar manufactures men's topcoats and regularly buys fabric from Maria. For the past five years, Maria has billed Azar for payment 90 days after delivery. Suddenly, without any prior arrangement, Maria bills Azar for payment within 10 days of delivery. Azar still has 90 days in which to pay. Because the parties have not specifically agreed to payment within 10 days of delivery, they are still bound by their past practices and dealings. If Maria wants to change the payment date, she must make that a specific part of her agreement with Azar.

2. Hazel orders "standard" copper piping from Daniel. Hazel and Daniel have dealt with each other for years, and Daniel always sells Hazel piping 3½ inches wide; the standard pipe in the industry is 4 inches. If Daniel sends Hazel 4-inch piping for this order, Hazel can complain of breach of contract. Because of the past practices of the parties, "standard" for them means 3½-inch piping, not the industry "standard" of 4 inches. The general provisions of Article I of the Code discussed above permeate all of the other provisions of the statute.

In 2012–2013, the National Conference of Commissioners on Uniform State Rules recommended several changes to certain provisions of the UCC, which some states have already adopted and which are currently being considered for adoption in others. With respect to Article 1, as herein discussed, the proposed revision includes the concept of "course of performance" as well as past business dealings and trade usage in determining the parties' performance obligations.

Article II, Sales

General Background

Article II §2-102 of the UCC states that contracts for the sale of goods must be in writing. This provision restates the Statute of Frauds (see Chapter 7) with respect to the sale of goods. In addition, this article reiterates the parol evidence rule and the rules of construction (see Chapter 7).

For the purposes of this chapter, Article II emphasizes three broad areas:

1. the type of contracts that are governed by the UCC;
2. specific contractual provisions regulated by the Code covering warranties and risk of loss; and
3. certain remedies that the contracting parties may be entitled to that differ from the general contractual remedies discussed in Chapter 11, Remedies.

The UCC both codifies the existing common law of contracts already discussed, as well as making some significant changes; all of those contract law concepts still apply unless otherwise stated.

Types of Contracts Covered by Article II

Generally, three types of contracts are regulated by UCC Article II:

1. contracts for the sale of goods;
2. contracts for the lease of goods; and
3. contracts between merchants.

Goods

As indicated above, Article II takes the place of the Statute of Frauds with respect to contracts for the sale of goods valued at $500 or more. **Goods** are defined by §2-105 as things that are existing and moveable. They may include such items as electricity, food or drink, or anything that can be removed from the land, such as minerals, oil, or crops.

In contracts for the sale of goods, the UCC holds the parties to a standard of **strict liability** with respect to the subject goods. Strict liability means that, regardless of how careful the manufacturer/seller may have been with respect to the making of the product, if the product proves defective, the seller is automatically liable to the injured party. Care, quality control, and like safeguards do not relieve the seller of its liability.

EXAMPLE:

Piedmont Pipes, Inc., sells 50,000 feet of copper pipes to Carl's Construction Company for the purpose of building several condominium units. After installation, the pipes disintegrate with the first use. Piedmont is automatically liable to Carl's because the contract, under the UCC, imposes strict liability on the manufacturer. It doesn't matter how careful Piedmont was in making the pipes; because the pipes failed to function properly, the maker is liable.

It is important to keep in mind that the UCC only covers transactions in goods; any contract for the sale of services is not governed by Article II (unless the provisions are specifically extended to contracts for mixed goods and services, which are addressed below).

EXAMPLE:

The law firm of Black & White, P.C., enters into an agreement with Elsie to represent her in pending litigation against her former employer. This contract is not covered by the UCC because the contract concerns services (legal representation), not goods.

If the contract is for the provision of services, the provider of the services will only be liable for injury to the other contracting party if the injured party can prove negligence, that is, that the provider failed to meet the standard of due care that exists for the particular service in question.

EXAMPLE:

Return to the example with Elsie and the law firm. After Elsie contracts with Black & White, the firm procrastinates and only files Elsie's suit after the Statute of Limitations has run. The case is thrown out, and Elsie sues the firm for negligence. In maintaining her action, Elsie must show that the firm failed to meet its standard of care.

What if the contract in question involves both goods and services? Is the standard one of strict liability or of negligence? According to Article II, if the contract cannot be determined to be one either strictly of goods or strictly of services, the court will determine the predominant category of the contract. Whatever the predominant category is determined to be will control the standard for the entire contract.

EXAMPLES:

1. Faye contracts with Ilona to have Ilona make Faye's wedding dress for $750. As Faye walks down the aisle, the dress starts coming apart at the seams and the embroidery falls off. Ilona is strictly liable. Why? Because, although services are involved in the contract (the sewing of the gown), the predominant object of the contract was to provide Faye with a wedding dress (a good). Consequently, the contract is deemed to be a contract for the sale of goods carrying strict liability.

2. Arnold is in a car accident and is rushed to City General Hospital, where he receives a nutrient solution intravenously. Later it is discovered that the solution was tainted, and Arnold develops hepatitis. Arnold sues the hospital. In this instance, the contract is for the providing of services (medical care), and the standard is one of negligence. If Arnold could sue the person who sold the solution to the hospital, that would be a suit for the sale of goods.

Article II of the UCC concerns itself with contracts for the sale of goods, not with contracts for the providing of services. Contracts for the sale of goods impose strict liability for the seller, and, as will be discussed below, the seller's liability can extend not only to the purchaser of the good, but to the ultimate user of the good as well. Contracts for the providing of services carry a standard of due care, and in order to be found liable, the service provider must be shown to have failed to meet the standard of care that exists for the particular service in question. Obviously, for the injured party, it is an easier burden to have the contract considered to be one for the sale of goods.

Leases

Several jurisdictions have added a new section to the UCC concerning the long-term lease of goods. Because this provision is fairly new and has not been universally adopted, each jurisdiction's version must be checked to determine whether the lease of goods is covered by the UCC or is found under general contract principles. See below. For an example of a contract for the lease of goods, see Chapter 12.

Contracts for the Sale of Goods Between Merchants

As discussed in Chapter 2, Offer, Article II makes several modifications to the general contract requirements if the contract is between merchants. The modifications exist so as to advance the Code's purpose to promote commerce, and it is assumed that merchants are the best judges of their own contractual needs. However, two problems may arise in these types of contracts.

The first problem arises from Article II's definition of **merchant** (§204). Because the UCC is to be liberally construed (Article I), Article II of the Code defines merchant as any person who regularly deals in the kind of goods covered by the contract, *or*, any person who, by his occupation, holds himself out as having knowledge or skill peculiar to the practice of dealing with the goods in question. What this means is that not only will a businessperson be deemed a merchant, but a hobbyist is considered a merchant for the purpose of Article II as well.

EXAMPLE:

Lola has been collecting stamps as a hobby for the past 12 years. When she contracts with Aldo, a vendor of rare stamps, it is a contract for the sale of goods between merchants.

The second problem regarding merchants arises as an exception to the mirror image rule of contract formation (see Chapter 2). Merchants may meet the requirements of a writing by using purchase order forms, billing receipts, and the like. However, because businesses usually use preprinted forms, and each form is designed to protect the interests of the preparer, the writings that act as the memoranda of the verbal agreement may conflict. This is known as the **battle of the forms.** In this instance, the UCC indicates that the contract will be enforced according to the most reasonable expectations of the parties based on their past practices and their actual actions. Furthermore, as discussed in Chapter 3, merchant traders may vary the terms of the offer without that variance being deemed a rejection or counter-offer, unless the offer is "iron clad." Under the common law, such negotiation would cause a significantly different result.

EXAMPLE:

Helen operates a business selling seeds to nurseries throughout the country. Helen sends her catalog to Randy, who sends Helen his printed purchase order form mandating a specific method of delivery. Helen acknowledges the order with her own preprinted form indicating a different method of delivery. Whose form created the contract? Under the common law, the catalog is an invitation to bid, the purchase order is an offer, and the acknowledgment would be a counteroffer (see Chapter 3, Acceptance); therefore, there is no contract. However, under the UCC, the parties would have a contract because a commercial understanding has been achieved. It would be necessary to determine whether the difference in method of delivery is a material change. If the difference is material, involving greater expense or time, it will not be considered part of the contract, and the parties' past practices and actions will determine the delivery provision.

Therefore, when the contract in question is between merchants, the UCC is particularly liberal and provides many exceptions to general contract principles in order to facilitate commercial transactions.

Contractual Provisions

Warranties

As stated above, when the contact involves a sale of goods, the manufacturer/seller may not only be liable to the buyer. He may also be strictly liable to the ultimate consumer of the good as well, because goods, unlike services, have UCC **warranties** that attach to them.

A warranty is a guarantee with respect to the goods covered by the sale. The manufacturer of the goods warrants, or guarantees, that the product is exactly what has been ordered, that it is fit as sold for its intended use, and that the seller has title sufficient to pass the goods to the buyer. A warranty can be created either by the express representations of the seller or be implied by the operation of law.

Express Warranties. Under §2-313, express warranties are created by the words or conduct of the seller. They can be created in three different ways:

1. An express warranty can be created by the specific promise or affirmation appearing in the contract itself. Many contracts contain special warranty clauses, and the parties are specifically held to the words of the warranty to which they have agreed.

EXAMPLE:

In a sales contract, a clause states that the "Seller warrants that all items furnished hereunder will be in full conformity with Buyer's specification." In this manner, the seller is guaranteeing that she will provide goods exactly meeting the buyer's expressed description.

2. An express warranty can be created by a description that the seller uses in a catalog.

EXAMPLE:

Dora's Dress Company sends out a catalog describing one of its dresses as having a 48-inch sweep. When Smart Shops orders 100 of the dresses, each one must have a 48-inch sweep, or the contract is breached.

3. Finally, an express warranty can be created by a sample or model used by the seller to induce the sale.

EXAMPLE:

A Fuller Brush salesperson comes to Myra's house to demonstrate a vacuum cleaner. Delighted with the results, Myra buys one; however, when the vacuum cleaner arrives it contains modifications that did not appear on the sample the salesperson used to demonstrate the product. The company has breached its express warranty.

Implied Warranties.   Implied warranties, **§2-314, come about by operation of law. There are two types of implied warranties: a** warranty of merchantability **and a** warranty of fitness for a particular use.

Warranty of Merchantability.   This warranty, §2-314, guarantees the buyer that the goods as sold are in a fit condition for the ordinary purpose for which they were intended. In other words, if a retailer buys 500 pairs of shoes from a shoe manufacturer, the manufacturer implicitly guarantees that the shoes can be used as they are without defect. A warranty of merchantability applies only to goods sold by merchants.

Warranty of Fitness for a Particular Use.   This warranty, §2-315, goes beyond that of a warranty of merchantability in that not only must the goods be capable of being used for their ordinary purposes, but the goods must be capable of performing any particular function the buyer has indicated. A warranty of fitness for a particular use applies both to merchants and nonmerchants.

 EXAMPLE:

Hikers, Unlimited, is a chain of retail stores that sells hiking equipment. In a contract, Hikers buys 500 pairs of shoes from Seth Shoes after having indicated that the shoes are meant for mountain hikers. The shoes sold, although perfectly good shoes, do not have soles appropriate for mountain hiking. Seth Shoes has breached an implied warranty. Even though the shoes meet the description in Seth's catalog and are capable of being used, they do not meet the hiker's specific needs, of which Seth Shoes had been informed.

For there to be a warranty of fitness for a particular use, the particular use must be made known to the seller, and the buyer must be relying on the seller's expertise in purchasing the appropriate goods. The specific use could be made an express warranty if the parties include it as a part of the contract itself.

Warranty of Title.   Finally, §2-312 states that the seller must have warranty of title: title sufficient to sell the object to the buyer. The law does not intend buyers to purchase lawsuits along with the goods. The warranty of title means that the seller must own and have the right to pass ownership of the goods to the buyer free and clear of the interests of any other party to the goods, such as secured creditors. (Secured transactions are discussed later in this chapter.)

An important aspect of all warranties is that they extend not only to the contracting buyer, but to all subsequent purchasers as well, down to the ultimate consumer of the product. For example, any woman who purchased a dress from Smart Shops hoping for a 48-inch sweep could sue Doris, and any hiker who had her shoes fall apart while on a hike could sue Seth. These situations are most usually encountered in suits for defects in children's clothing, products, and toys. Parents, on behalf of the child, sue the manufacturer for breach of warranty, even though no direct contract exists between them. As the ultimate consumer, the child can maintain a suit against the manufacturer.

Risk of Loss

Another important provision of Article II of the UCC concerns the question of who bears the risk of the goods being destroyed after the contract has been signed. As a general rule, the risk of loss of the goods falls on the person who has control over the goods; however, the parties may specifically contract to determine at what point the risk passes from the seller to the buyer. Note that the risk of loss is a different concept than title.

It is imperative to understand the liabilities involved. Whoever bears the risk of loss has the right to maintain an action for the damages caused by the goods' destruction and has the responsibility to insure the goods. If the goods are destroyed when the seller bears the risk, the seller must replace the goods at his own expense. If the goods are destroyed when the buyer bears the risk, the buyer is still obligated to pay the seller for the goods. Careful drafting is always needed in these types of contracts.

In a general mercantile agreement, many of these contractual provisions are indicated merely by abbreviations of the terms. These abbreviations appear in the contracts without any words of explanation because they are generally known. These provisions are extremely important in determining which party should insure the goods and who may maintain a suit should the goods be destroyed. A brief discussion of the most important of these clauses is in order and is given below.

Conditional Contracts. With conditional contracts, the sale is predicated upon certain conditions being met at the time of transferring the goods. There are four types of conditional contracts under Article II.

1. *Cost on Delivery (§2-310).* A **cost on delivery,** or **COD,** provision indicates that the risk of loss of the goods remains with the seller until the goods have been delivered to *and paid for* by the buyer. The contract itself will indicate the place of delivery (for example, COD Buyer's Warehouse,

1000 Main Street, Garden City), and the buyer has no right of inspection unless specifically agreed to by the parties.

2. *Sale on approval (§2-326).* In a **sale on approval** contract, the seller retains the risk of loss until the goods have been delivered to the buyer and the buyer has indicated his approval of the goods. Even if the goods meet the specifications, the buyer may choose to return the goods. In this type of arrangement, the buyer, who must be the ultimate consumer, has a right to inspect the goods, so the risk is retained by the seller for a longer period than with a COD contract.

3. *Sale or return (§2-326).* With a **sale or return** provision, the risk passes to the buyer on delivery. If the buyer does not approve of the goods or chooses to return them, it is he who bears the risk and cost of returning the goods to the seller.

4. *Consignment (§2-326).* In a **consignment** contract, the risk of loss remains with the seller until the buyer resells the goods; in other words, the buyer never has a risk of loss. Many small retail stores carry goods on consignment, in which the manufacturer leaves goods with the retailer/buyer in the hopes that the buyer can resell the items. If the goods are not sold by the buyer within a stated period of time, they are returned to the seller, who has born all the risk of loss.

Note that with all of the preceding types of contracts, the buyer may return the goods even if they conform to the contract specifications. These arrangements are only concerned with the risk of loss of the goods, not with other contractual rights of the parties.

Shipment Contracts.   If the goods are transferred to the buyer by means of an independent carrier (the U.S. Postal Service, Federal Express, UPS, and so forth), a new element is added to the relationship: the third party. In a general shipment contract, the contract merely requires the seller to send the goods to the buyer. Therefore, once the goods are shipped, the risk passes to the buyer. However, the parties may make special contractual arrangements whereby the seller retains the risk for a slightly longer period, but still not to the point of delivery. There are three types of these special shipment arrangements.

1. *FOB (place of shipment) (§2-314).* FOB stands for free on board, and the risk stays with the seller until he places the goods in the hands of the carrier—for example, FOB Kennedy Airport, Air Express. In this instance, the seller bears the risk until the goods are given to the Air Express office at Kennedy Airport.

2. *FAS (vessel) (§2-319).* FAS stands for free alongside, and the vessel is the actual name of the mode of transportation—for example, FAS American Airlines Flight #100, Air Express, Kennedy Airport. In this instance, the seller retains the risk until the goods are actually taken alongside the plane ready for loading, at which point the risk of loss passes to

the buyer. FAS (vessel) keeps the risk of loss with the seller for a longer period than with FOB (place of shipment).

3. *FOB (carrier) (§2-319).* With FOB (carrier), the seller bears the risk of loss until the goods are actually loaded onto the means of transportation. This arrangement keeps the risk of loss with the seller for a longer period than any of the preceding types of shipment contracts.

Regardless of the type of shipment arrangement employed, the seller may agree to pay for insuring the goods during transportation, even though the risk of loss has passed to the buyer who would normally pay to insure the goods. This arrangement is indicated as **CIF** (cost of insurance and freight). Even though the seller has paid for the insurance, if the goods are lost, it is the buyer who bears the risk and who receives the insurance proceeds.

Shipment contracts are most commonly used when the seller is in a better bargaining position than the buyer; the seller has desirable goods that are in limited supply. As can be seen, with these arrangements it is the buyer who has the greater risk. However, most commonly the buyer has the better bargaining position—all sellers need customers—and so instead of shipment contracts the parties use destination contracts.

Destination Contracts.   With destination contracts, the seller retains the risk of loss of the goods until the goods arrive at a specified destination point. There are three types of destination contracts.

1. *FOB (place of destination) (§2-319).* As with FOB (place of shipment), in FOB (place of destination) the risk passes when the carrier delivers the goods to a general destination point—FOB Port of San Diego.

2. *Ex (ship) (§2-322).* With **Ex (ship),** the risk only passes to the buyer when the goods are off-loaded from the mode of transportation. In the example above, if the contract read Ex American Airlines Flight #100, the risk would only pass to the buyer once the goods were unloaded from the plane.

3. *No Arrival, No Sale (§2-324).* With **no arrival, no sale,** the risk only transfers to the buyer when the goods have arrived at the destination point and have been tendered to the buyer by the seller.

In each of these destination contracts, the risk remains with the seller for a slightly longer period of time than with a shipping contract.

These provisions are important in the drafting and interpreting of contracts for the sale of goods when transportation of the goods is involved. Typically, shipment provisions are simply indicated by the abbreviations given above and are not spelled out in further detail.

Remedies

For the most part, the remedies specified in Article II for the buyer and seller in a sales contract are the same remedies, both legal and equitable, permitted for all injured parties under general contract law. Chapter 11, Remedies, discusses these general remedies in detail.

Article II of the UCC grants certain additional remedies that are unique to the Code, which deserve some mention at this point.

Remedies Available to Seller

If the seller is the injured party to the contract, Article II, Part 7, permits three additional methods of rectifying the situation.

1. *Withhold delivery.* The seller may withhold delivery of the goods to the buyer if any one of the following circumstances arises:

   a. The buyer wrongfully rejects the goods.
   b. The buyer fails to pay for the goods as required by the contract.
   c. The buyer does not cooperate with the seller.
   d. The buyer repudiates the contract.
   e. The buyer becomes insolvent before delivery.

EXAMPLE:

Under their contractual agreement, Rosie is obligated to send goods by a carrier that John is to name. John is prevaricating and won't specify a carrier. Rosie does not have to ship the goods because John is failing to cooperate according to the terms of the contract. Rosie has the right to resell the goods to another buyer.

2. *Stop delivery.* The seller may stop delivery of the goods in transit and resell them if one of the following circumstances arises:

   a. The buyer does not pay for the goods as required by the contract.
   b. The buyer repudiates the contract.
   c. The buyer becomes insolvent before delivery.

EXAMPLE:

John finally specifies a carrier to Rosie, who then ships the goods. Shipment will take two weeks. After one week elapses, John files for protection under the bankruptcy law. Under Article II, Rosie is permitted to stop delivery of the goods, provided John has not yet paid for them. The UCC does not require sellers to become creditors in the bankruptcy of insolvent buyers. Note, however, that if John had already paid for the goods, Rosie would be required to deliver them. If the goods are nonconforming, John still has the right to reject them.

3. *Reclaim goods from insolvent buyer.* The seller has the right to reclaim the goods from the buyer after delivery, but only if the goods are sold on credit, the buyer is insolvent, and the seller makes her demand within ten days of the buyer's receipt of the goods.

 EXAMPLE:

Assume that Rosie sells the goods to John on credit but is unaware that John has filed for bankruptcy. Ten days after John receives the goods, Rosie discovers that John is insolvent; she immediately demands that John return the goods. Under the UCC, Rosie can reclaim the goods and thus avoid becoming one of John's creditors.

Remedies Available to Buyer

If the buyer is the injured party, in addition to general contractual remedies, UCC Article II offers him four specific remedies. Note that under the UCC, a buyer is entitled to perfect performance and may reject nonconforming goods. The concept of substantial performance does not apply to merchant buyers unless the merchant buyer so wishes. This concept is known as **perfect tender.**

1. *Cover.* The buyer is entitled to **cover** if the seller breaches the contract. Cover is the purchase of goods that substitute for those that are the subject of the breached contract. The buyer can sue the seller for damages if the substituted goods cost more than what the buyer expected to pay under the original sales contract.

EXAMPLE:

Buymore Supermarkets has a contract to buy 1,000 bushels of plums from Farmer Jones. When the plums arrive, they do not meet Buymore's specifications, and so it rejects the plums. Buymore purchases plums from Farmer Hicks as cover. The contract with Hicks costs Buymore $1,000 more than the contract with Farmer Jones; Buymore can sue Jones for the extra $1,000.

2. *Replevin.* If cover is not available, the buyer may *replevy* the goods he had previously rejected from the seller. **Replevin** is an equitable remedy that means retaking, or recovering, the goods identified in the contract. The buyer may believe that nonconforming goods are better than none.

EXAMPLE:

If in the above situation, Buymore could not find plums anywhere else, it could replevy the plums it has already rejected from Farmer Jones.

3. *Revocation.* If the goods do not conform to the contract specifications, the buyer can **revoke** his acceptance. This means that no contract exists.

EXAMPLE:

Assume the above situation. Because the plums did not conform to Buymore's specifications, Buymore could revoke its acceptance. No contract is ever formed.

4. *Claim goods from insolvent seller.* If the seller becomes insolvent, the buyer can claim the goods from him, provided that the goods have been paid for. Just as the UCC will not require a seller to become a creditor of an insolvent buyer, neither will it require a buyer who has paid for goods to become a creditor of an insolvent seller. At this point, the goods are in fact the property of the buyer; the seller's creditors have the purchase price the buyer has already given to divide up among themselves.

Written Assurances

In addition to the foregoing, both parties to a contract under Article II have the right to demand assurances in writing that performance will occur. This can arise if either party becomes concerned about the other party's ability to perform. Note that this is different from a situation in which one party affirmatively states that she will not perform (see Chapter 10). Written assurances also have no applicability to situations in which a party has been judicially deemed bankrupt. If the assurances are not given within 30 days of the request, the requesting party can act as if the other party has breached the contract. Review the earlier discussion on anticipatory breach to see how the UCC interplays with contractual common law.

Summary

Article II is one of the most important provisions of the Uniform Commercial Code with respect to contract law. This article covers three main categories of contracts: contracts for the sale of goods valued at over $500; contracts between merchants; and contracts for the lease of property. Article II imposes warranties, or guarantees, with respect to the quality and usefulness of the subject goods. Additionally, it indicates special types of arrangements apportioning the risk of having the goods lost or destroyed while in transit between the seller and the buyer. Lastly, Article II details certain remedies for the injured party in a breach of one of the aforementioned contracts unique to the UCC.

Article II-A, Leases

Several years ago, many jurisdictions added a new subsection to Article II to deal with the lease of goods. There were several reasons for codifying the law with respect to such leases:

1. It was necessary to define the term "lease" so as to distinguish between a true lease and a hidden security agreement. A "true lease" is one in which, at the termination of the lease period, the item returns to the lessor. Conversely, with a hidden security agreement, the document reads like a lease but at its termination the lessee has the right to purchase the item at a nominal fee because its useful life has been exhausted during the leasehold. If the agreement is deemed to be a hidden security agreement, the provisions of Article IX must be complied with (see below).

2. If a lease exists, it must be analyzed to determine whether the lessor has made warranties to the lessee. If the contract is a sale, the regular warranties discussed above apply. However, without the codification of this article, the law was unclear as to whether lessors make any nonexplicit warranties to lessees. Under the provisions of Article II-A, the UCC imposes express and implied warranties, as well as warranties against infringement and interference of the lessee's right to the use and possession of the good, as well as the methods to be employed to exclude or modify warranties. The provisions of each state's version of this article must be analyzed to ascertain the extent of such provision in a given jurisdiction.

3. It was necessary to determine whether the remedies available under Article II are available under Article II-A. Once again, the extent to which such remedies would be applicable in a given instance is determined by the UCC version adopted by the jurisdiction in question.

In drafting the model version of UCC II-A, the Commissioners took the view that there was no need to include security interests disguised as leases, so "leases" were defined specifically to exclude such security devices. However, to avoid any conflict with specific state or federal laws, Article II-A makes its provisions subject to title and consumer protection laws.

The codification of this section was greatly influenced by the basic common law tenets of contract interpretation that have been discussed throughout this text. In other words, except where specifically noted, all common law rules and principles still apply to lease arrangements. Basically, the sales provisions of Article II have simply been extended to commercial leases of goods because of the current practice in the business community of leasing equipment rather than making an outright purchase, even if the lease in question provides for an option to purchase at the conclusion of the leasehold.

Article IX, Secured Transactions

Secured Transaction Defined

Article IX of the UCC defines a **secured transaction** as any transaction, regardless of form, that is intended to create a security interest in personal property or fixtures, including *tangible goods, intangibles,* and *documents.* A *tangible good* (§9-105) is any good that can be touched and moved and whose value is incorporated into the item itself. Examples of tangible goods are furniture, clothing, and automobiles. An intangible (§9-106) is a right to property, rather than a physical object. Examples of intangibles are stock certificates, bank savings account books, bonds, patents, and copyrights. Documents are such items as bills of lading and dock receipts.

A **security interest** represents the right of the holder of the interest to attach specific property in case of a default. In terms of contract law, this means that if the promissor defaults on his contractual obligation, and the promissee has a security interest, the promissee can attach the promissor's property that is subject to that interest to satisfy the default. It affords the innocent party greater protection in case of breach of contract because she knows that there will at least be the value of the secured property to lessen her injury.

EXAMPLE:

Heather goes to the state bank to take out a personal loan. Before the bank loans Heather the money, it asks her to put up some property as security. Heather gives the bank a pearl ring she owns. The bank retains this ring as **collateral** (property to secure payment of the debt) until Heather repays the loan. Should Heather default, the bank can sell the ring to satisfy Heather's debt. Physical possession is one method of creating a security interest.

Nearly all security interests in personal property and fixtures are covered under Article IX of the UCC. There are only six categories of property that are not subject to this article—enumerated in §9-104.

1. *Real estate.* As indicated by the definition of a secured transaction in Article IX, real property is automatically excluded from this UCC provision, except for fixtures. A fixture is property that has been attached to real property but is capable of being removed without destroying or disturbing the real estate. Examples of fixtures would be door knobs, chandeliers, and light switches.

2. *Interests perfected under federal statutes.* Certain types of property, such as patents and copyrights, are created by federal statutes that also provide methods for establishing security interests in that property.

3. *Wage assignments. Wage assignments,* or *garnishments,* are covered by separate laws that protect the wage earner from having all of her wages taken from her to satisfy debts.

4. *Mechanic's liens.* A **mechanic's lien** is the right of any person who works on a piece of property to attach that property if the owner does not pay for the work performed. Mechanic's liens have been in existence for hundreds of years, are part of the common law, and automatically afford protection to workers.

5. *Claims arising out of judicial proceedings.* If a court of competent jurisdiction grants the specific right to a piece of property, the court's authority supersedes that of the UCC, and these claims are excluded from Article IX.

6. *Consumer sales agreements regulated by state laws.* Many states have enacted laws to protect consumers from having property reclaimed by stores if the consumer fails to make a payment years after the purchase, and these sales are exempted from Article IX where such statutes exist.

A security interest gives the holder of the interest the right to attach specific property subject to the interest in the case of default. This type of creditor has greater rights to the specific property of the debtor than other creditors. Whenever payment for merchandise is not concurrent with delivery of the goods, contracts usually specify that the party who conveys the goods shall have a security interest in the goods until payment. This protects the person who has already given his consideration in case the other party defaults. However, merely having a clause in the contract may be insufficient to create a valid and enforceable security interest pursuant to Article IX.

Requirements to Create a Security Interest

To create a valid and enforceable security interest, the parties must intend to create a security interest and evidence such interest by meeting three requirements under Part Two of Article IX:

1. There must be a security agreement.
2. There must be attachment.
3. There must be perfection.

1. *Security agreement.* A **security agreement** is a writing signed by both parties. It describes the property that is subject to the security interest and states that a security interest is being created in that property. The property is generally referred to as the collateral. Usually, the contract between the parties for the sale of the goods satisfies this requirement, provided that it contains a statement creating the security interest. For an example of such a statement, see the sample clauses given below.

2. *Attachment.* **Attachment** is the timing element of the security interest; it indicates the moment when the creditor gives consideration for the security interest. Typically, this occurs when the agreement is signed, or the security holder conveys his consideration to the other party, or the debtor takes possession of the collateral. At this moment the security holder has an inchoate right to the collateral.

What happens if the contract is for a loan and the debtor is using the borrowed money to purchase the property that will become the collateral? The creditor's rights may not attach for several weeks. The reason that the attachment is delayed is because the property that is the subject of the security interest is not yet owned by the debtor. The debtor is using the borrowed money to purchase the collateral. During this time the debtor may default. Under these circumstances, the creditor has a **purchase money security interest** in the property the debtor buys with the creditor's funds. This interest is implied by law, and the debtor holds the property in trust for the creditor.

 EXAMPLE:

Leonard loans his brother-in-law Zack $50,000 to start a bottling company, and the loan states that Leonard will have a security interest in the bottling equipment. Zack orders the bottling equipment on credit and uses Leonard's money to buy office furniture and supplies. If Zack defaults prior to the equipment being delivered, Leonard has a purchase money security interest in the furniture and supplies because it was his money that paid for the items.

Another problem that can arise with respect to attachment occurs if the collateral is the inventory of the debtor. Many times, if money is loaned to a manufacturer, the creditor will take a security interest in the debtor's inventory. However, inventory is always being sold, so the specific items included in inventory one week are not the same items the following week.

In this situation, the creditor is deemed to have a **floating lien,** giving her the right to attach any item that is included in inventory at the moment of default. The actual collateral is always being changed.

EXAMPLE:

Assume that in the above example, instead of taking a security interest in Zack's equipment, Leonard takes a security interest in Zack's inventory. On the day the loan agreement is signed, Zack has 100,000 bottles in inventory; on the day Zack defaults, his inventory contains 200,000 bottles. Leonard has a right to claim the 200,000 bottles, even though these specific bottles were acquired by Zack after the agreement. The floating lien gives Leonard the right to all existing inventory on the day of default up to the value of the debt.

3. *Perfection.* The third requirement to create a valid and enforceable security interest is **perfection.** Perfection is the process of protecting a creditor's rights to the collateral from all other claimants and can be effectuated in three ways:

First, in certain circumstances, the attachment itself is sufficient to perfect the interest, as in the case of a purchase money security interest.

Second, perfection can come about by the creditor having physical possession of the collateral. An example would be the state bank in the earlier instance with Heather and the loan. Because the bank is actually holding Heather's pearl ring, no one else can get control of it.

Third, and most typically, perfection can be accomplished by filing a **financing statement.** A financing statement is a document, signed by the parties, that contains their names and addresses and describes the collateral. (See sample financing statement on the next page.) A security agreement can be used as a financing statement, but the reverse is not true. The financing statement does not create the security interest. However, it is very rare that anyone uses the security agreement as the financing statement, because once the document is filed, it becomes publicly available. Most people do not want all the terms of their contractual arrangements to be public knowledge. Usually creditors file financing statements. These forms can be purchased from legal stationery stores and only indicate the minimum information required by Article IX.

Filing is mandatory for perfecting security interests in intangibles, inventory goods, and equipment, but is permissive for all other property. Filing is effective for a period of five years. If the debt is not satisfied within this period, the financing statement must be refiled. Where the financing statements are filed depends on the nature of the collateral: either the County Filing Office where the property is located, the County Recorder's Office (typically for timber, minerals, and crops), or the Secretary of State's Office. Part 4 of Article IX specifies the appropriate office, and therefore the version of the Code adopted by the state in question must be checked.

Not only does filing afford the creditor some protection against other claimants, but because filing is public, prior to agreeing to accept a security interest in a particular piece of property, a potential creditor must check the appropriate office to make sure that no one else already has a security interest in the collateral. This is crucial for the formation of an enforceable security interest.

But what happens if there are conflicting claims to the same property? Which creditor prevails? Part 3 of Article IX has established an order of priorities in such situations to determine which creditor has superior rights to the collateral.

UCC FINANCING STATEMENT
FOLLOW INSTRUCTIONS

| A. NAME & PHONE OF CONTACT AT FILER (optional) |
| B. E-MAIL CONTACT AT FILER (optional) |
| C. SEND ACKNOWLEDGMENT TO: (Name and Address) |

| Print | Reset |

THE ABOVE SPACE IS FOR FILING OFFICE USE ONLY

1. DEBTOR'S NAME: Provide only one Debtor name (1a or 1b) (use exact, full name; do not omit, modify, or abbreviate any part of the Debtor's name); if any part of the Individual Debtor's name will not fit in line 1b, leave all of item 1 blank, check here ☐ and provide the Individual Debtor information in item 10 of the Financing Statement Addendum (Form UCC1Ad)

1a. ORGANIZATION'S NAME				
OR 1b. INDIVIDUAL'S SURNAME	FIRST PERSONAL NAME		ADDITIONAL NAME(S)/INITIAL(S)	SUFFIX
1c. MAILING ADDRESS	CITY		STATE	POSTAL CODE	COUNTRY

2. DEBTOR'S NAME: Provide only one Debtor name (2a or 2b) (use exact, full name; do not omit, modify, or abbreviate any part of the Debtor's name); if any part of the Individual Debtor's name will not fit in line 2b, leave all of item 2 blank, check here ☐ and provide the Individual Debtor information in item 10 of the Financing Statement Addendum (Form UCC1Ad)

2a. ORGANIZATION'S NAME				
OR 2b. INDIVIDUAL'S SURNAME	FIRST PERSONAL NAME		ADDITIONAL NAME(S)/INITIAL(S)	SUFFIX
2c. MAILING ADDRESS	CITY		STATE	POSTAL CODE	COUNTRY

3. SECURED PARTY'S NAME (or NAME of ASSIGNEE of ASSIGNOR SECURED PARTY): Provide only one Secured Party name (3a or 3b)

3a. ORGANIZATION'S NAME				
OR 3b. INDIVIDUAL'S SURNAME	FIRST PERSONAL NAME		ADDITIONAL NAME(S)/INITIAL(S)	SUFFIX
3c. MAILING ADDRESS	CITY		STATE	POSTAL CODE	COUNTRY

4. COLLATERAL: This financing statement covers the following collateral:

5. Check only if applicable and check only one box: Collateral is ☐ held in a Trust (see UCC1Ad, item 17 and Instructions)	☐ being administered by a Decedent's Personal Representative
6a. Check only if applicable and check only one box:	6b. Check only if applicable and check only one box:
☐ Public-Finance Transaction ☐ Manufactured-Home Transaction ☐ A Debtor is a Transmitting Utility	☐ Agricultural Lien ☐ Non-UCC Filing
7. ALTERNATIVE DESIGNATION (if applicable): ☐ Lessee/Lessor ☐ Consignee/Consignor ☐ Seller/Buyer ☐ Bailee/Bailor ☐ Licensee/Licensor
8. OPTIONAL FILER REFERENCE DATA:

FILING OFFICE COPY — UCC FINANCING STATEMENT (Form UCC1) (Rev. 04/20/11)

Priorities

Article IX has established an order of priorities for creditors in case of the debtor's default. Should there be conflicting claims for the same property, the claimant with the highest priority will prevail. The general rule is that secured creditors have greater priorities than unsecured creditors. Among secured creditors, priorities date from the time of filing *or* perfection of the security interest. The order of the priorities is:

1. creditors with a purchase money security interest;
2. creditors with a floating lien;
3. among creditors who perfect on the same day: creditors who filed first (this is the actual date of filing the financing statement, not the date the agreement was signed), then creditors with interests perfected other than by filing (attachment or possession); and
4. creditors whose interests attached first among nonperfected creditors.

EXAMPLE:

Julia loans $10,000 to Ariel, taking a security interest in Ariel's receivables. The loan agreement is signed and the money given on Monday. On Friday, Julia files her financing statement. In the interim, Ariel borrows $5,000 from Mark, signing a security agreement for the receivables on Wednesday. Mark also files his financing statement on Wednesday. When Ariel defaults, Mark prevails because he filed before Julia (Wednesday versus Friday).

If the debtor defaults, the creditor with a valid security interest may either retain the collateral in satisfaction of the debt, sell the collateral to satisfy the debt (any amount above the debt acquired by the sale of the collateral belongs to the debtor), or may simply sue the debtor in an action for debt.

Generally, paralegals who work with contracts subject to Article IX of the UCC have very specific functions to perform. First, they must draft a legally accurate description of the property that will be subject to the security interest. If the property is inaccurately or incompletely described, the client will not have an effective security interest. Second, the legal assistant must check the appropriate government office to determine that no other security interest is attached to the subject property. Finally, the paralegal must file the financing statement in a timely manner in the appropriate office.

The National Conference of Commissioners on Uniform State Rules has also recommended the following changes to Article 9:

1. When the debtor is an individual, the name that should be provided on the financing statement is to be the name that appears on the debtor's most recent driver's license, or unexpired nondriver

photo ID, issued by the state whose law governs the security
interest. If the debtor does not have such a document, the creditor
must include the individual's surname and first personal name.

2. When the debtor is a registered organization, the name that
    appears on the financing statement should be its name as reflected
    on the public organic record of the registered organization, rather
    than any electronic database maintained by the state.

3. If the debtor changes location, a new grace period is recommended
    for including after-acquired property; further a four-month grace
    period for refiling is recommended if the original debtor merges
    with an out-of-state entity.

SAMPLE CLAUSES

1

MANUFACTURER   HEREBY   WARRANTS   THAT   THE
MERCHANDISE WILL NOT FADE OR SHRINK.

This is an example of an express warranty made by a manufacturer.
Any person who purchases these goods or who is the ultimate consumer
(user) of these goods may sue the manufacturer if the goods do in fact fade
or shrink. The warranty is a covenant of the seller.

2

We hereby grant to you a security interest in all receivables, as defined
above, all present and future instruments, documents, chattel paper, and
general intangibles (as defined by the Uniform Commercial Code), and all
reserves, balances and deposits, and property at any time to our credit. All
of the foregoing shall secure payment and performance of all of our obligations at any time owing to you, fixed or contingent, whether arising out of
this or any other agreement, or by operation of law or otherwise.

The above is a contract clause intended to create a security agreement
in documents and intangibles. Taken in conjunction with the entire agreement, which would indicate the parties' names, addresses, and signatures,
this would constitute a valid security agreement, the first requirement to
create an enforceable security interest under Article IX of the UCC.

3

You want waterproof? Breathable? Look at our clothing on page 20,
all 100% waterproof and windproof, yet so breathable that overheating is
a thing of the past.

The above catalog description constitutes an express warranty by the
seller. Even though the word "warranty" is not used, because the description of the clothing appears in its sales literature, the manufacturer is held

to guarantee that the clothes are 100 percent waterproof and breathable so that the customer will not get wet or overheated.

CHAPTER SUMMARY

The Uniform Commercial Code was created to promote and facilitate commerce among the states and to provide some uniformity in state laws with respect to commercial transactions. The UCC is a state law, and versions of the model UCC have been adopted in every jurisdiction including the District of Columbia. Three UCC articles have a direct impact on the law of contracts.

Article I, General Provisions, establishes the general guidelines for interpretation of the entire Code. This article restates the purpose of the Code and indicates that the Code is to be liberally, not literally, construed, within the bounds of reasonable interpretation. Additionally, the state law will always prevail unless specifically superseded by the Code.

Article I also establishes three obligations for all persons whose transactions are covered by the UCC: (1) they are obligated to act in good faith; (2) they are obligated to perform within a reasonable time; and (3) they are expected to perform according to the custom, usage, and past practices of the parties and industry involved.

Article II, Sales, concerns itself with contracts for the sale of goods. It is the modern interpretation of the Statute of Frauds with respect to these types of contracts. The UCC does not cover contracts for the performance of services.

The UCC provisions on sales regulate the concept of warranties, or guarantees, with respect to contracts for the sale of goods. In this manner, Article II makes the manufacturer/seller of goods contractually bound not only to his direct purchaser, but to anyone who ultimately uses or consumes the goods. These warranties may be either express (created by words or conduct) or implied (created by operation of law).

Article II further establishes contractual methods of determining when the risk of loss of the goods transfers from the seller to the buyer. The Code specifies several different clauses or agreements that the parties may insert in their contract to make this determination.

Additionally, the article on sales provides specific remedies in case of breach of contract for both the seller and the buyer. These Article II remedies go beyond those generally afforded under contract law.

Note, several jurisdictions have enacted Article II-A, covering long-term leases of goods.

Finally, Article IX, Secured Transactions, indicates how a creditor may contractually provide for a security interest in specific property, property that he may then attach and sell to satisfy the debt in the case of the debtor's default. By meeting the UCC requirements for creating a security agreement and for attachment and perfection, a creditor is given greater protection for recovery in the case of breach of contract. Commerce is thus promoted by making credit and loans less risky for the creditor.

SYNOPSIS

UCC purpose: Modernizing, clarifying, and unifying state commercial law
    Article I, General provisions
Obligations
    1. Good faith
    2. Reasonable time
    3. Custom and usage
Article II, Sales
    1. Contracts covered
        a. Sale of goods (not services)
        b. Lease of goods
        c. Contracts between merchants
    2. Contract provisions
        a. Warranties
            i. Express
               (1) Affirmation or promise
               (2) Description
               (3) Sample or model
           ii. Implied
               (1) Merchantability
               (2) Fitness for a particular use
           iii. Title
        b. Risk of loss
            i. Conditional
           ii. Shipment
           iii. Destination
    3. Remedies
        a. Seller
            i. Withhold delivery
           ii. Stop delivery in transit
           iii. Redeem goods from insolvent buyer
        b. Buyer
            i. Cover
           ii. Replevin
           iii. Revoke acceptance
           iv. Reclaim goods from insolvent seller

Article IX, Secured Transactions
  1. Exceptions
  2. Requirements
     a. Security agreement
     b. Attachment
     c. Perfection (filing)
  3. Priorities

Key Terms

Attachment: time at which security interest becomes an inchoate right
Battle of the forms: difference in forms used by merchants for sales
        agreements
CIF: cost of insurance and freight paid for by seller, even though risk of loss
        has passed to the buyer
COD: cost on delivery; conditional contract in which the risk of loss passes
        to buyer only after goods have been delivered and paid for
Collateral: property pledged to secure a security interest
Consignment contract: conditional contract in which risk of loss remains
        with seller until buyer resells the goods
Cover: remedy whereby buyer can purchase goods in substitution for
        breached contract
Express warranty: guarantee created by words or conduct of the seller
Ex ship: destination contract in which risk of loss passes to buyer when
        goods are off-loaded from the mode of transportation
FAS: free alongside; a shipping contract in which risk of loss passes
        to buyer when goods are placed alongside vessel used for
        transportation
Financing statement: document filed in government office to protect a
        security interest
Floating lien: security interest in after-acquired property
FOB (carrier):   shipment contract in which risk of loss passes when goods
        are loaded onto third-party carrier
FOB (place of shipment):   free on board; shipment contract in which risk of
        loss passes when goods are given to third-party carrier
Implied warranty: guarantee created by operation of law
Mechanic's lien: security interest given under common law to persons who
        repair property
Merchant: person who regularly trades in goods or who holds himself out
        as having knowledge peculiar to a specific good
No arrival, no sale: destination contract in which risk of loss passes to
        buyer when goods are tendered to the buyer
Perfect tender: buyer's right to complete performance
Perfection: method of creating and protecting a security interest under
        Article IX of the UCC

Purchase money security interest: security interest created in the creditor whose money is used to buy the collateral

Replevin: equitable remedy in which buyer reclaims property previously rejected

Revocation: to recall an offer

Sale on approval: conditional contract in which risk of loss passes to buyer when buyer receives and approves goods

Sale or return: conditional contract in which risk of loss passes when buyer receives goods; buyer bears the cost of returning goods of which he does not approve

Secured transaction: any transaction, regardless of form, that creates a security interest in personal property or fixtures

Security agreement: document signed by debtor and creditor that names the collateral and creates a security interest in said collateral

Security interest: right acquired by a creditor to attach collateral in case of default by the debtor

Shipment contract: agreement whereby risk passes from seller to buyer when goods are transported by a third person

Strict liability: no standard of care; automatic liability if properly used goods do not meet the warranty

Warranty: guarantee made by manufacturer or seller with respect to quality, quantity, and type of good being sold

Warranty of fitness for a particular use: guarantee that goods can be used for a specified purpose

Warranty of merchantability: guarantee that goods can be used in their current condition

Warranty of title: guarantee that seller has a title sufficient to transfer goods to buyer

EXERCISES

1. Find two advertisements in your local newspaper that indicate warranties.
2. Discuss several methods of protecting a person's security interest.
3. Does the UCC in fact promote commerce? Explain.
4. Obtain and analyze a mortgage and chattel mortgage agreement.
5. Obtain the addresses of the appropriate government offices in your state for filing financing statements.
6. Check your own state statute for its version of the UCC.

Cases for Analysis

Wilson v. Brawn of California, Inc. highlights the concepts of risk of loss and sales on approval when purchasing items through an Internet catalog, and the battle of the forms is discussed in *Demarco California Fabrics, Inc. v. Nygard International, Ltd.*

Jacq Wilson et al. v. Brawn of California, Inc.

132 Cal. App. 4th 549; 33 Cal. Rptr. 3d 769 (2005)

The San Francisco Superior Court entered judgment against Brawn of California, Inc. (Brawn), a mail order company, ruling that Brawn had engaged in a deceptive business practice by charging its customers an "insurance fee" of $1.48 with every order placed. The ruling presumed that Brawn, rather than its customers, bears the loss of risk in transit, so that its customers received nothing of value in return for paying the fee. The court also awarded plaintiff litigation expenses in the amount of $24,699.21 and attorney fees in the amount of $422,982.50.

We reverse, concluding that Brawn did not bear the risk of loss of goods in transit under the applicable California Uniform Commercial Code sections discussed, post.

Background

Brawn markets clothing through its catalogs and over the Internet. When a customer places an order, Brawn packages it, and holds it at its warehouse, where it is picked up by a common carrier and delivered to the customer, using an address provided by the customer. At all times relevant, the terms of Brawn's mail order form required the customer to pay the listed price for the goods purchased, plus a delivery fee and a $1.48 "insurance fee." As to the last, the form recited: "INSURANCE: Items Lost or Damaged in Transit Replaced Free." Brawn based the insurance fee on the costs to it of replacing any goods lost in transit, and Brawn did indeed replace, without further cost to the customer, any goods that had been lost in transit. Brawn rarely, if ever, sold its goods to a customer unwilling to pay the insurance fee.

On February 5, 2002, and again on February 7, 2002, plaintiff Jacq Wilson (plaintiff) purchased items from Brawn's catalogue, each time paying the insurance fee. On February 13, 2002, Wilson, acting on behalf of himself and all other similarly situated persons, brought suit against Brawn, contending that in charging the fee, Brawn violated the unfair competition law, Business and Professions Code section 17200 et seq., prohibiting unfair competition, and Business and Professions Code section 17500 et seq., prohibiting false advertising.

Plaintiff's suit was premised on the theory that by charging customers an insurance fee, Brawn suggested to them that they were paying for and receiving a special benefit—insurance against loss in transit—when in fact, customers did not need insurance against loss in transit because Brawn already was required to pay for that loss as a matter of law. The trial court agreed, finding that irrespective of the insurance fee, Brawn bore the risk of loss of goods in transit, reasoning that the fee was an "illusory" benefit. The court found that Brawn's customers were likely to be deceived by the insurance fee, and that Brawn therefore had engaged in a deceptive business practice, entitling its customers to restitution.

Standard of Review

Our decision is based on our construction and application of statutory law, and not on any disputed issue of fact. Questions of law, such as statutory interpretation or the application of a statutory standard to undisputed facts, are reviewed de novo.

Discussion

Neither party has cited any significant source of law concerning mail order sales or the risk of loss in mail order consumer sales, resting their contentions on provisions of the California Uniform Commercial Code. As the California Uniform Commercial Code, and the cases cited there, typically involve arm's-length sales between fairly sophisticated parties, the fit is not perfect. Nonetheless, there appears to be little legislation or case law specifically concerned with mail order sales or risk of loss in consumer sales contracts, and we, too, turn to the California Uniform Commercial Code's provisions.

California Uniform Commercial Code section 2509 sets forth the general rules for determining which party bears the risk of loss of goods in transit when there has been no breach of contract. Subdivision (1) of section 2509 provides, as relevant: "(1) Where the contract requires or authorizes the seller to ship the goods by carrier (a) If it does not require him to deliver them at a particular destination, the risk of loss passes to the buyer when the goods are duly delivered to the carrier . . . ; but (b) If it does require him to deliver them at a particular destination and the goods are there duly tendered while in the possession of the carrier, the risk of loss passes to the buyer when the goods are there duly so tendered as to enable the buyer to take delivery."

Shipment Contract or Destination Contract

[U]nder this Article the "shipment" contract is regarded as the normal one and the "destination" contract as the variant type. The seller is not obligated to deliver at a named destination and bear the concurrent risk of loss until arrival, unless he has specifically agreed so to deliver or the commercial understanding of the terms used by the parties contemplates such a delivery. Of course, a seller will have to provide the carrier with shipping instructions. It follows that a contract is not a destination contract simply because the seller places an address label on the package, or directs the carrier to "ship to" a particular destination. "Thus a 'ship to' term has no significance in determining whether a contract is a shipment or destination contract for risk of loss purposes." The point is illustrated in *La Casse v. Blaustein*, where the plaintiff, a student in Massachusetts, purchased 23 pocket calculators by telephone from a New York manufacturer. The method of shipment was left to the seller, but the plaintiff wrote a check to cover postage, and directed the seller to ship the goods to the plaintiff's residence. The court held: "Under the Uniform Commercial Code, the sales contract which provides for delivery to a carrier is considered the usual one and delivery to a particular destination to a buyer the variant or unusual one. [Citations.] In view of the foregoing, the request of the plaintiff's letter to ship to his residence is insufficient to convert the contract into one requiring delivery to a destination rather than one to a carrier. The request was nothing more than a shipping instruction and not of sufficient weight and solemnity as to convert the agreement into a destination contract." Similarly, in *California State Electronics Assn. v. Zeos Internat. Ltd.*, one of the few California cases discussing the issue, the court held: "The evidence showed that Zeos's sales operation consists of telephone orders which are shipped at the buyer's expense via an overnight express service. The paperwork Zeos prepares and sends to the buyer, with the goods or shortly after their shipment, contains no provision requiring Zeos to deliver the goods to the buyer. These facts plainly mark Zeos's terms as 'shipment' contracts, which is the presumptive form."

In addition, although the risk of loss does not necessarily pass at the same time title to the goods passes, California Uniform Commercial Code section 2401, subdivision (2)(a), provides that "[i]f the contract requires or authorizes the seller to send the goods to the buyer but does not require him to deliver them at [a] destination, title passes to the buyer at the time and place of shipment." This section, therefore, also distinguishes between the seller's obligation to deliver goods to a carrier, and the seller's obligation to deliver goods to the buyer.

It is not at all uncommon for a contract to shift the risk of loss to the buyer at the point at which the seller delivers the goods to a common carrier, while calling for the seller to pay for delivery and insurance. The California Uniform Commercial Code recognizes this type of contract in its provisions pertaining to the term "C.I.F." "The term C.I.F. means that the price includes in a lump sum the cost of the goods and the insurance and freight to the named destination." (Cal. U. Com. Code, §2320, subd. (1).) Official comment to the section explains that "[t]he C.I.F. contract is not a destination but a shipment contract with risk of subsequent loss or damage to the goods passing to the buyer upon shipment if the seller has properly performed all his obligations with respect to the goods. Delivery to the carrier is delivery to the buyer for purposes of risk and 'title.'" Official Code comment 5 to Uniform Code section 2-503, similarly, explains that a term requiring the seller to pay the freight or the cost of delivery is not to be interpreted as the equivalent of a term requiring the seller to deliver to the buyer or to an agreed destination. In a standard "C.I.F." contract, then, the buyer bears the risk of loss in transit even though the cost of insurance is rolled into the purchase price and is in fact paid by the seller. By breaking out the cost of insurance, and requiring the buyer to pay it, Brawn's mail order contracts even more clearly place the risk of loss in transit on the buyer.

Other evidence, while not determinative, is consistent with the conclusion that Brawn, at least, intended the contracts to be shipment contracts. Brawn's own insurance covers goods lost while in Brawn's possession, but does not cover goods destroyed or lost after the goods left Brawn's physical possession. Brawn pays California use tax, rather than sales tax, on the theory that the goods were "sold" when they left Brawn's place of business, located outside of California. Brawn records the revenue for the goods sold at the point of shipment, and removes the goods from its inventory at the time of shipment.

In sum, nothing in Brawn's conduct, and nothing in the delivery or insurance terms of Brawn's mail order forms, suggests that it was offering anything other than a standard, C.I.F.-type shipment contract, which the customers agreed to when they used Brawn's mail order form to purchase goods.

Sales on Approval

Plaintiff, however, contended, and the trial court agreed, that Brawn's mail order contracts were "sales on approval," where, as a general rule, the seller bears the risk of loss in transit. The contention was and is based on the provision that Brawn's customers are entitled to return any goods with which they are not satisfied for a refund of the purchase price or credit toward another purchase. Plaintiff also contended that the practice of allowing customers to return goods for a full refund is so common in the industry as to establish a trade usage, asserting that even if the written terms of Brawn's contracts establish that they are shipment contracts, the written terms must be modified by trade usage so as to make the contracts "sales on approval."

The legal support for the claim that Brawn's contracts are "sales on approval" is contained in California Uniform Commercial Code sections 2326 and 2327. Section 2326, subdivision (1) provides: "Unless otherwise agreed, if delivered goods may be returned by the buyer even though they conform to the contract, the transaction is (a) A 'sale on approval' if the goods are delivered primarily for use, and (b) A 'sale or return' if the goods are delivered primarily for resale." California Uniform Commercial Code section 2327, subdivision (1)(a) provides that unless otherwise agreed, under a sale on approval, "the risk of loss and the title do not pass to the buyer until acceptance."

The initial flaw in plaintiff's contention is that a "sale on approval" places the risk of loss in transit on the seller "unless otherwise agreed." Brawn's contract specifically and expressly calls for the buyer to pay for shipping and insurance, placing the risk of loss in transit on the buyer. (CA(8)(8).) It also is well established that the express terms of the agreement controls usage of trade. (Cal. U. Com. Code, §2208, subd. (2).) Therefore, even if plaintiffs established that most contracts in the trade are "sales on approval" (and they did not), the express terms of Brawn's contract control.

In any event, California Uniform Commercial Code section 2326 is designed to distinguish between two forms of bailment, not to convert ordinary retail sales contracts into "sales on approval." The section addresses transactions where the parties intend the goods in question to continue to be the seller's property after the buyer takes possession of them. A common example is the consignment sale, where the buyer's responsibility is to sell the goods on behalf of the seller, or return them if they cannot be sold. Another example arises when the parties intend to postpone the change in ownership until sometime after delivery to allow the buyer an opportunity to decide whether or not to accept the goods. Section 2326 provides a means of distinguishing between these kinds of transactions, explaining that a sale is "on approval" when the goods are intended for the buyer's own use, and is a "sale or return" when the goods are to be resold by the buyer. (Id., subd. (1)(a) & (b).) A "sale on approval" is a bailment that gives the purchaser the right to use and the option to purchase after a reasonable period of time.

Comment 1 to Uniform Commercial Code section 2-326 elaborates, noting that the types of transaction governed by the section are "strongly delineated in practice and in general understanding," further providing, "Both a 'sale on approval' and a 'sale or return' should be distinguished from other types of transactions with which they frequently have been confused. A 'sale on approval,' sometimes also called a sale 'on trial' or 'on satisfaction,' deals with a contract under which the seller undertakes a risk in order to satisfy its prospective buyer with the appearance or performance of the goods that are sold. The goods are delivered to the proposed purchaser but they remain the property of the seller until the buyer accepts them." The ordinary retail sales contract is not a bailment, and the general presumption runs against a delivery to a consumer as being a sale on approval.

One reason for distinguishing between these types of transactions involves the competing interests of the buyer's creditors and the seller. California Uniform Commercial Code section 2326, subdivision (2) provides: "Goods held on approval are not subject to the claims of the buyer's creditors until acceptance; goods held on sale or return are subject to such claims while in the buyer's possession." Under plaintiff's interpretation, then, Brawn retains an interest in any goods shipped to its customers, superior to the rights of the customers' creditors, until some time after shipment, when the customers signal their approval of the goods.

It also has been recognized that a common attribute of "sales on approval" is that the obligation to pay for the goods does not arise until the goods have been tested and approved by the buyer. In *Copy Service, Inc. v. Florida Copy Corp.*, a purchaser argued that the sale of a copy machine was a sale on approval because the seller agreed that it would adjust the copier to the customer's satisfaction or replace it with a new unit. The court rejected the argument. It reasoned that the contract's denomination as an "Equipment and Sales Contract," and its recitation that the buyer entered an order for the equipment and agreed to pay cash for it, was "wholly inconsistent with a 'sale on approval' transaction." The court contrasted the contract with another, which was entitled "Demonstration and Trial Contract," under which the purchaser was given the right to use the copier in its business without any obligation to purchase—a transaction the court found to be a "classic embodiment of 'sale on approval.'" In *Buffalo Arms, Inc. v. Remler Co.*, the contract was for a sale of equipment on approval where the buyer did not pay for the equipment before, or upon, delivery, and the parties agreed that if, after the end of a 30-day trial period, the buyer decided against purchase, it would return the goods to the seller at no charge to the buyer. In *Imex Intern., Inc. v. Wires EL* the court suggested that a "sale on approval" contemplates a transaction allowing the buyer to inspect or test the goods after delivery, before becoming obligated to pay. Brawn's customers paid for their orders before they were shipped and before inspecting them, although they became entitled to a refund of the purchase price if they later decided to return the goods.

While we are not prepared to say that a sale on approval never can occur when the buyer pays for the goods before shipment, we think that for such a purchase to be a sale on approval there must be some provision or objective fact demonstrating an intent that, notwithstanding that the buyer has paid for the goods, they do not "belong" to the buyer until the buyer approves them, so that the seller's rights in the goods are superior to the rights of the buyer's creditors until the approval period has passed. That Brawn, or any other retailer, permits a customer to return goods for a refund is a benefit to the customer, but does not in and of itself suggest that the parties intended the seller to retain an interest in the goods until sometime after they are delivered to the customer, and does not convert a routine sale with a right to return into a sale on approval.

Conclusion

The judgment is reversed. The order awarding litigation expenses and attorney fees is reversed. Brawn is awarded its costs on appeal.

Questions

1. How is the risk of loss apportioned under the California UCC?
2. How does the court justify a sale on approval theory when the item is paid for prior to shipment?
3. Distinguish between a sale on approval and a sale or return.

Demarco California Fabrics, Inc. v. Nygard International, Ltd.
1990 U.S. Dist. LEXIS 3842 (S.D. N.Y. 1990)

DeMarco, a New York corporation, is a converter of textile fabrics. Nygard, a Canadian corporation, manufactures women's apparel. On or about May 11, 1989, Nygard ordered certain fabric from DeMarco by telephone. Nygard memorialized the order with a purchase order sent to DeMarco on or about May 15, 1989. In response to Nygard's purchase order, DeMarco immediately sent a sales confirmation form to Nygard. However, DeMarco did not sign Nygard's purchase order, and Nygard did not sign DeMarco's sales confirmation. On or about June 15, 1989, Nygard placed another order for DeMarco's fabric by mailing a second purchase order to DeMarco. DeMarco responded to Nygard's second purchase order by forwarding a second sales confirmation to Nygard. Again, neither party signed the other's form. It appears that DeMarco did deliver its fabric to Nygard, and Nygard did accept the fabric.

Nygard now alleges that the fabric it purchased from DeMarco was delivered late and was of unacceptable quality. Nygard withheld payment for the fabric due to these alleged defects. In addition, Nygard claims that it suffered damages of approximately $200,000 because of DeMarco's alleged breach of contract. DeMarco maintains that it fully performed all its obligations for the sale and delivery of the fabric ordered by Nygard, and seeks payment from Nygard for the merchandise.

DeMarco argues that arbitration is required in the instant case due to a provision included in the sales confirmation form which it sent to Nygard. The provision provides that, "[a]ll controversies arising out of, or relating to this contract, or any modification thereof, shall be settled by arbitration in the City of New York under the Rules of the General Arbitration Council of the Textile Industry." Far from being "prominently displayed" on the sales confirmation as DeMarco asserts, the arbitration provision is the smallest type on the printed, single-page form. The clause is clearly a "boilerplate provision."

Nygard, on the other hand, claims that the parties have not agreed to resolve their contractual disputes by arbitration. Nygard's purchase orders set forth, in the same size print as DeMarco's arbitration clause, a provision for settling disputes which arise concerning the agreement. Nygard's provision states that, "[i]n the event of a dispute the Seller and the Buyer consent to the exclusive jurisdiction of the Manitoba Court of Queen's Bench. . . . [I]n the event of any proceedings commenced by the parties, or if the parties agree to arbitrate any dispute, all such proceedings shall be initiated and conducted at Winnipeg, Manitoba, Canada." Nygard alleges that the above provision clearly demonstrates its intent not to arbitrate disputes arising under the purchase orders.

The Court's decision in the instant case turns on whether an arbitration agreement is to be inferred in the contract between the parties. For the reasons stated below, the Court grants Nygard's motion to stay arbitration.

Discussion

The parties' exchange of purchase orders and sales confirmations typifies the historic "battle of forms," which has received much attention in past court decisions. Apparently, the parties concur that an agreement was reached for the sale of DeMarco's fabric to Nygard. However, no memorial or contract embodying the agreement was properly executed. Absent such a memorial or contract, determining specific terms of the agreement depends upon the contractual intention of the parties, as construed under principles of New York contract law.

Section 2-207 of New York's Uniform Commercial Code provides the statutory rule to determine if additional terms included in a written confirmation are to become part of the parties' agreement. The New York Court of Appeals has held that the addition of an arbitration clause materially alters the parties' agreement. Thus, in New York, the well-settled rule is that "the parties to a commercial transaction 'will not be held to have chosen arbitration as the forum for the resolution of their disputes in the absence of an express, unequivocal agreement to that effect.'"

Under these principles of contract law, the parties have not agreed to arbitrate their disputes concerning the contract. DeMarco's sales confirmation form does include an arbitration clause. Nygard's purchase order, on the other hand, states that disputes will be resolved in Canadian court, unless the parties have otherwise agreed to arbitrate. No such agreement to arbitrate was reached by the parties. As provision for arbitration is "clearly a proposed additional term" to the parties' agreement which "materially alters" the agreement in the context of the battle of the forms, N.Y.U.C.C. §2-207(2) mandates that the provision not be included in the terms of the contract. The Court declines to compel arbitration where no arbitration agreement has been entered into under the clear rules of contract law.

DeMarco asserts that arbitration is required when a party fails to object within a reasonable time to the inclusion of an arbitration clause in a printed sales agreement. See *Imptex Int'l Corp. v. Lorprint Inc.*; *Lehigh Valley Industries, Inc. v. Armtex, Inc.* The rule of law put forward by DeMarco is not applicable in the context of the battle of the forms. In Imptex Int'l Corp., the parties entered into a sales contract through a broker. Both the broker's confirmation and the seller's sales confirmation contained arbitration clauses, yet the buyer claimed that since it had not signed the seller's or the broker's forms, there was no binding arbitration agreement. In *Lehigh Valley*, a case decided before *Matter of Marlene Indus. Co.*, the seller sent a signed contract containing an arbitration clause. The buyer did not object to the seller's contract, did not respond with a contract of its own, accepted goods under the contract, and ordered further goods referring to the seller's contract by number. The court held that the buyer's conduct, viewed in light of the common use of arbitration in the textile industry, waived his right to object to arbitration.

Neither of these cases involved a battle of the forms, and neither invoked N.Y.U.C.C. §2-207. In any case, Nygard did object to DeMarco's inclusion of an arbitration clause by returning a form which explicitly stated that disputes would be resolved in a Canadian court unless an agreement to arbitrate had been reached. Though the holding Matter of Marlene Indus. Co. has indeed been narrowed over the past decade, it is still the rule of law in battle of the forms cases. In recent years, courts have explicitly acknowledged this fact.

The Court recognizes the strong federal policy supporting arbitration articulated in recent cases. However, the federal policy favoring arbitration is most applicable in determining the scope of arbitration agreements, rather than whether an arbitration agreement actually exists. Mandating arbitration in this case will deprive Nygard of its "normal rights under the procedural and substantive law of the State, and it would be unfair to infer such a significant waiver on the basis of anything less than a clear indication of intent."

Conclusion

The parties have not agreed to arbitrate disputes which arise under their commercial agreement. Accordingly, defendant's motion to stay arbitration is granted.

Questions

1. How does the inclusion of an arbitration provision affect the battle of the forms?
2. What is the effect of a long relationship between the parties on the application of the battle of the forms?
3. What is your opinion of this decision?

Suggested Case References

1. For a discussion of the difference between an implied warranty of merchantability and an implied warranty of fitness for a particular use, read *Crysco Oilfield Services Inc. v. Hutchison-Hayes International Inc.*, 913 F.2d 850 (10th Cir. 1990).
2. A security agreement specified that the debtor's collateral could be his inventory of hogs, but it did not specifically state that it would include after-acquired property. Does this failure to specify after-acquired property destroy the creditor's ability to have a floating lien? *Coats State Bank v. Grey*, 902 F.2d 1479 (10th Cir. 1990).
3. To see how courts grappled with the concept of a lease versus a sale prior to the enactment of UCC II-A, read *Matka v. Tolland County Times*, 1993 Conn. Super. LEXIS 671 (1993).
4. If equipment is leased only for one day, do the provisions of the UCC still apply? See what the court said in *Kebish v. Thomas Equip.*, 541 Pa. 20, 660 A.2d 38 (1995).
5. To distinguish between honesty in fact and reasonable commercial standards, read *Sherrock v. Commercial Credit Corp.*, 290 A.2d 648 (Del. 1972).

Ethical Considerations

The ABA rules require that an attorney, and those working for the attorney, be truthful in all statements made by the law office to third persons. Rule 4.1. This means that, when assisting a client in drafting warranties, or any other document, UCC based or otherwise, the law office must be extremely careful not to include promises that the office knows are false, misleading, or incapable of being fulfilled.

Quick Quiz

Answer TRUE or FALSE. (Answers can be found in Appendix C on page 414.)

1. The Uniform Commercial Code supersedes state law.
2. The Uniform Commercial Code is designed to be strictly construed.
3. To enforce a security agreement, there must be attachment.
4. Collateral is property used to secure a debt.
5. Real estate and fixtures are covered by the secured transaction provisions of the UCC.

9 Third Party Contracts

Learning Objectives

After studying this chapter you will be able to:

- List the different types of third party contracts
- Discuss third party creditor beneficiary contracts
- Discuss third party donee beneficiary contracts
- Distinguish between an intended and an incidental beneficiary
- Define a contractual assignment
- Discuss the effect of an assignment on the original contracting parties
- Indicate how a gratuitous assignment may become irrevocable
- Differentiate between an assignment and a novation
- Distinguish a delegation from an assignment
- Explain the effect of the UCC on third party contracts

CHAPTER OVERVIEW

Typically, when a person enters into a contractual agreement, she expects to perform or deliver the consideration she has promised and to receive the consideration the other contracting party has promised her. Although this is the most usual contractual arrangement, there are situations in which the person who actually entered into the contract does not receive the promised consideration or does not perform her contractual promises herself.

One form of contract in which the promisee does not receive or expect to receive the bargained-for consideration is known as a third party beneficiary contract. In this contractual arrangement, the parties do not intend to contract to benefit themselves but intend to benefit some outside third person. All of the general contract rules and provisions still apply. The only difference between this and what would be considered the more usual contractual situation is that one of the parties to the contract agrees to convey the consideration not to the other contracting party, but to someone the other contracting party has designated when the contract was formed. In other words, the promisor conveys the consideration not to the promisee, but to a third party who, as a consequence, is benefiting from the contractual agreement.

If, in a similar situation, one party to the contract wishes, after the contract was formed, to have the consideration given not to her but to some third person, she may do so under certain circumstances. In this situation, known as an assignment, the promisor agrees, after formation of the contract, to convey the consideration not to the promisee but to the promisee's designee. Because this changes the promisor's contractual obligations, this type of arrangement may only be effectuated if the promisor agrees.

Finally, there are times when the promisor needs or desires assistance in fulfilling his contractual promise. Although a person may not relinquish his contractual obligation without being in default, in most instances a promisor may have some third person assist him in completing his promise. This situation is known as a delegation. Unlike the first two situations indicated above, this third person, the promisor's helper, receives no benefit from the contract itself.

When drafting and interpreting contract provisions, it is important to keep the above in mind. There are special contractual clauses that create or permit these arrangements, and these clauses become determinative of the contracting parties' rights and obligations under the contract. In each type of situation, the outside party may be entitled to some equitable relief for enforcement of the contract, even though he is not a contracting party himself.

Third Party Beneficiary Contracts: Generally

Third party beneficiary contracts are agreements in which the original intent of one of the contracting parties, when entering into the contractual arrangement, is to have the promised-for consideration pass not to her, but to some outside person. Generally, there are two reasons why a contracting party would desire this type of arrangement, and consequently, third party beneficiary contracts are divided into two categories.

The first category is a **third party creditor beneficiary** contract. In this type of third party contract, the purpose of the promisee's agreement is to extinguish a debt or obligation owed to some third person. In other words, the promisee was already obligated to the third person, his creditor, and the purpose for which he entered into the contract was to receive some consideration that would terminate his debt to the creditor.

EXAMPLE:

Last month Peter had extraordinary expenses and didn't have enough money to pay his rent. Wendy loaned Peter $500 to help him meet his expenses, and he promised to repay the loan this month with interest. Now, Peter has met all his regular expenses but doesn't have the money to repay the loan. To repay Wendy, Peter agrees to sell his CD player to Ralph, and Peter asks Ralph to give the money for the CD player to Wendy. Wendy agrees. This is a third party creditor beneficiary contract. The reason Peter entered into the sales contract with Ralph was to repay his debt to Wendy. Wendy was the person Peter intended to benefit from his contract with Ralph.

The second category of third party beneficiary contracts is a **third party donee beneficiary** contract. As the name might indicate, the purpose of this contract is to confer a gift on a third person. The promisee of the contract is under no preexisting obligation to the third person but wishes to give the third person a present. Under current legal terminology, both the creditor and donee beneficiaries are called **intended beneficiaries**.

EXAMPLE:

Peter suddenly comes into some money. He is still grateful to Wendy for helping him out when he had financial difficulties. Even though his debt to Wendy is now extinguished, he feels that he would like to do something nice for her. While watching a shopping channel on television, Peter sees a bracelet he thinks Wendy would like. He calls the station and orders the bracelet, telling the vendor that the bracelet is a gift. He directs the vendor to send the bracelet to Wendy and to bill him. This is a third party donee beneficiary contract. The reason Peter entered into the contract with the television vendor was to convey a gift to Wendy. He owed no debt, and he never intended the bracelet for himself.

The most important aspect of a third party beneficiary contract is the intent of the parties when the contract is formed. For the contract to be considered a third party beneficiary contract, it must be evidenced that the purpose of the contract is to benefit a person not a party to the contractual agreement. If the desire to benefit some outside person comes about after the contract already exists, it is not a third party beneficiary contract (but an assignment, which will be discussed later).

Bear in mind the specific terminology that is being used in a third party beneficiary contract. In every contractual situation, there must be a mutuality of consideration; in all bilateral contracts each party to the contract is both a promisor and a promisee. He is a promisor for the consideration he promises to convey, and a promisee for the consideration the other party promises to give him. When describing third party beneficiary contracts, the term **promisee** designates the person who entered the contract intending to benefit the third person. He is expecting to have the consideration he was promised conveyed to the outsider. **Promisor** describes the party conveying the consideration to the third person, because of the promisee's wishes and intent when contracting. This transfer to the third person is part of the promise the promisor makes when entering into the contract.

EXAMPLE:

In the examples discussed above with Peter, Wendy, Ralph, and the shopping channel, in both instances the contract was between Peter and either Ralph or the vendor. In the first instance, Peter promised to convey his CD player to Ralph, and Ralph promised to convey the purchase price of the CD player to Wendy. Peter is the promisee for the receipt of the money, and Ralph is the promisor who has agreed to convey the cash to Wendy as part of his contractual promise to Peter. In the second instance, Peter promised to pay for the bracelet that the vendor promised to convey to Wendy. Peter is the promisor for payment, and the promisee for the receipt of the merchandise. The shopping channel is the promisee of Peter's payment, and the promisor for sending the jewelry. In each instance, Wendy, the third party, is receiving the consideration from Peter's promisors.

In a third party beneficiary contract, the third party, although not a contracting party, is given certain rights with respect to the contract. Legally, the beneficiary may be able to bring the contracting parties into court to have the contract enforced in his favor. This is true even though the beneficiary is neither a party to the agreement nor has any enforceable obligation with respect to the agreement. To understand the rights and obligations that attach to the two categories of third party beneficiary contracts, each will be discussed separately.

When analyzing the enforceable rights of a third party beneficiary, it is important to note that enforceable rights attach only to third persons intended primarily to benefit from the contract. Should a third person benefit secondarily from the contract, i.e., his benefit was not the intent of the contract, that person is known as an **incidental beneficiary** and has no enforceable rights. For example, in the situation given above, the shipper the shopping channel uses to send its merchandise benefits from the channel's sales contract, but this benefit is totally incidental to the contract itself.

Third Party Creditor Beneficiary Contracts

The starting point for any discussion of a third party creditor beneficiary contract is the determination that the promisee owes some debt to a third person. The debt must be in existence prior to the third party contract being formed. Remember, the purpose of a third party creditor beneficiary contract is to extinguish a debt owed to a third person, so that debt must in fact exist.

Because the contract is formed to benefit this creditor, the creditor is considered to be a **real party in interest.** He becomes the focal point of the central contract between the debtor and the promisor. As a real party in interest, he may be entitled to enforce the contract if the promisor does not fulfill his contractual obligation.

To have enforceable rights, it must first be demonstrated that those rights exist. This means that the creditor must show that his rights have **vested** (become enforceable in a court of law). For a third party creditor beneficiary, the rights in the contract vest as soon as he detrimentally relies on the contract's existence.

What constitutes "detrimental reliance"? As discussed previously, detrimental reliance usually means some economic loss suffered in reliance on the promise. For creditor beneficiaries, this detrimental reliance is simply assumed to be his willingness to accept payment from the promisor. Because the debt must exist as a prerequisite to the formation of a third party creditor beneficiary contract, the creditor can always go to court to enforce the debt against the debtor/promisee. Because the creditor is forestalling taking that action in reliance on the contract between the debtor and the promisor, just as with an accord and satisfaction, it is deemed sufficient to vest his rights in the third party contract. Also, as soon as the intended beneficiary is aware of the contract, or institutes a suit to enforce it, the beneficiary's rights are deemed vested.

 EXAMPLE:

Pedro enrolls in his city's Paralegal Institute. Pedro doesn't have the money for the tuition but arranges for a student loan from a local bank at the school's suggestion. The loan contract is a third party creditor beneficiary contract, entered into between Pedro and the bank for the purpose of paying Pedro's debt to the Institute. The Institute's willingness to take payment from the bank on Pedro's behalf constitutes its reliance on the contract, and its rights have vested.

Once the third party creditor beneficiary's rights have vested, she has enforceable rights. This means that she may sue the promisor of the contract if the promisor fails to convey the consideration. Because the creditor is the real party in interest, and the promisor has agreed to convey the consideration to her, failure to fulfill this promise is a breach of contract that the real party in interest can sue to have remedied.

 EXAMPLE:

In the example given above with Peter, Wendy, and Ralph, if Ralph does not give Wendy the money he promised in his contract with Peter, Wendy can take Ralph to court. Because Ralph's promise is to convey the money to Wendy, his failure to do so is a breach. As the real party in interest, Wendy is the one whom the breach injures. Consequently, she has the right to enforce the contract against Ralph.

Should, for whatever reason, the creditor fail to get satisfaction from the promisor, he can always sue the promisee. Why? Because the promisee is still the debtor of the third party, and until that debt is extinguished he remains liable on the original obligation.

 EXAMPLE:

Wendy discovers that Ralph is insolvent. Because Peter still owes her $500 plus interest, she can enforce her claim directly against Peter because the third party contract has not extinguished his debt.

Of course, the creditor is limited to just one recovery. She cannot sue both the debtor and the promisor and recover from both. Recovery from one excuses the other.

If the creditor attempts to enforce his rights under the contract, the promisor can defend himself by asserting any defense he might have against the debtor/promisee. Because it is the contract between the debtor/promisee and the promisor that is in question, any defense that would render the contract unenforceable relieves the promisor of any obligation to the creditor.

EXAMPLES:

1. When Wendy sues Ralph for the purchase price of the CD player, Ralph can defend by asserting that Peter never gave him the CD player, or that the CD player delivered was not the one promised. In each instance, Ralph is claiming that Peter is in default, and Peter's default relieves Ralph of his contractual obligations to Peter. Because this obligation was to convey money to Wendy, if Ralph prevails, he is under no obligation to Wendy.

2. Pedro starts classes, but the Institute has not received the tuition from the bank. The Institute attempts to enforce the loan contract between Pedro and the bank. The bank defends by proving that its obligation was conditioned on Pedro's submitting proof of attendance, which he has failed to do. Consequently, the bank is not obligated under its loan agreement, and the Institute must look to Pedro directly for the tuition.

In addition to the third party creditor beneficiary having enforceable rights, the contracting parties themselves always have enforceable rights against each other. The promisee and the promisor of the contract can sue each other to have the contract enforced.

EXAMPLE:

When Wendy attempts to collect from Peter, Peter discovers that Ralph has not lived up to his obligation. Provided that Peter did in fact convey to Ralph the CD player he promised, Peter can sue Ralph to have the contract enforced because he, Peter, is a contracting party.

To summarize, in a third party creditor beneficiary contract, the third party creditor beneficiary has vested, enforceable rights in the contract once he has detrimentally relied on the contract. This detrimental reliance can simply take the form of agreeing to accept payment from the promisor rather than suing the debtor for payment. Once these rights have vested, the creditor beneficiary can sue the promisor of the contract to have these rights enforced. The promisor can defend by asserting any claim he may have against the promisee. The creditor may also sue the debtor on the original obligation if he receives no satisfaction from the promisor. Finally, the promisor and promisee of the contract can sue each other to have the contract provisions enforced.

Third Party Donee Beneficiary Contracts

The major difference between third party creditor beneficiary and third party donee beneficiary contracts is the element of the underlying debt. To have a creditor beneficiary contract, it must be shown that a debt exists between the promisee and the creditor. To have a donee beneficiary contract, it must be shown that the promisee intended to confer a gift on the donee (she is not repaying a debt).

Because the purpose of the contract is to convey a gift to the donee, the donee beneficiary is considered to be the real party in interest to the contract. As the real party in interest, she may have enforceable rights with respect to the contract once it is established that those rights have vested. For a third party donee beneficiary, the rights in the contract vest once she learns of the existence of the contract. No detrimental reliance is necessary.

EXAMPLE:

In the example given above with Wendy, Peter, and the shopping channel, when Peter calls Wendy to tell her that she should expect a bracelet that he has bought for her, her rights have vested. When two weeks pass without the bracelet arriving, Wendy can call the vendor to complain and to find out when the bracelet will arrive.

Once the donee beneficiary's rights have vested, she can sue the promisor of the contract to have the promise enforced. Just as with third party creditor beneficiary contracts, the promisor can defend against claims of the third party donee by asserting any defenses he would have against the promise of the contract.

EXAMPLES:

1. Several weeks pass, and Wendy still hasn't received the bracelet. She sues the shopping channel to have the contract enforced. The vendor can defend by proving that Peter attempted to pay for the bracelet with a check that bounced. Because Peter breached his promise to the shopping channel, the vendor is relieved of its contractual obligations.

2. Babs takes out a life insurance policy on her life with Connecticut Life, Inc., and names her best friend, Abdul, as the beneficiary. Babs is lost at sea, and Abdul claims the insurance. The company

can defend by saying that Babs failed to make the premium payments, or that there is no proof that Babs is actually dead.

Unlike a third party creditor beneficiary, because there is no obligation between the donee and the promisee, the donee beneficiary, under contract law, cannot sue the donor/promisee for enforcement of the contract. A promise to give a gift, unless a charitable donation, is not enforceable under contract law. However, if the donee can show that she detrimentally relied on the promised gift, under property law concepts, she may be able to recover against the donor.

 EXAMPLE:

When Peter tells Wendy about the bracelet, Wendy, in expectation of its arrival, buys a dress especially designed to show off the jewelry. When the bracelet doesn't arrive, Wendy may be able to recover the cost of the dress from Peter if she can prove that she only purchased it in expectation of the bracelet, and without the bracelet she has no use for the dress. Remember, the claim is based on property law concepts, and recovery may be permitted under the court's equitable jurisdiction to prevent injustice. It is not a contract case.

Of course, just as with creditor beneficiary contracts, the promisor and promisee of the contract can always sue each other for enforcement of the contract provisions.

 EXAMPLE:

When Peter finds out the shopping channel failed to send the bracelet to Wendy, he can sue the vendor directly. If Peter can show a cancelled check for payment, the vendor's original defense would fail, and it would have to ship out the bracelet.

In summary, a third party donee beneficiary contract is created for the purpose of conveying a gift to the third party. The donee has vested rights in the contract once she learns of its existence. Once the rights have vested, the donee can sue the promisor to have the contract enforced. Under contract law, the donee has no enforceable rights against the promisee (there is no consideration for a gift). The promisor and promisee of the contract can sue each other to have the contract enforced.

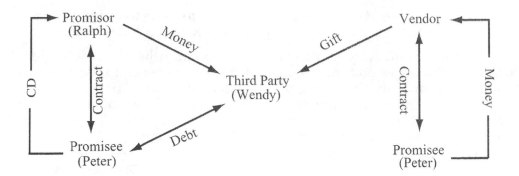

Creditor Beneficiary	*Donee Beneficiary*
Created to extinguish debt	Created to confer gift
Rights vest with detrimental reliance*	Rights vest on knowledge*
Can sue promisor or promisee	Can sue promisor only
Promisor/promisee can defend by asserting any claim he has against the other contracting party	Promisor can defend by asserting any claim he has against promise

   * With respect to the vesting of third party beneficiary rights, some courts have adopted the approach that a third party beneficiary's rights vest, regardless of whether he is a creditor or donee beneficiary, only if he assents to the contract, sues to have it enforced, or shows detrimental reliance. The standard followed by each jurisdiction should be specifically checked.

Assignment

   An **assignment** is the transfer of a promisee's rights under an existing contract. At first blush, it appears to be very similar to third party beneficiary contracts. Although they are similar, there are two important differences between assignments and third party beneficiary contracts:

   1. Assignments come into existence *after* the original contract is created. The benefit to the third party is not the reason the contract was formed; it is an afterthought.
   2. Because assignments are created *after* the original contract, a promisee may not assign his rights without the consent, express or implied, of the promisor.

Creating the Assignment

   An assignment may be oral or written, subject to requirements of the Statute of Frauds. If the basic contract must be in writing, so must the assignment.

EXAMPLE:

Sharona and Vince enter into a written contract for the sale of Vince's house. After the contract is signed, Vince wants to transfer his right to receive the purchase price to his son. The contract permits assignments. Because the contract concerns an interest in real estate, both the contract and the assignment must be in writing.

A person may assign her rights to a contract either gratuitously or for consideration. In other words, the promisee may use the assignment to confer a gift or to fulfill an obligation under a separate contract.

 EXAMPLES:

1. In the example given above, Sharona decides to give the house as an anniversary gift to her parents. In writing, she assigns her right to receive the house's title to her parents. This is a gratuitous assignment.

2. Sharona decides that she really doesn't want Vince's house, but her friend Wilma thinks that the house is "perfect." In writing, Sharona agrees to assign to Wilma her right to the title to Vince's house in consideration of Wilma giving Sharona $1,000. This is an example of an assignment for consideration. Sharona is transferring her rights under her contract with Vince to fulfill her promise under her contract with Wilma.

The **assignor,** the person who is transferring the contract right, may also make a partial assignment of rights to the **assignee** (the transferee of the rights). An assignment need not be an all-or-nothing situation.

 EXAMPLE:

Fabio sold his tape deck to Tom for $30. Before he receives payment, Fabio assigns $15 to Leon to extinguish a debt he owes to Leon. The assignment is valid, even though it transferred only part of Fabio's rights.

However, not all contracts are capable of being assigned. There can be no assignment if the rights assigned consist of personal services or are dependent on the personal confidence or circumstances of the recipient.

EXAMPLES:

1. Pavarotti has signed a contract with the New York Metropolitan Opera to perform *Pagliacci.* The Met cannot transfer its rights to the Omaha Civic Opera Company to have Pavarotti sing. Although Pavarotti may want to sing for the Met, he may not want to travel to Omaha. A person cannot be forced to perform for someone for whom he does not want to perform.

2. Sid purchases a health insurance policy from Connecticut Insurance, Inc. He cannot assign his contract's rights to Paul. The insurance company sold Sid the policy based on Sid's health and personal history; the same policy and premiums may not apply to someone with Paul's health and history. Because the insurance company's performance is dependent on the confidence it has in Sid's health, Sid cannot assign.

As with third party beneficiary contracts, if the assignment is valid, the assignee becomes the real party in interest and has enforceable rights against the promisor.

EXAMPLE:

In the situation given above, when Wilma gives Sharona $1,000 for Sharona's rights to receive title to Vince's house, should Vince fail to transfer the title after payment of the purchase price, Wilma can take Vince to court to have the right enforced. Wilma is the real party in interest, the person who is entitled to receive the property.

Consent of the Promisor

Because the assignment comes into existence after the contract is formed, it is usually necessary to get the consent of the promisor because conveying the consideration to a third person was not what he agreed to under the contract. The assignment has the effect of changing the promisor's contractual obligation, and this can only be done with his consent.

Under the law, most contracts are assignable, subject to the exceptions noted above. However, if the effect of the assignment would be to *materially* change the promisor's obligation or duty, the promisor's consent must be specifically given. The consent may take the form of a clause in the contract in which the promisor agrees to an assignment. This clause can also specify the terms on which the promisor's consent is given.

EXAMPLE:

Rhoda leases an apartment from Brenda. In the lease, Brenda agrees that Rhoda may assign her rights to occupy the apartment, provided that written notice be given to Brenda at least 30 days prior to the assignee taking occupancy, and further provided that Brenda meets the assignee prior to the assignment taking effect. This clause gives Brenda's consent prospectively, provided certain conditions precedent are met. (See Chapter 7.)

What is considered a "material" change in the promisor's duty? The term is not specifically defined but is determined on a case-by-case basis. As long as the assignment does not create an unnecessary burden on the promisor, it most probably will not be considered material.

EXAMPLE:

In the earlier example, when Peter purchased a bracelet from a television shopping channel as a gift for Wendy, suppose Peter and Wendy have a falling out before the bracelet is mailed and before Wendy is told about the gift. Peter calls the vendor and tells the vendor to send the bracelet to Peter's mother instead of to Wendy. This is an assignment of Peter's right to receive the bracelet. Because the cost of shipping was already paid for, it makes no difference to the vendor who the recipient is, and so this would not materially affect its obligations. However, if Peter's mother lived in a foreign country that had stringent requirements regarding importing jewelry, and in order to ship the bracelet the vendor would have to fill out many custom forms, shipping documents, and pay extra mailing fees, Peter could not make the assignment without the vendor's consent. This assignment to Mom creates a wholly different obligation on the part of the seller.

Under general contract law principles, most contracts are assignable if they are silent on the point. However, the contract may state affirmatively that its rights may not be assigned. Such a "nonassignment clause" is a common provision in many contracts. This clause is usually inserted to protect the contracting parties. With this clause, each party to the contract knows exactly to whom he must perform his promise. There are no late surprises.

Effect of Assignment

The effect of an assignment is to transfer the assignor's rights to the assignee. The assignee thereby becomes a real party in interest with enforceable rights against the promisor.

If the assignor makes the assignment for consideration, as in the example of Sharona assigning her rights to Vince's house to Wilma for $1,000, the assignment is irrevocable. When the promisor conveys the consideration to the assignee, he is relieved of all his obligations under the original contract. However, if he conveys the consideration to anyone other than the assignee, he does so at his own risk.

EXAMPLE:

After Sharona assigns her rights to Wilma, she informs Vince of the assignment. When Vince transfers the title to Wilma, he has fulfilled his contractual obligation to Sharona. Should Vince, however, transfer title to Sharona instead of Wilma, Wilma can take him into court. His obligation, after the assignment to which he has agreed, is to convey title to Wilma and to no one else.

On the other hand, if the assignment is gratuitous, the assignor may revoke, thereby cancelling the assignee's rights. Nevertheless, there are five situations in which a gratuitous assignment may become irrevocable:

1. delivery of a token chose;
2. writing;
3. estoppel;
4. performance; and
5. novation.

Delivery of a Token Chose.   A token chose is merely something symbolic of the assignment. Although it may not have much monetary value, its existence is considered sufficient to make a gratuitous assignment irrevocable.

EXAMPLE:

When Peter's mother hears about the bracelet Peter is having sent to her, she sends him a rose to commemorate the occasion. The rose is a token chose, and the assignment is irrevocable.

Writing.   Simply putting the assignment in writing, for historical legal reasons, makes the gratuitous assignment irrevocable.

EXAMPLE:

Peter writes to his mother telling her of the bracelet. The writing makes the assignment irrevocable.

Estoppel.   If the assignee is attempting to assert a claim of estoppel because the assignment is a gift, the donee/assignee must show detrimental reliance on the promise to make it irrevocable.

EXAMPLE:

When Peter's mother hears about the bracelet, she buys a dress to show off the jewelry. This may create detrimental reliance that would bar, or estop, Peter from changing his mind.

Performance.   It should be obvious that if the promisor has already performed and conveyed the consideration to the assignee before the assignor revokes, the assignment becomes irrevocable.

Novation.   A novation is a substitution of parties in a contract; it is an interesting subset of assignments. Generally, assignments only transfer rights; they never transfer contractual obligations. In a novation, the original party to the contract is substituted by a third person, and the third person not only receives the benefits of the transferor but also assumes all of the transferor's obligations. The contract, after the novation, reads as though the original contracting party never existed.

EXAMPLE:

When Sharona decides that she does not want to purchase Vince's house, she asks to novate her contract to Wilma. Vince agrees, and now the contract reads as though it always was a contract for the sale of Vince's house to Wilma. Sharona's rights and obligations are totally transferred to Wilma.

Novations are very rare because the other party to the contract must agree to the novation. Whereas a person may be willing to contract with one person, she may not have the same reliance with someone else. With few exceptions, a person cannot be forced to enter into a contractual agreement with someone with whom she does not want to contract. Therefore, there must be a clause in the contract specifying the novation. Typically, these clauses indicate specific conditions that must be met before the other contracting party's assent to the substitution will be given.

Multiple Assignees

If an assignor assigns his rights to more than one assignee, a problem arises with respect to which assignee is entitled to the transferred rights.

The general rule is that, with successive assignees, the first in time prevails, unless a later assignee has stronger equities (a greater equitable claim to the consideration).

EXAMPLE:

Lynn sells her car to Edward for $900. On Monday, Lynn assigns her right to receive the money to her mother as a birthday gift. The next day, Lynn buys Joan's pearl necklace and, instead of giving Joan a check, Lynn assigns to Joan her right to receive the $900 from Edward. When Mom and Joan both claim the money, the money will go to Joan. Even though Joan is a later assignee, because she gave consideration for the assignment, she has the greater equity. Also, because the first assignment is gratuitous it may be revoked. Making the second assignment acts as a revocation of the first, revocable, assignment.

Take note that under the Uniform Commercial Code (UCC), assignees of certain types of contracts, specifically those involving a security interest, are required to file a notice of their claims with various county and state offices. This filing constitutes notice to all subsequent assignees that the property in question has been previously assigned and cuts off the rights of later assignees. For a complete discussion of UCC filing requirements, see Chapter 8, The Uniform Commercial Code, and Chapter 12, Drafting Simple Contracts.

An assignment is only a transference of the assignor's contractual rights. The assignor is still liable for her performance as promised under the contract. A person cannot assign obligations; she may only assign rights.

Delegation

Unlike third party beneficiary contracts and assignments, a **delegation** does not involve a transfer of rights. In a delegation, the promisor of a contract authorizes another person to perform some duty owed by the promisor under the contract. In other words, the promisor delegates someone to assist him in fulfilling his contractual obligations. The delegated person has absolutely no rights under the contract, unlike third party beneficiaries or assignees, nor does she have any obligations under the contract. The delegate's only obligation is to the promisor, and the promisor remains totally liable under the contract.

EXAMPLE:

Rosario is a paralegal working for attorney Janet. Janet's firm has accepted a case from a client, and to assist her Janet has given Rosario several tasks to perform. The firm is the promisor under the contract with the client, and Rosario and Janet are delegates. The firm remains liable to the client, and Rosario is responsible to Janet.

Generally, all nonpersonal duties owed under a contract may be delegated. If the duty does not involve the personal services of the promisor, unless otherwise denied under the contract, the promisor may delegate. However, it is important to remember that the promisor *always* remains liable under the contract if the delegate fails to perform.

EXAMPLES:

1. Mel has a contract with Warner Brothers to play a leading role in a new film. After the contract is signed, Mel realizes that he has another commitment. He delegates his responsibilities to Paul. This is invalid. The contract between Mel and Warner Brothers involves personal services and consequently may not be delegated.

2. In the situation with Rosario and Janet, Janet tells Rosario to complete a summons and complaint and to file them with the appropriate court. Rosario forgets, and the statute of limitations runs, barring the action. The firm is the one responsible to the client, and it may be charged with malfeasance. As the promisor, the firm remains personally liable for the promised performance under the contract. (This is not a contract for personal services because these types of agreements assume the firm will act by delegation, unless otherwise specified in the contract.)

In summary, only rights can be assigned, and only duties can be delegated. The only obligations under a contract that may be assigned are those that do not involve personal services or confidence, and the promisor always remains liable under the contract. The delegate has no rights or obligations under the contract. Finally, a delegation may be gratuitous, as in asking a friend for assistance, or may be contractual, as with a lawyer and a paralegal.

SAMPLE CLAUSES

$\boxed{1}$

Notwithstanding anything to the contrary contained herein, X may not assign any right, or delegate any duty hereunder without the prior written consent of Y. Y may assign any right, or delegate any duty hereunder to any person or entity controlled, directly or indirectly, by it or any of its shareholders.

The above clause is an example of a contractual provision in which both parties have some rights to assign or delegate, but the contractual provision to do so is unequal. X must first obtain written approval from Y, and should X not obtain such approval, the contract with respect to X is nonassignable and nondelegable. On the other hand, Y, in the clause itself, has the automatic right to assign or delegate, but the assignee and/ or delegate is limited to certain described persons or entities. Therefore, as long as the assignee or delegate meets the definitional requirements of this provision, Y may assign or delegate without reference to X, and X must accept such action.

$\boxed{2}$ **Proxy**

The undersigned hereby constitutes and appoints X as his, her, or their proxy to cast the votes of the undersigned at all general, special, and adjourned meetings of the shareholders of Acme, Inc., from time to time and from year to year, when the undersigned is not present at any such meeting. This proxy shall be effective for one (1) year from the date hereof unless sooner revoked by written notice to the Secretary of the corporation.

Dated: /ss/ _____

The above is an example of a general proxy used by a corporation shareholder. The contract in question is the contract the shareholder has with the corporation for the purchase of the shares; voting is a right incident to the stock ownership. The shareholder is assigning his right to vote to the proxy holder. Although not specified above, the proxy may be gratuitous or may be subject to its own contractual relation between the shareholder and the proxy holder (the proxy holder paying the shareholder for the right to cast the vote). Remember, an assignment indicates a legal effect and is not necessarily determined by the words used. A proxy is an assignment, not a delegation, because it is a right of a shareholder, not a duty.

$\boxed{3}$ **Life Insurance Policy**

The _____ Life Insurance Company agrees, subject to the terms and conditions of this policy, to pay the Amount shown on page _____ to the beneficiary upon receipt at its home office of proof of the death of the insured.

The above is a clause from a whole-life insurance policy. A life insurance policy is an example of the third party donee beneficiary contract. The insured contracts with the insurance company (the promisor); the insured promises to pay the stated premiums; and the insurer, conditioned upon proof of the insured's death, promises to pay the policy amount to the beneficiary. After the insured's death, the beneficiary has enforceable rights against the insurer should the insurer fail to pay. The insurer can always defend by proving the insured failed to meet the premiums or lied about his age or physical condition, by showing that proof of death was not given, or by using any other defense against the insured's meeting the contract provisions.

CHAPTER SUMMARY

Not every party to a contract is the person who will receive the contract rights or who will perform the contractual obligations. There are several situations in which some outside individual will either reap the benefit of the contract or will perform the obligation imposed by the agreement.

A third party beneficiary contract is formed for the express purpose of benefiting some noncontracting party. This noncontracting party is intended to receive the contract right as the repayment of a debt owed to him by the promisee or as a gift to him from the promisee. In the first instance, this noncontracting party is known as a third party creditor beneficiary; in the second instance, the noncontracting party is a third party donee beneficiary. Once the contract right vests in this third person, he becomes the real party in interest and has enforceable rights against the promisor. The promisor can defend against suits instituted by the third party by asserting any defense he may have against the promisee. If the underlying contract is unenforceable, the third party beneficiary's rights are likewise incapable of enforcement. The creditor beneficiary may proceed against the promisee to enforce the original debt the promisee owed to him. Donee beneficiaries may proceed against the promisee only if the donee can prove detrimental reliance based on the third party beneficiary contract.

If the contract is already in existence when one of the parties wishes to transfer rights under the agreement, such transference of rights is known as an assignment. In an assignment, the assignee becomes the recipient of rights to a contract to which she was not an original party. Assignments can be distinguished from third party beneficiary contracts by determining the underlying purpose behind the contract's formation. If the contract was formed to benefit a third person, it is a third party beneficiary contract; if the intent to benefit a third person arose after the contract existed, it is an assignment.

Just as with a third party beneficiary, an assignee becomes a real party in interest and has enforceable rights against the promisor of the original contract. The promisor can defend by asserting any claim he may have against the assignor. The assignee's ability to proceed against the assignor is dependent on the nature of the assignment itself, gratuitous or for consideration.

If instead of assigning rights, the promisor is attempting to have a third person assist him in fulfilling his contractual obligations, then he is making a delegation. Rights may be assigned; duties may be delegated. However, unlike third party beneficiaries and assignees, the delegate never becomes a real party in interest to the contract, and the promisor remains fully liable for her own performance under the contract.

SYNOPSIS

Third party beneficiary contracts
    1. Third party creditor beneficiary contracts
        a. To extinguish existing debt
        b. Rights vest on detrimental reliance
        c. Creditor can sue promisor or promisee
        d. Promisor can defend by asserting any defense he has against promisee
    2. Third party donee beneficiary contracts
        a. To confer a gift
        b. Rights vest on knowledge of contract
        c. Donee can sue promisor
        d. Promisor can defend by asserting any defense she has against promisee
Assignment
    1. Transfer of contract right
    2. Assignee becomes real party in interest
    3. Can be gratuitous or for consideration
    4. Gratuitous assignments can be revoked unless certain situations exist
    5. Assignments for consideration are irrevocable
    6. UCC filing requirements
Delegation
    1. Having a third party assist in fulfilling contractual obligation
    2. Cannot delegate contracts based on personal services or confidence
    3. Promisor remains liable for contractual obligations

Key Terms

Assignee: transferee of contractual right
Assignment: transference of contractual right by the promisee to a third person

Assignor: transferor of contractual right
Delegation: promisor having assistance in fulfilling contractual duties
Estoppel: equitable term; barring certain actions in the interest of fairness
Incidental beneficiary: person who benefits tangentially from a contract
Intended beneficiary: third party donee or creditor beneficiary
Novation: substitution of a party to a contract; novated person takes over
       all rights and obligations under the contract
Promisee: one who receives consideration in a bilateral contract
Promisor: one who gives consideration in a bilateral contract
Real party in interest: person with enforceable contractual rights
Third party beneficiary contract: contract entered into for the purpose of
       benefiting someone not a party to the contract
Third party creditor beneficiary: person who receives the benefit of a
       contract in order to extinguish a debt owed him by the promisee
Third party donee beneficiary: person who receives the benefit of a
       contract in order to receive a gift from the promisee
Token chose: item of symbolic, rather than monetary, significance that
       makes a gratuitous assignment irrevocable
Vested: having a legally enforceable right

EXERCISES

1. How does an assignment differ from a delegation?
2. Give two examples of students being third party beneficiaries.
    Draft the clauses.
3. What factors would influence a third party beneficiary to sue the
    promisee rather than the promisor? Give examples.
4. How can you distinguish between a third party beneficiary and
    an incidental beneficiary?
5. Can a unilateral contract be a third party beneficiary contract?
    Explain.

Cases for Analysis

To exemplify the problems of interpreting third party contracts and
novations, the following case summaries are presented. *Delta Mech, Inc.
v Garden City Grp., Inc.* discusses asserting rights pursuant to such agreements, and *Bay Corrugated Container, Inc. v. Gould Electronics* highlights the
concept of a novation.

Delta Mech., Inc. v. Garden City Grp., Inc.
572 Fed. Appx. 554 (9th Cir 2014)

Rheem Manufacturing Company, American Water Heater Company,
the Bradford White Corporation, A.O. Smith Corporation, State Industries,

Inc., and Lochinvar Corporation (collectively, the "manufacturers") are manufacturers of water heaters. Delta Mechanical, Inc. ("Delta") is a plumbing company. This appeal arises out of a class action settlement between the manufacturers and the owners of defective water heaters that had been produced by the manufacturers. The settlement agreement required the manufacturers to pay authorized third-party contractors to replace or repair the defective water heaters. Delta served as one of the authorized third-party contractors. The settlement agreement set forth the claims protocol that class members were required to follow in order to obtain the replacement or repair.

While Delta received over $3,000,000 from the manufacturers for providing nearly 24,000 repairs or replacements, the manufacturers refused to reimburse Delta for approximately $500,000 because Delta's customers failed to follow the claims protocol in certain instances. Delta then filed the present action against the manufacturers. The district court granted summary judgment in favor of the manufacturers on the ground that Delta was not a third-party beneficiary of the settlement agreement under Missouri law because "any obligation assumed by [the manufacturers] was *indirect* and *conditional*." *Delta Mech., Inc. v. Garden City Grp., Inc.*, No. 2:06-CV-01095, 2012 U.S. Dist. LEXIS 3921, 2012 WL 94564, at *3-*4 (D. Ariz. Jan. 12, 2012) (emphasis in original). We reverse and remand.

While it is not entirely clear what the district judge meant by the phrase "indirect and conditional," we assume he was holding that, because Delta's right to recover was contingent on compliance with the claims protocol, it could not recover as a third-party beneficiary. In essence, the district court held that a conditional obligation was insufficient as a matter of law to confer third-party beneficiary status on Delta. 2012 U.S. Dist. LEXIS 3921, [WL] at *3. This holding is contrary to hornbook law. As Professor Corbin explains, "[m]erely attaching a condition to a promise to pay the promisee's debt or a promise to confer a gift on the third party does not affect the right of a third party any more than it would affect the right of a promisee. The condition, however, must occur to activate the right of the beneficiary just as it must occur to activate the right of a promisee." 9-46 *Corbin on Contracts* § 46.1; *see also Williston on Contracts* § 37:26 (same). The Restatement echoes both Williston and Corbin. *See Restatement (Second) of Contracts* § 303 (1981). One illustration of this principle, which is particularly apposite here, appears in comment a, as follows. "A owes C $100. B promises A to pay the debt if Dancer wins the Derby. *C is an intended beneficiary of the conditional promise.*" *Id.* at § 303 cmt. a, *Illustration 1* (emphasis added). Indeed, at oral argument, the counsel to the manufacturers conceded that the position of the Restatement (Second) likely is controlling in this case. Oral Argument at 19:30, *Delta Mech., Inc. v. Garden City Grp.*, No. 12-15285 (9th Cir. filed Feb. 10, 2012), *available at* http://www.ca9.uscourts.gov/media/view.php?pk_id=0000012356.

The primary case that the manufacturers rely on in arguing that a Missouri Court would not apply the position of the Restatement is *Stephens v. Great S. Sav. & Loan Ass'n*, 421 S.W.2d 332 (Mo. Ct. App. 1967). A careful reading of *Stephens* plainly supports the conclusion that Delta was a third-party beneficiary of the settlement agreement. Indeed, in the course of the opinion, the Missouri Court of Appeals cited the following example of what would and would not constitute an enforceable third-party beneficiary agreement: "B promises A for sufficient consideration to pay whatever debts A may incur in a certain undertaking. A incurs in the undertaking debts to C, D and E. If, on a fair interpretation of B's promise, the amount of the debts is to be paid by B to C, D and E, they are creditor beneficiaries; if the money is to be paid to A in order that he may be provided with money to pay C, D and E, they are at most incidental beneficiaries." *Stephens*, 421 S.W.2d at 336 (quoting *Restatement (First) of Contracts § 133*, Illustration 9 (1932)). The present case is one that fits neatly into the example of what would constitute an enforceable third-party beneficiary agreement. In this case, the manufacturers promised to pay Delta directly for the debt incurred by the customers on the condition that the claims protocol was followed. The manufacturers did not promise to provide the customers with money to pay Delta or the other approved plumbers for services that they had rendered under the settlement agreement.

Because the district court's decision rested solely on the ground that Delta was not a third-party beneficiary, it did not address the issue of whether Delta and its customers complied with the claims protocol for the disputed claims. Accordingly, we vacate the district court's ruling and remand to the district court for proceedings consistent with this disposition. Each side shall bear its own costs on appeal.

VACATED AND REMANDED.

Questions

1. Why was Delta awarded third-party beneficiary status?
2. How does the court distinguish between third-party creditor beneficiaries and incidental beneficiaries?
3. How would you argue against the court's holding?

Bay Corrugated Container, Incorporated v. Gould, Incorporated
2012 U.S. App. LEXIS 935 (6th Cir. 2012)

This case arises out of a consent judgment entered by the district court in 1994 in which Gould, Inc. agreed to pay for environmental investigation and remediation of property sold by Gould, Inc. to Bay Corrugated Container, Inc. In 1999, Bay filed a petition to enforce the consent judgment and Gould, Inc. In its petition, Bay acknowledged that Gould, Inc.'s successor, GNB, Inc. (now Exide Technologies) had assumed Gould, Inc.'s responsibilities under the settlement agreement. The parties entered mediation and Bay entered into a settlement with Exide. In 2009, Bay filed a "Notice Requesting Resolution of Petition to Enforce Consent Judgment." After soliciting status updates and holding a nonevidentiary hearing, the district court granted Gould, Inc.'s motion to dismiss.

Relying on a determination by the Seventh Circuit that GNB assumed all of Gould, Inc.'s environmental liabilities when it purchased Gould, Inc.'s battery business in 1984, and Bay's mediated settlement agreement with Exide, the district court determined that Gould, Inc. had no liability in this matter. In the alternative, the district court ruled that the "nine years of inactivity" in this case warranted dismissal under Federal Rule of Civil Procedure 41(b) and Eastern District of Michigan Local Rule 41.2. Bay moved the district court to reconsider its dismissal; the district court denied Bay's motion. In this same order, the court allowed Gould Electronics to respond to Bay's motion for reconsideration and to intervene for purposes of appeal. The district court also allowed Gould Electronics to intervene on appeal. Bay appeals, arguing that dismissal of the petition was error. We REVERSE.

Bay argues that Gould, Inc. remains liable to Bay under the 1994 settlement and judgment. Bay also argues that Bay's negotiation of the mediated settlement with Exide, in addition to other acknowledgments of GNB's assumption of Gould, Inc.'s liabilities, does not show that Bay released Gould, Inc. Gould, Inc.'s continued liability to Bay depends upon whether there has been a novation that substituted Gould, Inc.'s liability with that of GNB or Exide. The resolution of this issue depends upon whether Bay's discussions and negotiations with GNB and Exide actually extinguished its agreement with Gould, Inc. or whether GNB and Exide merely assumed Gould, Inc.'s obligations.

Under Michigan law, "[t]he elements of a novation require the creditor's intention both that the new debtor assume the obligation and that the old debtor be released." Consent to a novation "is not to be implied merely from the performance of the contract or the payment of money by the substitute, for that might well consist with the continued liability of the original party." "The circumstances surrounding a series of transactions may be considered, in addition to the text of any written instruments, in determining whether the parties reached a novation that extinguished the liability of one debtor and substituted for it the liability of another."

The district court based its dismissal on "its conclusion that [Gould, Inc.] has no liability for the contamination at issue because its liability transferred to GNB" and Bay's "extremely long period of inactivity warranted dismissal for lack of prosecution." The district court thus implicitly found or assumed that there had been a novation of Gould, Inc.'s liability to Bay, transferring it to GNB or Exide. However, we find the record contains insufficient facts to support this conclusion.

We hold that it cannot be determined from the record whether there has been a novation and whether, as the district court determined, Gould, Inc. is no longer liable to Bay. Likewise, the district court's summary dismissal under Rule 41(b) does not allow us to review the appropriateness of the decision. For the foregoing reasons, we REVERSE the district court's dismissal of the case and its denial of the motion for reconsideration, and REMAND for further proceedings consistent with this opinion.

Questions

1. According to the court, what is required under Michigan law to effect a novation? Is this the same requirement under your state's law?

2. What was the basis of the district court's implicit finding of a novation?

3. What would have to be shown to evidence a novation?

Suggested Case References

1. A municipality enters into a contract with a private company to construct sewers and make street repairs. The company agrees to be liable for any property damage resulting from its work. Are the citizens third party beneficiaries of this contract with enforceable rights against the company? Read *Lundt v. Parsons Construction Co.*, 181 Neb. 609 (1967), and *Anderson v. Rexroad*, 182 Kan. 676 (1954).

2. To be a third party beneficiary to a contract, must a person be specifically named in the contract? Read what the New Mexico court said in *Stotlar v. Hester*, 582 P.2d 403 (N.M. App. 1978).

3. Is any particular form needed to create a valid assignment? *Stoller v. Exchange National Bank of Chicago*, 199 Ill. App. 2d 674, 557 N.E.2d 438 (1990).

4. Is an insurer's right of subrogation the same as an assignment of rights by the insured to the insurer? The Missouri court discusses this question in *Farmer's Insurance Co., Inc. v. Effertz*, 795 S.W.2d 424 (Mo. App. 1990).

5. Are union members third party beneficiaries in a reorganization agreement between a corporation and its creditors? Read what the Iowa court said in *Bailey v. Iowa Beef Processors, Inc.*, 213 N.W.2d 642 (Iowa 1973).

Ethical Considerations

With respect to third party beneficiary contracts, ABA Rule of Professional Conduct 1.8(c) prohibits a lawyer from preparing a document in which a client gives a substantial gift to any close relative of the lawyer's, unless the client is also related to that third party donee beneficiary.

Quick Quiz

Answer TRUE or FALSE. (Answers can be found in Appendix C on page 414.)

1. A delegation concerns the transfer of contractual rights.
2. An incidental beneficiary is considered to be a real party in interest to a third party beneficiary contract.
3. "Vested" means having legally enforceable rights.
4. Pursuant to the Statute of Frauds, an assignment must be in writing.
5. Estoppel is an equitable defense.

10 Discharge of Obligations

Learning Objectives

After studying this chapter you will be able to:

- List the methods whereby a contractual obligation may be discharged
- Define "voluntary disablement"
- Discuss the concept of "anticipatory breach"
- Understand what is meant by tendering performance
- Differentiate between a material breach and a minor breach
- Define "mutual rescission"
- Explain the concept of impossibility of performance
- Exemplify frustration of purpose
- Understand which contracts are divisible contracts
- Discuss the effect of discharge on the parties to the agreement

CHAPTER OVERVIEW

The contract is now complete. Every clause has been analyzed and discussed, and the contract meets all of the legal requirements to be an enforceable agreement. Does this mean that the parties to the contract are required to fulfill their promised performances? The answer is a resounding "Not necessarily."

In several situations a contracting party's performance is discharged, or excused, without his actually having fulfilled his contractual obligations. The circumstances that create these situations generally involve occasions when either the other party or external situations negate the necessity of performance.

Suppose that one of the conditions specified or implied in the contract fails to occur. Because the condition is a timing element for performance, if the condition giving rise to that performance does not come to pass, no performance is expected under the terms of the contract.

A contracting party's performance is excused if the other contracting party breaches. Because a valid contract requires mutuality of consideration, when one side fails to deliver the promised-for consideration, the other side is excused from performance as well.

The parties to the contract, for one reason or another, may agree that the contract is not worth completing. In these circumstances the parties are perfectly free to rescind or modify their existing obligations. As a consequence of this new "meeting of the minds," the obligations imposed under the original contract are no longer applicable. The parties agree to be bound to a new contractual arrangement instead.

Finally, situations that occur through no fault of either side may discharge the parties' contractual obligations. These are cases where outside forces have made fulfillment of the contract impossible, such as a change in the law or the unforeseen destruction of the subject matter of the contract. The law does not require the parties to perform the impossible or the illegal simply because a contract is in existence. Changed circumstances can change contractual obligations.

In summary, once the contract itself is determined to be valid and enforceable, it is necessary to see what happens after the agreement has been entered into. Dependent upon what the parties themselves, or what external factors, do, a party to a contract may not be legally bound to fulfill his contractual promises. The specifics of these methods of discharging contractual obligations are discussed below.

Methods of Discharge

A party to a contract may be discharged, or excused, from her contractual obligation in the following eight circumstances:

1. excuse of conditions;
2. performance;
3. breach of contract;
4. agreement of the parties;
5. impossibility of performance/impracticability of performance;
6. supervening illegality;

7. death or destruction of the subject matter or parties; and
8. frustration of purpose.

Each of these eight methods of discharge will be discussed individually.

Excuse of Conditions

As discussed in a previous chapter, a **condition** is a timing element of a contractual agreement. The condition either creates or extinguishes a party's duty to perform. Consequently, if the condition fails to occur, the performance does not come into play; conversely, a condition subsequent can terminate the obligation to perform.

 EXAMPLES:

1. Abdul contracts to purchase Mamet's house. The contract is con-ditioned on Abdul finding financing for the purchase within 30 days. If Abdul is unable to find a mortgage within the 30 days, the contractual promises are excused. The condition precedent has not taken place, and so Abdul does not have to purchase Mamet's house. Mamet is free to sell the house to someone else.

2. Under their divorce settlement, Max has agreed to pay Fanny a set amount of alimony each month until one of them dies or Fanny remarries. When Fanny does remarry, Max is excused from his contractual obligation. The condition subsequent, Fanny's remarriage, discharges Max from his alimony obligations.

In each of the two examples above, the condition itself discharged the contractual obligation. In addition, because contractual conditions usually involve some element of time (either short, long, or indefinite), there exists the possibility that during the contractual time frame one of the parties will do something that will prevent or excuse the other side's performance. While such circumstances occur during the *time period* of the condition they are not situations in which *the condition itself* discharges the contractual obligation, as in the examples given above. Generally, there are four circumstances that fall into this category.

1. **Performance Prevented.** In this situation, one side, during the period of the condition, engages in some act that makes it impossible for the promisor to fulfill her obligation. The promisor will be excused from performing. The person who prevents the performance only excuses the counter performance of the other side; the wrongdoer is still contractually bound.

EXAMPLE:

Jessie agrees to paint Fred's house on Thursday. When Jessie arrives at Fred's, Fred has bolted and locked the gate, making entrance to the house impossible. Fred's conduct excuses Jessie's performance, but Fred will still be liable for Jessie's costs and expenses.

If the party who must perform *after* the condition occurs is the one who prevents the condition happening, he will not be excused and must perform. A person cannot benefit from his own wrongdoing.

EXAMPLE:

Ted hires Irene to remodel his house for a set sum and requires that after completion, Irene give Ted an architect's certificate stating the remodeling meets all current standards. Ted prevents the architect from giving the certificate. Ted must pay Irene. Because Ted is the one who prevented the condition from occurring, it does not excuse his contractual obligation.

2. **Voluntary Disablement.** **Voluntary disablement** means that one party to a contract voluntarily engages in some conduct that makes it virtually impossible for him to fulfill his obligation. It is not absolutely impossible, but the circumstances are such that it would be more than extremely unlikely that he will be able to perform. In these circumstances, the other side is excused from her obligations. The law will not force one side to perform if it is unlikely or impossible for the other side to perform. For contracts covered by the Uniform Commercial Code (UCC), voluntary disablement would give rise to the other party's right to seek written assurances of performance. (See Chapter 8.) If such assurances were not given within 30 days, the party seeking such assurances could consider the voluntary disablement a breach of contract.

EXAMPLE:

Becky agrees to purchase Patti's antique vase. Payment and delivery are to take place in two weeks. One week after their contract is entered into, Patti sells the vase to Rose. Because there is still one week left until Patti has to convey the vase to Becky, it is conceivable that she could repurchase the vase from Rose so as to be able to give it to Becky, but the likelihood is negligible. This is an example of voluntary disablement. Patti has voluntarily engaged in an action that makes it unlikely that she will be able to fulfill her contractual obligation to Becky. Consequently, Becky's obligation to Patti is discharged.

The majority of states considers that voluntary disablement constitutes a full breach of contract, entitling the injured party to sue immediately for contractual relief in the courts. In those jurisdictions where it is not considered a breach of contract, the promisee must wait until the time element has passed to ascertain whether the other party will perform before being able to seek judicial relief.

3. **Insolvency.** If one party to the contract becomes judicially insolvent, the other side is excused from performing. The law does not require that a person become a judicial creditor of a bankrupt, nor will it permit someone to attempt to fulfill a contract with a bankrupt resulting in increased debts for the insolvent party.

 EXAMPLE:

Farmer White has a contract to deliver 1,000 bushels of sweet potatoes to Eatwell Supermarkets, Inc., at the end of the month. Three weeks prior to delivery, Eatwell files for protection under the bankruptcy laws. Neither Eatwell nor Farmer White is required to fulfill their contractual obligations to each other.

4. **Anticipatory Breach.** **Anticipatory breach** occurs when one party to the contract, during the time of the condition, states that she has decided not to fulfill her contractual obligations. In other words, one party tells the other that she has no intention of conveying the promised-for consideration. In this situation, the innocent party does not have to perform.

For the contracting party's conduct to be considered anticipatory breach, the words indicating her intentions must be positive, unconditional, and unequivocal. A person cannot merely suggest that her performance will not be forthcoming; she must state that in no uncertain terms. In anticipatory breach, both sides must have executory duties to perform. If the innocent party has already performed, with no other duty to fulfill, there is no "anticipatory" breach; the other side is in total breach.

EXAMPLES:

1. Maura agrees to sell her used Property book to Wallace. Before payment and delivery, Maura tells Wallace that she has changed her mind, and that she is going to keep the book rather than sell it. This is anticipatory breach.

2. Maura agrees to sell her used Property book to Wallace. Wallace pays her and agrees to pick up the book the following week. Before the book is picked up, Maura tells Wallace that she has changed her mind, and that she is going to keep the book. This is not anticipatory breach; it is a breach of contract because Wallace has already performed, and his duties are executed.

In all of the situations discussed above, the injured, innocent party to the contract cannot simply sit back and sue the other person. The law imposes a duty on the injured party to a failed contract to attempt to minimize her injury. This is known as **mitigation of damages.** The injured party must make a reasonable attempt to find a replacement for the failed party's contractual performance. For example, in the situations given above, Jessie would have to find someone else's house to paint on Thursday, Farmer White would have to look for a new sweet potato purchaser, and Wallace would have to seek someone else's used book. In this fashion, the injured party will minimize the damages the injuring party will have to pay.

The injured party only need make "reasonable" attempts to mitigate. Extremely hard or expensive measures are not called for. What is "reasonable" is determined on a case-by-case basis. Also, should the innocent party make a better deal in attempting to mitigate what he originally had, the breaching party is totally excused from the contract.

One word about the antique vase and mitigation of damages: Because an antique vase is a unique piece of property, it is unlikely that the innocent party would be able to mitigate. This does not mean that she is not required to try, but the likelihood of success is reduced in these circumstances.

Performance

The simplest method of being excused from contractual obligations is to perform these obligations. Once performed, the duties are executed, and there is nothing more for the promisor to do. Fortunately, most contractual obligations are fulfilled in this fashion. The overwhelming majority of contractual duties are satisfied by the parties' actual performances.

Must a party perform completely to be excused from his obligations under the contract? The answer is no. Obviously, once a party has fully and completely performed nothing else could reasonably be expected. However, a party may be ready, willing, and able to perform, and the other side refuses the performance. The promisor in this instance is said to have **tendered complete performance,** which is legally sufficient to discharge him from his obligations. Remember the example above when Jessie arrived to paint Fred's house, only to find the entrance barred. In this instance, Jessie tendered complete performance. He arrived, ready, willing, and able to perform. His actual performance was forestalled by Fred's actions, and so Jessie was relieved of further obligations.

What happens if, instead of completely performing or tendering complete performance, a party only partially performs? Will she still be relieved of her contractual obligations? The answer depends on the nature of the promised performance and the extent of the performance actually given. Recall the case of Jimmy the Human Fly. In that instance, the court held that Jimmy climbing almost to the very top of the Washington Monument constituted "substantial" performance, satisfying his contractual obligation. If the performance is substantial, the performing party will be discharged, although she may have to compensate the promisee for the difference between the full performance and the substantial performance given.

EXAMPLE:

Lonnie agrees to sell 25 CDs to Bruce for $100. In fact, Lonnie only delivers 23 CDs. Lonnie did not breach her obligation; her performance is substantial. However, she is not entitled to the full $100. Bruce may deduct the price of two CDs from the total payment to Lonnie.

If, on the other hand, the performance delivered is insubstantial, the promisor is not relieved of his contractual obligation. Insubstantial performance never discharges a promisor's contractual obligation *unless* the promisee accepts that performance. Regardless of the performance actually given, if the promisee accepts the performance in complete satisfaction of the promisor's contractual obligation—be that performance complete, substantial, or insubstantial—that acceptance relieves the promisor of any further contractual responsibility.

As discussed in Chapter 8, part performance for merchant traders is unacceptable. A merchant buyer is entitled to perfect tender, and if the goods delivered do not completely conform to the contract specifications, the merchant buyer may reject the entire shipment or accept only conforming goods. The option is with the buyer. However, the UCC demands that the buyer give the seller the opportunity to remedy the defect within a reasonable time.

EXAMPLE:

Sally is a collector of old books. Bruce agrees to sell to Sally a 1902 edition of the Book of Knowledge, a set containing 20 volumes, for a certain price. On delivery day Bruce conveys only three volumes, all he actually has. Sally still thinks the sale is a good buy, and accepts the three volumes. Even though the performance is rather insubstantial, Sally's acceptance discharges Bruce from further performance.

Breach of Contract

To **breach** a contract means to break one's obligation made under the agreement. If a party to a contract breaches, the other side, the innocent party, has an immediate cause of action. A breach means the promisor has not lived up to what he has promised, and the injured party may sue to recover what she expected to receive under the contractual agreement.

EXAMPLE:

Harry agrees to buy Minnie's pearl necklace as a gift for his wife. Harry pays Minnie, but Minnie fails to deliver the necklace. Minnie has breached her promise, and Harry can sue her, either to get his money back or to have her convey the necklace.

Not all breaches give rise to an immediate cause of action. A **material breach** of contract always gives rise to an immediate cause of action for breach of the entire contract because it goes to the heart of the contract itself. A **minor breach** of contract, on the other hand, only gives rise to a cause of action for that minor, or insignificant, breach; the contract itself is still in force and effect.

EXAMPLES:

1. Corrinne agrees to sell Gary her car for $1,500. When Gary takes possession, he discovers that the car is totally broken down and does not meet the contract specifications. This is a breach of the entire contract, giving Gary an immediate cause of action for the full purchase price.

2. When Gary takes possession of the car, he discovers that the spark plugs are worn out. Although the contract specified that the car was in perfect working order, this is only a minor breach, because replacing spark plugs is basically insignificant. Gary has a cause of action against Corrinne for the cost of replacing the spark plugs, but the contract is still valid and enforceable.

What factors determine whether a breach is material or minor? There is no set standard, but generally the courts look at the intent of the parties, the words used in the contract, the degree of hardship the breach imposes, and the extent to which the injured party can be compensated. As a general rule, if any portion of a contract is deemed to be of special importance to one of the parties, it should be identified in the contract as a "material" clause. One such example would be a time of the essence clause discussed in Chapter 2.

The distinction between material and minor breaches gives rise to another legal concept, that of the **divisible contract**. As discussed in Chapter 7, one of the contractual rules of construction used by the courts is to attempt to uphold contracts if at all possible. As a consequence of this doctrine, the courts have created the concept of divisible contracts. A divisible contract is one that can be divided into several separate, but equal, portions. The contract can either expressly state that it is divisible (or that it is not divisible, if the parties so wish), or its divisibility can be implied from the contract terms themselves. If the contract is deemed divisible, then a breach would only affect that one small divided contract; the rest of the contract relationships would remain intact. In this method, even if the breach were material, the materiality may only go to one portion of the contract, and the remaining portions would still be in effect.

EXAMPLE:

Mitzi rents an apartment from Louise for a two-year period, with a monthly rent of $300. Mitzi pays her rent for the first six months, but in the seventh month her rent check bounces. Although Mitzi is in breach, the contract can be considered a divisible contract. The lease is for 24 months, with a monthly rent of $300, which could be looked at as 24 separate leases. In this context, Mitzi's breach is only a breach of one of those 24 contracts; all the remaining contracts are still deemed in effect.

The court will find a contract to be divisible only if it can be evenly and easily divided, and the parties themselves have not specified that the contract is nondivisible. Under the UCC, all contracts in which delivery is to be made in installments are deemed divisible unless such assumption would cause an undue hardship on the buyer merchant.

Agreement of the Parties

The parties to a contract are always free to rearrange their contractual agreements by mutual assent. As long as *both* parties agree to a change in the performances, the parties may be discharged from their original obligation without any negative consequences.

This mutual reagreement of the parties can come about in two ways. First, the original contract may contain a provision providing for the dissolution of the agreement. An example would be a lease providing for a tenancy at will where either party is free to terminate the relationship by providing notice to the other party. Or, a contract could contain a time period escape clause, meaning that during a specified period of time the parties could dissolve the contract without damage. An example of this type of arrangement would be a contract for schooling. From registration until the beginning of class, any student can change her mind and get a full tuition refund. Each contract must be individually analyzed to determine whether it contains some provision for the parties' termination of the contract without damage.

The second situation in which the parties can change their mutual obligations comes about not by the original contract, but by the parties forming a new contractual arrangement. There are six types of new agreements that have the effect of discharging the parties from their former contractual obligations.

1. **Mutual Rescission.**   A **mutual rescission** occurs when both parties to the contract agree that they do not want to proceed any further under the agreement. Both sides agree to rescind, or take back, the original obligation. The consideration supporting this agreement is the detriment incurred by each party of not receiving the promised-for consideration of the original contract. For rescission to be applicable the contract must be executory.

EXAMPLE:

Barry and Lynette agree to be partners in a retail store. The partnership is evidenced by a written partnership agreement. Prior to establishing the business they have a falling out and decide to rescind the contract. Because the provisions are executory, this is valid.

2. **Release.**   A **release** is a contract in which one side relieves the other of any obligation existing under a previous contract. Many times people hear the term "release" in the context of tort claims, but the concept is contractual as well. Usually, the releasing party receives some consideration for her agreement to release the other side from his original obligation.

EXAMPLE:

Tina has a contract with Melinda in which Melinda has agreed to supply Tina with 20 dresses each week for Tina's clothing store for a two-year period. After several problems arise, Tina agrees to release Melinda from the contract in consideration of a certain sum of money. The release is very much like a private settlement between parties to a contractual dispute.

3. **Accord and Satisfaction.**   An **accord and satisfaction** is a special contractual situation in which the parties to a disputed contract agree to settle their dispute by changing the obligations of the contract itself with the new agreement. Accord and satisfactions are discussed in Chapter 4, Consideration, and can be reviewed in that section.

4. **Substituted Agreement.**   A **substituted agreement** is a new contract that incorporates the original contract in the new provisions. Because the original obligations are now absorbed by the new agreement, the original contractual duties are deemed discharged.

EXAMPLE:

Judy is having a yard sale. Rise sees a shawl she likes, and the two women agree on a price. Before paying for the shawl, Rise spots a hat and a serving tray she would like to purchase. After some haggling, Judy agrees on one price for all three items. The original contract for the sale of the shawl is now absorbed into this substituted agreement, which covers three items instead of just one.

5. **Novation.** As discussed in Chapter 9, Third Party Contracts, a **novation** is a substitution of parties into an existing contractual agreement. When the novation is effectuated, the original party no longer has any rights or obligations under the contract. That person's contractual duties are discharged; they are now the responsibility of the novated party.

6. **Modification.** As discussed previously, if the contract is for the sale of goods between merchants, the merchants may make good faith modifications to their contractual obligations.

Impossibility of Performance/Impracticability of Performance

Under certain circumstances, a contracting party's performance may become impossible to fulfill through no fault of his own. The law feels it would be unfair and unjust to hold the person responsible to a contractual obligation that could not possibly be met.

What constitutes **impossibility of performance/impracticability of performance** depends on the facts and circumstances of each individual case. It also must be ascertained whether the performance is totally incapable of being performed or whether the impossibility is of a temporary nature. If the impossibility is only temporary, the promisor is not discharged from her obligation, but her performance is temporarily suspended until the situation rectifies itself; at that point the promisor must fulfill her original obligation. Take careful note that circumstances that merely make the performances more difficult or expensive than originally believed, but not impossible to perform, do not relieve the promisor of her obligations. This is the risk of contract. However, for contracts covered by the UCC, if performance becomes unduly expensive due to events that could not be foreseen or assumed when the contract was formed, the party *may* be discharged.

EXAMPLES:

1. Buycheap Markets has a contract with Australian Produce, Ltd. to purchase various food products from the latter. One contract

concerns the purchase of 5,000 bushels of Tasmanian oranges that Australian Produce has agreed to ship to the port of San Diego. As the ship pulls into the harbor, the longshoremen go on a national strike, and the oranges cannot be off-loaded anywhere in the United States. The oranges begin to perish. Australian Produce is relieved of its obligation by the impossibility of performance.

2. In a second contract, Buycheap has agreed to buy tinned lamb from Australian Produce, shipment to be to the port of Los Angeles. This ship arrives the same day as the one in the previous example, and the goods cannot be off-loaded. Australian Produce is not permanently relieved of its obligation. Because canned goods have an indefinite life, and time is not of the essence, Australian Produce's obligation is merely suspended until the strike is over.

Supervening Illegality

A **supervening illegality** will discharge contractual obligations because, since the inception of the contractual arrangement, the purpose for which the contract was created has become illegal. The law will not permit persons to engage in illegal activities, and therefore the parties are deemed discharged from their contractual duties.

EXAMPLE:

Jan and Dean enter into a contract to open and manage a gambling casino in Atlantic City, New Jersey. Six months after the casino opens, the town officials of Atlantic City rescind the ordinance permitting gambling in the town. Jan and Dean are now discharged from their contractual promises by a supervening illegality. The law will not allow them to break the law just to fulfill a contract.

Death of the Parties or Destruction of the Subject Matter

If the subject matter of the contract is destroyed, obviously the contract cannot be fulfilled. This is true provided that the object in question is unique and is not destroyed by an act of one of the parties. If the object is capable of near exact replacement, the promisor is expected to find a substitute product and fulfill his obligation. The fact that it might be more expensive for him is of no concern to the law. That is a risk of contract.

Death is self-evident; a person cannot be expected to perform from the grave. Note that a person's estate may be liable for contracts entered into by the deceased prior to death. If the decedent merely had to convey property she had sold or pay for property she had purchased, the estate is capable and expected to fulfill these obligations.

EXAMPLES:

1. Ian has agreed to buy Peg's house. Before closing, the house is destroyed by fire. Ian is discharged from his obligation by the destruction of the subject matter of the contract.

2. Willie has agreed to let his prize race horse stud with Liz's filly for a fee. Before consummation of the contract, Willie's horse dies. Willie and Liz are relieved of their contractual obligations.

Frustration of Purpose

Probably the least common method of discharge, but the most interesting, is **frustration of purpose.** Frustration of purpose occurs when the contract, on its face, is both valid and apparently capable of performance, but the underlying reason for the agreement no longer exists. This reason is not specified in the contract itself but is discernible by the circumstances surrounding the contract's creation.

EXAMPLE:

The most famous of the cases regarding frustration of purpose are known as the Coronation Cases, dealing with the coronation of Edward VII of England. At the turn of the century, after Queen Victoria's death, her son and heir, Edward, was to be crowned king after a 60-year wait. The procession route was announced months in advance, and people with homes and offices overlooking the route found themselves in possession of desirable real estate. One-day leases were entered into for the day of the coronation, so that the "tenants" could have a view of the parade. Two days before the ceremony Edward developed appendicitis, and the coronation was postponed for several months. The one-day landlords brought the tenants into court for rent when the tenants refused to pay. The court held that, while the contracts, on their faces, were valid and enforceable, the purpose of the contracts—to view the coronation procession—no longer existed. Consequently, the tenants were discharged from their rental obligations because of frustration of purpose.

SAMPLE CLAUSES

☐ 1

If, during the term of the lease, the described premises shall be destroyed by fire, the elements, or any other cause, or if they be so injured that they cannot be repaired with reasonable diligence within six (6) months, then this lease shall cease and become null and void from the date of such damage or destruction, and the lessee shall immediately surrender the premises to the lessor and shall pay rent only to the time of such surrender.

Here, the parties to the contract indicate a discharge caused by the loss or destruction of the subject matter. By having this clause in the original instrument specifying the grounds for discharge, the parties have hopefully avoided a lawsuit to have their obligations excused.

☐ 2

In the event bankruptcy or state proceedings should be filed against the lessee, his heirs or assigns, in any federal or state court, it shall give the right to said lessee, his heirs or assigns, immediately to declare this contract null and void.

This provision, as the preceding one, would appear in the original contract and specifies insolvency as a ground for discharging the contractual obligation.

☐ 3

If Subscriber within five (5) days after the execution of the Agreement notifies Seller in writing that Subscriber wishes to withdraw from the Agreement, the amount theretofore paid by him under the Agreement will be returned to him and thereafter all rights and liabilities of Subscriber hereunder shall cease and terminate.

This clause in the original sales contract provides a conditional time period during which the subscriber can withdraw from the contract without any negative effect. In this manner, the parties have agreed to a method of discharge in the original agreement.

☐ 4

If any obstacle or difficulty shall arise in respect to the title, the completion of the purchase, or otherwise, the vendor shall be at full liberty, at any time, to abandon this contract on returning the deposit money to the purchaser.

In this instance the parties in a contract for the sale of real estate have specified an excuse of conditions in the original contract. Of course, the specific obstacle or difficulty has not been definitely defined or described, which could create questions of interpretation later on. In drafting contracts, it is always a matter of judgment with respect to specificity. The more precise the clauses, the less leeway later on; the less precise the clauses, the more potential for a lawsuit.

CHAPTER SUMMARY

A party to a contract does not necessarily have to perform what he has promised under the agreement itself. There are several situations and circumstances that act to discharge a promisor from his duties without any negative consequences to the party himself. Generally, there are eight situations that have the effect of discharging the promisor's obligations. They are:

1. having the performance excused by a contractual condition not being met;
2. performing, either fully or partially, and having that performance accepted by the promisee;
3. by the other side's breach of contract;
4. by having the parties mutually agree to a new or different performance;
5. by impossibility of performance;
6. by having the law change so as to make the contract illegal;
7. by the death or destruction of the subject matter or parties; or
8. by frustration of purpose.

When any of these preceding situations occur, the promisor is excused from any further obligation under the contract.

SYNOPSIS

Methods of discharging or excusing performance
    1. Excuse of conditions
        a. Condition fails to create or extinguishes duties
        b. Other side prevents performance during time of condition
            i. Prevention
            ii. Voluntary disablement
            iii. Insolvency
            iv. Anticipatory breach
    2. Performance
        a. Full
        b. Tendered full performance
        c. Substantial v. insubstantial

3. Breach
   a. Material or minor
   b. Divisible contracts
4. Agreement
   a. In original contract
   b. New agreement
      i. Mutual rescission
      ii. Release
      iii. Accord and satisfaction
      iv. Substituted agreement
      v. Novation
5. Impossibility of performance
   a. Permanent
   b. Temporary
6. Supervening illegality
7. Death or destruction
8. Frustration of purpose: Coronation cases

Key Terms

Accord and satisfaction: new contract based on parties' agreement to settle dispute existing under a contract
Anticipatory breach: positive, unconditional, and unequivocal words that a party intends to breach his contractual obligations
Breach: breaking one's contractual promise
Condition: a fact or event, the happening or nonhappening of which creates or extinguishes an absolute duty to perform
Divisible contract: contract capable of being broken down into several equal agreements
Frustration of purpose: purpose for which the contract was formed no longer exists
Impossibility of performance: promisor's performance is incapable of being fulfilled due to outside forces
Material breach: breach of contract that goes to the heart of the agreement
Minor breach: breach of contract that goes to an insignificant aspect of the contract
Mitigation of damages: duty imposed on injured party to lessen, by reasonable means, the breaching party's liability
Mutual rescission: agreement by both contracting parties to do away with the contract
Novation: substitution of contracting parties
Release: contract relieving promisor from an obligation under an existing contract
Substituted agreement: a new contract that incorporates the original contract in the new provisions
Supervening illegality: change in law that makes the performance of the contract illegal

Tender complete performance: being ready, willing, and able to perform
Voluntary disablement: volitional act by a promisor that makes her
    obligation virtually incapable of being performed

EXERCISES

1. Give two examples of impossibility of performance.
2. What factors determine whether a contract is divisible? Draft a divisible contract.
3. What would be the result of an injured party failing to mitigate damages? Why?
4. Give an example of frustration of purpose other than the Coronation Cases.
5. What factors determine whether performance is substantial or insubstantial? Draft a contract clause that would help in this determination.

Cases for Analysis

The following case summaries are included to demonstrate how contracts may or may not be discharged by the contracting parties. In *Felt v. McCarthy* the court discusses the elements of frustration of purpose needed to discharge a contractual obligation, and in *Club Factorage, LLC v. Wood Duck Hiding, LLC* the court deals with anticipatory repudiation.

Felt v. McCarthy
130 Wn.2d 203 (Sup. Ct. 1996); 922 P.2d 90

Defendants defaulted on a promissory note that was given to Plaintiffs as part of the purchase price for a nine-acre lot, and Plaintiffs sued to enforce the note. Defendants claim "frustration of purpose" excuses them from making further payments on the note because newly-enacted wetlands regulations prevented them from developing the land as a business park. Both the trial court and the Court of Appeals granted summary judgment for Plaintiffs. We affirm.

Plaintiffs Dona and Charles Felt owned a nine-acre lot, which was dissected in the middle by the North Creek. The lot was zoned Rural Conservation, but the North Creek Comprehensive Plan designated the land as Business Park. Other properties in the immediate area had already been rezoned as Business Park, and there were completed and ongoing business developments on some of those neighboring properties.

In 1983, Thomas C. McCarthy and Ronald F. Tasso, who is not a party to this case, began gathering adjoining parcels of property in Snohomish County for the purpose of developing a business park. McCarthy approached the Felts to discuss his plan for developing a business park. In

1983 McCarthy and Tasso obtained an option agreement from the Felts to purchase the nine acres for $260,000. In the agreement, the Felts promised to help McCarthy and Tasso rezone the property to Business Park, and McCarthy and Tasso agreed to pay all costs associated with the rezone application.

McCarthy and Tasso applied to rezone 123 acres including the Felt property. In November 1985, the rezone application was denied without prejudice because McCarthy and Tasso held ownership interests in only 47 of the 123 acres.

Even though they failed to rezone the property, McCarthy and Tasso purchased the nine acres from the Felts in December 1986. The purchase price was $310,000. Part of the price was met by an $80,000 down payment, and McCarthy and Tasso each gave an unsecured promissory note for $89,627.84. The purchasers satisfied the remainder of the purchase price by assuming an old mortgage on the Felt property, paying closing costs, and receiving credit for option fees previously paid to the Felts. The Felts conveyed the property to McCarthy and Tasso by statutory warranty deed, and the Felts retained no interest in the land whatsoever. The sales contract placed no conditions on the sale.

In a transaction related to their purchase of the Felt property, McCarthy and Tasso borrowed $122,800 from Harry H. Olson, Inc. The lender obtained a deed of trust for the Felt property as security for this loan.

In January 1987, the Army Corps of Engineers released its Wetlands Delineation Manual. Soon thereafter, Snohomish County adopted several motions to protect wetlands. Although it was not immediately clear how these regulations affected the Felt property, by November 1990 McCarthy learned that the regulations rendered the Felt acreage useful only as a single homesite or as open space. In the trial court, McCarthy submitted a declaration from a real estate broker who set the estimated value of the Felt property at only $50,000 as a result of the wetlands regulations. Plaintiffs never contested this estimate.

Even before they were aware of the wetlands restrictions on the Felt property, McCarthy and Tasso defaulted on the loan repayments to Harry H. Olson, Inc. for the $122,800 loan which was secured by the Felt property. A notice of default was mailed to McCarthy and Tasso on May 24, 1988. On January 25, 1991, McCarthy and Tasso still had not cured the default, so the property was foreclosed and sold at public auction. According to the trustee's deed, the Felt property was sold for the sum of $240,338.30, in complete satisfaction of McCarthy's and Tasso's obligations under the original loan from Harry H. Olson, Inc.

Soon after the Felt property was sold in foreclosure, McCarthy defaulted on the promissory note held by the Felts. Dona Felt and the representative of her deceased husband's estate brought an action against McCarthy and his wife to collect the unpaid portion of the promissory note, plus interest and attorney fees. Tasso's note was not involved in the case. McCarthy raised the affirmative defense of commercial frustration, or frustration of purpose, and argued the court should excuse all unpaid portions of the note since the property was worth only $50,000. The trial court granted summary judgment for the Felts. The Court of Appeals found the frustration of purpose doctrine was not applicable to the facts of the case and affirmed the trial court. *Felt v. McCarthy*, 78 Wn. App. 362, 898 P.2d 315 (1995), *review granted*, 128 Wn.2d 1011 (1996). We also affirm.

McCarthy's frustration argument is fatally flawed. He claims his plans to develop a business park were frustrated by wetlands regulations. The facts show that McCarthy's plans were not frustrated by wetlands regulations; they were frustrated by his failure to repay the loan obtained from Harry H. Olson, Inc. McCarthy's first default on the loan payments occurred in 1988, two years before McCarthy even learned about the impact of the wetlands regulations on the Felt property. Nonetheless, because this court is reviewing a summary judgment favoring Plaintiffs, the facts should be considered in the light most favorable to the nonmoving party. *Degel v. Majestic Mobile Manor, Inc.*, 129 Wn.2d 43, 48, 914 P.2d 728 (1996). We will assume that wetlands regulations effectively prevented McCarthy from developing the business park.

Application of the doctrine of frustration is a question of law. *Washington State Hop Producers, Inc. Liquidation Trust v. Goschie Farms, Inc.*, 112 Wn.2d 694, 704, 773 P.2d 70 (1989). This court has adopted the doctrine as stated in RESTATEMENT (SECOND) OF CONTRACTS §265 (1979). *Hop Producers*, 112 Wn.2d at 700. This section, entitled "Discharge by Supervening Frustration," states:

> Where, after a contract is made, a party's principal purpose is substantially frustrated without his fault by the occurrence of an event the nonoccurrence of which was a basic assumption on which the contract was made, his remaining duties to render performance are discharged, unless the language or the circumstances indicate the contrary.

Restatement (Second) of Contracts §265 (1979).

Comment *a* to this section gives a detailed explanation of how the rule should be applied. It states, in part:

> The rule stated in this Section sets out the requirements for the discharge of that party's duty. First, the purpose that is frustrated must have been a principal purpose of that party in making the contract. It is not enough that he had in mind some specific object without which he would not have made the contract. The object must be so completely the basis of the contract that, as both parties understand, without it the transaction would make little sense. Second, the frustration must be substantial. It is not enough that the transaction has become less profitable for the affected party or even that he will sustain a loss. The frustration must be so severe that it is not fairly to be regarded as within the risks that he assumed under the contract. Third, the nonoccurrence of the frustrating event must have been a basic assumption on which the contract was made. . . .

The Court of Appeals applied section 265 to the facts and held McCarthy's successful development of the Felt property as a business park was *not* a basic assumption on which both the Felts and McCarthy entered into the contract. The Court of Appeals' decision focused on whether the frustrated purpose—McCarthy's attempt to develop a business park—was "so completely the basis of the contract that, as *both parties* understand, without it the transaction would make little sense.'" *Felt*, 78 Wn. App. at 367 (quoting *Hop Producers*, 112 Wn.2d at 700).

The Court of Appeals' reasoning closely follows comment *a* of section 265, and the facts of the case support the court's holding. None of the facts support McCarthy's claim that the Felts entered into the sales contract *on the basis* that McCarthy hoped to turn the property into a business park. If the Felts did not share McCarthy's assumption that the park would be successful, commercial frustration does not apply. See *Hop Producers*, 112 Wn.2d at 706 (the need to own hop base was an assumption central to the contract, without which there would neither have been an offer nor an acceptance); *Weyerhaeuser Real Estate Co. v. Stoneway Concrete, Inc.*, 96 Wn.2d 558, 562, 637 P.2d 647 (1981) (Stoneway's purpose for leasing the property formed the basis on which both parties entered the lease). Even though the Felts knew of McCarthy's business park goal, the Felts did not enter into the sales contract on the assumption that McCarthy would be successful in fulfilling his goal.

McCarthy claims the Felts' reasons for entering into the contract are irrelevant. According to McCarthy, the frustrated party's intentions for entering into the contract are considered under the frustration doctrine, but the other party's intentions are irrelevant. This contention is erroneous. As discussed above, RESTATEMENT (SECOND) requires both parties to the contract to share in the assumption that the particular purpose would not be frustrated.

The Felts sold their property free and clear, retaining not even a security interest in it. While the Felts promised to help rezone the property in the 1983 option agreement, the 1986 sales contract placed no requirements on the Felts. Once the sales contract closed, McCarthy, as the new owner of the property, implicitly assumed all risks that his planned use of the property would become frustrated due to any future occurrence, whether or not the occurrence was foreseeable. See *Scott v. Petett*, 63 Wn. App. 50, 816 P.2d 1229 (1991) (purchaser closed the real estate sale after expiration of 90-day contingency period, thereby assuming all risks of the land being unsuitable for his intended use); *cf. Pierce County v. King*, 47 Wn.2d 328, 287 P.2d 316 (1955) (if purchaser in an executory real estate contract has received either legal title or possession of the premises, purchaser is responsible for loss or destruction of property and is not thereby relieved from a duty to pay the price).

McCarthy drafted the sales contract for his purchase of the Felt property. If he wanted the real estate deal to be conditioned upon his successful development of a business park, he clearly had the power to include that condition in the contract. However, McCarthy failed to assign any risk of his business park failure to the Felts, and this court should not correct his mistake by using the frustration doctrine to implicitly read such an assignment into the sales contract. See RESTATEMENT (SECOND) OF CONTRACTS §206 (1979) ("In choosing among the reasonable meanings of an . . . agreement . . . , that meaning is generally preferred which operates against the party who supplies the words. . . ."); see also *Dudley v. St. Regis Corp.*, 635 F. Supp. 1468, 1472 (E.D. Mo. 1986) ("Public policy requires that the doctrine of commercial frustration 'be limited in its application so as to preserve the certainty of contracts.'") (quoting *Dutton v. Dutton*, 668 S.W.2d 585, 591 (Mo. Ct. App. 1984)).

Even if the Felts had shared in the assumption the business park would be successful, McCarthy's frustration was not "substantial" as required by section 265, comment *a*. McCarthy's claim of frustration rests on the property's alleged drop in value from $310,000 to $50,000. However, a decline in market value is not sufficient in and of itself to support a finding of frustration. *Hop Producers*, 112 Wn.2d at 703 (citing and quoting RESTATEMENT (SECOND) OF CONTRACTS §265 cmt. a (1979)). Furthermore, the expert's $50,000 valuation of the Felt property is brought into question by the fact that the land was sold at public auction in January 1991 for $240,338.30.

Since the commercial frustration doctrine fails to excuse McCarthy's payments under the promissory note, we affirm the Court of Appeals and uphold summary judgment for the Felts. The Felts are also awarded attorney fees on appeal in accordance with the terms of the promissory note and RAP 18.1.

Questions

1. How does the court define the concept of frustration of purpose?
2. What was the effect of the decline in the market value of the property on the court's determination? Why?
3. Create a scenario in which a contract could be discharged by frustration of purpose.

Club Factorage, LLC v. Wood Duck Hiding, LLC
2017 U.S. Dist. LEXIS 98354 (SD Ga 2017)

Background

Hampton Island Club, LLC (the "Club") is a private club on Hampton Island Preserve in Liberty County, Georgia. (Doc. 37, Attach. 1 at 8.) On July 11, 2006, Defendant Timothy Petrikin entered into a Purchase and Sale Agreement with Hampton Island Preservation Properties, Inc. to purchase a lot on Hampton Island Preserve. (Doc. 40, Attach. 1 at 1.) Defendant Petrikin assigned the rights to purchase that property to Defendant Wood Duck Hiding, LLC ("Wood Duck"). (Id. at 2.) Defendant Wood

Duck ultimately purchased the lot. (Id.) As part of the Purchase and Sale Agreement, Defendant Wood Duck agreed to buy a membership in the Club. In compliance with this term, Defendant Wood. Duck purchased a membership in the Club by signing a Club Agreement on July 31, 2006. (Doc. 38, Attach. 1 at 66.) The Club Agreement required a membership deposit of $150,000 to be made in three installments of $50,000, along with yearly dues payments. (Id.) However, the Purchase and Sale Agreement stated that Defendant Wood Duck's obligation to pay dues to the Club was to be waived "for the longer of (a) twelve (12) months from the Closing Date or (b) the date on which 18 holes of [the Club's golf course named] Ricefields Golf Course[,] become open for play." (Doc. 40, Attach. 1 at 3.)

Despite signing in his official capacity for Defendant Wood Duck, Defendant Petrikin was not absolved from all personal obligations under the Club Agreement. The Club Agreement listed Defendant Petrikin as the "designated user." (Id. at 4.) As the designated user, Defendant Petrikin agreed to become personally liable "for all dues, fees, charges and other amounts from time to time owing to the club." (Id. at 3.)

On January 17, 2008, Defendant Petrikin received correspondence (Id. at 4) from Ronald S. Leventhal—the president of the Club and Plaintiff Club Factorage, LLC ("Club Factorage") (id. at 9)—indicating that the Club's golf course would be opening sometime in 2008. On February 16, 2008, Defendant Petrikin received a second letter from Mr. Leventhal stating that all membership accounts should be in good standing by February 29, 2008 and that club members could not withhold dues payments on the basis that the golf course had not opened. (Id. at 4-5.) At that time, Defendants had made two payments of $50,000 each towards the membership deposit. On January 17, 2009, Defendant Petrikin informed Mr. Leventhal by email that he would be withholding club dues on the basis that the golf course was not open. (Id. at 5.)

Plaintiff disagreed that Defendants were entitled to withhold dues pending completion of the Club's golf course. Instead, Mr. Leventhal informed Defendant Petrikin that the Club was

> not bound by unrecorded side deals and we are in our view not being treated fair; if you want to leave, then please do so as a gentleman. Otherwise all payments must be current prior to further use. Also we are otherwise not bound by any [other] deal.

(Id.) On March 3, 2008, Defendant Petrikin advised Mr. Leventhal that Defendant Wood Duck would not make the final installment on the membership deposit and would pay no further dues. (Id. at 6.) On the same day, Mr. Leventhal responded stating that "I cannot agree to accept any agreements to which we were not a party; it would open the Pandora's Box if I did." (Id. at 7.) On October 8, 2008, Defendants followed this email correspondence with a formal letter indicating that they would not make any further payments. (Id.)

After this letter was sent, there was no development in this case for six years. On June 6, 2014, the Club assigned its rights in this action to Plaintiff Club Factorage. (Doc. 37, Attach. 1 at 18.) On July 9, 2014, Defendant Wood Duck received a letter from Plaintiff demanding the payment of the final membership deposit of $50,000, dues from 2009 to 2014, and associated interest. (Doc. 40, Attach. 1 at 9.) When Defendants refused to tender these payments, Plaintiff filed a complaint in the Superior Court of Cobb County. (Doc. 37, Attach. 1 at 6.) The complaint alleged that Defendants had breached the Club Agreement and that Defendants were liable in the amount of $135,300.00. (Id. at 11.)

On November 20, 2014, Defendants removed this case to the Northern District of Georgia. (Doc. 1.) On November 26, 2014, Defendants filed a motion to transfer the case to this district. (Doc. 2.) The Northern District granted that request on September 28, 2015. (Doc. 9.) On July 21, 2016, Defendants filed a motion for summary judgment. (Doc. 29.) However, this Court dismissed that motion and ordered Defendants to file an amended notice of removal because Defendants had failed to provide sufficient information to ascertain whether the Court had jurisdiction. (Doc. 35.) Defendants corrected that defect (Doc. 37) and refiled their motion for summary judgment (Doc. 38). Defendants argue that Plaintiff's claim under the Club Agreement is foreclosed by the statute of limitations, that Plaintiff's claim is barred because Plaintiff repudiated the Club Agreement, and that Defendant Petrikin is not personally liable. (Id.)

Analysis

* * *

III. Anticipatory Repudiation

Defendants also argue that Plaintiff cannot recover any payment because Plaintiff repudiated the contract. (Doc. 38, Attach. 2 at 5-6.) Specifically, Defendants point to Plaintiff's statement that it would not be bound by unrecorded side deals or any Shealy agreement in determining whether Plaintiff owed dues. (Id. at 6.) In Georgia, anticipatory repudiation occurs "when one party thereto repudiates his contractual obligation to perform prior to the time such performance is required under the terms of the contract." *Textile Rubber & Chem. Co. v. Thermo-Flex Techs., Inc.*, 301 Ga. App. 491, 494, 687 S.E.2d 919, 922 (2009) (quoting *Coffee Butler Svc. v. Sacha*, 258 Ga. 192, 193, 366 S.E.2d 672, 673 (1988)). When this happens the other party may elect to rescind the contract and recover in quasi contract, treat the repudiation as a breach, or wait until the time for performance of the contract and sue for breach. *Piedmont*, 103 Ga. App. at 234-35, 119 S.E.2d at 71 (citations ommitted).

In this case, Plaintiff and Defendant Petrikin exchanged a series of emails during a dispute as to dues payments. After Defendant Petrikin informed Mr. Leventhal that Defendants would make no further installment or dues payments, Mr. Leventhal informed Defendant Petrikin that the Club was not bound by unrecorded side deals and we are in our view not being treated fair; if you want to leave, then please do so as a gentleman. Otherwise all payments must be current prior to further use. Also, we are otherwise not bound by any Shealy deal.

(Doc. 38, Attach. 1 at 34.) Defendant Petrikin replied to this email by stating

I am sorry that the current management of the Hampton Island Club will not honor the agreement reached by Wood Duck Hiding and Wade Shealy's entity in July 2006. Since it is your position that no one is bound by those agreements, I do not think it is my best interest to make the final installment payment to purchase a trustee membership in the Club.

(Id.) Mr. Leventhal ended the exchange by informing Defendant Petrikin that

I cannot agree to accept any agreements to t [*sic*] which we were not a party, it would open the Pandora's Box if I did. I can with a guaranty from you of payment, delay until the first round is played by Steve in the next couple of months.

(Id. at 32.)

Defendants argue that this exchange is clear evidence of Plaintiff repudiating the contract which, in turn, allowed Defendants to breach by not paying the final installment or any future dues payments. Which contract Plaintiff repudiated—the Purchase and Sale Agreement or the Club Agreement—is less clear. From this exchange, the Court is unable to determine which contract Plaintiff allegedly repudiated and whether Plaintiff was successful in repudiating that contract. At first glance, it appears that Plaintiff is refusing to be bound by the Purchase and Sale Agreement. However, Plaintiff also appears willing to alter the terms of the Club Agreement by delaying the payment of dues with an appropriate guarantee. Defendants' motion for summary judgment is of little help in disentangling this conundrum as it alternatively suggests that Plaintiff repudiated the Purchase and Sale Agreement but also alleges that Plaintiff repudiated other "agreements." (Doc. 38, Attach. 2 at 6.) Because the Court itself is unclear which contract has been repudiated, it would be improvident to grant summary judgment to Defendants at this stage as a question of fact remains as to which contract was allegedly repudiated. Accordingly, Defendants are not entitled to summary judgment.

IV. DEFENDANT PETRIKIN'S INDIVIDUAL OBLIGATION

Defendants allege that Plaintiff's breach of contract claim against Defendant Petrikin fails because there was never a contract between Defendant Petrikin and Plaintiff. (Id.) Plaintiff disagrees. Plaintiff points to the terms of the Club Agreement, which state that Defendant Wood Duck "shall be jointly and severally liable with each Designated User for all dues, fees, charges and other amounts from time to time owing to the Club." (Doc. 38, Attach. 1 at 66.) Defendant Petrikin was the designated user on that Club Agreement. (Id. at 65.) In Georgia, as elsewhere, courts "interpret a contract in accordance with its plain language." *SCSJ Enters., Inc. v. Hansen & Hansen Enters., Inc.*, 319 Ga. App. 210, 212, 734 S.E.2d 214, 218 (2012) (citing *S. Point Retail Partners v. N. Am. Props. Atlanta*, 304 Ga. App. 419, 422, 696 S.E.2d 136 (2010)). Here the plain language of the contract states that Defendant Petrikin is personally liable as a designated user. Accordingly, Defendants' Motion for Summary Judgment on the basis that Defendant Petrikin is not individually liable is DENIED.

Conclusion

For the foregoing reasons, Defendants' Motion for Summary Judgment (Doc. 38) is GRANTED IN PART and DENIED IN PART. This case will proceed to trial on the issue of whether Defendants breached a contract when they failed to annual dues to Plaintiff.

Questions

1. How does the court define anticipatory repudiation?
2. Why did the court find that there was a contract between Petrikin and plaintiff?
3. What remedies are available to the other contracting party when one side repudiates the contract?

Suggested Case References

1. In a contract the parties have agreed to settle disputes by arbitration. A conflict arises regarding price, but the parties failed to set the arbitration process in motion. Is the action of not establishing the arbitration called for in the contract an example of mutual rescission by act of the parties? Read what the Louisiana court said in *Shell Oil Co. v. Texas Gas Transmission Corp.*, 210 So. 2d 554 (La. App. 1968).
2. Does a new agreement between the parties that covers the matters in a disputed contract absorb the original contract into the new agreement? Is this new agreement a separate contract or an accord and satisfaction? Read what the North Dakota court held in *First National Bank, Bismarck v. O'Callaghan*, 143 N.W.2d 104 (N.D. 1966).
3. If a party to a contract refuses to complete performance without additional consideration and continues to delay performance for a month, does that conduct constitute anticipatory breach? *Amberg Granite Co. v. Marinette County*, 247 Wis. 36 (1945).
4. May a written contract be verbally rescinded without any additional consideration? Read the decision in *Cowin v. Salmon*, 244 Ala. 285, 13 So. 2d 190 (1943).

5. Does the fact that the contract has become overly expensive to complete discharge a party's obligations? Read *Dunaj v. Glassmayer*, 61 Ohio Misc. 2d 493, 580 N.E.2d 98 (1990).

Ethical Considerations

A client always has the right to discharge an attorney, thereby terminating the contract, provided that the client pays the attorney for work performed. However, an attorney is not as free to terminate the attorney-client relationship. If the attorney's termination would have an adverse effect on the client, the court may not allow the attorney to withdraw. ABA Rule of Professional Conduct 1.16.

Quick Quiz

Answer TRUE or FALSE. (Answers can be found in Appendix C on page 414.)

1. A contract may be avoided by showing a frustration of purpose.
2. Any contractual promise may be excused.
3. A novation acts as an assignment of a contract.
4. The death of a contracting party always discharges all of his/her contractual obligations.
5. Contracting parties have a duty to mitigate their damages in case of a breach.

11

Remedies

Learning Objectives

After studying this chapter you will be able to:

- Distinguish between legal and equitable remedies
- Define "compensatory damages"
- Discuss when punitive damages may be sought
- Explain what is meant by consequential damages
- Distinguish between liquidated damages and limitation of damages
- Define "injunction"
- Understand when specific performance may be sought as a remedy
- Explain the effect of rescission and restitution on a contract
- List the quasi-contractual remedies
- Discuss the effect of waivers on a breach of contract

CHAPTER OVERVIEW

The time has finally come to answer the question everyone usually wants to start with: "What can I get?" The contract itself is complete, it has met every requirement of the law, all of the parties with vested interests in the agreement have been properly identified, and all conditions have been met. At this point, the promiser does not perform. The promisee is now injured; he has not received his promised-for consideration. What remedies are available to the injured party in a contractual relationship?

Historically, the judicial system was divided into **law** and **equity.** Law and the law courts were based on statutes and judicial precedents, and their purpose was to see that all citizens were treated equally and fairly. Equity and the equity courts were established from the concept of the sovereign's mercy and dealt with situations in which the legal outcomes might be just but were not merciful. These are situations in which, under legal principles, one party could "get away with something." To rectify this potentially unjust situation, equity was established. Equity prevents unjust enrichment that might result from a pure application of legal principles. Although today both these systems are merged into one, the theories proposed by the litigants follow the ancient concepts and precedents of law and equity, and the remedies are different depending on which theory, the legal or the equitable argument, prevails.

With respect to contract law, the concepts of legal and equitable remedies come into play whenever one party breaches her contractual obligations. A breach of contract is a broken promise. The promiser has failed to deliver what she had promised under the contract. When this occurs, the nonbreaching or innocent party to the contract is permitted to seek judicial relief to remedy the situation.

The injured party may seek *legal remedies* if her injury can be corrected simply by money. Legal remedies are known as *damages*, which denotes monetary relief. The type of damages available depends on the specific nature of the contract, the breach, and the injury incurred.

Equitable remedies are nonmonetary relief. They are awarded in those limited situations in which a monetary award would not compensate the innocent party for the injury occasioned by the breach. Equitable remedies are less frequently awarded than damages, and the circumstances must clearly meet all of the requirements of equitable doctrines.

Because the legal and equitable systems are now merged into one judicial process, an injured party may seek both legal and equitable remedies in the same action, and the court will determine which would be the most appropriate for the particular injury involved.

Legal Remedies

Legal remedies, or **damages,** are monetary awards granted to an injured party in a contractual dispute whenever money would be an appropriate method of rectifying the injury. The court awards four types of damages:

1. compensatory damages;
2. punitive damages;

3. consequential damages; and
4. liquidated damages.

Compensatory Damages

Compensatory damages are monetary awards designed to put the injured party in the same position he would have been in had the contract been completed as originally planned. The court determines the amount of the monetary loss the injured party suffered because of the breach.

The formula the courts use to determine the exact amount of compensatory damages was outlined in a judicial case decided many decades ago. The events of the case occurred in a rural community. A farmer's son was injured in a fire, and the palm of his hand was severely burned. In a nearby community, a doctor had been experimenting with skin grafts on farm animals, and when he heard about the farm boy, he offered to try a skin graft on the child for a specified sum of money. The doctor promised that the boy would have a "perfectly good hand."

The farmer agreed, and the operation took place. The doctor grafted skin from the boy's thigh onto the hand. After surgery, the hand healed, and the farmer was delighted. Unfortunately, a few years later the boy entered puberty, and hair started growing on the palm of his hand. The skin the doctor used for the graft was from a hair-producing part of the body. The farmer sued for breach of contract.

In determining that the boy was entitled to compensatory damages, the court arrived at the following formula for making the dollar determination: Take the value of what the injured party started with, add to it the value of what he was promised, and then subtract or add what he was left with to determine whether there was an injury, and the amount of the damage. Compensatory damages are used to put the party in the position he would have been in if the contract had not been breached. If he ends up with more than he was promised, there are no damages. In the case of the farm boy, he started with a burned hand, was promised a perfectly good hand, and was left with a hand with a hairy palm. The amount of his damage is the difference between a "perfectly good hand" and a hand with a hairy palm.

 EXAMPLES:

1. Alice purchases a pearl ring from Jean for $200. After the sale is complete, Alice discovers that the ring is phony and is only worth $2. The amount of Alice's compensatory damage would be $198, the difference between what she was promised (a genuine pearl ring worth $200) and what she actually received (a phony pearl ring worth $2).

2. Eatwell contracts to buy 100 bushels of Grade A plums from Farmer Grey at $10 per bushel. Farmer Grey delivers plums that are Grade B, worth $8 per bushel. Eatwell's compensatory damages are $2 per bushel, the difference between what it was promised and what it received.

To determine the amount of the compensatory damages, the courts have established certain guidelines depending on the type of contract in question. For instance, if the contract is for the sale of goods, compensatory damages are generally the difference between the market price and the contract price. If the buyer is the innocent party, she can recover the difference between the contract price and what she paid for substituted goods in mitigation. If the seller is the injured party, she can resell the goods and recover the difference from the buyer, or, if the goods cannot be resold, she is entitled to the full contract price.

For employment contracts, if the employer breaches, the employee gets the contract price; if the employee breaches, the employer can recover the cost of replacing the worker. Generally, in computing compensatory damages the court simply uses common sense under the given circumstance.

Compensatory damages are the most common remedy for breach of contract.

Punitive Damages

Punitive, or **exemplary, damages** are monetary awards granted by a court for a breach of contract that involves very unusual circumstances. Exemplary damages are intended not only to compensate the injured party but to punish the breaching party. Punishment is not a usual aspect of contract law. As a consequence, for a party to be entitled to punitive damages, there must be some statutory basis for the award under the state's law. Generally, punitive damages are only awarded by statute where the breach of contract is accompanied by some other violation of a breach of trust, such as fraud or antitrust. If a party is seeking punitive damages, he must be able to show the existence of a breach of contract as well as a statutory violation. The innocent party is awarded not only compensatory damages, but punitive damages as well.

EXAMPLE:

Ira is induced to buy a table from Harry for $500. Harry is an antique dealer, and although he claims that it *is* an antique, he knows that the table is not. Because a fraud is involved as well as a breach of contract, Ira may be entitled to punitive as well as compensatory damages if the state statute permits.

Consequential Damages

Consequential damages are monetary awards beyond the standard measure (compensatory damages) due to the special circumstances and expenses incurred because of the injury. For the innocent party to be entitled to consequential damages, when entering into the contractual relationship, she must make the other party aware of special losses that might result from a breach of contract. In this manner, the promisor can decide whether or not to enter into the contractual relationship.

In a famous case, a mill owner had contracted with several farmers in the area to mill their grain during a bumper season. Unfortunately, the mill shaft broke right before the harvest. The miller brought the shaft to a repairman who promised to repair the shaft in a week. The miller made no mention of any special need for the shaft. After the repair, the shaft broke during the first day of use, and the miller sued the repairman, not only for the value of the shaft, but for all his lost profit as well. It seems that because the shaft was the only one the miller had, when it broke he had to cancel his contract with the farmers. The court held that the miller was not entitled to lost profits. This was a loss that could not be foreseen by the repairman when the contract was entered into, and so he could not be responsible for those types of losses. The repairman did have to return to the miller the price of the repairs as compensatory damages.

Therefore, to be entitled to consequential damages, the promisee must make the promisor aware of any unusual or unforeseen consequences that could result from a potential breach at the time the contract is entered into; otherwise the breaching part will only be liable for compensatory damages.

Consequential and punitive damages must be distinguished from the concept of **speculative damages.** Speculative damages are monetary injuries the injured party believes she suffered because of the breach, but which are not readily ascertainable, provable, or quantifiable. An example of speculative damages would be profit the injured party had hoped to make as a result of the contract. Speculative damages cannot be recovered under any circumstances.

EXAMPLE:

Leane hires a limousine to take her to an important business meeting where she is to sign a $1 million contract. The limousine fails to appear, Leane cannot get to the meeting, and she loses the deal. She sues the limousine company for her lost profit of $300,000. Leane will not prevail. She would be entitled to the cost of the limousine, if she had paid for it, but her loss of a $1 million contract is not a foreseeable result of a car service failing to perform. Under these circumstances Leane would not be entitled to consequential damages. Also, her loss may be speculative; more information is needed to determine how realistic that contract was.

Liquidated Damages

Liquidated damages are reasonable damages that the parties themselves have agreed to in the contract itself. Normally, parties to a contract would specify liquidated damages if it would be difficult or impossible to compute compensatory damages because of the uncertain nature of the contract or the subject matter. When liquidated damages are specified, the court will usually award those damages, and the parties are generally precluded from arguing that the amount is too high or too low. Because liquidated damages are determined at the outset of the contract, in order to avoid lengthy litigation later on, the court will simply abide by the parties' agreement under the concept of freedom of contract. The parties never had to agree in the first place, so if they did, their agreement prevails.

However, for the liquidated damages provision of a contract to be enforced, it must be clear that the provision is in fact meant to ease recovery of hard-to-determine losses; if the liquidated damages clause is in fact meant as a punishment for the breaching party or to compensate for speculative damages, the court will not honor the provision.

EXAMPLE:

Gene and Elga have a contract to develop and patent an inexpensive process for creating a clotting agent. Because they don't know whether the idea is patentable or will be successful, they contract with a liquidated damages provision in the amount of $100,000. The contract is breached by Gene, and Elga sues. Regardless of the actual dollar amount of the loss, if Elga can show the existence of a valid contract and a breach by Gene, she will be awarded $100,000.

Liquidated damages should be distinguished from **limitation of damages,** another type of provision that can appear in contractual agreements. With limitation of damages, the parties agree when entering into the contract that, in case of breach, the breaching party will be liable for no more than the amount established as the ceiling, or limitation, in the contract. Unlike liquidated damages, with a limitation of damages provision the injured party must not only prove the contract and the breach, but must prove the actual damages as well. The financial award is limited to the amount contractually specified, but if the actual loss is less than that amount, the smaller sum is awarded. Liquidated damages set the amount of the recovery, regardless of actual loss, whereas a limitation of damages caps liability of actual loss to be no higher than the amount specified.

EXAMPLE:

Assume that instead of a liquidated damages provision, Gene and Elga insert a limitation of damages clause, setting the amount at $100,000. When Gene breaches, Elga now has to prove her actual loss. If she can only show a loss of $75,000, that is all she will recover. If she can show a loss of $250,000, she will only get $100,000, because she has contracted to limit her recovery to that amount.

As discussed in the previous chapter, whenever the court is computing the value of the damages suffered by the injured party, the court also looks to see whether the injured party attempted to **mitigate damages.** It is the duty of every innocent party in a breach of contract to attempt to lessen the damages the breaching party may have to pay, provided that such attempts are not unreasonable or unduly burdensome for the innocent person. The promisee does not have to go out of his way to mitigate but must make some attempt, if possible, to remedy the situation himself. The ultimate award will thereby be reduced by the amount of the mitigation.

EXAMPLES:

1. Ace Supermarkets has a contract to purchase 1,000 bushels of oranges from Farmer Jones at $10 per bushel. Farmer Jones fails to deliver, and Ace is able to find another farmer to sell it the oranges at $11 per bushel. Ace has mitigated its damages, and now is only entitled to $1,000 from Farmer Jones instead of $10,000 (the difference between the $10 per bushel it was to pay Farmer Jones and the $11 per bushel it actually had to pay).

2. In the same situation as above, Ace can find a farmer to sell it oranges at $9 per bushel. In this instance, Farmer Jones' breach has put Ace in a better position than it would have been in had the contract gone through, and so Ace is not entitled to any award from Farmer Jones.

3. Tiffany's contracts with a Thai mine to purchase a 50-carat sapphire for one of its customers. When the mine fails to deliver the jewel, Tiffany's cannot find a replacement stone. Because it is impossible for Tiffany's to mitigate, it is entitled to full compensatory damages.

Equitable Remedies

Whenever the legal remedy of damages is insufficient to compensate the injured party to a breach of contract, the innocent party can look for some equitable relief. **Equitable remedies** are designed to prevent unfairness and unjust enrichment. These largely nonmonetary awards are divided into five categories:

1. injunctions;
2. specific performance;
3. rescission and restitution;
4. reformation; and
5. quasi-contractual.

Injunction

An **injunction** is a court order to stop someone from engaging in a specific action. The verb is *to enjoin*, and the court will only order this when the innocent party could not otherwise be compensated.

 EXAMPLES:

1. Salim has a contract to purchase Whiteacre from Faruk, closing to take place in one month. Two weeks before the closing date, Salim discovers that Faruk is attempting to sell the property to someone else. Salim could go to court to have the court enjoin Faruk from selling the house to anyone other than Salim, pursuant to the contract. Although the injunction would stop Faruk from selling the property to anyone other than Salim, it does not mean that he will actually convey the property to Salim; he can still breach the contract by some other action later on.

2. Joe leaves Acme, Inc., after working there for 20 years. Joe and Acme have a contract in which Joe agreed that, should he leave Acme, he would not go into competition against them for two years. One week after Joe leaves Acme, he goes to work for Acme's biggest competitor. Acme can enjoin Joe from working for the competitor, pursuant to their contract.

Injunctions are permanent or temporary orders of the court to stop a particular action or activity. Because the courts do not usually order injunctions easily or without a full hearing (and only on a showing that irreparable harm would result from a refusal to order the injunction), until a full hearing can be arranged a litigant may be entitled to a **temporary restraining order (TRO)**. A TRO is only a temporary measure by the court until the hearing for full injunctive relief can take place. A TRO is for a short period of time; an injunction is more far reaching.

Specific Performance

Specific performance is a court order requiring the breaching party to perform exactly what she promised under the contract. Specific performance is only granted when the subject matter of the contract is considered unique and therefore not replaceable, or when no other remedy would rectify the injury to the innocent party. Unlike an injunction, in which the court orders a party to stop doing something, with specific performance the court is ordering a party to do something.

 EXAMPLES:

1. In the situation above with Salim and Faruk, on closing day Faruk refuses to convey the property to Salim. Because real estate is generally considered unique, Salim could go to court to seek specific performance. The court would order Faruk to convey Whiteacre to Salim, pursuant to the contract.

2. In the example with Joe and Acme, Acme could also have the court order specific performance of the contract provision. Joe would then have to abide by the agreement and not compete with Acme for two years. The injunction only stopped Joe from working for a specific competitor.

Rescission and Restitution

If a party to a contract finds that fulfillment of the contract would be unduly burdensome, he can ask the court for **rescission and restitution,** whereby the court will rescind, or revoke, the contract in the interest of fairness. It will then have each party restore to the other what the other has expended on the contract to date. If the parties can agree to this procedure by themselves, it is a form of discharge of obligation by a new agreement, as discussed in Chapter 10. If the parties cannot agree to terminate the relationship themselves, the court may do it for them.

Unlike the equitable remedies discussed previously, it is the party who wants to breach who is seeking relief from the court in the form of rescission and restitution. To be entitled to rescission and restitution, the party seeking the remedy must be able to demonstrate that fulfillment of the contract would be so burdensome as to be unjust. Mere economic loss, unless very substantial, is insufficient; economic loss is a risk of contract. What is deemed burdensome is determined by the court on a case-by-case basis.

 EXAMPLE:

Chad and Jeremy have entered into a partnership agreement to publish a magazine. Chad has an independent income; Jeremy does not. After two years of operation, the publication is still losing money with no change likely in the foreseeable future. Jeremy has gone through his money, and he needs to get a paying job. Chad wants to continue the magazine pursuant to the agreement. Under these circumstances, Jeremy could have the court rescind the contract because its fulfillment would be unduly burdensome.

Reformation

Reformation is an equitable remedy that allows a court, upon clear and convincing evidence, to conform a contract to the actual oral agreement of parties. When the parties to a contract cannot resolve their conflict, the court may do so for them by interpreting the contractual provisions according to the parties' intent. Under the rule of construction that contracts are to be upheld if at all possible (Chapter 7), if the dispute merely involves one of quantity or quality of subject matter, the court may reform the contract to reflect the parties' intent so that the contract may go forward.

EXAMPLE:

In the example discussed earlier in which Eatwell received the plums from Farmer Grey, Eatwell claimed the plums were Grade B, whereas Farmer Grey claimed they were in fact Grade A. The parties themselves could not resolve the dispute, but this was the first installment of a year's worth of deliveries. In court, instead of awarding damages, because of the long-term nature of the contract and the difficulty of proving grades of plums, the court could reform the contract to delete mention of the grade of plums and to change the price to $8.50 a bushel, because the clear evidence submitted indicated that the parties were more concerned with the price and total quantity than the actual grade of the plums. In this manner, the contract between Eatwell and Farmer Grey can be maintained.

Quasi-Contractual Remedies

The **quasi-contractual remedies** are the only equitable remedies that involve a monetary award. Quasi-contractual remedies are available in situations in which no contract exists, but there has been unjust enrichment to one of the parties of the dispute. To rectify the unjust enrichment, the court will order the injured party to be awarded the value of what she has lost (the value of the unjust enrichment). There are two types of quasi-contractual remedies:

1. *Quantum meruit* and
2. *Quantum valebant*.

Quantum Meruit

Quantum meruit means the value of the service rendered. If the defendant is unjustly enriched by receiving uncompensated-for services, she must pay the injured party the value of those services. Remember the paralegal who worked for her aunt with the expectation of receiving the aunt's property on the aunt's death (Chapter 1): Although no contract did in fact exist, the paralegal was entitled to the value of the services she performed for the aunt. This is *quantum meruit*.

Quantum Valebant

Quantum valebant means the value of the property received. If the injured party conveys property that unjustly enriches the recipient, the recipient is required to pay the innocent party for the value of the property. An example would be the newspaper that was left on the doorstep in Chapter 1. The person who kept accepting the newspaper is liable for the value of the paper to the publisher, who never intended to give the paper as a gift.

Both *quantum meruit* and *quantum valebant* are applied in cases involving quasi-contracts in the interests of justice.

Waivers and Their Effect

A party cannot be sued for breaching his obligation under a contract if the innocent party waives that breach. A **waiver** is the forgiveness by a party to a contract of the other side's failure to meet a contractual obligation. The waiver can be for a contractual covenant or for any condition specified in the contract.

A party can waive a contractual provision either expressly or implicitly. An **express waiver** occurs when the promisee specifically manifests that she intends to forgive the other side's breach. An **implied waiver** occurs, not by the words or manifestations of the promisee, but by the promisee's actions. In both instances, when a contractual provision has been waived, the other side is relieved of that specific obligation.

 EXAMPLES:

1. Leo contracts with Bob for the construction of an addition to his house. The contract states that Leo will only pay for the work when it is complete, and Bob gets an architect's certificate that the work meets all structural specifications. The work is done, and Leo pays Bob without having the architect's certificate. Leo has waived this condition of the contract by his actions.

2. Leona rents an apartment from ABC Realty, and the lease specifies that the apartment cannot be sublet. Leona has to go out of town for a long period of time and asks ABC if they would permit a short-term sublet to help her out. ABC agrees in writing to waive the nonsublet provision of the lease. Leona is now free to sublet without being in breach.

As a general rule, any party to a contract is free to waive any provision she wishes. However, the promisor cannot always rely on the waiver to relieve him of all liabilities, especially if the waiver waives an obligation that is an ongoing obligation, such as monthly rent during a two-year lease. To protect the parties, many contracts include a waiver provision in which it is specifically stated that waiving one provision of the contract does not necessarily waive any other provision, nor is a waiver at one time to be considered a continuing waiver of that contractual provision during the full term of the contract. Therefore, if one party to a contract is going to be unable to fulfill a particular contractual provision, it would behoove him to seek a waiver for the provision to avoid being in breach. The effect of an obligation being specifically waived is that the obligation cannot be reinstated or made the subject of a suit for breach of contract. The party who waives the provision is estopped, or barred, from raising that provision as the grounds of a lawsuit.

Arbitration Provisions

Despite the foregoing, many contracts specify that disputes will be decided not by going to court, but by having the matter resolved by **arbitration.** Arbitration is a nonjudicial method of settling legal disputes in which both sides agree to submit the claim to an agreed-on arbitrator for relief. Arbitration is usually a faster and less expensive method of resolving disputes than litigation.

Arbitrators are not bound by evidentiary rules and are free to determine liabilities and relief as they see fit. In most instances, the decision of the arbitrator is final and binding, precluding the parties from seeking further judicial relief. Examples of arbitration clauses appear in Chapter 12, Drafting Simple Contracts.

Because arbitration is now so popular, it must be considered when determining appropriate remedies for a contractual disagreement.

SAMPLE CLAUSES

1

The failure of the lessor to insist upon the strict performance of the terms, covenants, agreements and conditions herein contained, or any of them, shall not constitute or be construed as a waiver or relinquishment of the lessor's right to thereafter enforce any such term, covenant, agreement, or condition, but the same shall continue in full force and effect.

The above is an example of a waiver provision in a lease. By these words, the promisee is stating that he may, if he so desires, forgive enforcement of a contract promise, but that waiver is not to be considered a continuing waiver, or a waiver of all his rights. What he forgives once he may not forgive a second time, and the promisor is still contractually bound for all covenants and conditions not waived. Typically contracts will specify that waivers must be in writing; this protects both sides to the agreement. Remember, a promisor is not obligated to fulfill any promise that the promisee has waived. Failure to fulfill a waived obligation is *not* a breach of contract.

2

Should Seller breach any of the provisions of the agreement, Seller shall be liable for liquidated damages in the amount of $X.

The preceding is an example of a liquidated damages clause. The contracting parties, when entering into the agreement, have specified what the damages shall be in the case of breach. In this instance, the seller would be liable for $X, provided the buyer could prove the contract was breached.

No evidence need be given with respect to the actual damages involved; damages have already been contractually determined.

3

In the event of breach of any of the provisions of this agreement, damages shall be limited to $X, exclusive of attorneys' fees and court costs.

In the above example, the parties have set a limitation to their potential liability. In this case, the injured party not only has to prove breach but must also prove the amount of damages. Regardless of what can be proven, damages will not exceed the amount stipulated by the parties in their contract.

CHAPTER SUMMARY

Remedies are the awards the injured party in a contractual dispute can receive from the party who has breached her obligation. The type and the amount of the award depends on the nature of the injury occasioned by the breach; the purpose is to put the injured party in the same position she would have been in had there been no breach.

Legal remedies, known as damages, are monetary awards based on the injury suffered. The standard measure of damages is compensatory damages, which attempt to put the innocent party in the same position he would have been in had the contract been fulfilled as planned. In unusual circumstances, the injured party may be entitled to a monetary award different from the standard measure. If the nonbreaching party makes the promisor aware of some special losses that would be occasioned by a breach, he may be entitled to consequential damages to compensate him for this extraordinary loss. If the breach is accompanied by some other wrongdoing (such as fraud), the court, under statutory authority, may punish the breaching party. In this case, punitive, or exemplary, damages are awarded in addition to the standard measure.

When negotiating the agreement, the parties to the contract are always free to agree on liquidated damages or a limitation of liability. With liquidated damages, the parties agree that, in case of breach, the amount recovered by the nonbreaching party will be an amount established in the contract itself. With a limitation of liability provision, damages must be proven but cannot exceed the amount stipulated in the agreement.

If monetary awards would be insufficient, or inappropriate, to compensate the injured party, under the court's equitable jurisdiction the innocent party may be entitled to some nonmonetary relief. Examples of these equitable remedies are injunctions, to stop the breaching party from engaging in a specific action; specific performance, ordering the breaching party to fulfill the specific obligations of the contract; rescission and restitution, in which the court will rescind the contract and put the parties in the same position they were in before the contract was entered into; and reformation, in which the court will alter the terms of the agreement to keep the total contract in effect. In addition to these nonmonetary awards, if the source of the dispute is a quasi-contractual relationship, the court may order some monetary relief for the value of the unjust enrichment.

A promisee may waive any provision of a contract that she wishes, and the waiver relieves the promisor of that contractual provision without being in breach of contract. However, the waiver of one provision is usually not considered to be a waiver of any other provision, and except for the specifically waived obligation, the promisor remains contractually bound.

In court, the injured party may ask for as many different types of remedies as seem appropriate to the action. The court will make the ultimate decision as to which remedies to award.

SYNOPSIS

Legal remedies
  Damages (money)
    1. Compensatory
    2. Punitive
    3. Consequential
Equitable remedies (nonmonetary)
    1. Injunction
    2. Specific performance
    3. Rescission and restitution
    4. Reformation
    5. Quasi-contractual
Contract clauses
    1. Liquidated damages
    2. Limitation of damages
    3. Waivers
    4. Arbitration

Key Terms

Arbitration: nonjudicial method of resolving legal disputes
Compensatory damages: standard measure of damages; puts injured party
      in the position he would have been in had the contract been fulfilled
Consequential damages: damages above the standard measure due to
      special losses occasioned by the breach
Damages: legal remedies; monetary awards
Equitable remedies: nonmonetary awards
Equity: area of law concerned with preventing unfairness and unjust
      enrichment
Exemplary damages: additional monetary award designed to punish the
      breaching party

Express waiver: a waiver occurring when the promisee specifically
     manifests an intention to forgive the other side's breach
Implied waiver: a waiver occurring when the promisee's actions imply an
     intention to forgive the other side's breach
Injunction: court order to stop engaging in a specific action
Law: division of law concerned with historical legal principles designed to
     provide equal treatment to all persons
Legal remedies: monetary awards
Limitation of damages: contractual provision placing a ceiling on the
     amount of potential liability for breach of the contract
Liquidated damages: contractual provision providing a specified dollar
     amount for breach of the contract
Mitigation of damages: duty imposed on innocent party to make
     reasonable attempts to lessen the liability of the breaching party
Punitive damages: exemplary damages
QUANTUM MERUIT*:*   quasi-contractual award; value of the service performed
QUANTUM VALEBANT*:*   quasi-contractual award; value of the good given
Quasi-contractual remedy: an equitable remedy involving a monetary
     award
Reformation: a court-ordered accord and satisfaction
Rescission and restitution: a court order revoking a contract that would be
     unduly burdensome to fulfill
Specific performance: court order to perform contractual promise
Speculative damages: damages that are not specifically provable
Temporary restraining order (TRO):   preliminary step to an injunction
Waiver: forgiveness of a contract obligation

EXERCISES

1. Give an example of a situation in which punitive damages would
   be possible.
2. Your school decides to disband the paralegal program before you
   complete your studies. What damage would you claim, and how
   could you substantiate that claim?
3. What is the effect of a disclaimer on consequential damages?
4. Argue that a limitation of damages provision should not be considered valid.
5. Give two examples not discussed in the chapter in which quasi-
   contractual remedies would be appropriate.

Cases for Analysis

The following case summaries highlight the concepts of mutual
mistake in *Pioneer Exploration, Ltd. v. Rutherford* and the measurement
of damages and contract interpretation in *Fazio v. Cypress/GR Houston I,
L.P.*

Pioneer Exploration, Ltd. v. Rutherford

2009 U.S. App. LEXIS 14176 (5th Cir. 2009)

I. Facts and Proceedings Below

In the summer of 2005, a Pioneer representative, John Gilbert, approached the Rutherfords to discuss the possibility of leasing their property for the construction and operation of an oil and gas facility. The Rutherfords owned approximately twenty acres of land in Cameron Parish, Louisiana. The tract was divided approximately in half by a shell road, and though the portion north of the road was unused, the Rutherfords maintained their homesteads south of the road.[1]

During lease negotiations, the Rutherfords were represented by their attorney, Jennifer Jones (Ms. Jones), and Pioneer was represented by its vice president and general counsel, George Ruff (Mr. Ruff). Five drafts of the lease agreement were circulated prior to the final agreement. Each draft recited the following property description: "7 acres of land out of the SE/4 of the NE/4 of Section 34." But this property description was incorrect—the Rutherfords did not own any land in the northeast quarter of Section 34.[2] Thus, every draft prior to the final agreement contained a totally incorrect legal description of the property to be leased. Also, none of the prior drafts described which seven acres of the approximately twenty-acre tract were to be leased, and both parties admit that seven acres was an approximation and the exact amount of acreage to be included in the lease was uncertain.

Pioneer rejected each draft containing the incorrect legal description and repeatedly requested "a better property description." In January 2006, Mr. Ruff sent Ms. Jones a letter requesting a "good description of the 7 acres." In response, Ms. Jones faxed Mr. Ruff two documents: (1) a copy of the Cameron Parish Assessor's Office's record containing the legal description of the Rutherfords' property and (2) an approximately letter size copy of a "Tobin" map covering more than 20 sections in the area, including section 34, on which she had highlighted a some seven acre area.[3] The fax cover sheet read: "See attached property description from the Cameron Parish Assessor's Office." This record reflected that the Rutherfords owned 21.95 acres in the "W/2 NE/4 SE/4 SEC 34."

After receiving these documents, Mr. Ruff inserted the property description into the lease as follows: "All of the land owned by Lessor

---

1. While lease negotiations were ongoing, the Rutherfords' homesteads were destroyed by hurricane Rita; there is evidence that at all times, the Rutherfords have intended to rebuild their homes on the same site.

2. The Rutherfords own land in the western half of the northeast quarter of the southeast quarter of Section 34 (abbreviated as W/2 NE/4 SE/4 of Section 34); they do not own any land in the northeast quarter of Section 34.

3. The highlighted portion of the map was extremely small and the map was sent via facsimile, rendering it difficult, if not impossible, to ascertain what portion of land was highlighted.

in the W/2 NE/4 SE/4 of Section 34." This property description encompassed approximately twenty acres, though the parties repeatedly referred
to the lease as seven acres in previous drafts and correspondence. The
lease agreement, like all previous drafts, also states that the acreage is
only an estimate, that Pioneer would arrange to have the property sur-
veyed, and the survey description will replace the lease language property
description.

Pioneer then sent the lease agreement to the Rutherfords and attached
a cover sheet stating that Ms. Jones had supplied the lease's final property description. Pioneer also enclosed two checks for $5,000, each with
the following notation: "SURF. LS. ACQUISITION COVERING, 7 ACRES
IN THE W/2NE/4SE/4 OF, SEC. 34, 14S, 7W CAMERON PARI[SH]."
Though Mr. Ruff copied Ms. Jones on an email containing the cover sheet
and final lease agreement, Ms. Jones alleges that she did not receive a copy
of the lease agreement, either by email or mail. Three weeks later, the
Rutherfords signed the lease agreement in Ms. Jones's office and Ms. Jones
signed as a witness. Both the Rutherfords and Ms. Jones assert they did not
read the final lease agreement prior to signing it.

Nearly ten months later, Ms. Jones contacted Mr. Ruff asserting
that the property description contained in the final lease agreement
was erroneous. She requested that the property description be changed
to the following: "[a]pproximately seven (7) acres, more or less, located
North of shell road in the West one-half (1/2) of the NE/4 of the SE/4
of Section 34." Pioneer responded that it did not wish to amend the
lease, and Ms. Jones demanded renegotiation and threatened to sue
Pioneer.

Pioneer responded by filing suit in federal district court for a declaratory judgment against the Rutherfords. The Rutherfords counterclaimed,
alleging the contract was void due to (1) fraud, (2) unilateral error, and/
or (3) mutual error, and requested rescission or reformation. The district
court granted summary judgment in Pioneer's favor. The Rutherfords
now appeal to this court. The parties agree that in this diversity case the
applicable substantive law is that of Louisiana.

II.   Discussion

The Rutherfords argue that the district court erred in granting
Pioneer's summary judgment motion because the record evidence creates a genuine issue of fact as to the lease's validity. Under Louisiana
law, consent is required to form a valid contract. La. Civ. Code Ann. art.
1927. "Consent may be vitiated by error, fraud, or duress," which consequently would invalidate the contract. Id.[4] art. 1948. The Rutherfords
argue that, based upon the evidence presented, a reasonable trier of fact

---

4 Parol evidence is admissible where a party argues "vice of consent," either through
mistake or fraud. Condrey v. Suntrust Bank of Georgia, 429 F.3d 556, 563 (5th Cir. 2005); see
also La. Civ. Code Ann. art. 1848.

could determine that their consent to the lease was vitiated by (1) fraud, (2) unilateral error, or (3) mutual error; thus, Pioneer was not entitled to judgment as a matter of law.

This court reviews a district court's order granting summary judgment de novo, applying the same standard as the district court. *Aryain v. Wal-Mart Stores Texas LP*, 534 F.3d 473, 478 (5th Cir. 2008). Summary judgment is appropriate when "there is no genuine issue as to any material fact and . . . the movant is entitled to judgment as a matter of law." Fed. R. Civ. P. 56(c). With respect to issues on which the nonmovant would bear the burden of proof at trial, "[a] genuine issue of material fact exists if the summary judgment evidence is such that a reasonable jury could return a verdict for the nonmovant." *Aryain*, 534 F.3d at 478. "[A]ll facts and evidence must be taken in the light most favorable to the nonmovant." *LeMaire v. La. Dept. of Transp. and Dev.*, 480 F.3d 383, 387 (5th Cir. 2007). In reviewing the evidence at summary judgment, we must "refrain from making credibility determinations or weighing the evidence." *Turner v. Baylor Richardson Med. Ctr.*, 476 F.3d 337, 343 (5th Cir. 2007). We first address the Rutherfords' fraud and unilateral error claims before addressing the more difficult issue of mutual error.

A. *Fraud and Unilateral Error*

Under Louisiana law, "[i]t is well settled that a party who signs a written instrument is presumed to know its contents and cannot avoid its obligations by contending that he did not read it, that he did not understand it, or that the other party failed to explain it to him." *Aguillard v. Auction Mngt Corp.*, 908 So. 2d 1, 17 (La. 2005). Bearing this principle in mind, Louisiana courts have consistently held that a unilateral error cannot invalidate an agreement if it was caused by a complaining party's "inexcusable ignorance, neglect, or want of care" or where that party "through education or experience, had the knowledge or expertise to easily rectify or discover the error complained of." *Scott v. Bank of Coushatta*, 512 So. 2d 356, 362, 363 (La. 1987). This has become known as the contractual negligence defense and is most commonly used to bar rescission for errors "resulting from a party's failure to read the document in issue." *Ill. Cent. Gulf R. Co. v. R.R. Land, Inc.*, 988 F.2d 1397, 1405 (5th Cir. 1993). The defense also applies to fraud claims:

> "Fraud does not vitiate consent when the party against whom the fraud was directed could have ascertained the truth without difficulty, inconvenience, or special skill. This exception does not apply when a relation of confidence has reasonably induced a party to rely on the other's assertions or representations."

La. Civ. Code Ann. art. 1954. And again, this defense is consistently applied to bar a party's fraud claim where the complaining party failed to read a document before signing it. E.g., *Martin v. JKD Investments, LLC*, 961 So. 2d 575, 578 (La. App. 2d Cir. 2007); *Sonnier v. Boudreaux*, 673 So. 2d 713, 717-18 (La. App. 1st Cir. 1996).

The Rutherfords admit that neither they nor their attorney read the final lease agreement before signing it.[5] Had they read the document, they could have easily discovered the allegedly erroneous property description. The property description is contained in the "Premises Leased" provision, which is the first provision in the lease and is prominently located on the first page of the agreement. It is set off by double indents, contains no more than twenty-five words, and begins with "[a]ll of the land owned by Lessor." Further, the Rutherfords were experienced in leasing their property, had qualified counsel at their disposal, and were in possession of the lease for three weeks before signing it. The lease was signed by them, and signed as a witness by their counsel (and acknowledged by them before a notary who was their counsel's secretary) all in their counsel's office. It was then sent to Pioneer for execution by Pioneer. Clearly the Rutherfords could have easily discovered the alleged error simply by reading the document; thus, the contractual negligence defense bars the Rutherfords' claims that their consent is void due to fraud or unilateral error.

Contractual negligence, however, "does not bar reformation where mutual mistake has been pleaded and proved." *Ill. Cent.*, 988 F.2d at 1398. Thus, we now turn to whether a fact question regarding mutual mistake exists.

B.   *Mutual Error*

The Rutherfords contend that there clearly existed an antecedent agreement between the parties that the leased premises pertained to a seven-acre tract of land located north of the shell road. Further, they argue that this agreement was incorrectly reduced to writing, that the error was mutual, that their consent was vitiated, and reformation is warranted.[6]

Again, Louisiana law requires consent to have an enforceable contract, and consent can be rendered void by error. La. Civ. Code Ann. art. 1927, 1948. In the event that an error causes a contract to recite terms to which neither party agreed, Louisiana law provides contract reformation as an equitable remedy. *Phillips Oil Co. v. OKC Corp.*, 812 F.2d 265, 274 (5th Cir. 1987). "Before an instrument will be reformed, 'there must be clear proof of the antecedent agreement as well as an error in committing it to writing.'" *Ill. Cent.*, 988 F.2d at 1402 (quoting *Pat S. Todd Oil Co., Inc. v. Wall*, 581 So. 2d 333, 336 (La. App. 3rd Cir. 1991)). Reformation is only available to "'correct mistakes or errors in the written instrument when such instrument, as written, does not express the true contract or agreement of the parties.'" Phillips Oil, 812 F.2d at 274 (quoting *Fontenot v. Lewis*, 215 So. 2d 161, 163 (La. App. 3d Cir. 1968)). Most importantly, "[t]he error or

---

5. The Rutherfords also do not claim, nor is there any evidence to suggest, that a relationship of confidence existed between themselves and Pioneer.

6. Pioneer argues that the Rutherfords are barred from raising this claim on appeal because they did not press the issue to the district court. This argument is without merit because the Rutherfords alleged mutual error in their Counterclaim and in their Memorandum in Opposition to Summary Judgment, and the district court definitively ruled on the issue.

mistake must be **mutual**, and the party seeking reformation must establish the mutual error by clear and convincing evidence. *Id*." (emphasis added).

In light of the summary judgment standard and the Rutherfords' burden of proof at trial, this Court must ascertain whether, viewing all of the evidence in the light most favorable to the Rutherfords, enough evidence exists for a reasonable factfinder to determine that the Rutherfords have shown mutual error by clear and convincing evidence. In making this determination, "the court should focus on who reduced the proposed agreement to writing, who the parties to the agreement were, whether the provision at issue was central to the agreement, and what pains the parties took in reviewing the written instrument." Id. at 275.

The evidence in the present case demonstrates that Pioneer intended to modify the final lease to include all of the Rutherfords' land. First, the "Premises Leased" provision is central to the lease agreement and was written in clear and unambiguous terms, beginning with "[a]ll of the land owned by Lessor." Second, Pioneer reduced the agreement to writing, and it is undisputed that Pioneer inserted the final property description. Mr. Ruff's affidavit explains that he inserted this property description after Ms. Jones faxed him the Cameron Parish Assessor's records showing that the Rutherfords owned nearly twenty-two acres in Section 34. The lease's final property description is not limited by any reference to seven acres or a shell road. The significance of the provision and Pioneer's affirmative act to include "all land owned," rather than a limiting provision, demonstrates that this language was not included by accident. Additionally, both parties were experienced in leasing—Pioneer is an oil and gas producer with experience in surface leases, and the Rutherfords had leased their own land before and were also represented by qualified counsel. All of these factors evidence that Pioneer was not mistaken when it agreed to lease all of the Rutherfords' land.

Still, the Rutherfords maintain that clear and convincing evidence exists that a mutual mistake was made. They argue that during the lease negotiations both parties consistently referred to the lease as seven acres, as evidenced by the prior lease drafts and Pioneer's own correspondences with Ms. Jones. Additionally, in their affidavits, the Rutherfords explain that they were only willing to lease the land north of the shell road because they maintained their homesteads in the southern portion of the tract.[7] These arguments do not convince us that the record contains clear and convincing evidence of mutual mistake.

Though the parties consistently referred to seven acres, none of the previous drafts described land that the Rutherfords actually owned, nor did they mention a shell road or provide any means of identifying which seven acres of the twenty-acre tract were to be leased. It is also undisputed that seven acres was an approximation and neither party was certain as to the exact number of acres to be covered by the lease. When prompted

---

7. Again, the Rutherfords homesteads were destroyed by hurricane Rita during the negotiations. The Rutherfords maintain that they intended to rebuild their homesteads in the same location and never discussed the possibility of leasing the entire twenty-acre tract.

to provide a more detailed property description, the Rutherfords' attorney instructed Pioneer to "see [the] attached property description from the Cameron Parish Assessor's Office," which showed that the Rutherfords owned 21.95 acres in the "W/2 NE/4 SE/4 SEC 34." Ms. Jones also faxed Pioneer a map highlighting an area within section 34, but the fax cover sheet did not direct Pioneer's attention to this map, and the highlighted portion is largely unidentifiable because it was sent via fax and comprises only a very small portion of the map.

The Rutherfords' strongest evidence of mutual mistake is Pioneer's enclosure of two $5,000 checks with a notation referencing a surface lease of "7 acres." However, these still do not provide clear and convincing proof that Pioneer included the language "all land owned" in error. It may be that the individual writing the checks believed the lease was for seven acres, but the lease itself clearly describes all of the land owned by the Rutherfords in a twenty-acre tract. And there is no indication that the individual writing these checks had any involvement with the lease negotiations, the drafting of the final property description, or was aware of what the parties ultimately agreed upon.

Last, the Rutherfords' reliance on this court's opinion in *Illinois Central*, which upheld a district court's reformation of a contract after finding that a party's inadvertent omission of a term constituted a mutual error and warranted reformation, is unpersuasive in the present context. See 988 F.2d at 1404-05. In *Illinois Central*, there existed strong evidence that the parties had previously agreed to include a specific rider in the final sale. *Id.* at 1404. In fact, this very same rider had been included in a previous and related transaction between the parties. *Id.* at 1400, 1404. Yet, the drafting party inadvertently omitted the physical act of attaching the rider to the final agreement. *Id.* at 1404. And there was evidence that the other party was unaware of the rider's omission prior to signing because its actions were in accordance with the rider's terms. *Id.* at 1403 n. 17. Thus, the court determined that the physical omission of the rider was a mutual mistake, and reformed the agreement. *Id.* at 1404-05.

Unlike *Illinois Central*, the present case involves an intentional, affirmative act to include language in the most prominent provision of the contract. Pioneer did not inadvertently omit a term, it specifically altered a limiting phrase to extend the lease to "all of the land owned" in a twenty-acre tract. It is implausible that this could be done by accident or mistake. And, Pioneer, through Ruff, denied any such mistake. Every prior draft contained the language "7 acres," yet Pioneer consistently rejected this description, made repeated requests for a better property description, and ultimately revised the lease language to include "all of the land owned by Lessor."[8] This action reflects an affirmative, conscious choice

---

8. As appellants assert in their brief to this court (p. 32) "it is hard to imagine how, inter alia, deleting 'seven acres' and inserting 'all of the land owned by Lessor' into the sixth draft of the lease was accidental." Similarly, appellants also assert in their brief that "a close review of the record exposes the real motive behind Pioneer's last minute deception of the Rutherfords." (Id. at 39).

by Pioneer rather than an inadvertent omission—a stark contrast to *Illinois Central*, where a specific rider, used by the parties in a related past transaction, was inadvertently failed to be physically attached to the final sale document.

Viewing the above evidence in the light most favorable to the Rutherfords, a reasonable factfinder could not find mutual mistake by clear and convincing evidence.

Conclusion

For the aforementioned reasons, the district court did not err in granting summary judgment.

AFFIRMED.

Questions

1. Why does the court decide that a fraud defense does not apply in this instance?
2. What remedy is permitted if mutual mistake is proven?
3. What factors does the court look at to determine whether a mutual mistake exists?

Fazio v. Cypress/GR Houston I, L.P.
403 S.W.3d 390 (2013)

En Banc Opinion

In this suit arising from the sale of land, we examine the appropriate measure of damages for a sale obtained through fraudulent inducement. A jury concluded that the seller of the land had failed to disclose material information to the buyer about the financial state of a commercial tenant who leased the land. But the jury further concluded that the buyers suffered nothing in damages proximately caused by the fraud, measured at the time of the sale, and it awarded no damages in connection with the costs incurred with the termination of the tenant's lease, nor the legal fees the buyers incurred due to the tenant's bankruptcy, nor the interest expense the buyers incurred on loans they obtained to facilitate the purchase. The trial court entered a take-nothing judgment in favor of the seller.

A majority of a panel of our court reversed the trial court, concluding that the buyers were nonetheless entitled to damages based on the loss that the buyers took when they sold the land three years later. The majority also concluded, with one justice dissenting, that the buyers did not disclaim reliance on the seller's promise of full disclosure in a letter of intent that the seller had signed before the sale. The seller moved for rehearing and rehearing en banc. The panel majority granted the motion for rehearing and revised its opinion, mooting the en banc request, but its

disposition remained the same. The seller moved again for en banc consideration. Concluding that the case warranted en banc review, a majority
of our court has voted to reconsider this case. *See Tex. R. App. P. 49.7.* We
withdraw the panel's August 16, 2012 opinion on rehearing and judgment,
and substitute this opinion and judgment in its place.

We hold that the trial court properly entered a take-nothing judgment, because the jury found that no damages were proximately caused
by the fraud, measured at the time of the sale, and it found no incidental or
consequential damages relating to the sale. We further hold that the trial
court properly denied the seller's request for attorney's fees as the prevailing party, because the parties' contract did not provide for a recovery for
attorney's fees incurred in defense against claims of fraud. We therefore
affirm.

Background

Peter, Shari, and Eric Fazio sued Cypress/GR Houston I, L.P., Cypress/
GR Houston, Inc., and Cypress Equities, Inc. (collectively, Cypress) for
fraudulent inducement, relating to the Fazios' purchase, in October 2003, of
commercial land located on the frontage road of Interstate 10 in Houston.
At that time, Garden Ridge Pottery leased the site for one of its retail stores.

After identifying the land as an investment prospect, the Fazios notified Cypress of their interest in purchasing it. In early September 2003, the
parties executed a letter of intent, signed by Peter Fazio and a representative of Cypress Equities, in which Cypress agreed to allow the Fazios to
investigate "all aspects of the Property" and further agreed to provide the
Fazios with "all information in [Cypress's] possession." The Fazios and
their brokers subsequently conducted due diligence and inspected the
property. As part of this process, they requested "every scrap of paper"
that Cypress had regarding the property. The Fazios reviewed multiple
appraisals of the property; researched the property's primary tenant,
Garden Ridge; investigated the lease terms; reviewed Garden Ridge's
audited financial statements; and contacted Garden Ridge's CFO for an
assessment of Garden Ridge's financial condition. The Fazios' investiga-
tions revealed that Garden Ridge was restructuring and struggling finan-
cially, but that Garden Ridge had recently secured a line of credit for its
operations to continue through the 2003 Christmas season. During their
discussions with Garden Ridge's CFO, the CFO was optimistic that Garden
Ridge could work through its financial difficulties. The Fazios' own lenders were not as certain, and told the Fazios that Garden Ridge was not
a viable long-term tenant. Garden Ridge's audited financial statements,
which the Fazios reviewed, showed that Garden Ridge had defaulted on
its debt covenants and was in the process of corporate restructuring.

Despite its agreement in the letter of intent to provide to the Fazios
"all information in its possession," Cypress did not disclose to the Fazios
that, in February 2003, Garden Ridge had sent a letter to Cypress stating
that it was "restructuring" and needed "to reduce our occupancy costs

at your premises." Cypress also did not disclose that Garden Ridge had sought a 30% rent reduction for the 1-10 property as well as a similar reduction for another property owned by a separate Cypress entity and leased to Garden Ridge. Finally, Cypress failed to disclose that in early September 2003, Cypress's own lender was concerned about the financial condition of Garden Ridge and had asked that Cypress's President, Chris Maguire, execute a personal guaranty for the $5,704,000 loan that it had made to Cypress that had been formerly secured only by the property. Maguire eventually signed the guaranty—on September 25, one day after Cypress sold the land to the Fazios.

The parties executed the final purchase agreement on September 24, 2003 for a price of $7,667,000. The agreement contained various provisions disclaiming the Fazios' reliance on representations made by Cypress to the Fazios.

Garden Ridge paid its rent in October, November, and December, but it defaulted on its rent in January 2004, and shortly thereafter declared bankruptcy. Once in Chapter 11 bankruptcy protection, Garden Ridge rejected its lease. The Fazios attempted, unsuccessfully, to re-lease the land. They later sold it in 2007 for $3,750,000.

The jury found that Cypress Equities, but neither of the other Cypress entities, had defrauded the Fazios. It attributed 100% responsibility for any harm to the Fazios to Cypress Equities, but it found that the Cypress entities operated as a single business enterprise.

The trial court instructed the jury on two measures of direct damages, and various measures of incidental and consequential damages. The trial court's two measures for actual damages were distinctly different: Jury question 2(1) instructed the jury to determine "[t]he difference between the price the Fazios paid for the Property and the amount they received when they sold the Property"; to this question, the jury answered $3,961,524.60, which is the actual difference in the two amounts. Question 2(2), in contrast, instructed the jury to determine "the difference, if any, between the price the Fazios paid for the Property and the value of the Property at the time the Purchase Agreement was executed"; to this question, the jury answered $0. In response to each of four instructions on incidental and consequential damages, the jury also answered $0. But, finding clear and convincing evidence of fraud, the jury awarded $667,000 in exemplary damages.

Both parties moved for judgment in the trial court. Among other grounds, Cypress argued that the Fazios were not entitled to a judgment based on the jury's answer to question 2(1) because it was an improper measure of damages, and that it, Cypress, was entitled to judgment based on the jury's answer to question 2(2), in which the jury awarded nothing under the proper measure of damages. The Fazios requested judgment on the jury's verdict for the amount the jury found in answer to question 2(1), plus exemplary damages. After extensive post-verdict briefing, the trial court entered a take-nothing judgment for Cypress and denied Cypress's request for attorney's fees.

The Fazios appeal the trial court's judgment against them on their claim for fraudulent inducement, contending that the trial court erred in disregarding the jury's liability and damages findings in their favor. They contend that the trial court instead should have disregarded the damages questions the jury found against them. Cypress also appeals, challenging the trial court's denial of its motion for attorney's fees.

Damages

* * *

B. Measuring Direct Damages

There are two measures of direct damages in a fraud case: out-of-pocket and benefit-of-the-bargain. *Formosa Plastics Corp. USA v. Presidio Eng'rs & Contractors, Inc.*, 960 S.W.2d 41, 49 (Tex. 1998) (citing *Arthur Andersen & Co. v. Perry Equip. Corp.*, 945 S.W.2d 812, 817 (Tex. 1997)). Out-of-pocket damages measure the difference between the amount the buyer paid and the value of the property the buyer received. *Leyendecker & Assocs., Inc. v. Wechter*, 683 S.W.2d 369, 373 (Tex. 1984). Benefit-of-the-bargain damages measure the difference between the value of the property as represented and the actual value of the property. *Id.* Both measures are determined at the time of the sale induced by the fraud. *Id.*; *Arthur Andersen*, 945 S.W.2d at 817; *Woodyard v. Hunt*, 695 S.W.2d 730, 733 (Tex. App.—Houston [1st Dist.] 1985, no writ); *Highland Capital Mgmt., L.P. v. Ryder Scott Co.*, No.01-10-00362-CV, 402 S.W.3d 719, 2012 Tex. App. LEXIS 10120, 2012 WL 6082713, at *7-8 (Tex. App.—Houston [1st Dist.] Dec. 6, 2012, no pet. h.).

Losses that arise after the time of sale may be recoverable as consequential damages in appropriate cases. *Formosa Plastics*, 960 S.W.2d at 49 n.1 (citing *Arthur Andersen*, 945 S.W.2d at 817). Consequential damages must be foreseeable and directly traceable to the misrepresentation and result from it. *Arthur Andersen*, 945 S.W.2d at 816. An investor may not "shift the entire risk of an investment to a defendant who made a misrepresentation" if the loss is unrelated to the misrepresentation and due to market fluctuations or the chances of business. *Id.* at 817; *see Sw. Battery Corp. v. Owen*, 131 Tex. 423, 115 S.W.2d 1097, 1098 (Tex. 1938). Jury instructions on consequential damages must be explicitly premised on findings that the losses were foreseeable and directly traceable to the misrepresentation. *El Paso Dev. Co. v. Ravel*, 339 S.W.2d 360, 366-67 (Tex. App.—El Paso 1960, writ ref'd n.r.e.); *Turner v. PV Int'l Corp.*, 765 S.W.2d 455, 464 (Tex. App.—Dallas 1988, writ denied).

The jury instructions in this case included two questions on direct damages, questions 2(1) and 2(2). Jury question 2(1) instructed the jury to determine the difference between the actual price that the Fazios paid for the property and the actual price at which they sold it more than three years later, without consideration of any fluctuations in value absent any fraud. Because the question does not isolate the reduction in value attributable to the fraud, it asks a math word problem of basic subtraction, and is not a proper measure of damages.

In contrast, jury question 2(2) has it right, because that question parallels the rule for calculating out-of-pocket damages. Question 2(2) properly instructed the jury to determine the difference between the fraud-induced price that the Fazios paid for the property and the actual value of the property they received when they purchased it. See *Leyendecker*, 683 S.W.2d at 373; Arthur Andersen, 945 S.W.2d at 817. And, the question correctly focused the jury on the time of the sale, because direct damages for fraud, including out-of-pocket damages, are properly measured at the time of the sale induced by the fraud—in this case, when the purchase agreement was executed—and "not at some future time." *Woodyard*, 695 S.W.2d at 733; see *Leyendecker*, 683 S.W.2d at 373; *Arthur Andersen*, 945 S.W.2d at 817. The jury responded that such damages were $0. It found other sorts of incidental and consequential damage to be $0 as well, in questions 2(3), 2(4), 2(5), and 2(6). The Fazios did not challenge the legal sufficiency of any of these findings.

The Fazios contend, and the dissents agree, that jury question 2(1) instructed the jury on a proper measure of damages, and thus the trial court erred in disregarding it. The dissent cites *Henry S. Miller Co. v. Bynum* to support its position that fraud damages need not be measured at the time of sale, but may be measured as the loss on the Fazios' investment three years after the sale. 836 S.W.2d 160, 162-63 (Tex. 1992). But more than a decade ago, our court cast a similar erroneous interpretation of *Bynum* to hold that the plaintiff in a fraud action could recover the loss on its investment, and not merely time-of-sale damages, when the plaintiff invested in a business that went bankrupt just over a year later. The case was *Arthur Andersen & Co. v. Perry Equip. Corp.*, and the Texas Supreme Court reversed our court. See 898 S.W.2d 914 (Tex. App.—Houston [1st Dist.] 1995), rev'd, 945 S.W.2d 812 (Tex. 1997). In *Arthur Andersen*, the Texas Supreme Court expressly rejected such an interpretation, holding that, under the common law measure of fraud damages, direct damages must be measured at the time of the sale that induced the fraud. *Arthur Andersen*, 945 S.W.2d at 817. It further held that losses beyond the difference between the amount the plaintiff paid and the value it received at the time of sale could be recovered only as consequential damages. *Id*. Jury question 2(1) does not measure damages that were foreseeable and directly traceable to the misrepresentation, and thus, as the Fazios concede, was not an instruction on consequential damages. See *Ravel*, 339 S.W.2d at 366-67. The jury found $0 damages in response to four measures of incidental and consequential damages on which it was instructed.

Because jury question 2(1) did not instruct the jury on a valid measure of damages, and the jury found zero in damages in response to the proper instructions on direct and consequential damages, the trial court properly disregarded the damages found in response to question 2(1) and accorded judgment based on the jury's zero damages finding in answer to questions 2(2) through 2(6).

C. Rescission Damages

The Fazios also contend that jury question 2(1) instructs the jury on a rescission or restitution measure of damages. Out-of-pocket damages, if properly measured, are restitution damages. *Baylor Univ. v. Sonnichsen*, 221

S.W.3d 632, 636 (Tex. 2007) (per curiam). Rescission is a type of remedy in a fraud claim, but it is not a proper remedy if the amount the plaintiff pays for the property is equal to its value at the time the plaintiff purchased the property. *Bryant v. Vaughn*, 33 S.W.2d 729, 730 (Tex. 1930) (holding that plaintiff had no right to rescind in fraud action where jury found that value of property received by plaintiff was equal to amount plaintiff paid for property); see also *Cruz v. Andrews Restoration, Inc.*, 364 S.W.3d 817, 823 (Tex. 2012) ("[A] rescission award requires a showing of actual damages."); *Grundmeyer v. McFadin*, 537 S.W.2d 764, 769 (Tex. Civ. App.—Tyler 1976, writ ref'd n.r.e.); *Tex. Indus. Trust, Inc. v. Lusk*, 312 S.W.2d 324, 327 (Tex. Civ. App.—San Antonio 1958, writ ref'd). A plaintiff seeking to rescind a transaction induced by fraud "must surrender any benefits received" in the transaction, as "rescission is not a one-way street. It requires a mutual restoration and accounting, in which each party restores property received from the other." *Cruz*, 364 S.W.3d at 824, 826 (citing *Tex. Emp'rs Ins. Ass'n v. Kennedy*, 135 Tex. 486, 143 S.W.2d 583, 585 (1940)).

Jury question 2(2) properly instructed the jury on out-of-pocket damages. In finding no out-of-pocket damages in response to that question, the jury found no restitution damages. See *Sonnichsen*, 221 S.W.3d at 636. The jury's finding of no actual damages—that the amount the Fazios paid for the property equaled the value of the property when the Fazios purchased it, and that the Fazios suffered no consequential damages—precludes a money judgment based on a rescission theory. See *Bryant*, 33 S.W.2d at 730; *Cruz*, 364 S.W.3d at 823. Pursuant to a proper measure of rescission damages, the Fazios would have to reduce any amount of damages by whatever benefit they received in the transaction. See *Cruz*, 364 S.W.3d at 824. As the jury found that the Fazios received property equal in value to what they paid for it, and that the fraud did not proximately cause money damages under a proper measure, rescission is not a supportable remedy. *See id*. Question 2(1), in any event, does not ask about fraud-induced losses, albeit at a later time; rather, it asked the jury to mechanically subtract the price for which the Fazios sold the property three years later from the original purchase price. We hold that the trial court properly disregarded the jury's answer to question to 2(1), as it did not measure rescission or restitution damages. *Spencer*, 876 S.W.2d at 157 (holding that the jury question is immaterial and jury's answer should be disregarded if question is legally improper).

D. Exemplary Damages

Finally, because the jury found no direct or consequential damages, the Fazios could not recover exemplary damages. See *Wright v. Gifford-Hill & Co., Inc.*, 725 S.W.2d 712, 714 (Tex. 1987)("When a jury fails to find a plaintiff has sustained actual damages, the plaintiff is foreclosed from recovering exemplary damages."); see also *Sec. Inv. Co. of St. Louis v. Fin. Acceptance Corp.*, 474 S.W.2d 261, 270 (Tex. Civ. App.—Houston [1st Dist.] 1971, writ ref'd n.r.e.). The trial court therefore properly disregarded the jury's award of exemplary damages.

Attorney's Fees

Cypress requested that the trial court award it attorney's fees pursuant to section 7.3 of the purchase agreement, which requires,

> [i]n the event either party hereto is required to employ an attorney in connection with claims by one party against the other arising from the operation of this Agreement, the non-prevailing party shall pay the prevailing party all reasonable fees and expenses, including attorney's fees incurred in connection with such transaction.

The Fazios sued Cypress for common-law fraud, statutory fraud in a real estate transaction, and fraudulent inducement, but not for breach of contract. The trial court directed a verdict on the first two fraud claims, leaving the jury to decide only the fraudulent inducement claim. Cypress presented evidence that its attorney's fees through judgment in the trial court were $987,934.64 and its expenses were $53,703.58. The trial court denied Cypress's request for fees.

Although the Fazios' claims against Cypress sound in tort, Cypress contends that it may avail itself of the contractual remedy of attorney's fees, because the tort claims asserted against it should be read to "arise from the operation of ' the purchase agreement. The Fazios respond that Cypress reads the contract too broadly, and the provision at issue cannot require it to pay attorney's fees to a party defending against a tort claim that arose before the parties executed their agreement.

Standard of review

We review the trial court's construction of an unambiguous contract de novo. *J.M. Davidson, Inc. v. Webster*, 128 S.W.3d 223, 229 (Tex. 2003); *MCI Telecomms. Corp. v. Tex. Utils. Elec. Co.*, 995 S.W.2d 647, 650-651 (Tex. 1999). If a term is not defined by the parties, we use the term's plain, ordinary, and generally accepted meaning unless the instrument shows that the term has been used in a technical sense. *Heritage Res., Inc. v. NationsBank*, 939 S.W.2d 118, 121 (Tex. 1996).

Analysis

Cypress compares the prevailing party provision in the purchase agreement to prevailing party provisions in other agreements that provide for the recovery of attorney's fees in claims "related to" the agreement, which courts have interpreted to permit recovery of attorney's fees in fraudulent inducement claims. See *Robbins v. Capozzi*, 100 S.W.3d 18, 26-27 (Tex. App.—Tyler 2002, no pet.) (holding party entitled to recover attorney's fees for successfully defending fraud and DTPA claims under contract provision for such fees when agreement allowed their recovery by "[t]he prevailing party in any legal proceeding brought under or with respect to the transaction described in his contract"); *Rich v. Olah*, 274 S.W.3d 878, 888 (Tex. App.—Dallas 2008, no pet.) (holding that fraud and DTPA tort claims related to contract for purpose of provision awarding attorney's fees when contract provided for recovery by "prevailing party in any legal proceeding related to this contract"). Other prevailing party provisions that do not use the "with respect to" or "related" language have been construed more narrowly. See, e.g., *Oat Note, Inc. v. Ampro Equities, Inc.*, 141 S.W.3d 274, 280-81 (Tex. App.—Austin 2004, no pet.) (holding that prevailing party in misrepresentation claim could not recover attorney's fees under provision allowing party to recover attorney's fees if it "prevails in any litigation to enforce this Contract"). The language in this agreement is somewhere between the more broadly worded "related to" or "with respect to" and the more narrow "to enforce."

"Arising from the operation" of an agreement is more limited than "related to" an agreement. "Arising" means to originate or stem from. Black's Law Dictionary 122 (9th ed. 2009). "Operation" refers to the act or process of functioning or performing or "being in or having force or effect." See Merriam Webster's Collegiate Dictionary 869 (11th ed. 2003); Black's Law Dictionary 1201 (9th ed. 2009). Thus, "arising from the operation" of the agreement means originating from the performance of the agreement or the legal effect and obligations imposed by the agreement. See, e.g., *Pagel v. Pumphrey*, 204 S.W.2d 58, 64 (Tex. Civ. App.—San Antonio 1947, writ ref'd n.r.e.) (explaining that operation of agreement is its legal effect and obligations that it imposes on the parties); *Cont'l Sav. Ass'n v. U.S. Fid. & Guar. Co.*, 762 F.2d 1239, 1245 (5th Cir. 1985) (referring to contract's "operation" parties' performance of legal obligations imposed by contract). The language of section 7.3 of the purchase agreement more closely resembles the limited "to enforce" than the expansive "to relate."

The Fazios' claims are based on a failure to disclose information that Cypress promised to disclose before the parties ever entered into the purchase agreement. This is not a dispute about performance under the agreement or a suit for its breach. *See Formosa Plastics*, 960 S.W.2d at 47 ("[A]n independent legal duty, separate from the existence of the contract itself, precludes the use of fraud to induce a binding agreement."). While a contract undoubtedly can affect the scope of a legal duty to not commit fraud and is essential in determining the measure of damages for fraudulent inducement, the tort itself in this instance does not arise from the contract's operation—it was a pre-contract tort to induce a sale. The parties did not choose to allow for recovery of fees incurred in defending against extra-contractual tort claims by including torts or claims more broadly "relating to" the agreement. We hold that the Fazios' claims against Cypress do not "arise from the operation" of the purchase agreement; hence, the trial court correctly ruled that Cypress is not entitled to attorney's fees for defending against these claims.

Conclusion

The trial court properly entered a take-nothing judgment, because the jury found no actual damages under their correct measurement. The trial court properly denied Cypress's request for attorney's fees, because the Fazios' fraud and fraudulent inducement claims arose from conduct that occurred before the purchase agreement's execution, and not from its operation, and the agreement's attorney's fees provision does not encompass torts or extra-contractual claims. We therefore affirm the judgment of the trial court.

Questions

1. How does the court measure direct damages?
2. What does the court say about rescission damages?
3. Why can't the Fazios collect exemplary damages?

Suggested Case References

1. Read the requirements needed to be granted punitive damages in North Carolina. *Process Components v. Baltimore Aircoil Co., Inc.*, 89 N.C. App. 649, 366 S.E.2d 907 (1988).
2. Who has the burden of proving mitigation of damages, the breaching party or the injured party? *Cobb v. Osman*, 83 Nev. 415 (1967).
3. What circumstances are necessary before a court may order specific performance? *Mann v. Golub*, 182 W. Va. 523, 389 S.E.2d 734 (1990); In re Estate of Hayhurst, 478 P.2d 343 (Okla. 1970).
4. Does a party's actual performance under a contract in which performance was subject to a condition precedent constitute a waiver of the condition? See what the Montana court said in *Hein v. Fox*, 126 Mont. 514, 254 P.2d 1076 (1954).
5. Under what circumstances will a court award punitive damages for breach of contract? *Read Edens v. Goodyear Tire & Rubber Co.*, 858 F.2d 198 (4th Cir. 1988).

Ethical Considerations

A client who is dissatisfied with his or her attorney's representation, may always seek damages against the attorney in a malpractice or professional negligence action. In addition, the aggrieved client may propound a grievance against the attorney with the state's regulatory authority, and, if proven correct, the attorney may be disciplined by censor, suspension, or disbarment. See ABA Rules of Professional Conduct Article 8. It is important to note that the attorney may be disciplined for the actions of a paralegal over whom the attorney exercised supervisory authority.

Quick Quiz

Answer TRUE or FALSE. (Answers can be found in Appendix C on page 414.)

1. An innocent party to a breach of contract may always receive exemplary damages.
2. Damages are a form of equitable relief.
3. Injunctive relief may first occur as a temporary restraining order.
4. *Quantum meruit* is a type of quasi-contractual remedy.
5. Liquidated damages are only allowed if provided for in the contract itself.

12

Drafting Simple Contracts and Proving Their Terms in Court

Learning Objectives

After studying this chapter you will be able to:

- Deconstruct a basic contract.
- Create a tickler of important contractual clauses.
- Know how to describe the consideration in a contract.
- Understand when certain provisions are appropriate for a contract.
- List the special provisions and clauses that appear in most contracts.
- Discuss the grounds for terminating a contract that could appear in the agreement.
- Distinguish between the choice of law and submission to a particular jurisdiction.
- Explain the effect of arbitration clauses on contract enforcement.
- Know how to authenticate a contract.
- Understand the concept of hearsay.

CHAPTER OVERVIEW

This chapter incorporates all of the principles and ideas discussed in the previous chapters into one complete contract. Many people are daunted at the prospect of creating a contractual relationship, but in fact the process is quite interesting and challenging.

There are three keys to creating a contract that will truly reflect the parties' wishes: 1) start with a thorough understanding of the precise wishes of the contracting parties; 2) use a checklist of clauses, or topics, that should be covered; and 3) create the agreement by referring to existing contracts covering the same or similar subject matter. No lawyer or paralegal is expected to devise a contract out of whole cloth, and to this end there are many sources of sample contracts available to the drafter.

Before attempting to draft a contract, make sure that you have a clear idea of the precise nature of the relationship the parties intend. This must include all of the six major requirements of every valid contract (Chapter 1). Additionally, every industry has its own special terminology and relationships that must be included in an industry contract. To ascertain what those areas might be, use the library to read books about the particular area involved. Not only law libraries, but regular public libraries have innumerable volumes covering every conceivable industry, and this should always be a first reference before drafting a contract. These sources not only will indicate special areas of concern but usually will include sample agreements that can be used as models.

Always ask the parties themselves and the attorney whether they have old contracts that they wish to have used as a basis for the new agreement. This is usually the best source of a sample because the parties have already used, and presumably have been happy with, that format. Just bear in mind that these former contracts are usable only as samples; it is exceedingly rare that one contract will be perfect for several different parties. There is always going to be a need to make certain changes in the contractual provisions to reflect the current contractual relationship. And finally, always check the appropriate state law, both common and statutory, to insure compliance with any particular requirements.

The following section of this chapter will discuss many of the most typical types of clauses that appear in contracts. This section can be used as a checklist in preparing a draft contract. By going through the list, the paralegal will be able to determine that all of the important provisions have been discussed. Of course, the list is hardly exhaustive, but it does provide the basic guidelines for simple contract drafting. Additionally, sample contracts have been included that cover many different areas of law and that can be used as models by the novice drafter. After a while, attorneys and paralegals develop their own samples from the contracts they have drafted. To build an excellent resource for samples, paralegals should develop the habit of keeping copies of all legal documents that they come in contact with for future use, deleting the parties' names and identifying information. As long as a person has sample format to follow, drafting contracts becomes an easy process.

Always bear in mind that each clause in a sample contract must be read to determine whether its wording is in the best interests of a given client; if not, simple changes in the language can be made. To this end, it is always a good idea to use more than one sample contract; by having multiple samples, clauses can be compared and contrasted, and sentences can be taken from different contracts to create a clause that would suit the given client.

Reviewing existing contracts and contract interpretation should also be mentioned here. There will be many instances in which the paralegal must analyze an existing contract to determine the rights and liabilities of a client. The process of interpretation is the exact reverse of drafting. Simply read the contract to determine what is said in each clause, and use the checklist to make sure no major areas have been deleted or ignored. Pretend that the contract to be analyzed is a sample and go through it the same way you would if you were drafting the contract.

After the contract is executed, as long as all of the contracting parties are satisfied with each other's performance, even if the contract is poorly drafted, no legal problem will ensue. However, if any contracting party, or any person who believes that he or she is affected by the contract, is dissatisfied, there is a potential for litigation regarding the correct interpretation of the contract provisions. Hence, it is important for any legal professional involved in contractual work to be familiar with evidentiary rules so that the contract may be admitted into court for resolution of the dispute. This chapter will discuss some of the basic rules of evidence associated with contract law.

Checklist of Clauses

The following clauses are presented in an order most often followed in drafting contracts, but, of course, changes in the order can always be made.

Description of the Parties

The first clause of every contract usually contains a description of the parties to the agreement. The term *description* means the legal names and aliases of the parties, type of entity each party is, and the manner in which the parties will be referred to throughout the remainder of the contract.

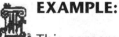 **EXAMPLE:**

This agreement is made this _____ day of _____, 20 _____, between Acme Realty, Inc., a New York corporation (hereinafter "Corporation"), and Lyle Roberts, an individual resident in the State of Pennsylvania (hereinafter "Roberts").

It is necessary to note the exact legal names of the parties and the type of entity each party is—corporation, limited partnership, individual, and so forth—in case of a potential dispute with respect to the agreement. When commencing a lawsuit and serving process, it is necessary to know exactly how the parties are legally designated. To this end, the introductory clause may also include the parties' addresses. Addresses usually appear at the end of a contract below the parties' signatures or may appear in provisions providing for notice to the parties.

Indicating a nomenclature for the parties other than their legal names is for the purpose of achieving simplicity throughout the remainder of the agreement. Many times, especially if the contract is a form contract used by one of the parties, this designation may indicate the roles the parties play in the agreement, such as Buyer, Seller, or Landlord. Any designation agreed on is appropriate. Simply make sure that the same designation is used throughout the remainder of the agreement. Be consistent.

Description of the Consideration

For the purpose of contract law, this section of the agreement assumes primary importance. In this clause, the offer, acceptance, and consideration coalesce into a binding contract. As indicated in the first four chapters of this book, it is mandatory that the consideration be specifically described, indicating a mutuality of consideration. This means the description must specify what each party to the contract is giving and receiving. It must include such terms as price, quantity, quality, and time of performance. This clause is generally the first covenant of the contract.

In addition to the specifics of the consideration, any conditions the parties wish to attach to their performances should be included in this clause. Such conditions could include such items as provisions for installment purchases, if and how the agreement may be modified, and how payments may be accelerated. It is important to ascertain exactly what covenants and conditions the parties expect to have placed on their performances.

Also remember that whereas most contracts make payment of money the consideration for a good or service received, a contract is just as valid if the consideration is a good for a good, a service for a service, or a service for a good. The concept of barter is a legal one.

EXAMPLE:

In consideration of Five Hundred Dollars ($500), Seller agrees to sell to Buyer the following: one used CD player.

Note that dollar amounts are usually written out as well as indicated numerically to avoid confusion and mistakes.

EXAMPLE:

It is agreed that Vendor will sell and Purchaser will buy all of the oranges growing at the farm of Vendor located at _____, during the year of _____, for the sum of Ten Thousand Dollars ($10,000.00), of which Four Thousand Dollars ($4,000.00) shall be paid upon the signing of this Agreement, Three Thousand Dollars ($3,000.00) shall be paid upon completion of the harvest, and Three Thousand Dollars ($3,000.00) shall be paid no later than one month after delivery of said oranges to Purchaser.

Purchaser shall, at his own expense, gather and harvest said fruit when it is sufficiently mature, and Purchaser and his employees shall have free access to the above-mentioned farm for the sole and exclusive purpose of harvesting said fruit.

In the above example, an output contract, the parties have agreed to an installment sale for the purchase of the oranges. All of the requisite terms and conditions have been specified.

EXAMPLE:

Seller agrees to convey to Buyer, for the sum of Eight Thousand Dollars ($8,000.00), upon the conditions set forth below, the following personal property:

(Exact description of the property)

The Buyer hereby agrees to pay to the Seller the sum of Two Thousand Dollars ($2,000) upon delivery of the above mentioned goods to the Buyer's place of business, and the sum of One Thousand Dollars ($1,000) on the first day of each month following the date of this agreement until the full amount is paid. It is further agreed that, in the event of failure by the Buyer to make any installment as it becomes due, the whole of the sum then outstanding shall immediately become due and payable. If the Buyer so wishes, he may accelerate payments. No modification of this agreement shall be effective unless executed in writing and signed by both parties.

The above example indicates an installment sales contract that provides for remedies if an installment is not made on time, and further permits acceleration of the payment schedule as well as a method of modifying the agreement.

EXAMPLE:

In consideration of Attorney drafting and executing the Last Will and Testament of Dentist, Dentist hereby agrees to perform root canal work on Attorney's number 18 tooth. All services shall be completed no later than two months from the date of this agreement.

This is an example of a contract clause in which each side performs services for the other, indicating exactly what services are to be performed and the timing of the performances.

In drafting the consideration clause, be sure to include the following:

1. A complete description of the consideration:
   a. for *money*, indicate the exact amount;
   b. for *real estate*, give a complete legal description or street address;
   c. for *personal property*, give as many identifying adjectives as are necessary to avoid confusion;
   d. for *services*, specify the service to be performed.
2. Indicate a mutuality of consideration.
3. Indicate the time of performance.
4. Specify any conditions or timing elements that attach to the performance.
5. Use words of present tense; don't use conditional words when indicating the covenants.
6. If the contract is covered by the UCC, determine whether a UCC form exists by checking the state statute book or legal stationery store.

Security Agreement

As discussed in Chapter 8, The Uniform Commercial Code, if a party to the agreement wishes to create a security interest in some property in the case of default, one of the requirements is to have a security agreement specifying that a secured interest is being created. Typically, the contract between the parties will satisfy this requirement of Article IX of the Code, provided that the contract indicates words to that effect. To this end, it becomes incumbent on the drafter to include such a clause in the contract.

EXAMPLE:

We grant to you a security interest in, and the right of set-off with respect to, all receivables as defined above, all present and future instruments, documents, chattel paper, and general intangibles (as defined in the Uniform Commercial Code), and all proceeds thereof. All of the foregoing shall secure payment and performance of all our obligations at any time owing to you, fixed or contingent, whether arising out of this agreement or by operation of law.

The preceding example constitutes a security agreement for receivables and intangibles under the UCC. This clause would read the same regardless of the collateral specified.

Warranties

As discussed in Chapter 8, The Uniform Commercial Code, whenever the agreement involves the sale of goods, certain warranties attach. Obviously the implied warranties exist regardless of what the contract says, but the contract itself is one method of creating express warranties between the parties. If the parties intend specific guarantees with respect to the subject goods, it is recommended to include provisions concerning these express warranties. These clauses may be part of the Description of the Consideration or may follow those provisions as indicated by the order given here. All express warranties become covenants of the seller.

EXAMPLE:

Seller hereby warrants that the (good) is in good and merchantable condition, and is free and clear of all liens, security interests and encumbrances. Seller further warrants that the (good) meets all of the following specifications: (specifications).

The preceding clause not only creates express warranties based on particular specifications of the parties but also makes express warranties of the implied warranty of merchantability and title.

Title

Title to the property indicates ownership, right of control, possession, and transfer, and the right to insure the property. As a consequence, it becomes important to indicate in a contract the moment at which title transfers from the seller to the buyer. In any transaction where the mutual consideration is exchanged at the same time, title is transferred simultaneously. Problems arise only when there is to be a delay in full payment for the property conveyed or a lag time due to delivery. Some examples of these situations would be installment sales or mortgaging real estate. In these instances, it is necessary to insert a clause in the contract indicating the condition that gives rise to the transfer of the title.

EXAMPLES:

1. Seller hereby agrees to convey all his right, title, and interest in and to the aforementioned property upon receipt of a certified check from the Buyer in the amount of _____.

2. In an installment sale:When the full sum above mentioned is fully paid, title to said property shall vest in the vendee, but until then title shall remain in the vendor.

The parties themselves are always free to determine the exact moment title passes; however, there are three timing elements that are typically used: (1) when the contract is signed; (2) when the goods are fully paid for; or (3) for installment sales, at the moment an agreed-on percentage of the total selling price has been paid. Simply insert the timing element the parties have agreed on into the contract.

Risk of Loss

Risk of loss, as discussed in Chapter 8, The Uniform Commercial Code, comes into play whenever there is some delay in having the goods transferred from the seller to the buyer, either because of a conditional sales agreement or because of transportation of the items. As exemplified in Chapter 8, there are several standard clauses that can be inserted into the contract to cover this contingency; simply refer to that chapter to find and use the appropriate description.

Waivers

See Chapters 7 and 8 for a discussion of waivers and their effects on a contract. There are certain standard clauses with respect to waivers that are usually inserted into contracts, examples of which appear below.

 EXAMPLES:

1. This Agreement shall constitute the entire Agreement between the parties, and no variance or modification shall be valid except by a written agreement, executed in the same manner as this Agreement.

2. No delay or failure on the part of _____ to fulfill any of these provisions shall operate as a waiver of such or of any other right, and no waiver whatsoever shall be valid unless in writing and signed by the parties, and only to the extent therein set forth.

3. The waiver of any one provision of this Agreement shall not constitute a continuing waiver.

Assignments

Most contracts are assignable (see Chapter 9, Third Party Contracts), but usually parties insert clauses into contracts specifically covering this topic, either by stating that the contract may not be assigned or, if assignable, by indicating the method of effectuating the transfer of rights. It is generally a good idea to have such a clause in every contract to avoid problems later on.

 EXAMPLES:

1. The rights herein permitted to _____ may be assigned, and upon such assignment, such Assignee shall have all of _____'s rights with respect thereto.

2. This contract is not transferable or assignable.

3. No assignment of this contract shall be effective unless executed in writing and signed by all parties.

In addition to specific assignment clauses, if a contract refers to assignees, that reference is sufficient to indicate that the contract is assignable. An example would be the phrase "the Agreement shall be binding on _____, his heirs, executors, assigns, etc." Also be aware that many states have specific case and statutory law with respect to the assignability of commercial leases, and for such contracts each Jurisdiction's law must be specifically checked.

Delegation

Just as with assignments discussed above, many contracts may be delegated, unless performance depends on personal services or confidence. (See Chapter 9.) Once again, a provision may be inserted into the agreement specifically covering this point.

EXAMPLES:

1. The obligations specified in this Agreement may not be delegated by the parties.

2. _____ may delegate his obligation to _____.

Terminology

Unless otherwise indicated, all contractual terms are construed in their ordinary meaning. Consequently, if the contracting parties expect specific words, terms, or designations to be defined in a particular manner, it is necessary to indicate that definition in the contract itself. Because many terms are peculiar to particular industries, it becomes imperative that the meaning the parties want to attach to those terms be stated. Also, because "custom and usage" is the standard under the UCC for interpreting sales contracts, it would best serve the parties to have the custom and usage delineated in the agreement so that it does not become a problem of interpretation later on.

It is impossible to give a detailed list of terms because terms are particular to each contracting party; however, some of the sample contracts that follow will have a terminology section that can be used as a model. Simply remember to define any important term in the agreement itself.

Special Provisions and Clauses

In the same way that terminology will be peculiar to particular industries, so will special contractual covenants and conditions. There are certain matters that must be contractually agreed on by the parties, but these clauses are dependent on the nature of the contract and the industry involved. Following is merely a sample of the types of special provisions that may appear in various agreements.

Covenant Not to Compete

"Employee hereby covenants and agrees that in the event of the termination of this Agreement for any reason, with or without cause, that Employee will not compete directly or indirectly with Employer on his own account or as an employee of any other person or entity in _____ for a period of _____ years."

Duties

In an employment or personal services contract, every one of the duties of the employee should be specified, including details of the authority of the employee, any limitations on her authority, and any special accounting methods that may be used to determine compensation. In addition, all other employee benefits to which the employee will be entitled should either be specified, or, if part of a general employee benefit and compensation package, should be incorporated by reference in the main body of the agreement.

Pronouns

"Any masculine personal pronoun as set forth in this Agreement shall be considered to mean the corresponding feminine or neuter personal pronoun, as the case may be."

Severability

"If, for any reason, any provision hereof shall be inoperative, the validity and effect of all other provisions shall not be affected thereby."

Successors

"This Agreement and all provisions hereunder shall inure to the benefits of and shall be binding upon the heirs, executors, legal representatives, next of kin, transferees, and assigns of the parties hereto."

Time of the Essence

Time in all respects is of the essence of this contract.

Trade Secrets

"_____ further covenants not to divulge, during the term of this Agreement, or at any time subsequently, any trade secrets, processes, procedures, or operations, including, but not limited to, the following: _____."

Work Product

"Employee hereby agrees that all inventions, improvements, ideas, and suggestions made by him and patents obtained by him severally or jointly with any other person or persons during the entire period of his employment, are and shall be the sole property of the Employer, free from any legal or equitable title of the Employee, and that all necessary documents for perfecting such title shall be executed by the Employee and delivered to the Employer."

It is usually a good idea to specify the type of property involved.

Duration and Termination

Every contract should specify the duration of its provisions. This is established in two ways: First, the contract should have a specific statement indicating the intended termination date. Second, the contract should specify grounds for terminating the agreement prior to the intended termination date without causing the parties to be in breach. The duration clause is usually as simple as a one-sentence statement indicating the number of years of duration from the date indicated in the contract, or indicating that the agreement shall terminate on a specified date or on the occurrence of a specified event.

Clauses involving grounds for termination are a bit more problematical. The usual grounds given for termination are

1. failure of a party to fulfill a covenant;
2. failure of a condition specified in the contract;
3. dissolution of one or more of the contracting entities;
4. bankruptcy;
5. death, illness, or disability of one or both of the parties;
6. destruction of the subject matter;
7. commission of a felony by one of the parties;
8. incarceration of one of the parties; or
9. change in circumstance (such changes must be delineated in the agreement).

All of the foregoing indicate grounds for terminating the agreement for cause. However, the parties may also provide that the contract may be terminated without cause by one or both of the parties by giving appropriate notice to the other party.

All properly drafted contracts should contain some provision with respect to duration and termination of the agreement; the specifics are dependent on the wishes of the parties to the contract.

Notice of Default

If a party fails to fulfill a contractual obligation, thereby being in default, the agreement should provide for notice by the injured party of the default. The notice provision should specify how such notice is to be given, and whether the defaulting party may be given the opportunity to cure the default.

EXAMPLE:

In the event of a default of any of these provisions, _____ shall notify _____ in writing by first class mail or fax, of such default. Should _____ fail to cure such default within _____ days, he or she shall be deemed to be in breach.

Remedies

A contract should contain some provision with respect to remedies available to the innocent party in the case of a breach.

In contracts that include a provision for a security interest, the security holder, in addition to rights granted to her under the UCC, usually specifies the right to dispose of the collateral so as to satisfy the default. Any money the injured party receives from the disposition of the property above the amount owed belongs to the defaulting party.

EXAMPLE:

Should the Buyer in any way default upon his obligation under this agreement, the Seller shall be at full liberty, at any time thereafter, to resell the (property), either by public auction or by private contract, and the expenses attending thereto shall be borne by the Buyer, but any excess in the price obtained shall belong to the Buyer.

As discussed and exemplified in Chapter 11, Remedies, the parties may specify liquidated damages, or include a limitation of damages clause. Any cost incurred in proceeding against the breaching party may be specified as being the breaching party's obligation.

EXAMPLE:

All costs, including reasonable attorney's fees, resulting from any dispute or controversy arising out of or under this Agreement shall be borne by _____.

Choice of Law

As a rule, contracts specify the state law that will govern its provisions and application.

EXAMPLE:

This Agreement shall be construed in accordance with and governed in all respects by the law of the State of _____.

Arbitration

Nowadays, to avoid the time and expense of judicial litigation for problems arising out of a conract, many parties include an arbitration clause by which the parties agree to submit disputes to an arbitrator instead of to the courts.

EXAMPLE:

All disputes, differences, and controversies arising under and in connection with this Agreement shall be settled and finally determined by arbitration according to the rules of the American Arbitration Association now in force or hereafter adopted.

Submission to Jurisdiction

Many contracts specify that the parties agree to submit to the jurisdiction of a particular court.

EXAMPLE:

The parties hereto agree that, in the case of any dispute or controversy arising under or out of this Agreement, to submit to the jurisdiction of the courts of the State of _____ for a settlement of said dispute or controversy.

Many contracts contain what is known as a *cognovit* provision, or a *confession of judgment*, whereby one party agrees to have the other party, in the case of a dispute, hire an attorney to represent and plead the alleged breaching party guilty. Many states do not favor these clauses, although they have been upheld by the U.S. Supreme Court, and so each jurisdiction should be researched to determine the appropriateness of such clauses.

Signatures

The final part of every contract is the signature of the parties. The signatures are usually introduced by the standard phrase: "IN WITNESS WHEREOF, the parties hereto, have hereunder signed this Agreement the day last above written." Following this introductory phrase, the parties sign above their typewritten names. If any of the parties is signing in a representative capacity, the full name of the organization should appear along with the signatory's name and title indicating the authority to sign the contract. If the party is a corporation, occasionally the corporate seal may be affixed as well.

Proving Contractual Terms

Despite how well a contract may be drafted, there is always the potential that questions regarding its validity or the interpretation of its terms may need to be resolved by a court or an arbitration. However, before the court can consider whether the contract is valid and enforceable, or whether its provisions have been breached, the contract must be introduced and taken into evidence.

Admitting a Contract into Evidence

In order to have the contract before the trier of fact, the agreement must meet certain evidentiary standards:

1. the contract must be property **authenticated**; and
2. it must not be **hearsay**.

Authentication is the process whereby a document being presented to a court is proven to be the actual document in controversy. To authenticate a written contract, the original signed document must be introduced by one of its signatories, testifying under oath that the contract is what it purports to be, that the signature is his or hers, and that the witness recognizes the signatures of the other contracting parties.

EXAMPLE:

Jason and Miranda signed a contract for the sale of Jason's car, but now Miranda is claiming that Jason failed to deliver the car to her as promised in the agreement. Based on this allegation, Miranda sues Jason in court.

In order to determine what the terms of the agreement are, the judge requires to see the contract. Miranda, under oath, produces the actual contract and confirms that the signatures are hers and Jason's. Miranda's testimony has authenticated the document as the contract in question.

However, what if the original contract cannot be found, but the proponent of the agreement has a copy, either a duplicated version or one on a computer that can be reprinted? Pursuant to the **best evidence rule**, the best evidence of a document is the original document itself. However, if the original cannot be found, a copy may be introduced as the best evidence available for proving the contract.

In order to introduce a copy into evidence as the best evidence available, the proponent must testify as to what he or she did to locate the original and swear or affirm that it cannot be located. In addition, the witness must testify as to the copy's genuiness in the same manner that he or she would testify to the original.

EXAMPLE:

Miranda cannot locate the original contract between her and Jason, but she found a duplicated copy among her papers. In order to have this copy admitted into evidence, Miranda must testify as to the diligent search that she made for the original, detailing all of the places where she looked, and aver that the copy she is presenting is a true and accurate copy of the original.

If neither the original nor a duplicate can be located, a party to the contract may testify under oath as to the contract's terms, as the best evidence available of the agreement. Note that, for oral contracts, the only way that their terms may be proven is by testimonial evidence, since no writing exists. Under those circumstances, the trier of fact must evaluate the credibility of the witness.

EXAMPLE:

Miranda cannot find any version of the contract that she had with Jason for the sale of the car. Under these circumstances, Miranda may testify as to what she remembers its terms to be.

The opponent to the introduction to the agreement has the right to question the witness regarding his or her authentication testimony. The process of challenging the witness who is authenticating the document is known as **voir dire**.

EXAMPLE:

When Miranda testifies that she could not find the original copy of the contract, Jason challenges her assertion by having her detail exactly where she looked, when she looked, and how much time she spent attempting to locate the original.

Note that the parties can agree that the document, whether it be the original or a duplicate, is the true agreement of the parties by **stipulation** (agreement).

After the document has been properly authenticated, before it can be admitted into evidence it must be determined that it is not hearsay. Hearsay is an out-of-court statement used to prove the truth of the matter asserted. A document is legally considered to be a statement. All hearsay statements are inadmissible, unless they fall into an exception to the hearsay rule excluding such statements.

If the issue before the court is the interpretation of the contract or its enforcement, it is the subject matter of the litigation and is not hearsay. However, there are many situations in which the contract is a secondary matter to the legal issue to be decided, at which point hearsay considerations must be addressed.

EXAMPLE:

A question has arisen as to whether Jason had a legally sufficient title to transfer ownership of the car to Miranda. Jason has based his ownership of the vehicle on his purchase of the car from Ira, Ira having bought the car from Joan, evidenced by contracts between Ira and Jason and Ira and Joan. In this situation, since the agreements between Ira and Jason and Ira and Joan are not the subject matter of the litigation, those contracts may only be admitted into evidence if they are not hearsay or fall into an exception to the rules regarding hearsay (the statement that Jason bought the car from Ira having been made out of court).

In the situation posited in the above example, the contract between Jason and Ira may be admitted because Jason, as a signatory, can authenticate it and as a witness, can testify as to its truth. However, neither Ira nor Joan are in court and, consequently, the agreement between those two persons is hearsay.

It is beyond the scope of this text to analyze all of the exceptions to the hearsay rule; however the most frequently used exception to the hearsay rule used to admit documents is called the **business record exception**.

The business record exception to hearsay allows documents to be entered into evidence if the document is prepared in the regular course of business of the person who is presenting it at court, is maintained by that person as part of his or her duties, and he or she can testify as to where and how it was retrieved from the business files so as to be brought to court. If these requirements are met, the document is considered properly authenticated and is admissible as an exception to the hearsay rule, which would otherwise prohibit its admission into evidence.

EXAMPLE:

Jason wants to introduce into evidence the contract of sale for the car between Ira and Joan; however, Joan has passed away and Ira has left the state with no current address available for him. Jason has found the name of Joan's lawyer who prepared the contract and saw to its execution. The lawyer has kept a copy of the contract in her files. When the lawyer comes to court, she testifies as to how she created the document, how she maintains her files, and the method by which she got the contract from her office. In this manner, the lawyer has authenticated the contract as her business record, and it may be admitted.

Note that for the business record exception to apply, the person testifying must be the one who has the responsibility of creating and maintaining the record for the business. In the prior example, if Jason had been given a copy of the contract between Ira and Joan by Ira, and he kept it, he could not introduce it as a business record, because he neither created the record nor was under a business duty to maintain it.

Once the contact is admitted into evidence, the court may consider whether the contract is valid.

Determining the Validity of a Contract

Whether or not a contract is valid depends on three separate issues: (1) whether the contract recites valid consideration, as discussed in Chapter 4; (2) whether the contract is legal, with respect to its subject matter and the contractual capacity of the parties, as discussed in Chapter 5; and (3) whether the parties had sufficient intent to enter into a valid contract, as discussed in Chapter 6.

Except for the contract's recitation of consideration and the legality of its terms as expressed therein, the other issues can only be determined by the court hearing evidence of extrinsic matters outside the written terms of the agreement. The exact rules of evidence regarding such testimonial and documentary evidence that would be necessary to prevail in a court of law are beyond the scope of this text. However, as a general rule, in order to prove a particular point in court, the proponent must submit legally sufficient evidence that would permit any person who is unconnected to the parties or the contract itself to believe that the proposition is true.

Analysis of a Contract's Terms

If the contract is challenged, an analysis must be made as to whether the contract's terms are either ambiguous or the result of a unilateral or mutual mistake.

An **ambiguity** exists when the term appearing in the contract is capable of more than just one meaning and is the result of poor or faulty draftsmanship. There are two types of ambiguities. A **patent ambiguity** in a contract is one that appears on the face of a document and arises from the language itself. A **latent ambiguity** does not readily appear in the language of a document, but instead arises from a collateral matter. Whether an ambiguity exists is a matter of law for the court to interpret. It is the court that decides whether the terms of the agreement are clear and unambiguous. Should the court determine that an ambiguity exists, the ambiguity is construed against the drafter.

EXAMPLE:

Miranda and Jason enter into a contract whereby Miranda agrees to purchase Jason's car for $7,000.00. However, the contract simply identifies the car as "Jason's car," but Jason owns three automobiles. In this situation, there is a latent ambiguity in the contract terms.

Where a contract is ambiguous, parol evidence of additional promises is admissible to complete the entire agreement. Parol evidence of the custom and practice of the parties may also be admitted.

However, extrinsic and parol evidence is not admissible to create an ambiguity in a written agreement which is complete and clear and unambiguous upon its face. An analysis that begins with consideration of extrinsic evidence of what the parties meant, instead of looking first to what they said and reaching extrinsic evidence only when required to do so because of some identified ambiguity, unnecessarily denigrates the contract and unsettles the law. Before looking to evidence of what was in the parties' minds, a court must give due weight to what was in their contract. A contract provision that is ambiguous may not be enforced.

In addition, agreements may be set aside or reformed based on the mutual mistake of the parties, provided that such mutual mistake existed at the time that the agreement was entered into and the mistake is so material that it goes to the very foundation of the agreement. However, the decision whether or not to grant such equitable relief lies with the sound discretion of the court.

A **mutual mistake** is a mistake wherein both or all parties to a bilateral transaction share the same erroneous belief and their acts do not in fact accomplish their mutual intent, while a **unilateral mistake** is one in which only one of the parties to a bilateral transaction is in error.

For a party to be entitled to reformation of a contract based on the ground of mutual mistake, the mutual mistake must be material, i.e., it must involve a fundamental assumption of the contract. A party need not establish that the parties entered into the contract because of the mutual mistake, only that the material mistake vitally affects a fact or facts on the basis of which the parties contracted. Moreover, proof of mistake must show clearly and beyond doubt that there has been a mutual mistake and must show, with equal clarity and certainty, the exact and precise form and import that the instrument ought to be made to assume, in order that it may express and effectuate what was really intended by the parties. Because the thrust of a reformation claim is that a writing does not set forth the actual agreement of the parties, generally neither the parol evidence rule nor the Statute of Frauds applies to bar proof, in the form or parol or extrinsic evidence, of the claimed agreement.

In order to substantiate a claim of mutual mistake, a party may rely on extrinsic evidence, because the essence of the assertion is that the writing does not set forth the actual agreement of the parties.

Conversely, a claim of unilateral mistake, must be evidenced by testimony that the party seeking to avoid the contract was induced to enter into the agreement by fraud, as discussed in Chapter 6.

CHAPTER SUMMARY

There are three preliminary rules of drafting a well-written contract:

1. Be conversant with the parties' wishes.
2. Use a checklist of clauses and topics incident to the subject matter involved.
3. Use several sample contracts to establish the format.

Most important in drafting a contractual agreement, be extremely precise in the choice of words. Do not be afraid to draft long clauses; precision requires words of limitation that may appear long-winded but that in fact create precision. For instance, the words "my house" are not nearly as precise as "my house located in Sunapee, New Hampshire," nor is that as precise as giving an exact street address or legal description. Laypersons confuse "lengthy" with "precise." Never be afraid of being wordy if the words create precision and avoid confusion. However, always scrutinize each clause you intend to use to make sure that it serves a useful purpose. Never insert a meaningless clause simply because it appears in a sample format.

After you have drafted a contract, go back over it to interpret what you have written, just as opposing counsel will do. Determine exactly what has been stated in each clause, whether anything has been left out, how each clause affects each party, whether the words are capable of multiple interpretations, and whether it truly reflects the parties' intent. If you are satisfied with what has been written, you now have a sample contract for your next assignment.

Key Terms

Ambiguity: contract provision with multiple interpretations
Authentication: process of proving the genuiness of a contract in court
Best evidence rule: rule stating that the best evidence of a written agreement is the original of that agreement
Business record exception: exception to the hearsay doctrine whereby a document kept in the regular course of business, authenticated by the person responsible for maintaining the document may be admitted into evidence
Hearsay: an out-of-court statement used to prove the truth of the matters asserted therein
Latent ambiguity: ambiguity that can only be proven by extrinsic evidence
Mutual mistake: misconception of the subject matter of a contract by both parties; makes the contract unenforceable
Patent ambiguity: contractual term that is ambiguous on the face of the contract

Stipulation: agreement of the parties
Unilateral mistake: misconception of the subject matter of a contract by
      only one party to the contract; may be enforceable
Voir dire: process used to challenge the authentication of a document
      proffered into evidence

EXERCISES

1. Draft an employment contract for yourself as a paralegal working for the firm of Pratt & Chase, a partnership of 25 attorneys working in your town. The contract is for a two-year period.

2. Go to the library and find two more sales contracts. Compare them to the samples in the Appendix. How would you use these contracts to create a new model for your own use?

3. What clauses would you include in a complex Antenuptial Agreement? Why?

4. Analyze the following draft of a contract:

Marketing Agreement

This document will outline the agreed to understanding between (Credit Union) and (Group); or any client of associate relationships presented to Credit Union and accepted in the membership of said Credit Union.

The Group will present said Credit Union with individuals and employer institutions that may wish to become members of Credit Union and become eligible to participate in said Credit Union benefits. It is understood by the management of said Credit Union that the Group is a life and health organization.

It is the intention of the Group to offer its insurance products to these marketed organizations, and any individuals within these organizations on a voluntary basis. The Credit Union may not enter into an agreement with any competing organization as it pertains to any group marketed by the Group, its clients or any of its associate organizations. The Credit Union will not impose any administrative fees to be paid by the Group on this block of premium production. The Credit Union may not directly compete against the Group.

The Credit Union will remit premiums to the selected insurance carriers from the Credit Union accounts of any individual who chooses to participate in said life and health plans provided proper documentation is presented to said Credit Union in a timely manner.

It is also understood that the Group will be responsible to provide said Credit Union members with sales and service and be accountable to the Board of Directors of the Credit Union as it pertains to their practices. Should the Group not sufficiently provide service to, or engage in unethical practices, the Credit Union may require that the Group be presented to the Board of the Credit Union to state its case. Should said inquiry result in the desire not to have the Group represent the Credit Union, this agreement can be terminated within 90 days, providing that the following items are enacted at the point of said termination:

The Group will secure an agreement with a properly bonded "third party administrator" that will assume the responsibility of collecting insurance premiums marketed by the Group or any of its clients and/or associate organizations, from the Credit Union in the form of a list bill.

The Credit Union will be given the option of keeping said Group marketed individuals in its membership with written request during said 90-day transition period, and may continue to provide benefits to said members. However, the Credit Union may not introduce a competitive insurance organization to this block of members. Should the Board of the Credit Union impose this clause, the Group will not represent to any Credit Union member that we are being sponsored by, or have any involvement with, the Credit Union.

The Credit Union will remit said insurance premiums to the "third party administrator" of the Group's choice, and will impose no administrative charge to either the Group or the third party administrator for this fee. The Credit Union will continue to provide the Group with any documentation pertaining to policy service on this block of business.

This Agreement between the Credit Union and the Group governs that block of business that is marketed by the Group.

There will be another Agreement that will govern premiums that were not introduced to the Credit Union and the Group.

_____

The Credit Union

_____

The Group

Date: _____
Witness: _____
Witness: _____

Cases for Analysis

The following two decisions have been included to underscore the problems that may be associated with drafting a contract. *Specialty Rental Tools & Supply, L.P. v. Shoemaker* concerns interpretation of a noncompetition clause in a contract, and *American Express Travel Related Services, Inc. v. Weppler* discusses contract construction.

Specialty Rental Tools & Supply, L.P. v. Shoemaker
2007 U.S. Dist. LEXIS 94520 (S.D. Miss. 2007)

Factual Background

From 1993 to 2002, Defendant William P. Shoemaker ("Shoemaker") owned and operated a company known as Southeastern Rentals, which was an oil field related service company that rented wireline tools. Sometime around March of 2001, Shoemaker was approached by a representative of Southeastern Rental Tools & Supply, L.P. ("STS"), who discussed the possible sale of Southeastern Rentals to STS. Some time passed, and in approximately November of 2001, there were further discussions regarding the sale of Southeastern Rentals to STS. Pursuant to these discussions, Shoemaker was sent a "Letter of Intent" regarding the sale on or about January 2, 2002. Shoemaker took this letter to his attorney for review and response.

The letter of intent states, in part in Section 7 that, "Shoemaker's employment agreement will also include certain noncompete provisions to be triggered should he leave the employment of STS." On January 24, 2002, Dal Williamson, Shoemaker's attorney, wrote to STS and, among other things, informed STS of Shoemaker's disagreement with the noncompetition part of the proposed agreement. STS responded by letter dated January 25, 2002 and specifically stated that, "STS will amend the noncompete agreement to extend for two years after STS is no longer compensating William Shoemaker. If Mr. Shoemaker leaves STS employment at the end of his five-year contract, the two-year noncompete will be enforced. Should Mr. Shoemaker terminate his employment within the five year contract period and compensation cease, the two-year noncompete will be enforced. This is consistent with STS employment policy."

Eventually, the parties agreed to terms and, on March 1, 2002, the parties closed the sale. As consideration for the sale of Southeastern Rentals to STS, Shoemaker was to be paid the sum of 1.5 million dollars. One of the closing documents was a Members Interest Purchase Agreement which contained a covenant not to compete as follows:

> 9.7 Covenant Not to Compete: During the period commencing on the Date of Closing and continuing until either the second anniversary of the Date of Closing or on the second anniversary of the termination of Seller's employment by the Company, whichever occurs later, the "Noncompetition Period", the Seller shall not (and shall cause each Noncompetition Party (as defined below) not to), directly or indirectly own, manage, operate or control or be employed by any business in competition with the business activities conducted by the Company on the Date of Closing or the date Seller is no longer an employee of the Company . . . .

As part of the closing, the parties also executed an Employment Agreement and a separate Noncompetition Agreement. The Noncompete

Agreement contained a paragraph which stated that "the parties hereto intend this Noncompetition Agreement to supersede any other noncompete agreements previously entered into by the parties, whether such agreements are written or orally made."

The Employment Agreement provided for a primary employment term of five years, subject to earlier termination. On February 21, 2007, the plaintiff informed Shoemaker that his contract of employment "would not be renewed." The plaintiff was very exact in its wording of this letter to make certain that Shoemaker's contract was not being "terminated" but only nonrenewed.

According to the Complaint, immediately after his employment with STS ended, Shoemaker opened an office for Professional Wireline Rentals, LLC ("PWR"), a Louisiana company engaged in oil field services in direct competition with STS. The plaintiff alleges that prior to March 1, 2007, PWR had no presence or office in the state of Mississippi, but that with Shoemaker's help, PWR opened an office in Ellisville, Mississippi, literally right down the road from STS's offices. The plaintiff asserts that since that time, Shoemaker has contacted and/or hired current and former employees of STS and that he has also contacted current and former clients of STS, solicited business, and performed work for these former or current clients of STS.

On April 27, 2007, the plaintiff filed its Complaint requesting: (1) injunctive relief from the court by prohibiting Shoemaker from competing against STS; (2) actual damages it has sustained as a result of Shoemaker interfering with business or contractual relations of STS; and (3) punitive damages; and (4) all expenses of litigation.

Standard of Review [omitted]

Analysis

The first rule of contract interpretation under the established jurisprudence of Mississippi is that the court give effect to the intent of the parties. Further, noncompetition agreements have been viewed by the Mississippi Supreme Court as "restrictive covenants [which] are in restraint of trade and individual freedom and are not favorites of the law." The enforceability of a noncompetition provision is "largely predicated upon the reasonableness and specificity of its terms."

The defendant points out that there is an ambiguity in the non-compete clauses in the Purchase Agreement and in the separate Noncompete Agreement. The plaintiff even admits as much but asserts, somewhat disingenuously, that the clause in the Purchase Agreement is "dominant" and should be given effect over that contained in the separate Noncompete Agreement. This is argument that carries little weight as the Noncompete Agreement signed concurrently with the Purchase Agreement states that "the parties hereto intend this Noncompetition Agreement to supersede any other noncompete agreements previously entered into by the parties, whether such agreements are written or orally made." Thus, if either clause is viewed as dominant, the one contained in the Noncompete Agreement would be. Regardless, there is an admitted ambiguity between the noncompete clauses of the two documents.

Mississippi Courts have long held that where the language of an otherwise enforceable contract is subject to more than one fair reading, the reading applied will be the one most favorable to the nondrafting party. In *Leach v. Tingle* the Mississippi Supreme Court, citing *Stampley v. Gilbert*, held:

> [W]e accept that, in a case where language of an otherwise enforceable contract is subject to more than one fair reading, we will give that language the reading most favorable to the nondrafting party.

If a court is unable to translate a clear understanding of the parties' intent, the court should apply the discretionary canons of contract construction. "Ambiguous words and terms should be construed against the party who has drafted them; and we accept that, in a case where language of an otherwise enforceable contract is subject to more than one fair reading, we will give that language the reading most favorable to the nondrafting party."

The plaintiff asserts that counsel for the defendant actually participated in the drafting of the closing documents and therefore discretionary construction unfavorable to the drafting party should not be utilized. The evidence, however, reveals that Shoemaker's counsel only provided minimal input into the actual drafting of the Purchase Agreement and no input into the drafting of the Employment Agreement or the Noncompete Agreement. Indeed, the first time Shoemaker or his counsel saw the latter two documents was on the day of closing.

Under Mississippi law, reviewing the construction of contracts involves questions of law that are committed to the court rather than the fact finder. However, "where a contract is ambiguous and uncertain, questions of fact are presented which are to be resolved by the trier of facts."

In the present case there is an ambiguity between the two noncompete agreements. The two agreements, in and of themselves, contain no such ambiguities and do not contain relevant questions of fact which require resolution by a separate finder of fact. While the clause in the Purchase Agreement may be subject to more than one interpretation, this clause is not controlling given the language of the Noncompete Agreement. Therefore, the canons of construction, and this court's duty to decide legal issues, require the court to resolve the ambiguity in the noncompete clauses more favorably to the defendant, as the nondrafting party.

In doing so, and viewing the two clauses together, the court finds that the parties intended for Shoemaker to work for the plaintiff for a period of five years and that if he quits or was terminated during that five year period, he would be subject to the noncompete clause for two years thereafter. However, the court finds that the parties clearly intended that once Shoemaker concluded his five year term of employment, he would no longer be prohibited from competing with the plaintiff.

As a final matter, the parties parse words over Shoemaker's ultimate dismissal from his employment. The defendant contends that he was never "terminated" according to the term as defined in the Employment Agreement. The court agrees that the term was defined in the employment documents to include termination for cause but also allows for termination by either party for any reason upon fourteen days written notice. There is no dispute that Shoemaker was not terminated for cause nor was he terminated under the fourteen day notice provision.

However, contrary to the defendant's contentions otherwise, termination also means conclusion of one's service. The contract of employment was fulfilled and it ended, i.e., it terminated. Noticeably, the plaintiff was very careful in its wording of the "termination" letter of February 21, 2007, by stating that Shoemaker was not being terminated, only that his contract was not being renewed. Thus, it is clear that the plaintiff understood and appreciated the differentiation, meaning and effect of the term "termination" versus a nonrenewal under the contract. The fact that the plaintiff chose to nonrenew the defendant's contract versus terminating it is further support for the court's conclusion that the parties did not intend the noncompete agreement to survive beyond the five year term of employment.

IT IS THEREFORE ORDERED AND ADJUDGED that the Motion for Summary Judgment filed on behalf of the defendant is Granted and the plaintiff's Complaint is dismissed with prejudice and that any other pending motions are denied as moot. A separate judgment shall be entered herein in accordance with Rule 58, Federal Rules of Civil Procedure.

Questions

1. What are the ambiguities identified by the court in the noncompete provisions?
2. What importance does the court place on the wording used in the termination letter?
3. How would you draft the provision, based on this decision, so as to avoid any ambiguity?

American Express Travel Related Services, Inc. v. Weppler
2003 Conn. Super. LEXIS 115

This is an action instituted by the plaintiff, American Express Travel Related Services, Inc., against the defendant, Jay Weppler, claiming money damages for the failure to pay amounts due from the purchase of commodities and services made under a credit agreement. The matter was tried to the court on September 11, 2002 and post-trial briefs were filed by the parties. The plaintiff's brief was filed on September 25, 2002 and the defendant's brief was filed on October 7, 2002. After consideration of the evidence and the issues as presented, the court enters a verdict in favor of the defendant.

The dispositive facts of this matter are undisputed. As part of a solicitation by the plaintiff, the defendant signed an application requesting the plaintiff to issue two credit cards, to himself and another employee of UNICO, Inc. The defendant was the president and employee of the company UNICO, Inc. The court finds on the basis of the defendant's testimony that the amounts sought by the plaintiff were for charges incurred by the defendant for the benefit of UNICO. Neither the plaintiff nor UNICO paid for the charges at issue which total $42,315.39.

The terms and conditions for the use of this card were contained in an "Agreement Between Corporate Cardmember and American Express Travel Related Services Company, Inc." The plaintiff relies on the following provisions in this agreement to support its claim against the defendant:

> You, as the Corporate Cardmember, are solely and personally liable to us for all Charges made in connection with Corporate Card issued to you. The company is not responsible to us for payment of such Charges. You should notify us immediately of any change in your billing address. Valid business expenses charged to the Corporate Card will be reimbursable by the company under the Company's expense reimbursement procedures applicable to you. This agreement has no effect on such procedures or your right to reimbursement by the Company.
>
> No other person is permitted to use this Corporate Card for charges, for identification, or any other reasons. We will look to you for payment of all Charges made with the Corporate Card issued to you, even if you have let someone else use the Corporate Card or relinquished physical possession of the Corporate Card.

The defendant, on the other hand, relies on a later provision of the agreement to support his defense that he is not personally liable for the charges. This provision is contained in what appears to be an addendum or a rider to the primary agreement:

> The Corporate Cardmember will be solely liable for all Charges on the Corporate Card Account except that the Company will be responsible to Amexco for Charges which benefitted the Company directly or indirectly and for which the Company has not reimbursed the Cardmember; and for any charges centrally billed to the Company.

In summary, one provision of the agreement indicates that "Cardmember" is solely responsible for all charges on the account and the company is not responsible for any of the payments, whereas another provision indicates that the company will be responsible for payments for those unreimbursed charges that are incurred for the benefit of the company. The courts agree with the defendant's position regarding the interpretation of this agreement. The plaintiff's view that the defendant is primarily and solely liable for the charges is rejected because it would construe the agreement in a manner which would make the later provision superfluous and meaningless.

The court finds that the latter language relied on by the defendant qualifies the earlier provisions of the Agreement so that the defendant was made responsible for charges on the card for his personal benefit; and the company, UNICO, was made responsible for charges on the card for UNICO's benefit for which UNICO failed to reimburse the defendant. This construction of the contract is the most reasonable interpretation of these provisions which appear facially inconsistent. The agreement consists of form documents created by the plaintiff, and the law is established that an ambiguity such as the one presented here must be construed against the drafter. *Hartford Electric Applicators of Thermalux, Inc. v. Alden*, 169 Conn. 177, 182, 363 A.2d 135 (1975) ("When there is ambiguity, we must construe contractual terms against the drafter").

Therefore, for the foregoing reasons, judgment shall enter in favor of the defendant, Jay Weppler, and against the plaintiff, American Express Travel Related Services, Inc.

So ordered.

Questions

1.   What are the terms of the conflicting provisions of the contract in question?

2.   Why is the contract construed against the drafter?

3.   What could have been done to avoid this problem of interpretation when the agreement was drafted?

Suggested Case References

1.   See what the court says about authentication and hearsay exceptions with respect to the introduction of a commercial lease in *Lyon Fin. Services, Inc. v. Manelle Fernando Med. Clinic, Inc.*, 2012 WI App 1 (2011).

2.   For problems associated with authenticating emails, read *Complete Conf. Coordinations, Inc. v. Kumon North Am., Inc.*, 394 Ill. 3d 103 (App, Ct. 2009).

3.   In *Walsh v. Nelson*, 622 N.W. 2d 499 (Iowa App. 2001), the court has to interpret a commercial lease to determine the parties' rights.

4.   The authentication of electronic writings is discussed in *Butler v. State*, 2014 Tex. App. Lexis 3269 (2014).

5.   Whether evidence of the drafting history of a contract may be used to interpret its terms is analyzed in *National Union Fire Ins. Co. v. Rhone-Poulenc*, 1993 Del. Super. Lexis 494 (1993).

Ethical Considerations

As a final reminder, the purpose of this, and all other textbooks, is to provide the reader with an understanding of the topics discussed. All legal professionals must be sure to review all relevant laws and authorities to ensure that the client is properly represented. As is stated in Rule 1.1 of the ABA's Rules of Professional Conduct:

"A lawyer shall provide competent representation to a client. Competent representation requires the legal knowledge, skill, thoroughness and preparation reasonably necessary for the representation."

Best wishes in your legal career!

APPENDIX A

Sample Contracts

Antenuptial Agreement (Simple Form)
Consulting Agreement
Employment Contract (Simple Form)
Employment Contract
Equipment Lease Agreement
General Partnership Agreement (Simple Form)
Limited Partnership Agreement
Real Estate Lease
Retainer Agreement
Shareholders Agreement
Subscription Agreement (Limited Partnership)
Work for Hire Agreement

Antenuptial Agreement (Simple Form)

Agreement entered into this _____ day of _____, 20 _____, by and between _____ and _____.

Whereas the parties agree to enter into the marriage relationship and hereafter live together as husband and wife,

NOW THEREFORE, in consideration of the marriage to be entered into by the parties they do hereby agree to the following:

1.   That all manner of property hereafter acquired or accumulated by them, or either of them, shall be held in joint or equal ownership.

2.   That each of the parties hereby grants, bargains, sells and conveys to the other an undivided one-half interest in all the property, real and personal, which he or she now owns, for the purpose and with the intent of vesting in both parties the joint ownership of all property at this date owned in severalty by either of them.

3.   In case of the death of one of the above mentioned parties, all said property shall, subject to the claims of creditors, vest absolutely in the survivor.

4.   That in the case of divorce of the above mentioned parties, all rights to property shall be equally divided between them pursuant to the terms of this Agreement.

IN WITNESS WHEREOF, the parties have executed this Agreement the day and year first above written.

_____

_____

Consulting Agreement

This Agreement is made this _____ day of _____, 20 _____ , by and between _____ (X), an individual residing at _____, and _____ (Consultant), an individual doing business at _____.

Consultant agrees to act as a financial consultant to X with respect to the development, production, and promotion of _____. Consultant shall meet and consult with X as the need arises, and shall perform services consistent with the duties of a financial consultant.

As full compensation for the services to be performed by Consultant, X agrees to pay Consultant 10% (ten percent) of the gross profit derived from the sale and marketing of the _____. The determination of the amount of said profit shall be made by an independent accounting firm should the parties to this Agreement disagree as to the amount of said profit.

Reasonable expenses actually incurred by Consultant incidental to the services performed shall be paid by X once money is received from the sale and marketing of _____ upon submission of a voucher of expenses to X by Consultant.

Should X willfully fail to develop, produce, and promote the _____, X shall pay Consultant reasonable compensation for work actually performed by Consultant on X's behalf.

Consultant, with respect to the services performed under this Agreement, is acting as an independent contractor and is not an employee. Consultant may be employed by other persons, firms, associations, or corporations not in conflict of interest with the terms of this Agreement during the term of this Agreement. Any employee or other personnel engaged by Consultant not for the express and direct benefit of X shall be under the exclusive direction and control of Consultant.

This Agreement is effective from the date above written and shall terminate when X no longer has any rights or title, direct or indirect, in _____.

This Agreement constitutes the entire Agreement between the parties relating to the subject matter contained in it, and supersedes all prior and contemporaneous representations, agreements, or understandings between the parties. No amendment or supplement of this Agreement shall be binding unless executed in writing by the parties. No waiver of one provision of this Agreement shall constitute a waiver of any other provision, nor shall any one waiver constitute a continuing waiver. No waiver shall be binding unless executed in writing by the party against whom the waiver is asserted.

This Agreement shall be construed and interpreted in accordance with, and governed by, the laws of the State of _____.

This Agreement may not be assigned by either party without the written consent of the other party.

If any provision of this Agreement is held by a court of competent jurisdiction to be invalid or unenforceable, the remainder of this Agreement shall remain in full force and shall in no way be impaired.

Any controversy or claim arising out of or relating to this Agreement, or the breach thereof, shall be settled by arbitration in accordance with the Rules of the American Arbitration Association, and judgment upon the award rendered by the arbitrator(s) may be entered in any court having jurisdiction thereof.

IN WITNESS WHEREOF, the parties have executed this Agreement on the date first above written.

X _____

_____

Consultant

Employment Contract (Simple Form)

Agreement made this _____ day of _____, 20 _____, between X of _____ (X), and Y, Inc., a corporation with principal offices at _____ (Y).

WHEREAS X is a well-known _____; and

WHEREAS Y is a well-known _____; and

WHEREAS Y wishes to make use of X's expertise; and

WHEREAS X accepts such employment,

NOW THEREFORE, in consideration of the mutual covenants herein contained, and other good and valuable consideration, it is agreed between the parties as follows:

1. Services

X shall provide Y with (describe specific services).

2. Compensation

Y shall compensate X in the sum of _____ Dollars ($ _____), payable in equal weekly installments.

3. No Further Obligations

All obligations with respect to the services to be performed by X shall cease upon _____.

4. Arbitration

Any controversy or claim arising out of or relating to this Agreement shall be settled by arbitration in the City of _____ in accordance with the Rules of the American Arbitration Association, and judgment upon the award rendered in such arbitration may be entered in any court having jurisdiction thereof.

5. Controlling Law

This Agreement shall be governed by the laws of the State of _____.

6. Entire Agreement

This Agreement expresses the whole Agreement between the parties hereto as of the date hereof. This Agreement shall not be changed, modified, terminated, or discharged except by a writing signed by the parties hereto.

7. Binding Effect

This Agreement shall be binding upon and ensure to the benefit of each of the parties hereto, their heirs, executors, administrators, or assigns.

IN WITNESS WHEREOF, the parties have executed this Agreement on the day and year first above written.

_____

X

_____

Y

By: _____

Employment Contract

Agreement dated _____, 20 _____, between X, Inc., a _____ corporation with principal offices at _____ (the Company), and Y, residing
at _____ (Y).

WITNESSETH:

WHEREAS the Company is doing business as a _____ and wishes
to avail itself of the services of Y; and
WHEREAS Y has substantial expertise and experience and is willing
to perform services for the Company, all in accordance with the following
terms and conditions;
NOW THEREFORE, it is agreed as follows:

1. Employment

The Company agrees to hire Y, and Y agrees to serve the Company as
its _____, with overall responsibility for _____.

2. Term

The term of employment shall be for one (1) year, commencing on
the _____ day of _____, 20 _____, and ending as of the _____ day
of _____ , 20 _____ (Termination Date). Sixty (60) days' written notice
prior to the Termination Date must be given by either party if the intention
of either party is not to negotiate a new Agreement.

3. Compensation

As compensation for the services hereunder, the Company shall pay
Y a total of (i) _____ Dollars ($ _____), payable in equal semimonthly
installments; and (ii) a sum equal to one-half (1/2) percent of the gross
sales volume accrued during the term of this Agreement, payable in one
installment not later than thirty (30) days after the Termination Date.

4. Records

The Company shall cause to be made available to Y, at least monthly, whatever figures are necessary to ascertain accurate records as to the gross volume of the Company.

5. Expenses

Y shall be reimbursed for all reasonable and necessary expenses incurred hereunder, upon the presentation of paid vouchers, or, as the case may be, the Company shall pay directly such expenses as may be determined in advance.

6. Travel

The Company agrees that it will consent to send Y at least twice yearly to the _____ in connection with the furtherance of his employment, and it is further agreed that Y will make two trips to _____ on behalf of the Company to introduce the Company's line.

7. Incidental Services

The Company shall make available to Y the various incidental services he deems necessary to successfully carry out his employment.

8. Responsibility

The Company intends that Y assume full responsibility for _____, maintaining a climate of maximum creativity within the Company's _____. It therefore agrees that Y shall be given substantial decision-making power in hiring and firing of all personnel.

9. Benefits

Y shall be entitled to receive those benefits which the Company provides for its key executive employees, including, without limiting the foregoing, hospitalization, major medical insurance, and disability insurance.

10. Life Insurance

The Company shall provide Y with life insurance of at least _____ Dollars ($ _____) during the term of this Agreement. Said insurance shall be convertible upon termination.

11. Vacation

Y shall be entitled to at least three (3) weeks' paid vacation per year, it being understood that said vacation shall be taken at times which are mutually convenient for the parties and shall not be taken consecutively.

12. Representation and Warranty

Y represents and warrants that he is not bound by any covenant or agreement, oral or written, which prohibits him from entering into this employment and from being employed by the Company.

13. Restrictive Covenant

Y will, during the term of this Agreement, devote his entire time, attention, and energies to the performance of his duties hereunder, and he will not directly or indirectly, either as a shareholder, owner, partner, director, officer, employee, consultant, or otherwise, be engaged in or concerned with any other commercial duties or pursuits whatsoever.

It is expressly understood and agreed that:

(a) All inventions, patents, copyrights, developments, and ideas and concepts developed by Y during the course of his employment under this Agreement shall be the exclusive property of the Company.

(b) Y shall have no right, either during or after employment under this Agreement, to use, sell, copy, transfer, or otherwise make use of, either for himself or for any other person other than the Company, any of the confidential information and trade secrets of the Company.

14. Illness or Disability

If during the term of this Agreement, Y becomes disabled or incapacitated by reason of illness, physical or mental, as to be unable to perform all duties to be performed hereunder, he shall be paid by the Company his salary during the first three (3) months of such disability, less a sum equal to the amount received by him under a disability insurance policy. In addition, Y shall be entitled to a sum equal to one-half (1/2) percent of the gross volume of the sales during said disability. Said sum shall be paid at the end of the three (3) months.

15. Severability

If any one or more of the provisions hereof shall be held to be invalid, illegal or unenforceable, the validity and enforceability of its other provisions shall not be affected thereby.

16. Notice

Any notice required to be given pursuant to the provisions of this Agreement shall be in writing and mailed prepaid to the parties at the addresses given at the beginning of this Agreement, by certified or registered mail, return receipt requested.

17. Arbitration

Any controversy or claim arising out of or relating to this Agreement, or the breach thereof, shall be settled by arbitration in the city _____ in accordance with the Rules of the American Arbitration Association, and the judgment upon the award rendered by the arbitrator(s) may be entered in any court having jurisdiction thereof.

18. Governing Law

This Agreement shall be governed by and construed according to the laws of the State of _____.

19. Modification

This Agreement contains the entire understanding of the parties and may not be amended, supplemented, or discharged except by an instrument in writing signed by the parties hereto.

20. Binding Effect

This Agreement shall enure to the benefit of and shall be binding upon the Company, its successors, and assigns.

IN WITNESS WHEREOF, the parties hereto have executed this Agreement as of the date and year first above written.

_____

Company

By: _____

_____

Y

Equipment Lease Agreement

Agreement made the _____ day of _____, 20 _____, between _____, Inc., with a place of business at _____ (Lessor) and _____ Inc. with a place of business at _____ (Lessee).

1. The Lessor hereby leases to the Lessee, and the Lessee hereby hires from the Lessor, subject to the terms and conditions hereinafter set forth, the following property consisting of _____ (Equipment).

2. The lease is for _____ months commencing on the _____ day of _____, 20 _____, and ending on the _____ day of _____, 20 _____. The total rent for said initial term is the sum of _____ Dollars ($ _____), plus sales tax payable as follows:

(a) _____ Dollars ($ _____) upon execution of the lease.

(b) The balance of the total rental of _____ Dollars ($ _____), i.e., $ _____, shall then be payable in equal monthly installments from and after payment of the initial $ _____ rental sum plus sales tax.

3. Lessee shall have the right and option to renew the said lease by the giving of ninety (90) days' advance written notice to the Lessor of its intention to do so. Lessee may renew the Lease for _____ terms (_____) of two (2) years each, with each term being renewed by the giving of the same ninety (90) days' advance written notice. Rent for each remaining term shall be as follows:

4. This Agreement creates a lease only of the Equipment and not a sale thereof or the creation of a security interest therein. The Lessor shall remain the sole owner of the Equipment, and nothing contained herein or the payment of rent hereunder shall enable the Lessee to acquire any right, title, or other interest in or to the Equipment.

5. Lessor agrees that neither it nor any principal or shareholder therein, nor any affiliate or entity in any way associated with Lessor, shall compete with the Lessee at any time during the term of this lease.

6. Upon delivery of the said Equipment by Lessor or Lessee, Lessor warrants that the same shall be in proper working order and fit for the purpose for which it was intended. The monthly rental payments by Lessee to Lessor specifically include consideration for Lessor's maintenance of the said Equipment, and during the term of the lease it shall be Lessor's responsibility to repair and maintain the same at Lessor's expense, provided that such repair and maintenance is for ordinary wear and tear.

7. (a) The Lessor shall pay all use taxes, personal property taxes, or other direct taxes imposed on the ownership, possession, use or operation of the Equipment or levied against or based upon the amount of rent to be paid hereunder or assessed in connection with the execution, filing, or recording of this Agreement. The term "direct taxes" as used herein shall include all taxes (except income taxes), charges, and fees imposed by any federal, state, or local authority.

(b) The Lessee assumes all responsibility and the cost and expense as may be required for the lawful operation of the Equipment. All certificates of title or registration applicable to the Equipment shall be applied for, issued, and maintained in the name of the Lessor, as Owner.

(c) The Lessee shall observe all safety rules and other requirements of regulatory bodies having jurisdiction and shall pay all fines and similar charges that may be duly and lawfully imposed or assessed by reason of the Lessee's failure to comply with the rules, regulations, and orders of regulatory bodies having jurisdiction.

(d) If the taxes, fines, or other charges, with the exception of permit fees, that the Lessee is responsible for under this Paragraph are levied, assessed, charged, or imposed against the Lessor, it shall notify the Lessee in writing of such fact. The Lessor shall have the option, but not the obligation, to pay any such tax, fine, or other charge, whether levied, assessed, charged, or imposed against Lessor or Lessee. In the event such payment is made by the Lessor, the Lessee shall reimburse the Lessor within seven (7) days after receipt of an invoice therefor, and the failure to make such reimbursement when due shall be deemed a default within Paragraph 8 hereof.

8. The Equipment shall be delivered by the Lessor to the Lessee at the Lessee's place of business. The Lessor shall have the right to place and maintain conspicuously on the side of the Equipment during the term of this lease the inscription _____, indicating the name of the owner of the Equipment or words of similar import in the event the lease is assigned by the Lessor, and the Lessee shall not remove, obscure, deface, or obliterate such inscription or suffer any other person to do so. Lessor can only assign its rights in this lease subject to all of the terms and conditions and rights that vest in Lessee herein.

9. The Lessee shall pay all operating expenses. The Lessee shall at all times provide suitable storage facilities and appropriate services for the Equipment including washing, polishing, cleaning, inspection, and storage space, and at the end or other expiration of this lease shall return the Equipment to the Lessor at the address above set forth in operating order and in the same condition and state of repair as it was at the date of delivery, ordinary wear and tear excepted.

10. The Lessee hereby indemnifies and shall hold the Lessor harmless from all loss and damage the Lessor may sustain or suffer by reason of the death of or injury to the person or property of any third person as a result, in whole or in part, of the use or maintenance of the Equipment during the term of this lease; and the Lessee shall procure, at the Lessee's cost and expense, a policy or policies of insurance issued by a company satisfactory to the Lessor with premiums prepaid thereon, insuring the Lessee against the risks and hazards specified above to the extent of the full value of the equipment and in the minimum amounts of _____ Dollars ($ _____) personal injury liability, together with fire and casualty loss. Such policy or policies shall name the Lessor as loss payee and not as co-insured. It shall be delivered to the Lessor simultaneously and prior to the delivery of the Equipment leased hereunder and shall carry an endorsement by the insurer either upon the policy or policies issued by it or by an independent instrument that the Lessor will receive thirty (30) days' written notice of the alteration or cancellation of such policy or policies. Failure by the Lessee to procure such insurance shall not affect the Lessee's obligations under the terms, covenants and conditions of this lease, and the loss,

damage to, or destruction of the Equipment shall not terminate the lease nor, except to the extent that the Lessor is actually compensated by insurance paid for by the Lessee, as herein provided, relieve the Lessee from the Lessee's liability hereunder. Should the Lessee fail to procure or maintain the insurance provided for herein, the Lessor shall have the option, but not the obligation, to do so for the account of the Lessee. In the event payment for procuring or maintaining such insurance is made by the Lessor, the Lessee shall reimburse the Lessor within seven (7) days after receipt of an invoice therefor, and the failure to make such reimbursement when due shall be deemed a default hereof.

11. The Lessee shall employ and have absolute control and supervision over the operator or operators of the Equipment and will not permit any person to operate the equipment unless such person is licensed.

12. In the event the Lessee fails to perform any material term, condition, and covenant contained herein in the manner and at the time or times required hereunder, including, but not limited to, the payment in full of any rental payment or the reimbursement of the Lessor for a disbursement made hereunder, or if any proceedings in bankruptcy or insolvency are instituted by or against the Lessee, or if reorganization of the Lessee is sought under any statute, state or federal, or a receiver appointed for the goods and chattels of the Lessee, or the Lessee makes an assignment for the benefit of creditors or makes an attempt to sell, secrete, convert, or remove the Equipment, or if any distress, execution, or attachment be levied thereon, or the Equipment be encumbered in any way, or if, at any time, in the Lessor's judgment (reasonable standard is applicable), its rights in the Equipment shall be threatened or rendered insecure, the Lessee shall be deemed to be in default under this Agreement, and the Lessor shall have the right to exercise either of the following remedies:

(a) To declare the balance of the rental payable hereunder to be due and payable whereupon the same shall become immediately due and payable, but Lessor shall use due diligence to release all Equipment covered in this Agreement; or

(b) To retake and retain the Equipment with demand on five (5) days' notice or legal process free of all right of the Lessee, in which case the Lessee authorizes the Lessor or its agents to enter upon any premises where the Equipment may be found for the purpose of repossessing the same, and the Lessee specifically waives any right of action it might otherwise have arising out of such entry and repossession, whereupon all rights of the Lessee in the Equipment shall terminate immediately. If the Lessor retakes possession of the Equipment and at the time of such retaking there shall be in, upon, or attached to the Equipment any property, goods, or things of value belonging to the Lessee or in the custody or under the control of the Lessee, the Lessor is hereby authorized to take possession of such property, goods, or things of value and hold the same for the Lessee or place such property, goods, or things of value in public storage for the account of and at the expense of the Lessee.

13. Forbearance on the part of the Lessor to exercise any right or remedy available hereunder upon the Lessee's breach of the terms, conditions, and covenants of this Agreement, or the Lessor's failure to demand the punctual performance thereof, shall not be deemed a waiver:

(a) Of such right or remedy;
(b) Of the requirement of punctual performance; or
(c) Of any subsequent breach or default on the part of the Lessee.

14. Neither this lease nor the Lessee's rights hereunder shall be assignable by the Lessee without any prior written consent of the Lessor, which consent shall not unreasonably be withheld.

15. The Lessee shall make available to the Lessor the Equipment for inspection as required by any governmental agency. The Equipment shall be available on forty-eight (48) hours' notice to Lessee at Lessee's place of business. Failure to make the Equipment available for said inspection shall be a substantial breach of this Agreement, and the operator will surrender the Equipment immediately upon notice.

16. The Lessee shall be responsible for obeying all laws, rules, and regulation of the State of _____ and the City of _____ , and any other governmental authority having jurisdiction. Further, any fines or penalties imposed because of the Lessee's failure to obey such laws, rules, and regulations shall be the sole responsibility of the Lessee, and paid for solely by him or her.

17. The Lessee acknowledges that he or she is not in the employ of the Lessor but is an independent contractor responsible for his or her own acts. Further, the Lessee shall maintain records and be responsible for the payment of any and all taxes and fees as previously mentioned. Any substantial violation by the Lessee to this Agreement shall render the entire Agreement in default, and the Lessee will be responsible to return the Lessor's Equipment within forty-eight (48) hours.

18. All notification from one party to the other as set forth in this Agreement must be in writing and forwarded by certified mail at the address specified on the first page of this lease.

19. Lessor represents that the permits and/or licenses it has in order to effectuate the said terms and conditions of this lease are in good standing and that the Lessor has the authority to enter into the within lease. Lessor further warrants that there are no assessments, taxes, levies, charges, encumbrances, liens, security interests, or other rights presently outstanding that would in any way interfere with or affect Lessee's intended operation.

20. The parties hereto specifically agree that Lessee has the right to cure any default provided the same occurred within ten (10) days' of written notification by Lessor to Lessee of the same.

21. This instrument contains the entire Agreement between the parties and shall be binding on their respective heirs, executors, administrators,

legal representatives, successors, and assigns. This Agreement may not be amended or altered except by a writing signed by both parties.

22. This Agreement is subject to the laws of the State of _____.

IN WITNESS WHEREOF, the parties hereto have executed this Agreement on the day and year first above written.

_____

Lessor

By: _____

_____

Lessee

By: _____

General Partnership Agreement (Simple Form)

This Agreement, made this _____ day of _____, 20 _____, by and between _____, First Party, _____, Second Party, and _____, Third Party, witnesses as follows:

That the said parties hereby agree to become partners in the business of _____ under the firm name of _____ for the term of _____ years from the date hereof, upon the terms and conditions hereinafter stated:

1. That the business shall be carried on at _____ or at any other place that may hereinafter be mutually agreed upon by the parties.

2. That proper books of account shall be kept, and therein shall be duly entered, from time to time, all dealings, transactions, matters, and things whatsoever in or relating to the said business; and each party shall have full and free access thereto at all times, but shall not remove the same from the premises.

3. That the capital requirements for carrying on the said business shall be borne by said partners in equal parts, and the said capital, and all such stock, implements, and utensils in trade purchased out of the partnership funds as well as the gains and profits of the said business, shall belong to the said partners in equal parts.

4. That each partner shall be at full liberty to have _____ Dollars ($ _____) monthly for his own private use, on account, but not in excess of his presumptive share of the profits, so long as the said business shall be found profitable.

5. That an account of the stock, implements, and utensils belonging to the said business, and of the book debts and capital, shall be taken, and a statement of the affairs of the said partnership to be made yearly, to be computed from the date hereof, when the sums drawn by each partner during the preceding year shall be charged to his share of the profits of said business; but, if, at the end of any one year of the said partnership it shall be found to be unprofitable, the said partnership shall thereupon be dissolved, unless it shall be occasioned by some accidental circumstances.

6. That each party shall sign duplicate copies of each of such statement of affairs, and shall retain one of these for his own use, and another copy shall be written in one of the partnership books, and likewise signed by each of them.

7. That all partners of the same class shall have identical and equal rights except as herein otherwise provided: _____. Each partner shall devote his best efforts to the firm and its clients and customers, and each partner shall follow the rules and policies of the business that may from time to time be adopted by them.

8. That no partner may be added to the firm unless each additional partner be unanimously elected by all of the existing partners.

9. That the death of a partner shall terminate all his interest in the partnership, its property and assets. The continuing firm shall pay in cash to his estate, or to his nominee, the following amounts to be paid in installments at the times indicated: _____ .

10. That any partner may voluntarily withdraw from the partnership at any time on notice of thirty (30) days to the other partners. At the expiration of the thirty- (30-) day period, or sooner if mutually agreed upon, the withdrawal shall become effective. The withdrawing partner's rights, title, and interests in the firm shall be extinguished in consideration of the payments to him by the continuing firm on the following basis: _____.

11. That any partner may be expelled from the firm for cause when it has been determined by a vote of the partners that any of the following reasons for his expulsion exist:

   (a) Loss of professional license;
   (b) Professional misconduct;
   (c) Insolvency;
   (d) Breach of any of the provisions of this Agreement;
   (e) Any other reason that the other partners unanimously agree warrants expulsion.

Upon expulsion, the expelled partner shall have no further rights, duties, or interest in the firm or any of its assets, records, or affairs. He shall immediately remove himself and his personal effects from the firm's offices. A partner so expelled shall be entitled to the same rights, the same payments by, and be subject to the same duties to the continuing firm as if he were voluntarily withdrawing from the firm.

12. That all provisions of this Agreement shall be construed and shall be enforced according to the laws of the State of _____.

13. That any controversy or claim arising out of or relating to any provision of this Agreement or the breach thereof shall be settled by arbitration in accordance with the Rules then in effect of the American Arbitration Association, to the extent consistent with the laws of the State of _____.

14. That no partner may assign or in any way transfer his interest in the partnership, all such rights and interests being personal to him.

15. That the invalidity or unenforceability of any one provision of this Agreement shall not affect the validity or enforceability of the other provisions of this Agreement.

IN WITNESS WHEREOF, the parties hereto have executed this Agreement on the day and year first above written.

_____
First Party

_____
Second Party

_____
Third Party

Limited Partnership Agreement

Agreement of Limited Partnership (the Agreement) of (the Partnership), entered into this _____ day of _____, 20 _____, by and among _____, Inc. (the General Partner), and each of the persons executing this Agreement (the Limited Partners). Reference herein to "Partners" without designation to "General" or "Limited" includes the General Partner and the Limited Partners except as the context otherwise requires.

PREAMBLE

The Partnership has been organized as a Limited Partnership under the laws of the State of _____ for the purpose of _____.

NOW THEREFORE, in consideration of the promises and mutual covenants hereinafter set forth, the parties hereto do hereby agree and certify as follows:

Article I

Definitions

1.0   Whenever used in this Agreement, the following terms shall have the following meanings:

(a) "Affiliate" shall mean (i) any person directly or indirectly controlling, controlled by or under common control with another person, (ii) a person owning or controlling ten percent (10%) or more of the outstanding voting securities of such other person, (iii) any officer, director, or partner of such person, and (iv) if such other person is an officer, director, or partner, any company for which such person acts in any such capacity.

(b) "Capital Account" means with respect to each partner his Capital Contribution, to the extent contributed, *increased* by: (i) any additional contributions and (ii) his distributive share of Partnership income and gains, and *decreased* by (i) cash and the Partnership's adjusted basis of property distributed to him and (ii) his distributive share of Partnership losses.

(c) "Capital Contribution" means the capital contributed by the General Partner and Limited Partners as set forth in Article IV and as hereinafter contributed to the Partnership by any Partner.

(d) "Cash Flow" means cash form revenues to the Partnership available for distribution after payment of Partnership expenses, advances made by the General Partner and others, and after amounts reserved to meet future contingencies as determined in the sole discretion of the General Partner.

(e) "Closing Date" shall mean the date the offering of the Units is complete.

(f) "Code" shall mean the Internal Revenue Code of 1986, as amended.

(g) "General Partner's Contribution" shall mean the contribution of the General Partner pursuant to Section 4.2 hereof.

(h) "Interest" shall mean the individual interest of each Partner in the Partnership.

(i) "Limited Partners' Contributions" shall mean the aggregate cash contributors of the Limited Partners.

(j) "Original Limited Partner" shall mean the Limited Partner who executed the original Certificate of Limited Partnership of the Partnership.

(k) "P&L Percentage" shall mean the percent of Profits and Losses allocable to each Partner.

(l) "Partnership Property" or "Partnership Properties" shall mean all interest, properties, and rights of any type owner or leased by the Partnership.

(m) "Permitted Transfer" shall mean a transfer by a Limited Partner of his Interest to: (i) his spouse, unless legally separated, child, parent, or grandparent; or (ii) a corporation, partnership, trust or other entity, fifty-one percent (51%) of the equity interest of which is owned by such Limited Partner individually or with any of the persons specified in subparagraph (i) hereof.

(n) "Profits and Losses" shall mean the Profits and Losses of the Partnership as reflected on its Federal Partnership Income Tax Return.

(o) "Unit" shall have the same meaning ascribed to such a term in a Private Placement Memorandum of the Partnership and any and all amendments thereto (the Memorandum).

Article II

Organization

2.1 *Addition of Limited Partners.* Promptly following the execution hereof, the General Partner, on behalf of the Partnership, shall execute or cause to be executed an Amended Certificate of Limited Partnership reflecting the withdrawal of the Original Limited Partner and the addition of the Limited Partners to the Partnership and all such other certificates and documents conforming thereto and shall do all such filing, recording, publishing and other acts, as may be necessary or appropriate from time to time to comply with all requirements for the operation of a limited partnership in the State of _____ and all other jurisdictions where the Partnership shall desire to conduct business. The General Partner shall cause the Partnership to comply with all requirements for the qualification of the Partnership as a Limited Partnership (of a partnership in which the Limited Partners have limited liability) in any jurisdiction before the Partnership shall conduct any business in such jurisdiction.

2.2 *Withdrawal of Original Limited Partner.* Upon execution of this Agreement by the Limited Partners, the Original Limited Partner shall withdraw as a Limited Partner and acknowledge that he shall have no interest in the Partnership as a Limited Partner and no rights to any of the profits, losses, or other distributions of the Partnership from the inception of the Partnership.

2.3 *Partnership Name.* The name of the Partnership shall be _____.

2.4 *Purposes of the Partnership.* The purposes of the Partnership shall be to acquire, own and continue to acquire, own, lease, and deal in or with real and personal property, securities, and investments of every kind, nature and description consistent with the best interests of the Limited Partners.

2.5 *Principal Place of Business and Address.* The principal office of the Partnership shall be maintained as _____, or such other address or addresses as the General Partner may designate by notice to Limited Partners. The Partnership may maintain offices and other facilities from time to time at such locations, within or without the State of _____, as may be deemed necessary or advisable by the General Partner.

2.6 *Term.* The Partnership shall dissolve on December 31, 20_____, unless sooner terminated or dissolved under the provisions of this Agreement.

Article III

Operation of the Partnership

3.1 *Powers and Duties of the General Partner.* Except as set forth in Section 3.2 below, the General Partner (if more than one, then such General Partners shall act by any one of the General Partners with the consent of the majority of the General Partners) shall have full, exclusive, and irrevocable authority to manage and control the Partnership and the Partnership Properties, and to do all reasonable and prudent things on behalf of the Partnership including, but not limited to, the following:

(a) To acquire any additional Partnership Property, including all property ancillary thereto and obtain rights to enable the Partnership to renovate, construct, alter, equip, staff, operate, manage, lease, maintain, and promote the Partnership Property, as well as all of the equipment and any other personal or mixed property connected therewith, including, but not limited to, the financial arrangements, development, improvement, maintenance, exchange, trade, or sale of such Property (including, but not limited to, all real or personal property connected therewith) at such price or amount for cash, securities, or other property, and upon such terms as it deems in its absolute discretion to be in the best interests of the Partnership;

(b) To sell or otherwise dispose of the Partnership Property and terminate the Partnership;

(c) To borrow or lend money for operation and/or for any other Partnership purpose, and, if security is required therefor, to mortgage or subject to any other security device any portion of the Partnership Property, to obtain replacements of any mortgage or other security device, and to prepay, in whole or in part, refinance, increase, modify, consolidate, or extend any mortgage or other security device, all of the foregoing at such terms and in such amounts as it deems, in its absolute discretion, to be in the best interest of the Partnership;

(d) To enter into contracts with various contractors and subcontractors for the maintenance of the Property;

(e) To enter into employment or other agreements to provide for the management and operation of the Partnership Property (including the right to contract with affiliates of the General Partner on behalf of the Partnership for such services);

(f) To place record title to, or the right to use, Partnership assets in the name or names of a nominee or nominees for any purpose convenient or beneficial to the Partnership;

(g) To acquire and enter into any contract of insurance that the General Partner deems necessary and proper for the protection of the Partnership, for the conservation of its assets, or for any other purpose, convenience, or benefit of the Partnership;

(h) To employ persons in the operation and management of the Partnership business, including, but not limited to, supervisory managing agents, consultants, insurance brokers, and loan brokers on such terms and for such compensation as the General Partner shall determine;

(i) To employ attorneys and accountants to represent the Partnership in connection with Partnership business;

(j) To pay or not pay rentals and other payments to lessors;

(k) To sell, trade, release, surrender, or abandon any or all of the Partnership Properties, or any portion thereof, or other assets of the Partnership;

(l) To settle claims, prosecute, defend, and settle and handle all matters with governmental agencies;

(m) To purchase, acquire, lease, construct, and/or operate equipment and any other type of tangible, real or personal property;

(n) To open bank accounts for the Partnership and to designate and change signatories on such accounts;

(o) To invest the funds of the Partnership in certificates of deposit or evidence of debt of the United States of America or any state, or commonwealth thereof, or any instrumentality of either;

(p) To enter into any other partnership agreement whether general or limited, or any joint venture or other similar agreement; and

(q) Without in any manner being limited by the foregoing, to execute any and all other agreements, conveyances, and other documents and to take any and all other action which the General Partner in its sole discretion deems to be necessary, useful, or convenient in connection with the Partnership Properties or business.

In accomplishing all of the foregoing, the General Partner may, in its sole discretion, but shall not be required to, use its own personnel, properties, and equipment, and may employ on a temporary or continuing basis outside accountants, attorneys, brokers, consultants, and others on such terms as he deems advisable. Any or all of the Partnership Properties, and any or all of the other Partnership assets, may be held from time to time, at the General Partner's sole discretion, in the name of the General Partner, the Partnership, or one or more nominees; and any and all of the powers of the General Partner may be exercised from time to time, at the General Partner's sole discretion, in the name of any one or more of the foregoing.

3.2 *Limitations of the Powers of the General Partner.* The General Partner may not act for or bind the Partnership without the prior consent of the holders of fifty-one percent (51%) of Limited Partnership Interests on the following matters:

(i) Amendment of the Partnership Agreement (except as set forth in Section 12.4); or

(ii) A change in the general character or nature of the Partnership's business.

3.3 *Powers and Liabilities of the Limited Partners.* No Limited Partner shall have any personal liability or obligation for any liability or obligation of the Partnership or be required to lend or advance funds to the Partnership for any purpose. No Limited Partner shall be responsible for the obligations of any other Limited Partner. No Limited Partner shall take part in the management of the business of the Partnership or transact any business for the Partnership, and no Limited Partner shall have power to sign for or bind the Partnership. No Limited Partner shall have a drawing account. No Limited Partner shall be entitled to the return of his capital contribution, except to the extent, if any, that distributions are made or deemed to be made to such Limited Partner otherwise than out of Profits pursuant to this Agreement. No Limited Partner shall receive any interest on his capital account. Upon the consent of fifty-one percent (51%) in interest of the Limited Partners, the Limited Partners shall have a right to call a meeting of the Partnership upon written notice to all of the Partners of the time, date, and place of such meeting. Upon the written request of twenty-five percent (25%) in interest of the nonaffiliated Limited Partners, the General Partner shall promptly call an informational meeting of the Partnership upon written notice to all of the Partners of the time, date, and place of such meeting.

3.4 *Exculpation and Indemnification of the General Partner.* (a) The Limited Partners recognize that there are substantial risks involved in the Partnership's business. The General Partner is willing to continue to serve as General Partner only because the Limited Partners hereby accept the speculative character of the Partnership business and the uncertainties and hazards which may be involved, and only because the Limited Partners hereby agree, that despite the broad authority granted to the General

Partner by Section 3.1, the General Partner shall have no liability to the Partnership or to the Limited Partners because of the failure of the General Partner to act as a prudent operator, or based upon errors in judgment, negligence, or other fault of the General Partner in connection with its management of the Partnership, so long as the General Partner is acting in good faith. Accordingly, the Limited Partners, for themselves, their heirs, distributees, legal representatives, successors, and assigns, covenant not to assert or attempt to assert any claim or liability as against the General Partner for any reason whatsoever except for gross negligence, fraud, bad faith, or willful misconduct in connection with the operation of the Partnership. It shall be deemed conclusively established that the General Partner is acting in good faith with respect to action taken by him on the advice of the independent accountants, legal counsel, or independent consultants of the partnership.

(b) In the event of any action, suit, or other legal proceeding, including arbitration, instituted or threatened against the General Partner or in which he (or if more than one, any of them) may be a party, whether such suit, action, or proceeding is brought on behalf of third parties or Limited Partners, individually or as a class, or in a derivative or representative capacity, the General Partner shall have the right to obtain legal counsel and other expert counsel at the expense of the Partnership and to defend or participate in any such suit, action, or proceeding at the expense of the Partnership, and he shall be reimbursed, indemnified against, and saved harmless by the Partnership for and with respect to any liabilities, costs, and expenses incurred in connection therewith. It is understood and agreed that the reimbursement and indemnification herein provided for shall include and extend to any suit, action, or proceeding based upon a claim of misrepresentation or omission to reveal any act of substance in any document pursuant to which the Limited Partnership Interests have been offered. It is expressly agreed that any claim of the nature referred to in the preceding sentences is and shall be subject to the provisions of this Subsection 3.4(b), other provisions of this Section, and other provisions of this Agreement relating to the nonliability, reimbursement, and indemnification of the General Partner. This Agreement is part of the consideration inducing the General Partner to accept the Limited Partners as members of the Partnership. The foregoing provisions for the indemnification and reimbursement of the General Partner shall apply in every case except in which it is affirmatively determined in any proceeding that the General Partner shall not be entitled to have indemnification or reimbursement by reason of his having been guilty of gross negligence, fraud, bad faith, or willful misconduct.

(c) Nothing herein shall be deemed to constitute a representation or warranty by the General Partner with respect to the title to or value of any Partnership Property or with respect to the existence or nonexistence of any contracts or other encumbrances with regard thereto, whether as against its own acts in the normal course of business or otherwise.

3.5 *Power of Attorney.* (a) Each Limited Partner by the execution of this Agreement does irrevocably constitute and appoint the General

Partner or any one of them, if more than one, with full power of substitution, as his true and lawful attorney in his name, place, and stead to execute, acknowledge, deliver, file, and record all documents in connection with the Partnership, including but not limited to (i) the original Certificate of Limited Partnership and all amendments thereto required by law or the provisions of this Agreement, (ii) all certificates and other instruments necessary to qualify or continue the Partnership as a limited partnership or partnership wherein the Limited Partners have limited liability in the states or provinces where the partnership may be doing its business, (iii) all instruments necessary to effect a change or modification of the Partnership in accordance with this Agreement, (iv) all conveyances and other instruments necessary to effect the dissolution and termination of the Partnership, and (v) all election under the Internal Revenue Code governing the taxation of the Partnership. Each Limited Partner agrees to be bound by any representations of the attorney-in-fact under this power of attorney, and hereby ratifies and confirms all acts which the said attorney-in-fact may take as attorney-in-fact hereunder in all respects as though performed by the Limited Partner.

(b) The Power of attorney granted herein shall be deemed to be coupled with an interest and shall be irrevocable and survive the death of a Limited Partner. In the event of any conflict between this Agreement and any instruments filed by such attorney-in-fact pursuant to the power of attorney granted in this Section, this Agreement shall control, and no power granted herein shall be used to create any personal liabilities on the part of the Limited Partners.

(c) By virtue of the power of attorney granted herein, the General Partner, or any one of them, if more than one, shall execute the Certificate of Limited Partnership and any amendments thereto by listing all of the Limited Partners and executing any instrument with the signature of the General Partner(s) acting as attorney-in-fact for all of them. Each Limited Partner agrees to execute with acknowledgement of affidavit, if required, any further documents and writings which may be necessary to effectively grant the foregoing power of attorney to the General Partner(s).

Article IV

Capitalization and Capital Contribution

4.1 *Capitalization.* The total initial capital of the Partnership shall be a minimum of _____ ($ _____) and a maximum of _____ ($ _____), exclusive of any capital contribution by the General Partner.

4.2 *General Partner's Contribution.* The General Partner has contributed _____ ($ _____) in cash to the capital of the Partnership and will be reimbursed at Closing for amounts that he has expended on behalf of the Partnership prior to Closing.

4.3 *Limited Partner's Contribution.* Each Limited Partner has made the contribution of capital to the Partnership in the amount set forth on Schedule A annexed hereto. Subscription for a Unit shall be made upon the execution hereof by the payment of ($ _____) in cash on subscription.

4.4 *Capital Accounts.* A separate Capital Account shall be maintained for each Partner and shall be credited with his Capital Contribution and his allocable share of all revenues, income, or gain and shall be debited with his allocable share of costs, expenses, deductions, and losses of the Partnership and any distributions made to him.

Article V

Fees and Compensation

In consideration of various services to be rendered to the Partnership by the General Partner, the General Partner will receive the compensation and fees as described in the Memorandum.

In furtherance of the provisions of Article III hereof, the General Partner may contract with any person, firm, or corporation (whether or not affiliated with the General Partner) for fair value and at reasonable competitive rates of compensation, for the performance of any and all services which may at any time be necessary, proper, convenient, or advisable to carry on the business of the Partnership.

Article VI

Distribution of Proceeds from Operations and Profit and Loss Allocations

6.1 *Distribution of Cash Flow.* Subject to the right of the General Partner to retain all or any portion of the annual cash flow for the anticipated needs of the Partnership, the net annual cash flow of the Partnership available for distribution from operations will be allocated ninety-nine percent (99%) to the Limited Partners (pro rata among them in the proportion that each Unit owned by a Limited Partner bears to the total number of Units owned by all Limited Partners) and one percent (1%) to the General Partner, until such time as the Limited Partners shall have received their capital contributions (Payout) and thereafter, fifty percent (50%) to the Limited Partners, pro rata, and fifty percent (50%) to the General Partner.

6.2 *Allocation of Profits and Losses.* Profits and losses of the Partnership from operation will be allocated ninety-nine percent (99%) to the Limited

Partners (pro rata among them in proportion that each Unit owned by a Limited Partner bears to the total number of Units owned by all Limited Partners) and one percent (1%) to the General Partner until Payout. After Payout, profits and losses will be allocated fifty percent (50%) to the Limited Partners, pro rata, and fifty percent (50%) to the General Partner.

6.3 *Allocation of Income for Certain Tax Purposes.* (a) Anything contained in this Agreement to the contrary notwithstanding, in the event an allocation of income in any calendar year pursuant to Section 6.2 above would cause the General Partner to have a positive Capital Account at the end of such year at a time when the Limited Partners have negative Capital Accounts, the amount of such income which would have been allocated to the General Partner pursuant to Section 6.2 in excess of the aggregate negative Capital Accounts of the Limited Partners shall instead be allocated to the Capital Accounts of the Limited Partners on a pro rata basis. For purposes of computing what a Partner's Capital Account would be at the end of a year, any cash available for distribution at such time which is intended to be distributed shall be deemed to have been distributed to such Partner on the last day of such year.

(b) Anything contained in this Agreement to the contrary notwithstanding, a Partner or Partners with deficit Capital Account balances resulting, in whole or in part, from an interest or other expense accrual, shall be allocated income resulting from the forgiveness of indebtedness of such deficit Capital Account balances no later than the time at which the accrual is reduced below the sum of such deficit Capital Account balances.

(c) If any Partner is, for income tax purposes, allocated additional income or denied a loss because of Section 6.3(b) above, a compensating allocation shall be made, for income tax purposes, at the first time such an allocation would be permissible thereunder.

Article VII

Allocation of Profits and Losses on a Sale or Other Taxable of Partnership Property

7.1 Any gain realized by the Partnership in connection with the sale or other taxable disposition of the Partnership Property shall be allocated to the Partners in the following order of priority:

(a) If any Partner has a negative Capital Account, any gain from the sale or other disposition of the Partnership Property shall be allocated to such Partners in the amount of their respective negative account balances, until the balance of each such Partner's Capital Account is equal to zero; and

(b) Any remaining gains shall be allocated ninety-nine percent (99%) to the Limited Partners, pro rata, and one percent (1%) to the General

Partner until Payout, and thereafter fifty percent (50%) to the Limited Partners, pro rata, and fifty percent (50%) to the General Partner.

7.2   Any loss realized by the Partnership in connection with the sale or other taxable disposition of the Partnership Property shall be allocated to the Partners in the following order of priority:

(a) If any of the Partners has a positive Capital Account, any loss from the sale or other disposition of the Partnership Property shall be allocated to such Partners in the amount of their respective positive account balances, until the balance of each such Partner's Capital Account is equal to zero; and

(b) Any remaining losses shall be allocated to the Partners as set forth in Section 7.1(b) above.

7.3   It is the intention of the General Partner that the allocation set forth herein have "substantial economic effect" within the meaning of regulations promulgated under Internal Revenue Code Section 704. In the event such allocations are deemed by the Internal Revenue Service or the courts not to have substantial economic effect, the General Partner reserves the right to modify allocations of profits and losses, after consulting with counsel, to achieve substantial economic effect. Nothing herein shall be construed to require the General Partner to so modify the allocation as set forth herein.

Article VIII

Limited Partners' Covenants and Representation with Respect to Securities Act

8.1   *Investment Representations.* Each of the Limited Partners, by signing this Agreement, represents and warrants to the General Partner and to the Partnership that he (a) is acquiring his Interest in the Partnership for his own personal account for investment purposes only and without any intention of selling or distributing all or any part of the same; (b) has no reason to anticipate any change in personal circumstances, financial or otherwise, which would cause him to sell or distribute, or necessitate or require any sale or distribution of such Interest; (c) is familiar with the nature of and risks attending investments in securities and the particular financial, legal, and tax implications of the business to be conducted by the Partnership, and has determined on his own or on the basis of consultation with his own financial and tax advisors that the purchase of such Interest is consistent with his own investment objectives and income prospects; (d) has received a copy of the Private Placement Memorandum, to which a copy of this Agreement is attached as Exhibit A, and has had access to any and all information concerning the Partnership which he and his financial, tax, and legal advisors requested or considered necessary to make proper evaluation of this investment; (e) is aware that no trading market for

Interests in the Partnership will exist at any time and that his Interest will at no time be freely transferable or be transferable with potential adverse tax consequences; and (f) is aware that there is a substantial risk that the federal partnership tax returns will be audited by the Internal Revenue Service and that, upon such audit, a part of the deductions allocated to the Limited Partners could be disallowed, thereby reducing the tax benefits of investing in the Partnership.

8.2 *Covenant Against Resale.* Each of the Limited Partners agrees hereby that he will, in no event, sell or distribute his Interest in the Partnership or any portion thereof unless, in the opinion of counsel to the Partnership, such Interest may be legally sold or distributed without registration under the Securities Act of 1933, as amended, or registration or qualification under then applicable state or federal statutes, or such Interest shall have been so registered or qualified and an appropriate prospectus shall then be in effect. *Notwithstanding the foregoing, no Limited Partner will be permitted to sell, distribute, or otherwise transfer his Interest in the Partnership or any portion thereof without the written consent of the General Partner (except as otherwise provided in Paragraph 9.1(b) below), the granting of which consent is in the absolute discretion of the General Partner.*

8.3 *Reliance on Private Offering Exemption.* Each of the Limited Partners represents and warrants hereby that he is fully aware that his Interest in the Partnership is being issued and sold to him by the Partnership in reliance upon the exemption provided for by Section 4(2) of the Securities Act of 1933, as amended, and Regulation D promulgated under such Act, and exemptions available under state securities laws, on the grounds that no public offering is involved, and upon the representations, warranties, and agreements set forth in this Article VIII.

Article IX

Transfer of Partnership Interests

9.1 *Limited Partnership Interest.* (a) No transfer of all or any part of a Limited Partner's Interest (including a transferee by death or operation of law and including a transferee in a Permitted Transfer) shall be admitted to the Partnership as a Limited Partner without the written consent of the General Partner, which consent may be withheld in the complete discretion of the General Partner. In no event shall the General Partner consent to the admission of the transferee as a Limited Partner unless the transferee executes this Agreement and such other instruments as may be required by law, or as the General Partner shall deem necessary or desirable to confirm the undertaking of such transferee to: (i) be bound by all the terms and provisions of this Agreement; and (ii) pay all reasonable expenses incurred by the Partnership in conjunction with the transfer, including, but not limited to, the cost of preparation, filing, and publishing such amendments to the Certificate as may be required by law of such other instruments as the General Partner may deem necessary and desirable.

A sale, assignment, or transfer of a Limited Partner's Interest will be recognized by the Partnership when it has received written notice of such sale or assignment, signed by both parties, containing the purchaser's or assignee's acceptance of the terms of the Partnership Agreement and a representation by the parties that the sale or assignment was lawful. Such sale or assignment will be recognized as of the date of such notice, except that if such date is more than thirty (30) days prior to the time of filing of such notice, such sale or assignment will be recognized as of the time the notice was filed with the Partnership. For purposes of allocating Profits and Losses, the assignee will be treated as having become a Limited Partner as of the date of which the sale, assignment, or transfer was recognized by the Partnership.

(b) Except for: (i) a Permitted Transfer and/or transfer by operation of law other than transfers in excess of the "forty percent (40%) limitation" (see subsection (c) below); or (ii) a transfer by gift, bequest, or inheritance, on Limited Partner may transfer all or any part of his Interest without first giving written notice of the proposed transfer to the General Partner (setting forth the terms thereof and the name and address of the proposed transferee) and obtaining the written consent of the General Partner to such transfer. Such consent shall be within the complete discretion of the General Partner and subject to such conditions, if any, as it shall determine.

(c) Anything else to the contrary contained herein notwithstanding:

(i) in any period of twelve (12) consecutive months, no transfer of an Interest may be made which would result in increasing the aggregate Profit and Loss Percentages of Partnership Interests previously transferred in such period above forty percent (40%). This limitation is herein referred to as the "forty percent (40%) limitation";

(ii) a Permitted Transfer is fully subject to the forty percent (40%) limitation;

(iii) subparagraph (i) hereof shall not apply to a transfer by gift, bequest, or inheritance, or a transfer to the Partnership, and for the purposes of the forty percent (40%) limitation, any such transfer shall not be treated as such;

(iv) if, after the forty percent (40%) limitation is reached in any consecutive twelve- (12-)month period, a transfer of a Partnership Interest would otherwise take place by operation of law (but not including any transfer referred to in subparagraph (iii) hereof), then such Partnership Interest shall be deemed sold by the transferor to the Partnership immediately prior to such transfer for a price equal to the fair market value of such interest on such date of transfer. The price shall be paid within ninety (90) days after the date of the sale out of the assets of the Partnership and the General Partner. If the Partnership and the transferor do not agree upon the fair market value of the Partnership Interest, then the purchase prices shall be determined in accordance with Section 9.3. The purchase price shall be paid by the Partnership out of its assets in cash within ten (10) days after such determination.

9.2 *Events Requiring Sale of Partnership Interest.* (a) The Interest of a Limited Partner shall be deemed offered for sale to a person designated by the General Partner upon the happening of any of the following events:

(i) a petition in bankruptcy having been filed by or against a Limited Partner and not discharged within ninety (90) days from the date of such filing; or

(ii) a receiver or committee having been appointed to manage a Limited Partner's property; or

(iii) a creditor of a Limited Partner having attached his Interest and such attachment not being discharged or vacated within ninety (90) days from the date it became effective.

The General Partner shall have ninety (90) days after the occurrence of any of the foregoing within which to accept such offer, designate such a purchaser (including the General Partner), and transmit written notice thereof to such Limited Partner. If the General Partner fails to make such designation within ninety (90) days as aforesaid, the offer shall be deemed withdrawn. The purchase price for such Interest shall be its appraised value as determined in accordance with Section 9.3. The purchaser shall pay over to the selling Limited Partner the purchase price in cash within ten (10) days after such determination. Upon payment of the purchase price to the selling Limited Partner, his Interest shall be deemed transferred to the aforesaid designated person.

(b) If any of the events described in Subsection 10.1(a)(v) should occur to the General Partner, or any one of them if more than one, and the Partnership shall not thereafter be dissolved but shall continue as a successor Limited Partnership with a successor General Partner, then upon the happening of any of such events the Interest of such General Partner shall be deemed offered for sale to the successor General Partner at its appraised value determined in accordance with Section 9.3 (except in the case of a voluntary withdrawal by a General Partner, in which event the value shall be determined by the withdrawing General Partner and the proposed successor General Partner, as selected by the withdrawing General Partner). The successor General Partner shall not become a General Partner of the Partnership until such former General Partner's Interest has been paid for in full in cash.

9.3 *Appraisal.* For the purpose of this Agreement, the appraised value of an Interest shall be the average of the values determined by three appraisers who are experts in evaluating property similar to the Partnership Property selected at the request of the General Partner. The appraisal made by such appraisers shall be binding and conclusive as between the selling Partner or Partners and the persons purchasing such Interest. The cost of such appraisal shall be borne equally by the selling and purchasing parties, and by each set of parties, among themselves, in proportion to their respective shares.

9.4 *Death, Bankruptcy, Incompetence, or Dissolution of a Limited Partner.* (a) Upon the death, bankruptcy, or legal incompetency of an individual Limited Partner, his legally authorized personal representative shall have all of the rights of a Limited Partner for the purpose of settling or managing his estate, and shall have such power as the decedent, bankrupt, or incompetent possessed to make an assignment of his Interest in the Partnership in accordance with the terms hereof and to join with such assignee in making application to substitute such assignee as a Limited Partner.

(b) Upon bankruptcy, insolvency, dissolution, or other cessation to exist as a legal entity of any Limited Partner which is not an individual, the authorized representative of such entity shall have all of the rights of the Limited Partner for the purpose of effecting the orderly winding up and disposition of the business of such entity, and such power as such entity possessed to make an assignment of its Interest in the Partnership in accordance with the terms hereof and to join with such assignee in making application to substitute such assignee as a Limited Partner.

9.5 *Voluntary Withdrawal or Transfer by a General Partner.* (a) A General Partner may resign as General Partner at any time, but only upon compliance with the following procedures:

(i) The General Partner shall give notification to all Limited Partners that he proposes to withdraw and that he proposes that there be substituted in his place a person designated and described in such notification.

(ii) Enclosed with such notification shall be (a) an opinion of counsel to the Partnership that the proposed General Partner qualifies to serve as a General Partner under federal law, and (b) a certificate, duly executed by or on behalf of such proposed successor General Partner, to the effect that he is experienced in performing (or employs sufficient personnel who are experienced in performing) functions of the type then being performed by the resigning General Partner.

(iii) The consent of the remaining General Partner and the holders of at least fifty-one percent (51%) in interest of the Limited Partner shall be required for the appointment of the proposed successor General Partner pursuant to this Section 9.5(a). If the proposed successor General Partner shall not receive such consent within sixty (60) days after the date of the withdrawing General Partner's notification, then, at the sole option of the General Partner seeking to withdraw, the Partnership may be terminated and dissolved and its assets liquidated in accordance with Article VIII of this Agreement.

(iv) The General Partner who has withdrawn pursuant to this Section shall cooperate fully with the successor General Partner so that the responsibilities of such withdrawn General Partner may be transferred to such successor General Partner with as little disruption of the Partnership's business and affairs as is practicable.

(b) Except as part of a transfer to a successor General Partner pursuant to Section 9.5(a), the General Partner shall not have the right to retire or to transfer or assign his General Partner's Interest.

9.6 *Removal of a General Partner.* (a) A General Partner may be removed as General Partner only without his consent or the consent of the other General Partners only for cause upon the consent of 51% in Interest of the Limited Partners, such removal to be effective upon the service of written notice upon the General Partner to be removed by posting said notice in the United States mails. Upon such removal, the Partnership shall continue and the remaining General Partners shall continue the Partnership. If all the General Partners are removed, then the Partnership shall be dissolved unless 51% in Interest of the Limited Partners vote to continue the Partnership as a successor limited partnership and appoint a successor General Partner who (i) in the opinion of counsel to the Partnership qualifies to serve as General Partner under federal law, and (ii) agrees to purchase the Interest of the other General Partners in accordance with Sections 9.2(b) and 9.3 hereof.

(b) Any successor General Partner appointed by the Limited Partners to replace the General Partner shall, beginning on the effective date of such replacement, have the same rights and obligations under this Agreement as the General Partner would have had subsequent to such date if the General Partner continued to act as General Partner.

9.7 *Death, Retirement, Bankruptcy, Legal Incapacity, etc. of a General Partner.* Upon the death, retirement, or legal incapacity of a General Partner, or the filing by or against a General Partner of a petition in bankruptcy, the adjudication of the General Partner as a bankrupt, or the making by the General Partner of an assignment for the benefit of creditors, the remaining General Partners shall continue the Partnership unless all of the General Partners are subject to the foregoing events, in which case the Partnership shall terminate unless fifty-one percent (51%) in Interest of the Limited Partners (or one hundred percent (100%) in the case of the death, retirement, or insanity of a General Partner) vote to continue the Partnership as a successor Limited Partnership and appoint a successor General Partner, who (i) in the opinion of counsel to the Partnership qualifies to serve as General Partner under federal law, and (ii) agrees to purchase the Interest of the General Partner in accordance with Sections 9.2(b) and 9.3 hereof.

9.8 *Admission of a Successor General Partner.* The admission of a successor General Partner shall be effective only if the Interests of the Limited Partners shall not be affected by the admission of such successor General Partner.

9.9 *Liability and Rights of Replaced General Partner.* Any General Partner who shall be replaced as General Partner shall remain liable for his portion of any obligation and liabilities incurred by him as General Partner prior to the time such replacement shall have become effective, but he shall be free of any obligation or liability incurred on account of the activities of the Partnership from and after such time. Such replacement shall not affect any rights of the General Partner which shall mature prior to the effective date of such replacement.

Article X

Dissolution, Liquidation, and Termination

10.1 *Dissolution.* (a) The Partnership shall be dissolved upon the earliest of:

(i) the expiration of its term as provided in this Agreement;

(ii) the sale of all or substantially all of the Partnership Property;

(iii) the occurrence of any event which causes the dissolution of a limited partnership under the laws of the State of _____;

(iv) the written election of Limited Partners owning eighty percent (80%) of the Limited Partnership Interests; or

(v) except as otherwise provided herein, the withdrawal or removal of, the death, retirement, or legal incapacity of, or the filing of a petition in bankruptcy, the adjudication as a bankrupt, or the making of an assignment for the benefit of creditors by the last remaining General Partner, unless fifty-one percent (51%) in Interest of the Limited Partners (or one hundred percent (100%) in the case of the death, retirement, or legal incapacity of the General Partner) appoint a successor General Partner and vote to continue the Partnership as a successor Limited Partnership.

(b) The Partnership shall not be dissolved upon the death of a Limited Partner.

(c) In the event of such dissolution, the assets of the Partnership shall be liquidated and the proceeds thereof distributed in accordance with Section 7.1 hereof.

10.2 *Liquidating Trustee.* Upon the dissolution of the Partnership, the liquidating trustee (which shall be those General Partners which are not subject to any of the events set forth in subparagraph 10.1(a)(v), or, in the event all General Partners are subject to such events, a trustee appointed by the Limited Partners representing a majority in interest of the profit and loss percentages of the Limited Partners), shall proceed diligently to wind up the affairs of the Partnership and distribute its assets in accordance with Section 7.1 hereof. All saleable assets of the Partnership may be sold in connection with any liquidation at public or private sale, at such price and upon such terms as the liquidating trustee in his sole discretion may deem advisable. Any Partner and any partnership, corporation, or other firm in which any Partner is in any way interested may purchase assets at such sale. Distributions of Partnership assets may be made in cash or in kind, in the sole and absolute discretion of the liquidating trustee. The liquidating trustee shall make a proper accounting to each Limited Partner of his Capital Account and of the net profit or loss of the Partnership from the date of the last previous accounting to the date of dissolution.

Article XI

Accounting, Records, Reports, and Taxes

11.1 *Fiscal Year and Reports.* The fiscal year of the Partnership for both accounting and federal income tax purposes shall be the calendar year. At all times during the continuance of the Partnership, the General Partner shall keep or cause to be kept full and faithful books of account in which shall be entered fully and accurately each transaction of the Partnership. All of the books of account shall be open to the inspection and examination of the Limited Partners or their duly authorized representatives upon reasonable notice during normal business hours. Annual financial statement of the Partnership shall be transmitted by the General Partner to each Limited Partner. The General Partner shall further transmit to each Limited Partner annually, within a reasonable time after the end of each calendar year (but in no event later than seventy-five (75) days after the end of the calendar year or as soon as practicable thereafter), a report setting forth the Limited Partner's share of the Partnership's Profits or Losses for each such year, and such Limited Partner's allocation of cash receipts. The reports and statements delivered in accordance herewith may be changed from time to time to cure errors or omission and to give effect to any retroactive costs or adjustments. All costs and expenses incurred in connection with such reports and statements shall constitute expenses of Partnership operation.

11.2 *Income Tax Elections.* (a) No elections shall be made by the Partnership, the General Partner or any Limited Partner to be excluded from the application of the provision of Subchapter K of Chapter I of Subtitle A of the Code or from the application of any similar provisions of state tax laws.

(b) All other elections required or permitted under the Code shall be made by the General Partner in such manner as will, in the opinion of the Partnership's accountants, be most advantageous to a majority in Interest of the Limited Partners.

11.3 *Tax Matters Partner.* The General Partner shall be designated the tax matters partner of the Partnership pursuant to Section 6231(7) of the Internal Revenue Code.

Article XII

General

12.1 *Notices.* Any notice, communication, or consent required or permitted to be given by any provision of this Agreement shall, except as otherwise expressly provided herein, be deemed to have been sufficiently given or served for any purpose only if in writing, delivered personally, or sent by registered mail, postage and charges prepaid, or by standard prepaid telegram.

12.2 *Further Assurances.* Each of the Partners agrees hereafter to execute, acknowledge, deliver, file, record, and publish such further certificates, instruments, agreements and other documents and to take all such further actions as may be required by law or deemed by the General Partner to be necessary or useful in furtherance of the Partnership's purposes and the objectives and intentions underlying this Agreement and not inconsistent with the terms hereof.

12.3 *Banking.* All funds shall be deposited in the Partnership's name in such checking accounts as shall be designated by the General Partner. All withdrawals therefrom shall be made upon checks signed by the General Partner.

12.4 *Amendment of Certificate of Limited Partnership.* The General Partners may amend the Certificate of Limited Partnership and the Agreement when any one of the following events occur: (a) there is a change in the name of the Partnership, or the amount of character of the contribution of any Limited Partner; (b) a person is substituted as a Limited Partner; or (c) an additional Limited Partner is admitted.

12.5 *Voting Rights of Limited Partners.* This Agreement may not be modified or amended in any manner whatsoever except with the written consent of the General Partner and the written consent of Limited Partners whose Profit and Loss percentages at that time are sixty-six and two-thirds percent (66 2/3%) of the total Profit and Loss Percentages of all Limited Partners.

12.6 *Meetings.* Any vote of the Limited Partners on any matters upon which Limited Partners are entitled to vote hereunder may be accomplished at a meeting of Limited Partners called for such purposes by the General Partner or by the nonpromoted, nonaffiliated Limited Partners whose Profit and Loss Percentages at that time exceed fifty-one percent (51%) of the total Profit and Loss Percentages of all such Limited Partners, upon not less than ten (10) days' prior notice or, in lieu of a meeting, by the written consent of the required percentage of Limited Partners.

12.7 *Access to Records.* The Limited Partners and their designated representatives shall be permitted access to all records of the Partnership at the office of the Partnership during reasonable hours. The Partnership records shall include a list of the names and addresses of the Limited Partners.

12.8 *Miscellaneous.* (a) Except as otherwise expressly provided herein, the headings in this Agreement are inserted for convenience of reference only and are in no way intended to describe, interpret, define, or limit the scope, extent, or intent of this Agreement or any provision hereof.

(b) Every provision of this Agreement is intended to be severable. If any term or provision hereof is illegal or invalid for any reason whatsoever, such illegality or invalidity shall not affect the validity of the remainder of this Agreement.

(c) This Agreement, and the application and interpretation hereof, shall be governed exclusively by the terms hereof and by the laws of the State of _____ .

(d) The rights and remedies provided by this Agreement are cumulative, and the use of any one right or remedy by any party shall not preclude or waive its right to pursue any or all other remedies. Such rights and remedies are given in addition to any other rights the parties may have by law, statute, ordinance, or otherwise.

(e) This Agreement may be executed in any number of counterparts with the same effect as if the parties had all signed the same instrument. All counterparts shall be construed together and shall constitute one Agreement. Limited Partners may become parties to this Agreement by executing and delivering to the General Partner a signature page hereto in the form approved by the General Partner.

(f) Time is of the essence hereof.

(g) Each and all of the covenants, terms, provisions and agreements therein contained shall be binding upon and inure to the benefit of each party and, to the extent permitted by this Agreement, the respective successors and assigns of the parties.

(h) No person, firm, or corporation dealing with the Partnership shall be required to inquire into the authority of the General Partner to take any action or to make any decision.

(i) This instrument incorporates the entire agreement between the parties hereto, regardless of anything to the contrary contained in any certificate of limited partnership or other instrument or notice purporting to summarize the terms hereof, whether or not the same shall be recorded or published.

(j) The General Partner shall prepare or cause to be prepared and shall file on or before the due date (or any extension thereof) any federal, state, or local tax returns required to be filed by the Partnership. The General Partner shall cause the Partnership to pay any taxes payable by the Partnership.

IN WITNESS WHEREOF, the undersigned have executed this Agreement as of the day and year first above written.

_____

General Partner

_____

Limited Partner

Real Estate Lease

Agreement made this _____ day of _____, 20 _____, between X, Inc., a _____ corporation (Lessor), and _____, an individual (Lessee).

The Lessor hereby devises and lets to the Lessee the premises known as _____ for the term of one year, commencing on the _____ day of _____, 20 _____, and ending on the _____ day of _____, 20 _____, for which the Lessee agrees to pay the Lessor, at his place of business, promptly on the first day of each month, in advance, a monthly rental of _____ Dollars ($ _____). On the failure of the Lessee to pay said rent when due, all further rent under this contract shall immediately become due and payable, and the Lessor has the right, at his option, to declare this lease void, cancel the same, enter and take possession of the premises.

It is further agreed that:

(Indicate all specific covenants the parties agree to, for example:
Allocation of cost of repairs
Maintenance of premises
Right of Lessor to enter
Subletting
Destruction of property due to fire or act of God
Alteration of premises
Payment of damages due to negligence
Notice to quit
Security deposit)

All of the aforementioned agreements, covenants, and conditions shall apply to and be binding upon the parties hereto, their heirs, executors, administrators, and assigns.

IN WITNESS WHEREOF, the parties hereto have set their hands and seals this _____ day of _____, 20 _____.

_____
Lessor

By: _____

_____
Lessee

Retainer Agreement

Names and Addresses of the Parties

THIS AGREEMENT FOR LEGAL SERVICES by and between

Client, and

        , Esq.

Attorney

constitutes a binding legal contract and should be reviewed carefully.

Nature of the Services to Be Rendered

The Client authorizes the Attorney to take any steps which, in the sole discretion of the Attorney, are deemed necessary or appropriate to protect Client's interest in the matter.

Amount of the Advance Retainer, If Any, and What It Is Intended to Cover

In order for Attorney to begin the representation, Client agrees to pay Attorney, and Attorney has agreed to accept a retainer payment of $ _____ . This retainer payment does not necessarily represent the amount of the overall fee which may be incurred by virtue of Attorney's services. This retainer constitutes a Minimum Fee and is nonrefundable. This retainer shall entitle Client to up to _____ hours of Attorney's time. The amount of Attorney's eventual fee will be based upon Attorney's regular schedule of established hourly time charges, along with any out-of-pocket disbursements (such as court costs, messenger services, transcripts of proceedings, long distance telephone calls, faxes, process service fees, mileage, deposition and court transcripts, and excess postage) which are incurred on Client's behalf.

The Client further understands that the hourly rates apply to all time expanded relative to the Client's matter, including but not limited to, office meetings and conferences, telephone calls and conferences, either placed by or placed to the Client, or otherwise made or had on the Client's behalf or relative to the Client's matter, preparation, review and revision of correspondence, pleadings, motions, disclosure demands and responses, affidavits and affirmations, or any other documents, memoranda, or papers relative to the Client's matter, legal research, court appearances, conferences, file review, preparation time, travel time, and any other time expended on behalf of or in connection with the Client's matter.

Client's Right to Cancel This Agreement

Client has the absolute right to cancel this agreement at any time. Should Client exercise this right, Client will be charged only the fee expenses (time charges and disbursements) incurred within that period that exceeds the amount of the Earned Retainer, based upon the hourly rates set forth in the Retainer Agreement.

Client's Duty to Pay Fee

Client agrees to pay Attorney amounts that may be due not later than ten (10) days from the date that Attorney shall submit a bill to Client for the same. If an amount due is not paid within ten (10) days after Attorney's statement to Client for the amount due, interest at the rate of 10% per annum shall be added to the balance due to Attorney.

Hourly Fee

Client shall be charged an hourly fee of $ _____ . In addition, Client is responsible for direct payment or reimbursement of Attorney for disbursements advanced on Client's behalf.

The hourly fee set forth in this Retainer Agreement shall remain in effect throughout this period of Attorney's representation for the matter set forth in this Retainer Agreement, unless changed by mutual consent of Client and Attorney, in which event any modification of this Retainer Agreement will be reduced to writing and signed by Attorney and Client.

Frequency of Billing

Client will be billed periodically, generally each month but in no event less frequently than 60 days. Included in the bill will be a detailed explanation of the services rendered and the disbursements incurred in connection with Client's matter. Upon receipt of the bill Client is expected to review the bill and promptly bring to Attorney's attention any objection Client may have to the bill. While Attorney strives to keep perfectly accurate time records, Attorney recognizes the possibility of human error and Attorney shall discuss with Client any objection raised with respect to the bill. Client will not be charged for time expended in discussing any aspect of the bill rendered to Client.

Client's Right to Copies of Documents and to Be Apprised of the Status of the Case

Attorneys shall keep Client informed of the status of the case and agrees to explain the laws pertinent to Client's situation, the available course of action, and the attendant risks. Attorney shall notify Client promptly of any development in Client's case, and will be available for meetings and telephone conversations with Client at mutually convenient times. Copies of all papers will be supplied to Client unless Client requests the contrary, and Client will be billed reasonable photocopy charges for these materials which will be included in the periodic bill.

Attorney's Right to Withdraw

Client is advised that if, in the judgment of Attorney, Attorney decides that there has been an irretrievable breakdown in the attorney-client relationship, or a material breach of the terms of his Retainer Agreement, Attorney may decide to make application to the court in which Client's action is pending, or by letter to Client in the situation in which no case is pending before a court, to be relieved as Clients' Attorney. In such event, Client will be provided with notice of such application and an opportunity to be heard. Should any fees be due and owing to Attorney at the time of such discharge or withdrawal, Attorney shall have the right, in addition to any other remedy, to seek a charging lien, i.e., a lien upon the property that is awarded to Client as a result of any conclusion of this matter.

In the event that any bill from Attorney remains unpaid beyond a 90-day period, Client agrees that Attorney may withdraw his representation, at the option of the Attorney. In the event that an action is pending, and absent Client's consent, an application must be made to the Court for such withdrawal. Where the fee is unpaid for the period set forth above, the Client acknowledges that in connection with any such withdrawal application, that the account delinquency shall be good cause for withdrawal.

Arbitration

Should a dispute arise with respect to this agreement, the parties agree to submit such dispute to arbitration for resolution pursuant to Article 75 of the CPLR.

Acknowledgment and Understanding

Client acknowledges that he or she has read this Retainer Agreement in its entirety, has had full opportunity to consider its terms, and has had full and satisfactory explanation of same, and fully understands its terms and agrees to such terms.

Client fully understands and acknowledges that there are no additional or different terms or agreements other than those expressly set forth in the Retainer Agreement.

Client acknowledges that he or she was provided with and read the Statement of Client's Rights and Responsibilities, a copy of which is attached hereto.

Certifications

Attorney has Informed Client that pursuant to court rules, Attorney may be required to certify court papers submitted by Client which contain statements of fact and specificity to certify that Attorney has no knowledge that the substance of such submission is false. Accordingly, Client agrees to provide Attorney with complete and accurate information, which forms the basis for court papers and to certify in writing to Attorney, prior to the time the papers are actually submitted to the court, the accuracy of the court submission which Attorney prepares on Client's behalf, and which Client shall review and sign.

No Guarantees

It is specifically acknowledged by Client that Attorney has made no representations, express or implied, concerning the outcome of this representation. Client further acknowledges that the Attorney has not guaranteed and cannot guarantee the success of any action taken by Attorney on Client's behalf.

Other Matters

Closing

Client acknowledges that no guarantees have been made with respect to any phase of this representation.
Dated:

_____
, Attorney

I have read and understand the above, received a copy and accept all of its terms.

_____
, Attorney

Statement of Client's Rights and Responsibilities

Your attorney is providing you with this document to inform you of what you, as a client, are entitled to by law or by custom. To help prevent any misunderstanding between you and your attorney please read this document carefully.

If you ever have any questions about these rights, or about the way your case is being handled, do not hesitate to ask your attorney. He or she should be readily available to represent your best interests and keep you informed about your case.

An attorney may not refuse to represent you on the basis of race, creed, color, sex, sexual orientation, age, national origin, or disability.

You are entitled to an attorney who will be capable of handling your case; show you courtesy and consideration at all times; represent you zealously; and preserve your confidences and secrets that are revealed in the course of the relationship.

You are entitled to a written retainer agreement which must set forth, in plain language, the nature of the relationship and the details of the fee arrangement. At your request, and before you sign the agreement, you are entitled to have your attorney clarify in writing any of its terms, or include additional provisions.

You are entitled to fully understand the proposed rates and retainer fee before you sign a retainer agreement, as in any other contract.

You may refuse to enter into any fee arrangement that you find unsatisfactory.

Your attorney may not request a fee that is contingent on the securing of a divorce or on the amount of money or property that may be obtained.

Your attorney may not request a retainer fee that is nonrefundable. That is, should you discharge your attorney, or should your attorney withdraw from the case, before the retainer is used up, he or she is entitled to be paid commensurate with the work performed on your case and any expenses, but must return the balance of the retainer to you. However, your attorney may enter into a minimum fee arrangement with you that provides for the payment of a specific amount below which the fee will not fall based upon the handling of the case to its conclusion.

You are entitled to know the approximate number of attorneys and other legal staff members who will be working on your case at any given time and what you will be charged for the services of each.

You are entitled to know in advance how you will be asked to pay legal fees and expenses, and how the retainer, if any, will be spent.

At your request, and after your attorney has had a reasonable opportunity to investigate your case, you are entitled to be given an estimate of approximate future costs of your case, which estimate shall be made in good faith but may be subject to change due to facts and circumstances affecting the case.

You are entitled to receive a written, itemized bill on a regular basis, at least every 60 days.

You are expected to review the itemized bills sent by counsel, and to raise any objections or errors in a timely manner. Time spent in discussion or explanation of bills will not be charged to you.

You are expected to be truthful in all discussions with your attorney, and to provide all relevant information and documentation to enable him or her to competently prepare your case.

You are entitled to be kept informed of the status of your case, and to be provided with copies of correspondence and documents prepared on your behalf or received from the court or your adversary.

You have the right to be present in court at the time that conferences are held.

You are entitled to make the ultimate decision on the objectives to be pursued in your case, and to make the final decision regarding the settlement of your case.

Your attorney's written retainer agreement must specify under what circumstances he or she might seek to withdraw as your attorney for nonpayment of legal fees. If an action or proceeding is pending, the court may give your attorney a "charging lien," which entitles your attorney to payment for services already rendered at the end of the case out of the proceeds of the final order or judgment.

You are under no legal obligation to sign a confession of judgment or promissory note, or to agree to a lien or mortgage on your home to cover legal fees. Your attorney's written retainer agreement must specify whether, and under what circumstances, such security may be requested. In no event may such security interest be obtained by your attorney without prior court approval and notice to your adversary. An attorney's security interest in the marital residence cannot be foreclosed against you.

You are entitled to have your attorney's best efforts exerted on your behalf, but no particular results can be guaranteed.

If you entrust money with an attorney for an escrow deposit in your case, the attorney must safeguard the escrow in a special bank account. You are entitled to a written escrow agreement, a written receipt, and a complete record concerning the escrow. When the terms of the escrow agreement have been performed, the attorney must promptly make payment of the escrow to all persons who are entitled to it.

In the event of a fee dispute, you may have the right to seek arbitration. Your attorney will provide you with the necessary information regarding arbitration in the event of a fee dispute, or upon your request.

Receipt Acknowledged:

Attorney's signature:

Client's signature:

Date:

Shareholders Agreement

Agreement made this _____ day of _____, 20 _____, by and between _____, residing at _____ (hereinafter X), and _____, residing at _____ (hereinafter Y).

IN CONSIDERATION OF the mutual covenants and conditions contained herein, it is hereby agreed as follows:

1. Organization of the Corporation

1.1 The parties agree that upon the execution of this Agreement, they will cause a corporation to be formed under the laws of the State of _____ to be named _____ (hereinafter called the Corporation). The Corporation shall be authorized to issue _____ shares of common voting stock, all with(out) a par value (of $ _____).

1.2 (a) Each party hereto agrees that he will subscribe for and purchase shares of the common stock of the Corporation as follows:

X—_____ shares
Y—_____ shares

(b) Each party agrees that in consideration of the shares of the Corporation's stock to be purchased by him he will pay to the Corporation the sum of $ _____.

1.3 The parties hereto shall vote (as shareholders or directors, as the case may be) as follows:

(a) To elect the following as Directors of the Corporation so long as they are stockholders thereof: X and Y.

(b) To elect the following as Officers of the Corporation so long as they are stockholders, directors, and/or employees thereof:

X—President
Y—Secretary-Treasurer

(c) To cause the Corporation to become a party to this Agreement by adopting same after the Corporation has been organized and to take all necessary action to carry out the terms of this Agreement.

2. Operation of the Corporation

2.1 The business of the Corporation shall be _____.

2.2 X and Y each agrees to make available to the Corporation, as additional working capital, up to $ _____ each, upon such terms as they and the Corporation may from time to time agree.

2.3 It is agreed by the parties hereto that no action shall be taken with respect to any of the following matters except by a unanimous vote of all of the stockholders and directors:

(a) Sale of all or substantially all of the assets of the Corporation;

(b) The merger, consolidation, or reorganization of the Corporation;

(c) The issuance or sale, or the offer to sell, any additional shares of stock to existing shareholders or third parties;

(d) The commitment of the Corporation to any lease or distributorship;

(e) The creation of indebtedness on behalf of the Corporation to any one person or firm in excess of $ _____ .

The Bylaws of the Corporation shall set out and include a statement of the foregoing action requiring the unanimous consent of the directors and/or shareholders, as the case may be.

2.4 The Corporation shall select as its depository the _____ Bank. The resolution authorizing the opening and maintenance of such bank account shall provide that all checks, notes, drafts, and other evidence of indebtedness, etc., drawn on the account of the Corporation at such bank, shall be executed by the President and the Secretary-Treasurer.

2.5 The Corporation shall enter into an employment agreement with X in the form annexed hereto, which shall also contain the following terms:

(a) X shall be paid a salary of $ _____ per week during the first five (5) years of his employment or until its earlier termination, plus _____ % of the net profits of the Corporation.

(b) X agrees that he shall devote all of his business time to the Corporation and agrees that so long as he is an employee and a stockholder of the Corporation and for such further period of two (2) years thereafter, he will not directly or indirectly, engage as a principal, owner, stockholder, employee, officer, or director, or in any other capacity in any business venture or enterprise which deals directly or indirectly, or by association, in the business from time to time conducted by the Corporation or by any wholly owned subsidiary corporation or affiliate.

(c) The salary of X shall from time to time be increased as determined by the Board of Directors of the Corporation.

(d) The parties hereto shall each be entitled to receive as benefits under their respective employment with the Corporation, at the expense of the Corporation, health insurance coverage and such other benefits as the Corporation from time to time may determine.

3. Transfer for Shares

3.1 No share of stock of the Corporation, whether preferred or common, and whenever issued, shall be sold, assigned, transferred or otherwise disposed of, encumbered, pledged or hypothecated except as hereinafter provided. A stockholder desiring to sell all (and not a part) of his stock shall offer to sell all of his shares in the Corporation in writing, which offer shall be mailed to the Corporation and to each of the stockholders. The Corporation shall have the first option to accept or reject the offer. Such option must be exercised within thirty (30) days and no longer from the date of receipt of the offer, which acceptance must be in writing and mailed to the offeror. Failure on the part of the Corporation to respond to the offer shall constitute rejection as of the end of the thirtieth (30th) day following receipt of the offer. If the Corporation rejects the offer (and any partial acceptance or partial rejection shall constitute a total rejection), the other stockholders or stockholder, as the case may be, shall pro rata to their then shareholdings in the Corporation, have second option to accept or reject the offer. Such option must be exercised within fifteen (15) days (and no longer) from the date of the rejection and must be exercised in writing and mailed to the offeror. Failure to timely respond by such other stockholders (or any of the stockholders) shall likewise constitute a total rejection. Thereafter, for an additional fifteen (15) days (and no longer) the remaining stockholders who have not rejected the offer made to them, may, in proportion to their shareholdings, accept the entire offer of all such offered shareholdings. If all of the offered shares are not wholly accepted as provided above, all of the shares of the offeree stockholders shall, without further act, be automatically deemed counteroffered for sale to the original offeror, which counteroffer must be accepted by the original offeror within fifteen (15) days (and no longer) from the making of the counteroffer. Such counteroffer shall be deemed to have been made as of the date of the rejection by the remaining stockholders as provided above. Failure to timely respond to such original offeror shall likewise constitute a total rejection of such counteroffer. In all cases a partial acceptance or a partial rejection shall constitute a total rejection.

If all of the offered shares are not wholly accepted as provided above, the parties covenant to and shall take immediate steps thereafter to dissolve and liquidate the Corporation and its assets; and for such purposes, the offeror is hereby, without further act or document, constituted, appointed, and delegated as attorney-in-fact and as irrevocable agent (which agency shall be deemed to be "coupled with an interest") with all proxy rights in connection therewith, to dissolve and liquidate the Corporation on behalf and at the pro rata cost and expense of all of the then shareholders.

The price and terms of any offer shall be as a hereinafter set forth. Closing shall take place on the fifteenth (15th) business day following the receipt of the acceptance at the Corporation's then principal office at 10:00 A.M. of that day.

(a) The stockholders, simultaneously herewith, have executed a "Certificate of Agreed Value," setting forth the total net value of the Corporation as of this date. They agree to execute new such Certificates semiannually or more often. The term "total net value" as used herein shall be deemed to mean the agreed total value of all of the assets of the Corporation, after deducting therefrom any and all liabilities, howsoever characterized.

(b) The price for the offered shares in the Corporation shall be computed as follows:

The total number of common shares of stock then issued and outstanding in such Corporation shall be divided into the total net value set forth in such Certificate of Agreed Value, and the quotient shall be the price for each share of common stock of the Corporation sold, subject to no adjustments, except as hereinafter provided. The latest dated such Certificate of Agreed Value shall control, except that if any such Certificate, at the time of any total acceptance by any offeree is dated prior to one (1) year from the date of such total acceptance, there shall be added to or subtracted from the total net value set forth in the last dated such Certificate of Agreed Value the difference between the "book value" of the Corporation (as hereinafter defined) as of the date of the last dated such Certificate and such "book value" as of the date of the total acceptance. In computing book value, if necessary, as hereinbefore provided, the established accounting practices, including, but not limited to, Reserves for Bad Debts, Contingent Liabilities, Depreciation, and Amortization, theretofore employed by the Corporation, shall be applied, subject to and in accordance with the following rules:

1. Goodwill, franchises, trademarks, and trade names shall in no way be considered assets for the purpose of determining the "book value";

2. The value of the fixed assets and merchandise inventory shall be fixed by agreement amongst the parties or, if the parties cannot agree, by arbitration, as hereinafter provided;

3. All other assets and liabilities shall be taken at the net figures at which they appear on the books of account;

4. Any life insurance policy owned by the Corporation shall be valued at its cash surrender value.

(c) The price, as hereinbefore determined, shall be adjusted as follows: (i) by subtracting therefrom all personal debts and interest thereon, if any, owed by the offeror to the Corporation, whether or not due; and (ii) by adding thereto all debts and interest thereon, if any, owed by the Corporation to the offeror, whether or not due. If the purchaser is another stockholder, and not the Corporation, an assignment without recourse shall be delivered to him at the closing by the offeror of such corporate debt due to the offeror; and likewise, such other stockholder-purchaser shall be liable (in such same percentage) for debts due to the Corporation from the offeror if an adjustment was made therefor in computing the price, as aforesaid, and the offeror and the Corporation shall execute and deliver unto the offeror a Release in connection with such obligation.

(d) If any offering stockholder shall be indebted to any other stockholder of the Corporation, such selling-stockholder shall, at the closing hereinabove provided for, discharge any such indebtedness by payment thereof to such other stockholder, with all interest due thereon, whether or not such debt is then due. Furthermore, should any offering-stockholder have monies or other collateral deposited as security for any corporate indebtedness, such monies or collateral shall be returned in full at such closing. In addition, and at the same time, the Corporation and each purchasing-stockholder thereof shall indemnify the selling-stockholder and agree to hold him harmless against any and all claims, losses, demands, and expenses of every nature, arising out of or which may result from or be based upon any guarantee executed or given by the selling-stockholder with respect to any corporate obligation.

(e) The price, as adjusted, shall be paid as follows: twenty-five percent (25%) in cash or by good, certified check, at the closing, and the balance in twelve (12) equal monthly installments, with interest as set forth below. The installments shall be evidence by a series of twelve (12) negotiable promissory notes to be made by the offeree as "Maker" to the order of the offerer as "Payee," dated the date of the closing, the first note being due one (1) month after the closing and monthly consecutively thereafter; each of the notes to bear interest at the rate of _____ percent (____ %) per annum and contain a grace period of ten (10) days, and shall be payable at the bank of the Maker. The notes shall contain an acceleration clause, but failure to assert such right of acceleration shall not be deemed a waiver thereof. If the Corporation is the Maker, the other stockholders shall, jointly and severally, endorse each note and guarantors.

(f) The notes may be prepaid without penalty on any installment date, upon thirty (30) days' prior written notice, in inverse order, with all accrued interest on each note so prepaid; provided, however, that at the option of the offeror: (i) no prepayment shall be allowed in the same calendar year of the closing; and (ii) the payment of all or any part of the notes ordinarily due in such calendar year shall be deferred (and all interest thereon shall run) to January 2 of the next calendar year.

(g) Should the surplus and/or the net assets of the Corporation be insufficient to authorize the purchase of all of the stock so offered in accordance with the provisions of the (State corporation law) as the same is or may be from time to time amended, and should the Corporation exercise the option to purchase, then and in such event, the Corporation shall purchase so much as it is authorized by law and the other stockholders shall purchase (such obligation being mandatory upon such other stockholders) the balance of such offered shares, which obligation shall be joint and several.

3.2 In the event of the death of X or Y, his estate or his personal representative shall sell his stock to the Corporation. The Corporation shall purchase the same upon the following terms: the price per share shall be as determined in paragraph 3.1 and shall be payable as therein set forth, except as may be hereinafter provided. Should there be insurance on the life of such deceased stockholder (of which insurance the Corporation shall be the beneficiary in whole or in part), then, upon the death of X or Y, the Corporation shall proceed immediately to collect the proceeds of such insurance on his life and upon such collection of all such proceeds and the qualification of a legal representative of such deceased stockholder, the Corporation shall use such insurance proceeds by payment thereof in cash against the purchase price; provided, however, that if the insurance proceeds be greater than the purchase price, the entire price shall be paid in cash at the closing, and the Corporation may retain the balance of the proceeds for its own corporate purposes, but if the purchase price is greater than the insurance proceeds, the entire proceeds shall be applied as the cash deposit against the price and the balance of the price shall be paid in twelve (12) equal monthly installments, the first such installment to be due thirty (30) days after the closing and each installment to bear interest at the rate of _____ percent (_____ %) per annum and which said install-ments are to be evidenced by a series of promissory notes as hereinabove provided in paragraph 3.1, and the same provisions as therein set forth shall apply herein with respect to such notes, except that the said notes may be prepaid in inverse order in whole or in part at any time with all accrued interest on any notes so prepaid.

4. Escrow

At the option of the seller, all of the documents required to be deliv-ered at the closing by the seller shall be retained in escrow with his attor-neys, pending full payment of the "adjusted" price. Should the escrowee receive notice of a default, he shall forthwith deliver the documents to the seller of his representative, who shall, upon ten (10) days' written notice to the defaulting purchaser, by certified or registered mail, return receipt requested, sell the shareholdings at public or private sale, at which sale the seller or his representative may purchase. Any sales proceeds received in excess of the unpaid balance due and interest, and the expenses of the sale, shall forthwith be turned over to the defaulting purchaser, who shall be liable for any deficiency. There shall be included as a cost of sale legal fees calculated on the unpaid balance and interest, at _____ percent (_____ %), together with the costs and disbursements of the sale. Upon the escrowee receiving written notice from the seller of full payment, he shall forthwith deliver the escrowed documents to the purchaser or pur-chasers. At the closing, the seller and the purchasers shall execute general releases, excepting therefrom the provisions of this Agreement applicable to the purchaser and the provisions of all Agreements and notes executed at the closing provided for deferred payments and indemnification by the purchaser.

5. Endorsement of Stock Certificates

The Certificates of Stock of the Corporation shall be endorsed as follows:
"The shares of stock represented by this Certificate are subject to all the terms and conditions of an Agreement made on the _____ day of _____, 20 _____, a copy of which is on file in the office of the Corporation."

6. Voting

At any stockholders' meeting called by the Corporation, for the purpose of accepting or rejecting any offer made by a stockholder to sell his shares in accordance with this Agreement, such stockholder shall be deemed to have voted for the Corporation's purchasing or redeeming the offered shares.

7. Equity

The provisions of this Agreement may be enforced in a court of equity by injunction or specific performance. Such remedies shall be cumulative and not exclusive and shall be in addition to any other remedies which the parties may have. Should any part or parts of this Agreement be determined to be void by a court of competent jurisdiction, the remaining provisions hereof shall nevertheless be binding.

8. Notices

All notices, options, offers, and acceptances hereunder (unless deemed to have been made by the operation of the terms of this Agreement) shall be in writing and served by certified or registered mail, return receipt requested and, unless otherwise herein specified, shall be deemed to have been made as of the date of mailing.

9. Arbitration

Any question or controversy with respect to any question arising hereunder shall be resolved by arbitration in accordance with the laws of the State of _____ and pursuant to the Rules of the American Arbitration Association.

10. Entire Agreement

This Agreement constitutes the entire understanding of the parties concerning the subject matter herein contained. No modification of any provision of this Agreement shall be valid, and the same may not be terminated or abandoned except by a writing signed by the parties to this Agreement.

IN WITNESS WHEREOF, the parties have hereunto set their hands and seals the day and year first above written.

X _____

Y _____

Subscription Agreement (Limited Partnership)

1. The undersigned hereby subscribes for the number of Units of limited partnership interests set forth below in _____, a _____ limited partnership (the Partnership), each Unit of _____ Dollars ($ _____) payable in full on subscription.

2. The undersigned understands that the General Partner will notify him prior to _____, 20 _____, as to whether this subscription has been accepted or rejected. If rejected, the check tendered by him will be returned to him forthwith without interest or deduction. The undersigned understands that the payments made under this Subscription Agreement will be held in escrow by the Partnership for his benefit at a commercial bank in _____ with assets of at least $10,000,000. If accepted, the check tendered by the undersigned will be applied in accordance with the use of proceeds description set forth in the Private Placement Memorandum relating to the Partnership (the Memorandum).

3. The undersigned had been furnished with and has carefully read the Memorandum relating to the Partnership and the documents attached as Exhibits thereto, including the Partnership Agreement. The undersigned is aware that:

(i) The Partnership has no financial or operating history;

(ii) There are substantial risks incident to an investment in the Partnership, as summarized under "Risks" and "Tax Risks" in the Memorandum;

(iii) No federal or state agency has passed upon the Units or made any finding or determination as to the fairness of the investment;

(iv) The discussion of the tax consequences arising from investment in the Partnership set forth in the Memorandum is general in nature, and the tax consequences to the undersigned of an investment in the Partnership depend upon his particular circumstances;

(v) There can be no assurance that the Internal Revenue Code or the regulations thereunder will not be amended in such manner as to deprive the Partnership and its Partners of some of the tax benefits they might now receive; and

(vi) The books and records of the Partnership will be available for inspection of the undersigned at the Partnership's place of business.

4. The undersigned understands that investment in the Partnership is an illiquid investment. In particular, the undersigned recognizes that:

(i) The undersigned must bear the economic risk of investment in the Units for an indefinite period of time since the Units have not been registered under the Securities Act of 1933, as amended, and, therefore, cannot be sold unless either they are subsequently registered under said Act or an exemption from such registration is available and a favorable opinion of counsel for the Partnership to such effect is obtained;

(ii) There will be no established market for the Units and it is not likely that any public market for the Units will develop; and

(iii) The undersigned's rights to transfer his Units will be restricted, as provided for in the Partnership Agreement.

5. The undersigned represents and warrants to the Partnership and to the General Partner that:

(i) The undersigned has carefully reviewed and understands the risks of, and other considerations relating to, a purchase of Units, including the risks set forth under "Risk Factors" and "Tax Risks" in the Memorandum and the considerations described under "Federal Income Tax Consequences" in the Memorandum;

(ii) The undersigned has been furnished with all materials relating to the Partnership and its proposed activities, the offering of Units, or anything set forth in the Memorandum which he has requested, and has been afforded the opportunity to obtain any additional information necessary to verify the accuracy of any representations or information set forth in the Memorandum;

(iii) The General Partner has answered all inquiries of the undersigned concerning the Partnership and its proposed activities, the offering of Units, or any other matter relating to the business of the Partnership as set forth in the Memorandum;

(iv) The undersigned has not been furnished any offering literature other than the Memorandum and the documents attached as Exhibits thereto, and the undersigned has relied only on the information contained in the Memorandum and such Exhibits and the information furnished or made available by the Partnership or the General Partner, as described in subparagraphs (ii) and (iii) above;

(v) The undersigned is acquiring the Units for which he hereby subscribes for his own account, as principal, for investment and not with a view to the resale or distribution of all or any part of such Units;

(vi) The undersigned, if a corporation, partnership, trust, or other form of business entity, is authorized and otherwise duly qualified to purchase and hold Units in the Partnership, such entity has its principal place of business as set forth on the signature page hereof and such entity has not been formed for the specific purchase of acquiring Units in the Partnership;

(vii) The undersigned has adequate means of providing for his current needs and personal contingencies and has no need for liquidity in this investment;

(viii) All the information which the undersigned has heretofore furnished the General Partner, or which is set forth in his Purchase Questionnaire and elsewhere with respect to his financial position and business experience, is correct and complete as of the date of this Agreement and, if there should be any material change in such information prior to the completion of the Offering, the undersigned will immediately furnish such revised or corrected information to the General Partner;

(ix) The undersigned further agrees to be bound by all of the terms and conditions of the Offering made by the Memorandum and Exhibits thereto, and by all of the terms and conditions of the Partnership Agreement and to perform any obligations therein imposed upon a Limited Partner thereof.

6. In order to facilitate the admission of the undersigned and other subscribers into the Partnership, the undersigned hereby irrevocably

constitutes and appoints the General Partner, or any one of them if more than one, as his agent and attorney-in-fact, in his name, place and stead, to make, execute, acknowledge, swear to, file, record, and deliver the Amended Certificate of Limited Partnership of the Partnership to admit the undersigned into the Partnership, and any and all other instruments which may be required to effect the admission of the undersigned into the Partnership as a Limited Partner thereof or otherwise comply with applicable law. It is expressly understood and intended by the undersigned that the grant of the foregoing power of attorney is coupled with an interest, and such grant shall be irrevocable. Said power of attorney shall survive the death, bankruptcy, or mental incapacitation of the undersigned, to the extent he may legally contract for such survival, or the assignment or transfer of all or any part of the undersigned's interest in the Partnership. Any person dealing with the Partnership may conclusively presume and rely upon the fact that any instrument referred to above, executed by such agents and attorneys-in-fact, is authorized, regular, and binding without further inquiry. If required, the undersigned shall execute and deliver to the General Partner, within five (5) days after the receipt of a request therefor, such further designations, powers of attorney, or other instruments as the General Partner shall reasonably deem necessary for the purpose of this provision.

7. This subscription is not transferable or assignable by the undersigned.

8. If the undersigned is more than one person, the obligations of the undersigned shall be joint and several and the representations and warranties herein contained shall be deemed to be made by and be binding upon each such person and his heirs, executors, administrators, successors, and assigns.

9. This subscription, upon acceptance by the Partnership, shall be binding upon the heirs, executors, administrators, successors, and assigns of the undersigned.

10. This Subscription Agreement shall be construed in accordance with and governed in all respects by the laws of the State of _____.

11. Any masculine personal pronoun as set forth in this Subscription Agreement shall be considered to mean the corresponding feminine or neuter personal pronoun, as the context requires.

12. The undersigned represents that the information furnished in the Purchaser Questionnaire is true and complete as of the date hereof, and the undersigned agrees to notify the Partnership of any changes in the information prior to completion of the Offering.

13. The undersigned is subscribing for the following number of Units:

Number of Units subscribed for: _____
Amount of check enclosed: $ _____

Dated:_____
/s/_____
Printed Name:_____
Address:_____
_____

Work for Hire Agreement

This Agreement is made and entered into this _____ day of _____ 20_____ by and between Jones (Jones) whose address is _____ and Smith (Smith) whose address is _____, and Brown whose address is _____.

Whereas the parties to this Agreement are collaborating on a musical entitled "_____" (hereinafter known as "Musical") in which each of the parties has made a unique contribution and for which parties have composed the music and lyrics for the Musical.

Now, therefore, the parties do agree as follows:

1. The parties acknowledge that Composers have composed the music for the Musical, and the parties are engaging the services of Brown as an arranger (Brown will hereinafter be referred to as "Arranger") for the Musical.

2. Arranger, for good and valuable consideration of thirty percent (30%) of any royalties received by the parties for the use of said music, said payment not to exceed a maximum of fifty thousand dollars ($50,000.00), (which sum Arranger may be entitled), certifies and agrees that all of the results and proceeds of the services of every kind heretofore rendered by and hereafter to be rendered by Arranger in connection with the Musical are and shall be deemed works "made-for-hire" for Composers and/or works assigned to Composers, as applicable. Accordingly, Arranger further acknowledges, certifies and agrees that Composers shall be deemed the authors and/or exclusive owners of the music for the Musical throughout the world, and of all the rights comprised in the copyright thereof (expressly including the copyrights in and to the "sound recordings" and any renewal or extension rights in connection therewith and of any and all other rights thereto), and that Composers shall have the right to exploit any or all of the foregoing in any and all media, now known or hereafter devised, throughout the universe, in perpetuity, in all configurations as Composers determine.

3. Arranger hereby agrees not to make any claim against Composers or any party authorized by Composers to exploit said Musical based on such moral or like rights.

4. Composers warrant that all lyrics and other material, including, without limitation, so-called "samples" and all compositions, ideas, designs, and inventions of Composers, furnished by Composers in connection with the Musical are or will be original or in the public domain throughout the world or used with the consent of the original owner thereof, and shall not infringe upon or violate any copyright of, or infringe upon or violate the right or privacy or any other right of, any person.

5. Composers agree that Arranger shall have billing credit as arranger on all programs, billings, posters, advertisements, and so forth connected with a production of the Musical.

6. Arranger agrees to hold Composers and their respective successors, licensees, and assigns harmless from and against all damages, losses, costs, and expenses (including reasonable attorneys' fees and costs) which Arranger and their respective successors, licensees, or assigns may suffer or incur by reason by the breach of any of the warranties made in this Agreement.
7. This Agreement shall be deemed to have been made in New York, New York and shall be construed, interpreted, and enforced in accordance with the laws of the State of New York applicable to agreements executed, delivered, and to be performed wholly within such State.
8. This Agreement shall be the complete and binding agreement between the parties and arranger and may not be amended except by an agreement in writing signed by the arranger and the parties hereto.

IN WITNESS WHEREOF, the parties have duly executed this Agreement on the day and year first above written.

_____

Jones
_____

Smith
_____

Brown

APPENDIX B

Supplemental Cases

The following cases are presented to highlight certain material discussed in the text:

1. *Don King Productions, Inc. v. Douglas*: discusses the concept of consideration and what may be legally valuable at the time of contract
2. *Matter of Baby M*: concerns the legality of relinquishing certain parental rights
3. *Hong v. Marriott Corp.*: highlights, in an amusing fashion, the concept of warranties under UCC Article II
4. *In re Peregrine Entertainment, Ltd*: details the method of perfecting a securities interest under Article IX of the UCC

Don King Productions, Inc. v. Douglas
742 F. Supp. 741 (S.D.N.Y. 1990)

. . . Indefiniteness of Consideration

According to Johnson and Douglas, the Promotion and Bout Agreements are unenforceable because they are indefinite as to the essential term of consideration. The facts are undisputed: the Promotion Agreement provided for payment of $25,000 to Douglas in return for his granting DKP the exclusive right to promote his bouts for a stated term. Compensation for the individual bouts that were contemplated by the Promotion Agreement (numbering no fewer than three per year, with the exception of the first contract year) was made subject to further negotiation and agreement, with the agreed-to terms to be set forth in the individually-negotiated bout agreements. The Promotion Agreement specified a floor level of compensation of $25,000, plus $10,000 in training expenses, for these fights, except that in the case of a title bout or defense of such a bout, no floor (or ceiling) was provided, the purse to be "negotiated and mutually agreed upon between us."

One such subsequent agreement as to Douglas' purse for a title fight was reached, as set forth in the Bout Agreement executed for the match with then-world champion Tyson. The Bout Agreement stated that "in full consideration of [Douglas'] participation in the [Tokyo] Bout and for all of the rights herein granted to Promoter," Douglas would be paid $1.3 million. That agreement further provided that with respect to Douglas' first three fights post-Tokyo, upon which DKP was given an exclusive option, the purse per fight would be $1 million, unless Douglas was the winner in Tokyo, in which case the amount would be subject to negotiation with that sum of $1 million as a floor.

In the face of this contractual language, Douglas and Johnson are forced to take the position that "although a minimum purse of $1,000,000 was specified, this is insufficient to render the contract sufficiently definite for enforcement" because "the 'minimum' consideration is obviously a token, at best." The factual predicate for the argument is that the market at present values the world champion heavyweight fighter at considerably more than one million dollars a pop (Johnson states he has received offers as high as $50 million for Douglas to fight, and King apparently offered him $15 million plus a percentage of gross receipts). Therefore, the contractually-specified million dollar compensation floor is asserted to be nothing other than the proverbial "peppercorn" of consideration.

Assuming the factual premise as to Douglas' present value, the argument, nevertheless, suffers once one considers that the appropriate yard-stick for making the judgment. Whether one million dollars is token consideration must be assessed by reference to Douglas' expected future value as a fighter at the time the agreement was entered into, i.e., before his unexpected defeat of Tyson. No one has contended on this record that $1 million was a "mere token" vis-a-vis Douglas' value at the time he, Johnson and their lawyer Enz, negotiated the Bout Agreement, and, in fact, the parties, after such negotiations, fixed a figure reasonably proximate to that—$1.3 million—for services to be rendered in a title fight with an undefeated heavy-weight champion. Thus, when Douglas and Johnson signed the Bout Agreement they evidently did not regard one million dollars as a "peppercorn," even if they did not regard it as the full (as opposed to minimum) value to be affixed to Douglas' services when defending a championship. The subsequent change in Douglas' relative fortunes does not provide a legal basis now to disregard his prior agreement as to the reasonable floor at which to begin discussion of the value of his services as defending heavyweight champion.

It is standard contract law that a contract, to be binding, must address without "impenetrable vagueness" the terms material to its subject matter. *Joseph Martin, Jr. Delicatessen, Inc. v. Schumacher*, 52 N.Y.2d 105, 109, 436 N.Y.S.2d 247, 249, 417 N.E.2d 541, 543 (1981). Just as well settled is the proposition that

> to render a contract enforceable, absolute certainty is not required; it is enough if the promise or agreement is sufficiently definite and explicit so that the intention of the parties may be ascertained "to a reasonable

certainty." *Varney v. Ditmars*, 217 N.Y. 223, 228, 111 N.E. 822, 824, Ann. Cas. 1916B, 758. A contract cannot be ignored as meaningless, except as a last resort. "Indefiniteness must reach the point where construction becomes futile." *Cohen & Sons v. M. Lurie Woolen Co.*, 232 N.Y. 112, 114, 133 N.E. 370, 371.

Here, the Promotional Agreement and Bout Agreement addressed their essential subject matter in a manner that is far from impenetrable. While leaving certain terms open to future negotiation, the contracts were explicit and definite about Douglas' commitment to fight only for DKP during the life of those contracts and about the minimum consideration he could receive for making that commitment. Thus, the contracts, at least with respect to their exclusivity terms, are much more than "mere agreements to agree." *Joseph Martin, Jr. Delicatessen*, 52 N.Y.2d at 109, 436 N.Y.S.2d at 249, 417 N.E.2d at 543.

The parties agreed to leave open the compensation that would be payable under certain contingencies, such as after Douglas' becoming world champion (in contrast to the fixed purse for title fights against another champion, which were priced at $1 million a bout) and this may have repercussions as to Douglas' obligation to fight a particular title defense at a particular price named by King, since no separate bout agreement has been executed for such fight pursuant to the process of negotiation contemplated by the Promotion Agreement for fights to be held under its provisions. Nevertheless, the writing manifests in definite language Douglas and DKP's agreement to deal exclusively with one another with respect to title defenses and to negotiate in an effort to reach a mutual understanding as to the open price term for such a defense.

For that reason, the exclusivity provisions of the Agreements are not void *ab initio* on grounds of price indefiniteness. See *R.S. Stokvis & Sons v. Kearney & Trecker Corp.*, 58 F. Supp. 260, 267 (S.D.N.Y. 1944) (agreement containing definite grant of "exclusive representation" valid as to that term, notwithstanding that agreement contained "no provisions with respect to quantities, prices, deliveries, payments, or even discounts," all of which were "left 'to be arranged separately.'"). Whether $1 million turns out to be a definite default price—or merely a minimum price—simply does not control the question of whether Douglas and Johnson have violated the definite right they granted to DKP to exclusively "secure and arrange all [of Douglas'] professional boxing bouts" and their definite duty under the Agreement to refrain from "render[ing] services as a professional boxer to any person, firm or entity" other than DKP. That is because the minimum price terms, together with DKP's upfront payment of $25,000 and its commitments to hold a set number of bouts, clearly did provide an expectancy of compensation for Douglas that was sufficiently definite to induce his promise to fight exclusively for DKP. Accordingly, Douglas/Johnson fail to sustain their burden as movants seeking dismissal of the complaint on the ground that the underlying instruments are too illusory to be breached.

Adequacy of the Term

Douglas and Johnson next urge that this case is an appropriate one for application of the maxim that "an option actually intended by the parties to run for an unlimited time, i.e., forever is void." *Mohr Park Manor, Inc. v. Mohr*, 83 Nev. 107, 424 P.2d 101 (1967).

The Promotional Agreement and Bout Agreement do not fall into that class of contracts, as both contain clauses explicitly addressing duration and neither contemplates an indefinite term. The former provides that it shall run for three years and shall be "automatically extended to cover the entire period [Douglas is] world champion and a period of two years following the date on which [Douglas] thereafter cease[s], for any reason, to be so recognized as world champion." So extensive a commitment of one's services might be questioned as excessive, but clearly does not suffer from indefiniteness or ambiguity. Nor does the Bout Agreement: it grants DKP an exclusive option on the promotion of Douglas' "next three fights," which must be exercised within thirty days of the Tokyo bout.

Both are contracts "of the type . . . which do provide for termination or cancellation upon the occurrence of a specified event," *Payroll Express Corp. v. Aetna Casualty & Sur. Co.*, 659 F.2d 285, 291 (2d Cir. 1981), and are therefore not jeopardized by the void-for-indefiniteness rule. Id. Contracts which "provide no fixed date for the termination of the promisor's obligation but condition the obligation upon an event which would necessarily terminate the contract" remain in force until that event occurs. *Warner-Lambert Pharmaceutical Co. v. John J. Reynolds, Inc.*, 178 F. Supp. 655 (S.D.N.Y. 1959), *aff'd*, 280 F.2d 197 (2d Cir. 1960) (upholding contract entered into in 1881 that lacked termination date but which obligated pharmaceutical manufacturer to pay royalties on every gross of "Listerine" made and sold by it as long as it continued to manufacture the product); *Ketcham v. Hall Syndicate, Inc.*, 37 Misc. 2d 693, 236 N.Y.S.2d 206, 212-213 (Sup. Ct. 1962) (agreement for syndication of cartoons sufficiently definite as to term where duration of contract was made subject to termination in event artist's share of revenue fell below stipulated amount), *aff'd*, 19 A.D.2d 611, 242 N.Y.S.2d 182 (1st Dep't 1963) . . . .

The Unconscionable Contracts Defense

Douglas and Johnson plead as an affirmative defense that the contracts they entered into with DKP are unconscionable. Under New York law, a determination of unconscionability

> requires a showing that the contract was both procedurally and substantively unconscionable *when made*— i.e., "some showing of an 'absence of meaningful choice on the part of one of the parties together with contract terms which are unreasonably favorable to the other party.'"

Gillman v. Chase Manhattan Bank, N.A., 73 N.Y.2d 1, 10, 537 N.Y.S.2d 787, 791, 534 N.E.2d 824, 828 (1988) (citations omitted and emphasis supplied).

The factual contentions set forth in the Douglas/Johnson interrogatories to support the unconscionability defense—that the Tokyo conduct of King was unconscionable, that King is a powerful promoter, and that exclusive, extendable terms of the contracts are unreasonably favorable to King—are as a matter of law insufficient.

The Douglas/Johnson contention that the contracts "became unconscionable" *after* their inception owing to King's conduct during the Tokyo fight is unavailing, as the underlined language in Gillman illustrates. The doctrine of unconscionability implicates the circumstances and terms of a contract at the time of formation—not the parties' subsequent performance under it. See *State v. Avco Financial Service of New York, Inc.*, 50 N.Y.2d 383, 390, 429 N.Y.S.2d 181, 185, 406 N.E.2d 1075, 1079 (1980) (referring to "circumstances existing at the time of the making"). The Tokyo performance by King is, of course, relevant to whether King breached his obligations of good faith and fair dealing under the contracts, an issue discussed at length in the May 18 Opinion and which has been reserved for trial to a jury. That conduct has, however, absolutely no bearing on the defense of unconscionability, which relates to substantive and procedural fairness of a contract "when made." *Gillman*, 73 N.Y.2d at 10, 537 N.Y.S.2d at 791, 534 N.E.2d at 828.

Douglas/Johnson next contend that King so dominates promotion of heavyweight fights that the Douglas-King contracts are inherently procedurally unconscionable. That assertion, if true, sounds more probative of an antitrust claim for monopolization than it is demonstrative of the particularized showing of an unfair bargaining process that is requisite to the defense of unconscionability. Douglas/Johnson make no allegation here that deceptive or high-pressure tactics were employed in concluding the contracts, that contract terms were concealed in fine print, or that there was a gross asymmetry in the experience and education of the parties, each of whom was represented by counsel throughout the course of their arms-length negotiations. See May 18 Opinion at 747; cf. *Gillman*, 73 N.Y.2d at 11, 537 N.Y.S.2d at 791, 534 N.E.2d at 828 (identifying relevance of these and other factors to establishment of procedural unfairness).

At least as stated in the responses to the contention interrogatories, the unconscionability defense does not here implicate its primary use as "a means with which to protect the commercially illiterate consumer beguiled into a grossly unfair bargain by a deceptive vendor or finance company." *Marvel Entertainment Group, Inc. v. Young Astronaut Council*, No. 88-5141, 1989 WL 129504 (S.D.N.Y. October 27, 1989). Without some definite allegation of a defect in the contract negotiation process apart from King's stature in the boxing field, which alone does not suggest "inequality so strong and manifest as to shock the conscience and confound the judgment," id. (quoting *Christian v. Christian*, 42 N.Y.2d 63, 71, 396 N.Y.S.2d 817, 823, 365 N.E.2d 849, 855 (1977)), defendants have failed to create an issue of procedural unconscionability requiring resolution by jury.

The contention that the contracts require Douglas to fight exclusively for DKP for the extendable terms of such contracts, which could amount to the rest of the boxer's professional life, equally fails to satisfy the requirement of substantive unconscionability. Only in "exceptional cases" is "a provision of [a] contract . . . so outrageous as to warrant holding it unenforceable on the ground of substantive unconscionability alone." *Gillman*, 73 N.Y.2d at 12, 537 N.Y.S.2d at 792, 534 N.E.2d at 829 (omitting citations); see also *Marvel Entertainment* (citing *Christian v. Christian*, 42 N.Y.2d 63, 71, 396 N.Y.S.2d 817, 823, 365 N.E.2d 849, 855 (1977)) (terms must be "such as no [person] in his senses and not under delusion would make on one hand, and no honest and fair [person] would accept on the other").

Douglas and Johnson fail to make any proffer as to what makes this term of their contract so exceptional as to fit within the line of cases referred to in *Gillman*, and they cite to no case considering or holding an exclusive services contract unconscionable on grounds of duration . . . . The court therefore declines to revisit its prior legal determinations that the contract durational terms were definite in nature and the contracts were supported by sufficiently-definite price consideration to induce Douglas' promise to fight exclusively for DKP. See May 18 Opinion at 761-764. The unconscionability defense accordingly shall be stricken, there having been no proffer or allegation sufficient to establish either its procedural or substantive elements . . . .

Matter of Baby M
109 N.J. 396 (1988)

WILENTZ, C. J.

In this matter the Court is asked to determine the validity of a contract that purports to provide a new way of bringing children into a family. For a fee of $10,000, a woman agrees to be artificially inseminated with the semen of another woman's husband; she is to conceive a child, carry it to term, and after its birth surrender it to the natural father and his wife. The intent of the contract is that the child's natural mother will thereafter be forever separated from her child. The wife is to adopt the child, and she and the natural father are to be regarded as its parents for all purposes. The contract providing for this is called "surrogacy contract," the natal mother inappropriately called the "surrogate mother."

We invalidate the surrogacy contract because it conflicts with the law and public policy of this State. While we recognize the depth of the yearning of infertile couples to have their own children, we find the payment of money to a "surrogate" mother illegal, perhaps criminal, and potentially degrading to women. Although in this case we grant custody to the natural father, the evidence having clearly proved such custody to be in the best interests of the infant, we void both the termination of the surrogate mother's parental rights and the adoption of the child by the wife/step-parent. We thus restore the "surrogate" as the mother of the child. We remand the issue of the natural mother's visitation rights to the trial court, since that issue was not reached below and the record before us is not sufficient to permit us to decide it *de novo*.

We find no offense to our present laws where a woman voluntarily and without payment agrees to act as a "surrogate" mother, provided that she is not subject to a binding agreement to surrender her child. Moreover, our holding today does not preclude the Legislature from altering the current statutory scheme, within constitutional limits, so as to permit surrogacy contracts. Under current law, however, the surrogacy agreement before us is illegal and invalid . . . .

Invalidity and Unenforceability of Surrogacy Contract

We have concluded that this surrogacy contract is invalid. Our conclusion has two bases: direct conflict with existing statutes and conflict with the public policies of this State, as expressed in its statutory and decisional law.

One of the surrogacy contract's basic purposes, to achieve the adoption of a child through private placement, though permitted in New Jersey "is very much disfavored." *Sees v. Baber*, 74 N.J. 201, 217 (1977). Its use of money for this purpose—and we have no doubt whatsoever that the money is being paid to obtain an adoption and not, as the Sterns argue, for the personal services of Mary Beth Whitehead—is illegal and perhaps criminal. N.J.S.A. 9:3-54. In addition to the inducement of money, there is the coercion of contract: the natural mother's irrevocable agreement, prior to birth, even prior to conception, to surrender the child to the adoptive couple. Such an agreement is totally unenforceable in private placement adoption. *Sees*, 74 N.J. at 212-214. Even where the adoption is through an approved agency, the formal agreement to surrender occurs only *after* birth (as we read N.J.S.A. 9:2-16 and 9:2-17, and similar statutes), and then, by regulation, only after the birth mother has been offered counseling. N.J.A.C. 10:121A-5.4(c). Integral to these invalid provisions of the surrogacy contract is the related agreement, equally invalid, on the part of the natural mother to cooperate with, and not to contest, proceedings to terminate her parental rights, as well as her contractual concession, in aid of the adoption, that the child's best interests would be served by awarding custody to the natural father and his wife—all of this before she has even conceived, and, in some cases, before she has the slightest idea of what the natural father and adoptive mother are like.

The foregoing provisions not only directly conflict with New Jersey statutes, but also offend long-established State policies. These critical terms, which are at the heart of the contract are invalid and unenforceable; the conclusion therefore follows, without more, that the entire contract is unenforceable.

Conflict with Statutory Provisions

The surrogacy contract conflicts with: (1) laws prohibiting the use of money in connection with adoptions; (2) laws requiring proof of parental unfitness or abandonment before termination of parental rights is ordered or an adoption is granted; and (3) laws that make surrender of custody and consent to adoption revocable in private placement adoptions.

(1) Our law prohibits paying or accepting money in connection with any placement of a child for adoption. N.J.S.A. 9:3-54a. Violation is a high misdemeanor. N.J.S.A. 9:3-54c. Excepted are fees of an approved agency (which must be a nonprofit entity, N.J.S.A. 9:3-38a.) and certain expenses in connection with childbirth. N.J.S.A. 9:3-54b.

Considerable care was taken in this case to structure the surrogacy arrangement so as not to violate this prohibition. The arrangement was structured as follows: the adopting parent, Mrs. Stern, was not a party to the surrogacy contract; the money paid to Mrs. Whitehead was stated to be for her services—not for the adoption; the sole purpose of the contract was stated as being that "of giving a child to William Stern, its natural and biological father"; the money was purported to be "compensation for services and expenses and in no way . . . a fee for termination of parental rights or a payment in exchange for consent to surrender a child for adoption"; the fee to the Infertility Center ($7,500) was stated to be for legal representation, advice, administrative work, and other "services." Nevertheless, it seems clear that the money was paid and accepted in connection with an adoption.

The Infertility Center's major role was first as a "finder" of the surrogate mother whose child was to be adopted, and second as the arranger of all proceedings that led to the adoption. Its role as adoption finder is demonstrated by the provision requiring Mr. Stern to pay another $7,500 if he uses Mary Beth Whitehead again as a surrogate, and by ICNY's agreement to "coordinate arrangements for the adoption of the child by the wife." The surrogacy agreement requires Mrs. Whitehead to surrender Baby M for the purposes of adoption. The agreement notes that Mr. *and* Mrs. Stern wanted to have a child, and provides that the child be "placed" with Mrs. Stern in the event Mr. Stern dies before the child is born. The payment of the $10,000 occurs only on surrender of custody of the child and "completion of the duties and obligations" of Mrs. Whitehead, including termination of her parental rights to facilitate adoption by Mrs. Stern. As for the contention that the Sterns are paying only for services and not for an adoption, we need note only that they would pay nothing in the event the child died before the fourth month of pregnancy, and only $1,000 if the child were stillborn, even though the "services" had been fully rendered. Additionally, one of Mrs. Whitehead's estimated costs, to be assumed by Mr. Stern, was an "Adoption Fee," presumably for Mrs. Whitehead's incidental costs in connection with the adoption.

Mr. Stern knew he was paying for the adoption of a child; Mrs. Whitehead knew she was accepting money so that a child might be adopted; the Infertility Center knew that it was being paid for assisting in the adoption of a child. The actions of all three worked to frustrate the goals of the statute. It strains credulity to claim that these arrangements, touted by those in the surrogacy business as an attractive alternative to the usual route leading to an adoption, really amount to something other than a private placement adoption for money.

The prohibition of our statute is strong. Violation constitutes a high misdemeanor, N.J.S.A. 9:3-54c, a third-degree crime, N.J.S.A. 2C:43-1b, carrying a penalty of three to five years imprisonment. N.J.S.A. 2C:43-6a(3).

The evils inherent in baby-bartering are loathsome for a myriad of reasons. The child is sold without regard for whether the purchasers will be suitable parents. N. Baker, Baby Selling: The Scandal of Black Market Adoption 7 (1978). The natural mother does not receive the benefit of counseling and guidance to assist her in making a decision that may affect her for a lifetime. In fact, the monetary incentive to sell her child may, depending on her financial circumstances, make her decision less voluntary. Id. at 44. Furthermore, the adoptive parents may not be fully informed of the natural parents' medical history.

Baby-selling potentially results in the exploitation of all parties involved. Ibid. Conversely, adoption statutes seek to further humanitarian goals, foremost among them the best interests of the child. H. Witmer, E. Herzog, E. Weinstein, & M. Sullivan, Independent Adoptions: A Follow-Up Study 32 (1967). The negative consequences of baby-buying are potentially present in the surrogacy context, especially the potential for placing and adopting a child without regard to the interest of the child or the natural mother . . . .

The provision in the surrogacy contract stating that Mary Beth Whitehead agrees to "surrender custody . . . and terminate all parental rights" contains no clause giving her a right to rescind. It is intended to be an irrevocable consent to surrender the child for adoption—in other words, an irrevocable commitment by Mrs. Whitehead to turn Baby M over to the Sterns and thereafter to allow termination of her parental rights. The trial court required a "best interests" showing as a condition to granting specific performance of the surrogacy contract. 217 N.J. Super. at 399-400. Having decided the "best interests" issue in favor of the Sterns, that court's order included, among other things, specific performance of this agreement to surrender custody and terminate all parental rights.

Mrs. Whitehead, shortly after the child's birth, had attempted to revoke her consent and surrender by refusing, after the Sterns had allowed her to have the child "just for one week," to return Baby M to them. The trial court's award of specific performance therefore reflects its view that the consent to surrender the child was irrevocable. We accept the trial court's construction of the contract; indeed it appears quite clear that this was the parties' intent. Such a provision, however, making irrevocable the natural mother's consent to surrender custody of her child in a private placement adoption, clearly conflicts with New Jersey law.

Our analysis commences with the statute providing for surrender of custody to an approved agency and termination of parental rights on the suit of that agency. The two basic provisions of the statute are N.J.S.A. 9:2-14 and 9:2-16. The former provides explicitly that

> [e]xcept as otherwise provided by law or by order or judgment of a court of competent jurisdiction or by testamentary disposition, no surrender of the custody of a child shall be valid in this state unless made to an approved agency pursuant to the provisions of this act . . . .

There is no exception "provided by law," and it is not clear that there could be any "order or judgment of a court of competent jurisdiction" validating a surrender of custody as a basis for adoption when that surrender was not in conformance with the statute. Requirements for a voluntary surrender to an approved agency are set forth in N.J.S.A. 9:2-16. This section allows an approved agency to take a voluntary surrender of custody from the parent of a child but provides stringent requirements as a condition to its validity. The surrender must be in writing, must be in such form as is required for the recording of a deed, and, pursuant to N.J.S.A. 9:2-17, must

> be such as to declare that the person executing the same desires to relinquish the custody of the child, acknowledge the termination of parental rights as to such custody in favor of the approved agency, and acknowledge full understanding of the effect of such surrender as provided by this act.

If the foregoing requirements are met, the consent, the voluntary surrender of custody

> shall be valid whether or not the person giving same is a minor and shall be irrevocable except at the discretion of the approved agency taking such surrender or upon order or judgment of a court of competent jurisdiction, setting aside such surrender upon proof of fraud, duress, or misrepresentation. [N.J.S.A. 9:2-16.]

The importance of that irrevocability is that the surrender itself gives the agency the power to obtain termination of parental rights—in other words, permanent separation of the parent from the child, leading in the ordinary case to an adoption. N.J.S.A. 9:2-18 to 9:2-20.

This statutory pattern, providing for a surrender in writing and for termination of parental rights by an approved agency, is generally followed in connection with adoption proceedings and proceedings by DYFS to obtain permanent custody of a child. Our adoption statute repeats the requirements necessary to accomplish an irrevocable surrender to an approved agency in both form and substance. N.J.S.A. 9:3-41a. It provides that the surrender "shall be valid and binding without regard to the age of the person executing the surrender," ibid.; and although the word "irrevocable" is not used, that seems clearly to be the intent of the provision. The statute speaks of such surrender as constituting "relinquishment of such person's parental rights in or guardianship or custody of the child *named therein* and consent by such person to adoption of the child." Ibid. (emphasis supplied). We emphasize "named therein," for we construe the statute to allow a surrender only after the birth of the child. The formal consent to surrender enables the approved agency to terminate parental rights.

Similarly, DYFS is empowered to "take voluntary surrenders and releases of custody and consents to adoption[s]" from parents, which surrenders, releases, or consents "when properly acknowledged . . . shall be valid and binding irrespective of the age of the person giving the same, and shall be irrevocable except at the discretion of the Bureau of Children's Services [currently DYFS] or upon order of a court of competent jurisdiction." N.J.S.A. 30:4C-23. Such consent to surrender of the custody of the child would presumably lead to an adoption placement by DYFS. See N.J.S.A. 30:4C-20.

It is clear that the Legislature so carefully circumscribed all aspects of a consent to surrender custody—its form and substance, its manner of execution, and the agency or agencies to which it may be made—in order to provide the basis for irrevocability. It seems most unlikely that the Legislature intended that a consent not complying with these requirements would also be irrevocable, especially where, as here, that consent falls radically short of compliance. Not only do the form and substance of the consent in the surrogacy contract fail to meet statutory requirements, but the surrender of custody is made to a private party. It is not made, as the statute requires, either to an approved agency or to DYFS.

These strict prerequisites to irrevocability constitute a recognition of the most serious consequences that flow from such consents: termination of parental rights, the permanent separation of parent from child, and the ultimate adoption of the child. See *Sees v. Baber*, supra, 74 N.J. at 217. Because of those consequences, the Legislature severely limited the circumstances under which such consent would be irrevocable. The legislative goal is furthered by regulations requiring approved agencies, prior to accepting irrevocable consents, to provide advice and counseling to women, making it more likely that they fully understand and appreciate the consequences of their acts. N.J.A.C. 10:121A-5.4(c).

Contractual surrender of parental rights is not provided for in our statutes as now written. Indeed, in the Parentage Act, N.J.S.A. 9:17-38 to 59, there is a specific provision invalidating any agreement "between an alleged or presumed father and the mother of the child" to bar an action brought for the purpose of determining paternity "[r]egardless of [the contract's] terms." N.J.S.A. 9:17-45. Even a settlement agreement concerning parentage reached in a judicially-mandated consent conference is not valid unless the proposed settlement is approved beforehand by the court. N.J.S.A. 9:17-48c and 9:17-48d. There is no doubt that a contractual provision purporting to constitute an irrevocable agreement to surrender custody of a child for adoption is invalid.

In *Sees v. Baber*, supra, 74 N.J. 201, we noted that a natural mother's consent to surrender her child and to its subsequent adoption was no longer *required* by the statute in private placement adoptions. After tracing the statutory history from the time when such a consent had been an essential prerequisite to adoption, we concluded that such a consent was now neither necessary nor sufficient for the purpose of terminating parental rights. Id. at 213. The consent to surrender custody in that case was in writing, had been executed prior to physical surrender of the infant, and had been explained to the mother by an attorney. The trial court found that the consent to surrender of custody in that private placement adoption was knowing, voluntary, and deliberate. Id. at 216. The physical surrender of the child took place four days after its birth. Two days thereafter the natural mother changed her mind, and asked that the adoptive couple give her baby back to her. We held that she was entitled to the baby's return. The effect of our holding in that case necessarily encompassed our conclusion that "in an unsupervised private placement, since there is no statutory obligation to consent, there can be no legal barrier to its retraction." Id. at 215. The only possible relevance of consent in these matters, we noted, was that it *might* bear on whether there had been an abandonment of the child, or a forsaking of parental obligations. Id. at 216. Otherwise, consent in a private placement adoption is not only revocable, but, when revoked early enough, irrelevant. Id. at 213-215.

The provision in the surrogacy contract whereby the mother irrevocably agrees to surrender custody of her child and to terminate her parental rights conflicts with the settled interpretation of New Jersey statutory law. There is only one irrevocable consent, and that is the one explicitly provided for by statute: a consent to surrender of custody and a placement with an approved agency or with DYFS. The provision in the surrogacy contract, agreed to before conception, requiring the natural mother to surrender custody of the child without any right of revocation is one more indication of the essential nature of this transaction: the creation of a contractual system of termination and adoption designed to circumvent our statutes.

Public Policy Considerations

The surrogacy contract's invalidity, resulting from its direct conflict with the above statutory provisions, is further underlined when its goals and means are measured against New Jersey's public policy. The contract's basic premise, that the natural parents can decide in advance of birth which one is to have custody of the child, bears no relationship to the settled law that the child's best interests shall determine custody. See *Fantony v. Fantony*, 21 N.J. 525, 536-537 (1956); see also *Sheehan v. Sheehan*, 38 N.J. Super. 120, 125 (App. Div. 1955) ("Whatever the agreement of the parents, the ultimate determination of custody lies with the court in the exercise of its supervisory jurisdiction as *parens patriae*."). The fact that the trial court remedied that aspect of the contract through the "best interests" phase does not make the contractual provision any less offensive to the public policy of this State.

The surrogacy contract guarantees permanent separation of the child from one of its natural parents. Our policy, however, has long been that to the extent possible, children should remain with and be brought up by both of their natural parents. That was the first stated purpose of the previous adoption act, L. 1953, c. 264, §1, codified at N.J.S.A. 9:3-17 (repealed): "it is necessary and desirable (a) to protect the child from unnecessary separation from his natural parents . . . . " While not so stated in the present adoption law, this purpose remains part of the public policy of this State. See, e.g., *Wilke v. Culp*, 196 N.J. Super. 487, 496 (App. Div. 1984), *certif. den.*, 99 N.J. 243 (1985); In re Adoption by J.J.P., supra, 175 N.J. Super. at 426. This is not simply some theoretical ideal that in practice has no meaning. The impact of failure to follow that policy is nowhere better shown than in the results of this surrogacy contract. A child, instead of starting off its life with as much peace and security as possible, finds itself immediately in a tug-of-war between contending mother and father.

The surrogacy contract violates the policy of this State that the rights of natural parents are equal concerning their child, the father's right no greater than the mother's. "The parent and child relationship extends equally to every child and to every parent, regardless of the marital status of the parents." N.J.S.A. 9:17-40. As the Assembly Judiciary Committee noted in its statement to the bill, this section establishes "the principle that regardless of the marital status of the parents, all children *and all parents* have equal rights with respect to each other." Statement to Senate No. 888, Assembly Judiciary, Law, Public Safety and Defense Committee (1983) (emphasis supplied). The whole purpose and effect of the surrogacy contract was to give the father the exclusive right to the child by destroying the rights of the mother . . . .

The only legal advice Mary Beth Whitehead received regarding the surrogacy contract was provided in connection with the contract that she previously entered into with another couple. Mrs. Whitehead's lawyer was referred to her by the Infertility Center, with which he had an agreement to act as counsel for surrogate candidates. His services consisted of spending one hour going through the contract with the Whiteheads, section by section, and answering their questions. Mrs. Whitehead received no further legal advice prior to signing the contract with the Sterns . . . .

Under the contract, the natural mother is irrevocably committed before she knows the strength of her bond with her child. She never makes a totally voluntary, informed decision, for quite clearly any decision prior to the baby's birth is, in the most important sense, uninformed, and any decision after that, compelled by a pre-existing contractual commitment, the threat of a lawsuit, and the inducement of a $10,000 payment is less than totally voluntary. Her interests are of little concern to those who controlled this transaction.

Although the interest of the natural father and adoptive mother is certainly the predominant interest, realistically the *only* interest served, even they are left with less than what public policy requires. They know little about the natural mother, her genetic makeup, and her psychological and medical history. Moreover, not even a superficial attempt is made to determine their awareness of their responsibilities as parents.

Worst of all, however, is the contract's total disregard of the best interests of the child. There is not the slightest suggestion that any inquiry will be made at any time to determine the fitness of the Sterns as custodial parents, of Mrs. Stern as an adoptive parent, their superiority to Mrs. Whitehead, or the effect on the child of not living with her natural mother.

This is the sale of a child, or, at the very least, the sale of a mother's right to her child, the only mitigating factor being that one of the purchasers is the father. Almost every evil that prompted the prohibition on the payment of money in connection with adoptions exists here.

The differences between an adoption and a surrogacy contract should be noted, since it is asserted that the use of money in connection with surrogacy does not pose the risks found where money buys an adoption. Katz, "Surrogate Motherhood and the Baby-Selling Laws," 20 Colum. J.L. & Soc. Probs. 1 (1986).

First, and perhaps most important, all parties concede that it is unlikely that surrogacy will survive without money. Despite the alleged selfless motivation of surrogate mothers, if there is no payment, there will be no surrogates, or very few. That conclusion contrasts with adoption; for obvious reasons, there remains a steady supply, albeit insufficient, despite the prohibitions against payment. The adoption itself, relieving the natural mother of the financial burden of supporting an infant, is in some sense the equivalent of payment.

Second, the use of money in adoptions does not *produce* the problem—conception occurs, and usually the birth itself, before illicit funds are offered. With surrogacy, the "problem," if one views it as such, consisting of the purchase of a woman's procreative capacity, at the risk of her life, is caused by and originates with the offer of money.

Third, with the law prohibiting the use of money in connection with adoptions, the built-in financial pressure of the unwanted pregnancy and the consequent support obligation do not lead the mother to the highest paying, ill-suited, adoptive parents. She is just as well-off surrendering the child to an approved agency. In surrogacy, the highest bidders will presumably become the adoptive parents regardless of suitability, so long as payment of money is permitted.

Fourth, the mother's consent to surrender her child in adoptions is revocable, even after surrender of the child, unless it be to an approved agency, where by regulation there are protections against an ill-advised surrender. In surrogacy, consent occurs so early that no amount of advice would satisfy the potential mother's need, yet the consent is irrevocable.

The main difference, that the unwanted pregnancy is unintended while the situation of the surrogate mother is voluntary and intended, is really not significant. Initially, it produces stronger reactions of sympathy for the mother whose pregnancy was unwanted than for the surrogate mother, who "went into this with her eyes wide open." On reflection, however, it appears that the essential evil is the same, taking advantage of a woman's circumstances (the unwanted pregnancy or the need for money) in order to take away her child, the difference being one of degree.

In the scheme contemplated by the surrogacy contract in this case, a middle man, propelled by profit, promotes the sale. Whatever idealism may have motivated any of the participants, the profit motive predominates, permeates, and ultimately governs the transaction. The demand for children is great and the supply small. The availability of contraception, abortion, and the greater willingness of single mothers to bring up their children has led to a shortage of babies offered for adoption. See N. Baker, Baby Selling: The Scandal of Black Market Adoption supra; Adoption and Foster Care, 1975; Hearings on Baby Selling Before the Subcomm. On Children and Youth of the Senate Comm. on Labor and Public Welfare, 94th Cong. 1st Sess. 6 (1975) (Statement of Joseph H. Reid, Executive Director, Child Welfare League of America, Inc.). The situation is ripe for the entry of the middleman who will bring some equilibrium into the market by increasing the supply through the use of money.

Intimated, but disputed, is the assertion that surrogacy will be used for the benefit of the rich at the expense of the poor. See, e.g., Radin, "Market Inalienability," 100 Harv. L. Rev. 1849, 1930 (1987). In response it is noted that the Sterns are not rich and the Whiteheads not poor. Nevertheless, it is clear to us that it is unlikely that surrogate mothers will be as proportionately numerous among those women in the top twenty percent income bracket as among those in the bottom twenty percent. Ibid. Put differently, we doubt that infertile couples in the low-income bracket will find upper income surrogates.

In any event, even in this case one should not pretend that disparate wealth does not play a part simply because the contrast is not the dramatic "rich versus poor." At the time of trial, the Whiteheads' net assets were probably negative—Mrs. Whitehead's own sister was foreclosing on a second mortgage. Their income derived from Mr. Whitehead's labors. Mrs. Whitehead is a homemaker, having previously held part-time jobs. The Sterns are both professionals, she a medical doctor, he a biochemist. Their combined income when both were working was about $89,500 a year and their assets sufficient to pay for the surrogacy contract arrangements.

The point is made that Mrs. Whitehead *agreed* to the surrogacy arrangement, supposedly fully understanding the consequences. Putting aside the issue of how compelling her need for money may have been, and how significant her understanding of the consequences, we suggest that her consent is irrelevant. There are, in a civilized society, some things that money cannot buy. In America, we decided long ago that merely because conduct purchased by money was "voluntary" did not mean that it was good or beyond regulation and prohibition. *West Coast Hotel Co. v. Parrish*, 300 U.S. 379, 57 S. Ct. 578, 81 L. Ed. 703 (1937). Employers can no longer buy labor at the lowest price they can bargain for, even though that labor is "voluntary," 29 U.S.C. §206 (1982), or buy women's labor for less money than paid to men for the same job, 29 U.S.C. §206(d), or purchase the agreement of children to perform oppressive labor, 29 U.S.C. §212, or purchase the agreement of workers to subject themselves to unsafe or unhealthful working conditions, 29 U.S.C. §§651 to 678. (Occupational Safety and Health Act of 1970). There are, in short, values that society deems more important than granting to wealth whatever it can buy, be it labor, love, or life. Whether this principle recommends prohibition of surrogacy, which presumably sometimes results in great satisfaction to all of the parties, is not for us to say. We note here only that, under existing law, the fact that Mrs. Whitehead "agreed" to the arrangement is not dispositive.

The long-term effects of surrogacy contracts are not known, but feared—the impact on the child who learns her life was bought, that she is the offspring of someone who gave birth to her only to obtain money; the impact on the natural mother as the full weight of her isolation is felt along with the full reality of the sale of her body and her child; the impact on the natural father and adoptive mother once they realize the consequences of their conduct. Literature in related areas suggests these are substantial considerations, although, given the newness of surrogacy, there is little information. See N. Baker, Baby Selling: The Scandal of Black Market Adoption, supra; Adoption and Foster Care, 1975: Hearings on Baby Selling Before the Subcomm. on Children and Youth of the Senate Comm. on Labor and Public Welfare, 94th Cong. 1st Sess. (1975).

The surrogacy contract is based on principles that are directly contrary to the objectives of our laws. It guarantees the separation of a child from its mother; it looks to adoption regardless of suitability; it totally ignores the child; it takes the child from the mother regardless of her wishes and her maternal fitness; and it does all of this, it accomplishes all of its goals, through the use of money.

Beyond that is the potential degradation of some women that may result from this arrangement. In many cases, of course, surrogacy may bring satisfaction, not only to the infertile couple, but to the surrogate mother herself. The fact, however, that many women may not perceive surrogacy negatively but rather see it as an opportunity does not diminish its potential for devastation to other women.

In sum, the harmful consequences of this surrogacy arrangement appear to us all too palpable. In New Jersey the surrogate mother's agreement to sell her child is void . . . .

We have found that our present laws do not permit the surrogacy contract used in this case. Nowhere, however, do we find any legal prohibition against surrogacy when the surrogate mother volunteers, without any payment, to act as a surrogate and is given the right to change her mind and to assert her parental rights. Moreover, the Legislature remains free to deal with this most sensitive issue as it sees fit, subject only to constitutional constraints . . . .

The judgment is affirmed in part, reversed in part, and remanded for further proceedings consistent with this opinion.

Hong v. Marriott Corp.
656 F. Supp. 445 (D. Md. 1987)

SMALKIN, District Judge.

The plaintiff, Yong Cha Hong, commenced this case in a Maryland court with a complaint alleging counts of negligence and breach of warranty against defendants, the proprietor of a chain of fast food restaurants called Roy Rogers Family Restaurants (Marriott) and the supplier of raw frying chicken to the chain (Gold Kist). The case was removed to this Court on diversity grounds. It seems that the plaintiff was contentedly munching away one day on a piece of Roy Rogers take-out fried chicken[1] (a wing) when she bit into something in the chicken that she perceived to be a worm. She suffered, it is alleged, great physical and emotional upset

---

1. The court takes judicial notice (because it is so well-known in this jurisdiction) that Roy Rogers specializes in fried chicken, to eat in or take out. Fed. R. Evid. 201.

from her encounter with this item, including permanent injuries, in consequence of which she prays damages in the amount of $500,000.00.

The defendants moved for summary judgment on plaintiff's warranty count, and also, later, as to the entire complaint, on the ground that there is no genuine dispute of material fact and that, as a matter of law, there was no breach of warranty or negligence. If they are right, they are entitled to summary judgment. Fed. R. Civ. P. 56(c); *Anderson v. Liberty Lobby, Inc.*, 106 S. Ct. 2505 (1986).

It appears that the item encountered by plaintiff in the chicken wing was probably not a worm or other parasite, although plaintiff, in her deposition, steadfastly maintains that it was a worm, notwithstanding the expert analysis. If it was not in fact a worm, i.e., if the expert analysis is correct, it was either one of the chicken's major blood vessels (the aorta) or its trachea, both of which (the Court can judicially notice) would appear worm-like (although not meaty like a worm, but hollow) to a person unschooled in chicken anatomy. The Court must presume plaintiff to be inexpert as to chickens, even though she admits some acquaintance with fresh-slaughtered chickens. See *Ross v. Communications Satellite Corp.*, 759 F.2d 355, 364 (4th Cir. 1985). For the purposes of analyzing the plaintiff's warranty claim, the Court will assume that the item was not a worm. Precisely how the aorta or trachea wound up in this hapless chicken's wing is a fascinating, but as yet unanswered (and presently immaterial), question.

Thus, the warranty issue squarely framed is, does Maryland law[2] provide a breach of warranty[3] remedy for personal injury flowing from an unexpected encounter with an inedible[4] part of the chicken's anatomy in a piece of fast food fried chicken? Defendants contend that there can be no warranty recovery unless the offending item was a "foreign object," i.e., not a part of the chicken itself.

In *Webster v. Blue Ship Tea Room, Inc.*, 347 Mass. 421, 198 N.E.2d 309 (1964), a favorite of commercial law teachers,[5] the plaintiff was injured when a fish bone she encountered in a bowl of New England fish chowder, served in a "quaint" Boston restaurant, became stuck in her throat. She was denied warranty recovery (on a theory of implied warranty of merchantability) on grounds that are not altogether clear from the court's opinion. The opinion can be read in several ways: (1) There was no breach because the bone was not extraneous, but a natural substance; (2) There was no breach because New England fish chowder always has bones as an unavoidable contaminant; or (3) The plaintiff, an undoubted Yankee,

---

2. Of course, Maryland law applies in this diversity case. *Erie Railroad v. Tompkins*, 304 U.S. 64 (1938).

3. The relevant warranty is found in Md. Comm. Law Code Ann. [UCC]§2-314(2) (1975). The Maryland UCC warranty of merchantability applies to sales of food in restaurants, including take-out sales. UCC §2-1314(1).

4. Although perhaps digestible, the aorta and the trachea of a chicken would appear indisputably to belong to the realm of the inedible in that fowl's anatomy.

5. Of which this Judge is one (part-time).

should have expected to find a bone in her chowder and should have slurped it more gingerly.

In their respected hornbook, UCC, §9-7 (2d Ed. 1979) at 351, Professors White and Summers classify *Webster* in a category of warranty cases involving "the presence of unexpected objects," along with several other cases illustrative of that genre. Id. at n.96. In *DeGraff v. Myers Foods*, 19 Pa. D&C2d 19, 1 UCC Rep. 110 (C.P. 1958), the unexpected object was a chicken bone in a chicken pot pie. (The plaintiff won.) In *Flip-po v. Mode O'Day Frock Shops*, 248 Ark. 1, 449 S.W.2d 692 (1970), the unexpected object was a poisonous spider lurking in a newly bought pair of trousers. (It bit plaintiff. Plaintiff lost.)

Unlike New England Fish Chowder, a well-known regional specialty, fried chicken (though of Southern origin) is a ubiquitous American dish. Chicken, generically, has a special place in the American poultry pantheon:

> The dream of the good life in America is embodied in the promise of "a chicken in every pot." Domestic and wild fowl have always been abundant and popular, and each wave of immigrants has brought along favorite dishes—such as paella and chicken cacciatori—which have soon become naturalized citizens.

The Fannie Farmer Cookbook (Knopf: 1980) at 228.

Indeed, as to fried chicken, Fannie Farmer lists recipes for three varieties of fried chicken alone—pan-fried, batter-fried, and Maryland Fried chicken.[6] Id. at 238-239. As best this Judge can determine (and he is no culinary expert) the fast-food chicken served in Roy Rogers most resembles Fannie Farmer's batter-fried chicken. That is, it is covered with a thick, crusty (often highly spiced) batter, that usually conceals from inspection whatever lurks beneath. There is deposition testimony from plaintiff establishing that she saw the offending item before she bit into it, having torn the wing asunder before eating it. A question of fact is raised as to just what she saw, or how carefully she might reasonably be expected to have examined what she saw before eating. It is common knowledge that chicken parts often harbor minor blood vessels. But, this Judge, born and raised south of the Mason-Dixon Line (where fried chicken has been around longer than in any other part of America), knows of no special heightened awareness chargeable to fried chicken eaters that ought to caution them to be on the alert for tracheas or aortas in the middle of their wings.[7]

Certainly, in *Webster* and many other cases that have denied warranty recovery as a matter of law, the injurious substance was, as in this case,

---

6. Oddly enough, Maryland Fried Chicken is seldom encountered in Maryland restaurants, though this Judge has seen it on restaurant menus in Ireland and England.

7. Of course, if as a matter of fact and law plaintiff abandoned her reliance on defendants' warranty by eating the wing with "contributory negligence," the defendants would have a good warranty defense, as well as a good negligence defense, under Maryland law. *Erdman v. Johnson Bros. Radio & Television*, 260 Md. 190, 271 A.2d 744 (1970). But this is quintessentially a question of fact for the jury. Id. at 303-304, 271 A.2d at 751.

a natural (though inedible) part of the edible item consumed. Thus, in *Shapiro v. Hotel Statler Corp.*, 132 F. Supp. 891 (S.D. Cal. 1955), recovery was denied for a fish bone in "Hot Barquette of Seafood Mornay." And in *Allen v. Grafton*, 170 Ohio St. 249, 164 N.E.2d 167 (1960), recovery was denied for oyster shell in fried oysters.[8] But in all these cases, the natural item was, beyond dispute, reasonably to be expected in the dish by its very nature, under the prevailing expectation of any reasonable consumer. Indeed, precisely this "reasonable expectation" test has been adopted in a number of cases. See, e.g., *Morrison's Cafeteria of Montgomery, Inc. v. Haddox*, 431 So. 2d 975, 35 UCC 1074 (Ala. 1983); *Battiste v. St. Thomas Diving Club*, 26 UCC 324 (D.V.I. 1979); *Jeffries v. Clark's Restaurant Enterprises, Inc.*, 20 Wash. App. 428, 580 P.2d 1103, 24 UCC 587 (1978); *Williams v. Braum Ice Cream Stores, Inc.*, 534 P.2d 700, 15 UCC 1019 (Okla. App. 1974); *Stark v. Chock Full O'Nuts*, 77 Misc. 2d 553, 356 N.Y.S.2d 403, 14 UCC 51 (1974). The "reasonable expectation" test has largely displaced the natural/foreign test adverted to by defendants. In the circumstances of this case and many others, it is the only one that makes sense. In the absence of any Maryland decisional law, and in view of the expense and impracticality of certification of the question to the Court of Appeals of, Maryland in this case, this court must decide the issue by applying the rule that that Court would likely adopt some time in the future. See, e.g., *Wilson v. Ford Motor Co.*, 656 F.2d 960 (4th Cir. 1981). This court is confident that Maryland would apply the "reasonable expectation" rule to this warranty case, especially in view of the Court of Appeals' holding in *Bryer v. Rath Packing Co.*, 221 Md. 105, 156 A.2d 442 (1959), recognizing a negligence claim for the presence in a prepared food item of "something that should not be there" which renders the food unfit. Id. at 112, 156 A.2d at 447.

Applying the reasonable expectation test to this case, the court cannot conclude that the presence of a trachea or an aorta in a fast food fried chicken wing is so reasonably to be expected as to render it merchantable, as a matter of law, within the bounds of UCC §2-314(2). This is not like the situation involving a 1 cm. bone in a piece of fried fish in *Morrison's Cafeteria*. Everyone but a fool knows that tiny bones may remain in even the best filets of fish. This case is more like *Williams*, where the court held that the issue was for the trier of fact, on a claim arising from a cherry pit in cherry ice cream. Thus, a question of fact is presented that precludes the grant of summary judgment. See *Celotex Corp. v. Catrett*, 106 S.Ct. 2548 (1986). The jury must determine whether a piece of fast food fried chicken is merchantable if it contains an inedible item of the chicken's anatomy. Of course, the jury will be instructed that the consumer's reasonable expectations form a part of the merchantability concept (under the theory of ordinary fitness, UCC §2-314(2)(c)), as do trade quality standards (under UCC §2-214(2)(a)).

---

8. Although the item encountered by plaintiff in this case does not carry the same potential for physical harm as do fish bones and oyster shells, plaintiff alleges compensable personal injury damage under UCC §2-715(2)(b).

In short, summary judgment cannot be awarded defendants on plaintiff's warranty count, and their motion for partial summary judgment is, accordingly, denied.

Defendants' motion for summary judgment as to the entire complaint is mainly predicated upon plaintiff's insistence at her deposition that the offending item was in fact a worm, notwithstanding the independent analysis showing it not to be a worm. It is true that a party having the burden of proof cannot carry that burden by "evidence which points in both directions," see *N.L.R.B. v. Patrick Plaza Dodge, Inc.*, 522 F.2d 804, 809 (4th Cir. 1975), but it is also the undoubted common law of all American jurisdictions that a plaintiff can advance alternative legal theories of recovery. Here, the negligence and breach of warranty counts (as interpreted by this court's preceding discussion of the scope of the warranty) would permit recovery whether the item was worm or nonworm. Of course, plaintiff's credibility may be severely damaged by her insistence (on deposition and perhaps even at trial) that the item was a worm, despite the contrary expert analysis, which stands unimpugned by contrary expert evidence. This, however, is a risk that plaintiff must assume as part of her right to have the issues of fact tried by a jury under the Seventh Amendment, and summary judgment cannot be used to foreclose that right under the state of this record.

Finally, the court perceives genuine, material disputes of fact and law on plaintiff's negligence count, precluding summary judgment thereon. Fed R. Civ. P. 56(c). Neither expert testimony nor other direct evidence of any sort is needed (except in professional malpractice cases) to prove negligence under Maryland law; negligence can be inferred. *Western Md. R. Co. v. Shivers*, 101 Md. 391, 393, 61 A. 618, 619 (1905). Although perhaps weak, all inferences, including inferences establishing negligence, must be taken in plaintiff's favor at this stage of the proceedings. *Ross v. Communications Satellite Corp.*, 759 F.2d at 364.

For these reasons, the defendant's motion for summary judgment *in toto* is also denied.

In re Peregrine Entertainment, Ltd.
116 Bankr. 194 (C.D. Cal. 1990)

This appeal from a decision of the bankruptcy court raises an issue never before confronted by a federal court in a published opinion: Is a security interest in a copyright perfected by an appropriate filing with the United States Copyright Office or by a UCC-1 financing statement filed with the relevant secretary of state?

I

National Peregrine, Inc. (NPI) is a Chapter 11 debtor in possession whose principal assets are a library of copyrights, distribution rights and licenses to approximately 145 films, and accounts receivable arising from the licensing of these films to various programmers. NPI claims to have an outright assignment of some of the copyrights; as for the others, NPI claims it has an exclusive license to distribute in a certain territory, or for a certain period of time.

In June 1985, Capitol Federal Savings and Loan Association of Denver (Cap Fed) extended to American National Enterprises, Inc., NPI's predecessor by merger, a six million dollar line of credit secured by what is now NPI's film library. Both the security agreement and the UCC-1 financing statements filed by Cap Fed describe the collateral as "[a]ll inventory consisting of films and all accounts, contract rights, chattel paper, general intangibles, instruments, equipment, and documents related to such inventory, now owned or hereafter acquired by the Debtor." Although Cap Fed filed its UCC-1 financing statements in California, Colorado and Utah, it did not record its security interest in the United States Copyright Office.

NPI filed a voluntary petition for bankruptcy on January 30, 1989. On April 6, 1989, NPI filed an amended complaint against Cap Fed, contending that the bank's security interest in the copyrights to the films in NPI's library and in the accounts receivable generated by their distribution were unperfected because Cap Fed failed to record its security interest with the Copyright Office. NPI claimed that, as a debtor in possession, it had a judicial lien on all assets in the bankruptcy estate, including the copyrights and receivables. Armed with this lien, it sought to avoid, recover and preserve Cap Fed's supposedly unperfected security interest for the benefit of the estate.

The parties filed cross-motions for partial summary judgment on the question of whether Cap Fed had a valid security interest in the NPI film library. The bankruptcy court held for Cap Fed. See Memorandum of Decision re Motion for Partial Summary Adjudication (Nov. 14, 1989) [hereinafter "Memorandum of Decision"] and Order re Summary Adjudication of Issues (Dec. 18, 1989). NPI appeals.

II

A. Where to File

The Copyright Act provides that "[a]ny transfer of copyright ownership or other document pertaining to a copyright" may be recorded in the United States Copyright Office. 17 U.S.C. §205(a); see Copyright Office Circular 12: Recordation of Transfers and Other Documents (reprinted in 1 Copyright L. Rep. (CCH) ¶15,015) [hereinafter "Circular 12"]. A "transfer" under the Act includes any "mortgage" or "hypothecation of a copyright," whether "in whole or in part" and "by any means of conveyance or by operation of law." 17 U.S.C. §§101, 201(d)(1); see 3 Nimmer on Copyright §10.05[A], at 10-43—10-45 (1989). The terms "mortgage" and "hypothecation" include a pledge of property as security or collateral for a debt.

See Black's Law Dictionary 669 (5th ed. 1979). In addition, the Copyright Office has defined a "document pertaining to a copyright" as one that

> has a direct or indirect relationship to the existence, scope, duration, or identification of a copyright, or to the ownership, division, allocation, licensing, transfer, or exercise of rights under a copyright. That relationship may be past, present, future, or potential.

37 C.F.R. §201.4(a)(2); see also Compendium of Copyright Office Practices II ¶¶1602-1603 (identifying which documents the Copyright Office will accept for filing).

It is clear from the preceding that an agreement granting a creditor a security interest in a copyright may be recorded in the Copyright Office. See G. Gilmore, Security Interests in Personal Property §17.3, at 545 (1965). Likewise, because a copyright entitles the holder to receive all income derived from the display of the creative work, see 17 U.S.C. §106, an agreement creating a security interest in the receivables generated by a copyright may also be recorded in the Copyright Office. Thus, Cap Fed's security interest *could* have been recorded in the Copyright Office; the parties seem to agree on this much. The question is, does the UCC provide a parallel method of perfecting a security interest in a copyright? One can answer this question by reference to either federal or state law; both inquiries lead to the same conclusion.

1

Even in the absence of express language, federal regulation will preempt state law if it is so pervasive as to indicate that "Congress left no room for supplementary state regulation," or if "the federal interest is so dominant that the federal system will be assumed to preclude enforcement of state laws on the same subject," *Hillsborough County v. Automated Medical Laboratories, Inc.*, 471 U.S. 707, 713, 105 S. Ct. 2371, 2375, 85 L. Ed. 2d 714 (1985) (internal quotations omitted). Here, the comprehensive scope of the federal Copyright Act's recording provisions, along with the unique federal interests they implicate, support the view that federal law preempts state methods of perfecting security interests in copyrights and related accounts receivable.

The federal copyright laws ensure "predictability and certainty of copyright ownership," "promote national uniformity" and "avoid the practical difficulties of determining and enforcing an author's rights under the differing laws and in the separate courts of the various States." *Community for Creative Non-Violence v. Reid*, _____ U.S. _____ , 109 S. Ct. 2166, 2177, 104 L. Ed. 2d 811 (1989); H.R. Rep. No. 1476, 94th Cong., 2d Sess. 129 (1976), U.S. Code Cong., & Admin. News 1976, p. 5659. As discussed above, section 205(a) of the Copyright Act establishes a uniform method for recording security interests in copyrights. A secured creditor need only file in the Copyright Office in order to give "all persons constructive notice of the facts stated in the recorded document." 17 U.S.C. §205(c). Likewise, an interested third party need only search the indices maintained by the

Copyright Office to determine whether a particular copyright is encumbered. See *Northern Songs, Ltd. v. Distinguished Productions, Inc.*, 581 F. Supp. 638, 640-641 (S.D.N.Y 1984); Circular 12, at 8035-4.

A recording system works by virtue of the fact that interested parties have a specific place to look in order to discover with certainty whether a particular interest has been transferred or encumbered. To the extent there are competing recordation schemes, this lessens the utility of each; when records are scattered in several filing units, potential creditors must conduct several searches before they can be sure that the property is not encumbered. See *Danning v. Pacific Propeller, Inc.*, (In re Holiday Airlines Corp.), 620 F.2d 731 (9th Cir.), *cert. denied*, 449 U.S. 900, 101 S. Ct. 269, 66 L. Ed. 2d 130 (1980); *Red Carpet Homes of Johnstown, Inc. v. Gerling* (In re Knapp), 575 F.2d 341, 343 (2d Cir. 1978); UCC §9401, Official Comment ¶1. It is for that reason that parallel recordation schemes for the same types of property are scarce as hens' teeth; the court is aware of no others, and the parties have cited none. No useful purposes would be served—indeed, much confusion would result—if creditors were permitted to perfect security interests by filing with either the Copyright Office or state offices. See G. Gilmore, Security Interests in Personal Property §17.3, at 545 (1965); see also 3 Nimmer on Copyright §10.05[A] at 10-44 (1989) ("a persuasive argument . . . can be made to the effect that by reasons of Sections 201(d)(1), 204(a), 205(c) and 205(d) of the current Act . . . Congress has preempted the field with respect to the form and recordation requirements applicable to copyright mortgages").

If state methods of perfection were valid, a third party (such as a potential purchaser of the copyright) who wanted to learn of any encumbrances thereon would have to check not merely the indices of the U.S. Copyright Office, but also the indices of any relevant secretary of state. Because copyrights are incorporeal—they have no fixed situs—a number of state authorities could be relevant. See, e.g., note 4 supra. Thus, interested third parties could never be entirely sure that all relevant jurisdictions have been searched. This possibility, together with the expense and delay of conducting searches in a variety of jurisdictions, could hinder the purchaser and sale of copyrights, frustrating Congress's policy that copyrights be readily transferable in commerce.

This is the reasoning adopted by the Ninth Circuit in *Danning v. Pacific Propeller. Danning* held that 49 U.S.C. App. §1403(a), the Federal Aviation Act's provision for recording conveyances and the creation of liens and security interests in civil aircraft, preempts state filing provisions. 620 F.2d at 735-736. According to *Danning*,

> [t]he predominant purpose of the statute was to provide one central place for the filing of [liens on aircraft] and thus eliminate the need, given the highly mobile nature of aircraft and their appurtenances, for the examination of State and County records.

620 F.2d at 735-736. Copyrights, even more than aircraft, lack a clear situs; tangible, movable goods such as airplanes must always exist at some

physical location; they may have a home base from which they operate or where they receive regular maintenance. The same cannot be said of intangibles. As noted above, this lack of an identifiable situs militates against individual state filings and in favor of a single, national registration scheme.

Moreover, as discussed at greater length below, see pp. 205-207 infra, the Copyright Act establishes its own scheme for determining priority between conflicting transferees, one that differs in certain respects from that of Article Nine. Under Article Nine, priority between holders of conflicting security interests in intangibles is generally determined by who perfected his interest first. UCC §9312(5). By contrast, section 205(d) of the Copyright Act provides:

> As between two conflicting transfers, the one executed first prevails if it is recorded, in the manner required to give constructive notice under subsection (c), *within one month after its execution in the United States or within two months after its execution outside the United States*, or at any time before recordation in such manner of the later transfer . . . .

17 U.S.C. §205(d) (emphasis added). Thus, unlike Article Nine, the Copyright Act permits the effect of recording with the Copyright Office to relate back as far as two months.

Because the Copyright Act and Article Nine create different priority schemes, there will be occasions when different results will be reached depending on which scheme was employed. The availability of filing under the UCC would thus undermine the priority scheme established by Congress with respect to copyrights. This type of direct interference with the operation of federal law weighs heavily in favor of preemption. See generally *Bonito Boats, Inc. v. Thunder Craft Boats, Inc.*, 489 U.S. 141, 109 S. Ct. 971, 103 L. Ed. 2d 118 (1989).

The bankruptcy court below nevertheless concluded that security interests in copyrights could be perfected by filing either with the copyright office or with the secretary of state under the UCC, making a tongue-in-cheek analog to the use of a belt and suspenders to hold up a pair of pants. According to the bankruptcy court, because either device is equally useful, one should be free to choose which one to wear. With all due respect, this court finds the analogy inapt. There is no legitimate reason why pants should be held up in only one particular manner: Individuals and public modesty are equally served by either device, or even by a safety pin or a piece of rope; all that really matters is that the job gets done. Registration schemes are different in that the *way* notice is given is precisely what matters. To the extent interested parties are confused as to which system is being employed, this increases the level of uncertainty and multiplies the risk of error, exposing creditors to the possibility that they might get caught with their pants down.

A recordation scheme best serves its purpose where interested parties can obtain notice of all encumbrances by referring to a single, precisely defined recordation system. The availability of parallel state recordation systems that could put parties on constructive notice as to encumbrances on copyrights would surely interfere with the effectiveness of the federal recordation scheme. Given the virtual absence of dual recordation schemes in our legal system, Congress cannot be presumed to have contemplated such a result. The court therefore concludes that any state recordation system pertaining to interests in copyrights would be preempted by the Copyright Act.

2

State law leads to the same conclusion. Article Nine of the Uniform Commercial Code establishes a comprehensive scheme for the regulation of security interests in personal property and fixtures. By superseding a multitude of pre-Code security devices, it provides "a simple and unified structure within which the immense variety of present-day secured financing transactions can go forward with less cost and greater certainty." UCC §9101, Official Comment. However, Article Nine is not all encompassing; under the "step back" provision of UCC §9104, Article Nine does not apply "[t]o a security interest subject to any statute of the United States to the extent that such statute governs the rights of parties to and third parties affected by transactions in particular types of property."

For most items of personal property, Article Nine provides that security interests must be perfected by filing with the office of the secretary of state in which the debtor is located. See UCC §§9302(1), 9401(1)(c). Such filing, however, is not "necessary of effective to perfect a security interest in property subject to . . . [a] statute or treaty of the United States which provides for a national or international registration . . . or which specifies a place of filing different from that specified in [Article Nine] for filing of the security interest." UCC §9302(3)(a). When a national system for recording security interests exists, the Code treats compliance with that system as "equivalent to the filing of a financing statement under [Article Nine,] and a security interest in property subject to the statute or treaty can be perfected only by compliance therewith . . . ." UCC §9302(4).

As discussed above, section 205(a) of the Copyright Act clearly does establish a national system for recording transfers of copyright interests, and it specifies a place of filing different from that provided in Article Nine. Recording in the Copyright Office gives nationwide, constructive notice to third parties of the recorded encumbrance. Except for the fact that the Copyright Office's indices are organized on the basis of the title and registration number, rather than by reference to the identity of the debtor, this system is nearly identical to that which Article Nine generally provides on a statewide basis. And, lest there be any doubt, the drafters of the UCC specifically identified the Copyright Act as establishing the type of national registration system that would trigger the §9302(3) and (4) step back provisions.

> Examples of the type of federal statute referred to in [UCC §9302(3)(a)] are the provisions of [Title 17] (copyrights) . . . .

UCC §9302, Official Comment ¶8; see G. Gilmore, Security Interests in Personal Property §17.3, at 545 (1965) ("[t]here can be no doubt that [the Copyright Act was] meant to be within the description of §9-302(3)(a)").

The court therefore concludes that the Copyright Act provides for national registration and "specifies a place of filing different from that specified in [Article Nine] for filing of the security interest." UCC §9302(3)(a). Recording in the U.S. Copyright Office, rather than filing a financing statement under Article Nine, is the proper method for perfecting a security interest in a copyright.

In reaching this conclusion, the court rejects *City Bank & Trust Co. v. Otto Fabric, Inc.*, 83 B.R. 780 (D. Kan. 1988), and *In re Transportation Design & Technology Inc.*, 48 B.R. 635 (Bankr. S.D. Cal. 1985), insofar as they are germane to the issues presented here. Both cases held that, under the UCC, security interests in patents need not be recorded in the U.S. Patent and Trademark Office to be perfected as against lien creditors because the federal statute governing patent assignments does not specifically provide for liens:

> Applications for patent, patents, or any interest therein, shall be assignable in law by an instrument in writing. The applicant, patentee, or his assigns or legal representatives may in like manner grant and convey an exclusive right under his application for patent, or patents, to the whole or any specified part of the United States . . . .
>
> An assignment, grant or conveyance shall be void as against *any subsequent purchaser or mortgagee* for a valuable consideration, without notice, unless it is recorded in the Patent and Trademark Office within three months from its date or prior to the date of such subsequent purchase or mortgage.

35 U.S.C. §261 (emphasis added).

According to *In re Transportation*, because section 261's priority scheme only provides for a "subsequent purchaser or mortgagee for valuable consideration," it does not require recording in the Patent and Trademark Office to perfect against lien creditors. See 48 B.R. at 639. Likewise, *City Bank* held that "the failure of the statute to mention protection against lien creditors suggests that it is unnecessary to record an assignment or other conveyance with the Patent Office to protect the appellant's security interest against the trustee." 83 B.R. at 782.

These cases misconstrue the plain language of UCC section 9104, which provides for the voluntary step back of Article Nine's provisions "*to the extent* [federal law] governs the rights of [the] parties." UCC §9104(a) (emphasis added). Thus, when a federal statute provides for a national system of recordation or specifies a place of filing different from that in Article Nine, the methods of perfection specified in Article Nine are supplanted by that national system; compliance with a national system of recordation is equivalent to the filing of a financing statement under Article Nine. UCC §9302(4). Whether the federal statute also provides a priority scheme different from that in Article Nine is a separate issue, addressed below. Compliance with a national registration scheme is necessary for perfection regardless of whether federal law governs priorities. Cap Fed's security interest in the copyrights of the films in NPI's library and the receivables they have generated therefore is unperfected.

B. Effect of Failing to Record with the Copyright Office

Having concluded that Cap Fed should have, but did not, record its security interest with the Copyright Office, the court must next determine whether NPI as a debtor in possession can subordinate Cap Fed's interest and recover it for the benefit of the bankruptcy estate. As a debtor in possession, NPI has nearly all of the powers of a bankruptcy trustee, see 11 U.S.C. §1107(a), including the authority to set aside preferential or fraudulent transfers, as well as transfers otherwise voidable under applicable state or federal law. See 11 U.S.C. §§544, 547, 548.

Particularly relevant is the "strong arm clause" of 11 U.S.C. §544(a) (1), which, in respect to personal property in the bankruptcy estate, gives the debtor in possession every right and power state law confers upon one who has acquired a lien by legal or equitable proceedings. If, under the applicable law, a judicial lien creditor would prevail over an adverse claimant, the debtor in possession prevails; if not, not. *Wind Power Systems, Inc. v. Cannon Financial Group, Inc. (In re Wind Power Systems, Inc.)*, 841 F.2d 288, 293 (9th Cir. 1988); *Angeles Real Estate Co. v. Kerxton (In re Construction General Inc.)*, 737 F.2d 416, 418 (4th Cir. 1984). A lien creditor generally takes priority over unperfected security interests in estate property because, under Article Nine, "an unperfected security interest is subordinate to the rights of . . . [a] person who becomes a lien creditor before the security interest is perfected." UCC §9301(1)(b). But, as discussed previously, the UCC does not apply to the extent a federal statute "governs the rights of parties to and third parties affected by transactions in particular types of property." UCC §9104. Section 205(d) of the Copyright Act is such a statute, establishing a priority scheme between conflicting transfers of interests in a copyright:

> As between two conflicting *transfers*, the one executed first prevails if it is recorded, in the manner required to give constructive notice under subsection (c), within one month after its execution in the United States or within two months after its execution outside the United States, or at any time before recordation in such manner of the later transfer. Otherwise, the later *transfer* prevails if recorded first in such manner, and if taken in good faith, for valuable consideration or on the basis of a binding promise to pay royalties, and without notice of the earlier *transfer*.

17 U.S.C. §205(d) (emphasis added). The federal priority scheme preempts the state priority scheme.

Section 205(d) does not expressly address the rights of lien creditors, speaking only in terms of competing transfers of copyright interests. To determine whether NPI, as a hypothetical lien creditor, may avoid Cap Fed's unperfected security interest, the court must therefore consider whether a judicial lien is a transfer as that term is used in the Copyright Act.

As noted above, the Copyright Act recognizes transfers of copyright ownership "in whole or in part by any means of conveyance or by operation of law." 17 U.S.C. §201(d)(1). Transfer is defined broadly to include any "assignment, mortgage, exclusive license, or any other conveyance, alienation, or hypothecation of a copyright . . . whether or not it is limited in time or place of effect." 17 U.S.C. §101. A judicial lien creditor is a creditor who has obtained a lien "by judgment, levy, sequestration, or other legal or equitable process or proceeding." 11 U.S.C. §101(32). Such a creditor typically has the power to seize and sell property held by the debtor at the time of the creation of the lien in order to satisfy the judgment or, in the case of general intangibles such as copyrights, to collect the revenues generated by the intangible as they come due. See, e.g., Cal. Civ. P. Code §§701.510, 701.520, 701.640 . . . . Thus, while the creation of a lien on a copyright may not give a creditor an immediate right to control the copyright, it amounts to a sufficient transfer of rights to come within the broad definition of transfer under the Copyright Act. See *Phoenix Bond & Indemnity Co. v. Shamblin (In re Shamblin)*, 890 F.2d 123, 127 n.7 (9th Cir. 1989) (under the Bankruptcy Code, "[t]his court has consistently treated the creation of liens on the debtor's property as a transfer").

Cap Fed contends that, in order to prevail under 17 U.S.C. §205(d), NPI must have the status of a bona fide purchaser, rather than that of a judicial lien creditor. See *Pistole v. Mellor (In re Mellor)*, 734 F.2d 1396, 1401 n.4 (9th Cir. 1984) (judicial lien creditor does not have the same rights as a bona fide purchaser); cf. 11 U.S.C. §544(a)(3) (for real estate in the bankruptcy estate, debtor in possession has the rights of a bona fide purchaser). Cap Fed, in essence, is arguing that the term transfer in section 205(d) refers only to consensual transfers. For the reasons expressed above, the court rejects this argument. The Copyright Act's definition of transfer is very broad and specifically includes transfers by operation of law. 17 U.S.C. §201(d)(1). The term is broad enough to encompass not merely purchasers, but lien creditors as well. NPI therefore is entitled to priority if it meets the statutory good faith, notice, consideration and recording requirements of section 205(a). As the hypothetical lien creditor, NPI is deemed to have taken in good faith and without notice. See 11 U.S.C. §544(a). The only remaining issues are whether NPI could have recorded its interest in the Copyright Office and whether it obtained its lien for valuable consideration.

In order to obtain a lien on a particular piece of property, a creditor who has received a money judgment in the form of a writ of execution must prepare a notice of levy that specifically identifies the property to be encumbered and the consequences of that action. See Cal. Civ. P. Code §699.540. If such a notice identifies a federal copyright or the receivables generated by such a copyright, it and the underlying writ of execution, constitute "document[s] pertaining to a copyright" and, therefore, are capable of recordation in the Copyright Office. See 17 U.S.C. §205(a); Compendium of Copyright Office Practices II ¶¶1602-1603 (identifying which documents the Copyright Office will accept for filing). Because these documents could be recorded in the Copyright Office, NPI as debtor in possession will be deemed to have done so.

Finally, contrary to Cap Fed's assertion, a trustee or debtor in possession is deemed to have given valuable consideration for its judicial lien. Section 544(a)(1) provides:

> The trustee [or debtor in possession] shall have, as of the commencement of the case . . . the right and powers of, or may avoid any transfer of property of the debtor or any obligation incurred by the debtor that is voidable by . . . a creditor *that extends credit to the debtor at the time of the commencement of the case*, and that obtains, at such time and with respect to such credit, a judicial lien on all property on which a creditor on a simple contract could have obtained such a judicial lien . . . .

11 U.S.C. §544(a)(1) (emphasis added). The act of extending credit, of course, constitutes the giving of valuable consideration. See *First Maryland Leasecorp v. M/V Golden Egret*, 764 F.2d 749, 753 (11th Cir. 1985); *United States v. Cahall Bros.*, 674 F.2d 578, 581 (6th Cir. 1982). In addition, the trustee's lien—like that of any other judgment creditor—is deemed to be in exchange for the claim that formed the basis of the underlying judgment, a claim that is extinguished by the entry of the judgment.

Because NPI meets all of the requirements for subsequent transferees to prevail under 17 U.S.C. §205(b)—a transferee who took in good faith, for valuable consideration and without notice of the earlier transfer—Cap Fed's unperfected security interest in NPI's copyrights and the receivables they generated is trumped by NPI's hypothetical judicial lien. NPI may therefore avoid Cap Fed's interest and preserve it for the benefit of the bankruptcy estate.

Conclusion

The judgment of the bankruptcy court is reversed. The case is ordered remanded for a determination of which movies in NPI's library are the subject of valid copyrights.

APPENDIX C

Answers to the Quick Quizzes

Chapter 1

1. True
2. False
3. False
4. True
5. False

Chapter 2

1. False
2. True
3. False
4. False
5. True

Chapter 3

1. True
2. True
3. True
4. False
5. False

Chapter 4

1. False
2. True
3. True
4. False
5. False

Chapter 5

1. False
2. True
3. True
4. False
5. True

Chapter 6

1. False
2. False
3. True
4. True
5. True

Chapter 7

1. True
2. False
3. True
4. False
5. False

Chapter 8

1. True
2. False
3. True
4. True
5. False

Chapter 9

1. False
2. False
3. True
4. False
5. True

Chapter 10

1. True
2. True
3. False
4. False
5. True

Chapter 11

1. False
2. False
3. True
4. True
5. True

GLOSSARY

Acceptance: manifestation of assent in the manner requested or authorized by the offeror.

Accord and satisfaction: a special agreement in which the parties to a disputed contract agree to new terms in exchange for forbearing to sue under the original contract.

Ambiguity: contract provision with multiple interpretations.

Antenuptial agreement: contract entered into prior to marriage determining the parties' rights on dissolution of the marriage; must be in writing to be enforceable.

Anticipatory breach: positive, unconditional, and unequivocal words that a party intends to breach his contractual obligations.

Arbitration: nonjudicial method of resolving legal disputes.

Assignee: transferee of contractual rights.

Assignment: transference of contractual rights by the promisee to a third party.

Assignor: transferor of a contractual right.

Attachment: the time a security interest becomes an inchoate right under Article IX of the UCC.

Auction with reserve: parties have the right to revoke any time before gavel comes down.

Auction without reserve: property owner relinquishes the right to revoke.

Authentication: process of proving the genuiness of a contract in court.

Battle of the forms: difference in forms used by merchants for sales agreements pursuant to Article II of the UCC.

Best evidence rule: rule stating that the best evidence of a written agreement is the original of that agreement.

Bilateral contract: a promise for a promise.

Breach: breaking one's contractual promise.

Breach of contract: failure of a promisor to fulfill a contractual obligation.

Business record exception: exception to the hearsay doctrine whereby a document kept in the regular course of business, authenticated by the person responsible for maintaining the document may be admitted into evidence.

Caveat emptor: let the buyer beware.

Caveat venditor: let the seller beware.

Charitable subscription: promise to donate to a charity, given the enforceability of a contract under law.

Children of tender years: children between the ages of 7 and 14.

CIF: cost of insurance and freight.

Class: a group of persons identified as a group rather than as named individuals.

COD: cost on delivery, the moment when risk passes to the buyer.

Collateral: property subject of a security agreement under Article IX of the UCC.

Compensatory damages: standard measure of damages; puts the injured party in the same position he would have been in had the contract been fulfilled.

Condition: fact or event, the happening or nonhappening of which creates or extinguishes an absolute duty to perform.

Condition concurrent: promise to perform and performance occur simultaneously.

Condition precedent: fact or event that creates an absolute duty to perform.

Condition subsequent: fact or event that extinguishes as absolute duty to perform.

Conditional promise: a promise dependent on the happening or nonhappening of some event.

Consequential damages: damages above the standard measure due to special losses occasioned by the breach.

Consideration: a benefit conferred or a detriment incurred; a basic requirement of every valid contract.

Consignment contract: agreement whereby risk of loss to the subject goods remains with the seller until the buyer resells the goods.

Constructive condition: an implied-in-fact condition.

Contract: a legally enforceable agreement between two or more parties in which each agrees to give and receive something of legal value.

Contract of adhesion: a contract entered into where one party has an unfair bargaining advantage; voidable.

Contractual capacity: the legal ability to enter into a contractual relationship.

Contractual intent: the purposefulness of forming a contractual relationship.

Co-signer: person who agrees to be equally liable with a promisor under a contract.

Counteroffer: a variance in the terms of an offer that constitutes a rejection of the original offer and results in a new offer by the offeree to the original offeror.

Covenant: an absolute, unconditional promise to perform.

Cover: remedy whereby the buyer can purchase goods in substitution for the goods designated in a breached contract.

Cross-offer: see Counteroffer.

Damages: legal remedies; monetary awards.

Delegation: promisor having assistance in fulfilling contractual duties.

Divisible contract: contract capable of being broken down into several equal agreements.

Duress: force or coercion used to induce agreement to a contract.

Economic duress: threatening the loss of an economic benefit if the person refuses to contract.

Emancipation: a minor no longer under the legal care of an adult.

Equitable remedies: nonmonetary awards.

Equity: the branch of the legal system that deals with fairness and mercy.

Estoppel: equitable term; the doctrine bars certain actions in the interest of fairness.

Executed contract: a contract that is complete and final with respect to all of its terms and conditions.

Executory contract: a contract in which one or both of the parties still have obligations to perform.

Exemplary damages: additional monetary award designed to punish the breaching party.

Express condition: a condition created by the words of the parties.

Express contract: a contract manifested in so many words, oral or written.

Express waiver: a waiver occurring when the promisee specifically manifests an intention to forgive the other side's breach.

Express warranty: a guarantee created by words or conduct of the seller.

Ex ship: risk passes to buyer of the goods when the goods are offloaded from the means of conveyance.

FAS: free alongside; risk passes to buyer when goods are placed alongside the vessel used for transportation.

Financing statement: document filed in government office to protect a security interest under Article IX of the UCC.

Firm offer: offer made by a merchant under the provisions of the UCC that cannot be revoked for a period of time.

Floating lien: security interest in after-acquired property.

FOB: free on board; risk passes to buyer when the goods are loaded on the vessel used to transport the goods.

Formal contract: historically, a written contract under seal; currently, any contract so designated by a state statute.

Fraud: a misrepresentation of a material fact made with the intent to deceive, relied on by the other party to his or her detriment.

Frustration of purpose: the purpose for which the contract was formed no longer exists.

Goods: things that are existing and moveable.

Guarantee: promise to answer for the debts of another; must be in writing.

Guarantor: person who agrees to be responsible to answer for the debts of another should the debtor default.

Hearsay: an out-of-court statement used to prove the truth of the matters asserted therein.

Implied-in-fact condition: condition created by the reasonable expectation of the parties.

Implied-in-fact contract: a contract in which the promises of the parties are inferred from their actions as opposed to specific words.

Implied-in-law condition: a condition imposed by law in the interests of fairness.

Implied-in-law contract: see Quasi-contract.

Implied waiver: a waiver occurring when the promisee's actions imply an intention to forgive the other side's breach.

Implied warranty: guarantee created by operation of law.

Impossibility of performance: promisor's performance cannot be fulfilled due to outside forces.

Incidental beneficiary: person who benefits tangentially from a contract.

Informal contract: any nonformal contract.

Injunction: court order to stop engaging in a specific action.

Intended beneficiary: third party beneficiary.

Ironclad offer: offer under the UCC whose terms cannot be modified by the offeree.

Latent ambiguity: ambiguity that can only be proven by extrinsic evidence.

Law: division of the legal system concerned with historical legal principles designed to provide equal treatment to all persons.

Legal remedies: monetary awards.

Limitation of damages: a contractual provision placing a ceiling on the amount of potential liability for breach of the contract.

Liquidated damages: a contractual provision providing a specified dollar amount for breach of the contract.

Mailbox rule: the acceptance of a bilateral contract is effective when properly dispatched by an authorized means of communication.

Majority: adulthood; above the legal age of consent.

Malum in se: bad in and of itself, against public morals.

Malum prohibitum: regulatory wrong; violates a statute.

Material breach: breach of contract that goes to the heart of the agreement.

Mechanic's lien: security interest given under common law to persons who repair property.

Mental duress: psychological threats used to induce a person to contract.

Merchant: under the UCC, any person who regularly trades in goods or who holds himself out as having knowledge peculiar to a specific good.

Minor breach: breach of contract that goes to an insignificant aspect of the agreement.

Minority: persons under the legal age of consent.

Mirror image rule: an acceptance must correspond exactly to the terms of the offer.

Misrepresentation: mistakes of a material fact relied on by the other party to his or her detriment; no intent to defraud.

Mistake: misconception of the subject matter of the contract.

Mitigation of damages: duty imposed on injured party to lessen, by reasonable means, the breaching party's liability.

Mutual assent: a meeting of the minds; agreeing to the same terms at the same time; the offer and acceptance combined.

Mutual mistake: misconception of the subject matter of a contract by both parties; makes the contract unenforceable.

Mutual rescission: agreement by both contracting parties to do away with the contract.

Mutuality of consideration: the bargain element of the contract; that each side must give and receive something of legal value.

Natural infant: a child under the age of seven.

Necessaries: food, clothing, shelter, and medical aid.

No arrival, no sale: risk passes to the buyer when the goods are tendered to the buyer.

Nominal consideration: consideration of insufficient legal value to support a contract.

Novation: substitution of a party to a contract; novated person takes over all rights and obligations under the contract.

Offer: a proposition made by one party to another manifesting a present intention to enter into a valid contract and creating a power in the other person to create a valid contract by making an appropriate acceptance.

Offeree: the person to whom an offer is made; the party who has the power to create a valid contract by making an appropriate acceptance.

Offeror: the person who initiates a contract by proposing the offer.

Operation of law: a manner in which rights and obligations devolve on a person without the act or cooperation of the party himself.

Option: a contract to keep an offer open for a specified time.

Output contract: an agreement whereby one person agrees to buy or sell all the goods produced by the other party.

Palimony: payment made to a person under certain circumstances pursuant to the break-up of a nonmarital relationship.

Parol evidence rule: oral testimony may not be used to vary the terms of a writing.

Patent ambiguity: contractual term that is ambiguous on the face of the contract.

Perfect tender: under the UCC the buyer's right to complete, not substantial, performance.

Perfection: method of creating and protecting a security interest under Article IX of the UCC.

Physical duress: threatening physical harm to force a person to contract.

Pre-existing duty rule: promises to do what one is already legally bound to do is not consideration.

Prenuptial agreement: see antenuptial agreement.

Principal-agent: an agent is one who acts for and on behalf of another, the principal, for the purpose of entering into contracts with third persons.

Promisee: the one who receives consideration in a bilateral contract.

Promisor: the one who gives consideration in a bilateral contract.

Promissory estoppel: doctrine in which promises not supported by consideration are given enforceability if the promisee had detrimentally relied on the promises.

Promissory note: promise to pay money; repayment of a loan.

Punitive damages: exemplary damages.

Purchase money security interest: security interest created in the person whose money was used to buy the collateral.

Quantum meruit: quasi-contractual award; value of the service performed.

Quantum valebant: quasi-contractual award; value of the good given.

Quasi-contract: a legal relationship that the courts, in the interests of fairness and equity, treat in a manner similar to a contractual relationship, but one in which no contract exists.

Quasi-contractual remedy: an equitable remedy involving a monetary award.

Quid pro quo: this for that; the mutuality of consideration.

Real party in interest: person with enforceable contractual rights.

Reformation: a court-ordered accord and satisfaction.

Rejection: to refuse an offer.

Release: contract relieving the promisor from an obligation under an existing contract.

Replevin: equitable remedy in which buyer reclaims property previously rejected.

Requirements contract: agreement whereby one person agrees to buy all his supplies from the other person.

Rescission and restitution: a court order revoking a contract that would be unduly burdensome to fulfill.

Reverse unilateral contract: a contract in which the performer, rather than the promisor, makes the offer.

Revocation: to recall an offer.

Rules of construction: guidelines used by the courts to interpret contractual provisions.

Sale on approval: risk passes to the buyer when the buyer receives and approves the goods.

Sale or return: risk passes to the buyer when the buyer receives the goods, but the buyer bears the cost of returning any goods of which she does not approve.

Secured transaction: any transaction, regardless of form, that intends to create a security interest in personal property or fixtures.

Security agreement: document signed by debtor and creditor naming the collateral and creating a security interest in said collateral.

Security interest: right acquired by a creditor to attach collateral in case of default by the debtor.

Severability: the ability to separate a contract into its legal and illegal portions.

Sham consideration: legally insufficient consideration used to mask a gift in words of contract.

Shipment contract: agreement whereby risk passes from seller to buyer when goods are transported by a third person under Article II of the UCC.

Specific performance: court order to perform contractual promises.

Speculative damages: damages that are not specifically provable.

Statute of Frauds: statute mandating that certain contracts must be in writing to be enforceable.

Stipulation: agreement of the parties.

Strict liability: no standard of care; automatic liability if properly used goods do not meet warranties.

Substituted agreement: a new contract that incorporates the original contract in the new provisions.

Sufficiency of the consideration: doctrine that each party to a contract must contribute something of legal value for which he has bargained.

Supervening illegality: change in law that makes the subject matter of the contract illegal.

Temporary restraining order (TRO):   preliminary step to an injunction.

Tender complete performance: being ready, willing, and able to perform.

Third party beneficiary contract: contract entered into for the purpose of benefiting someone not a party to the contract.

Third party creditor beneficiary: person who receives the benefit of a contract in order to extinguish a debt owed to him by the promisee.

Third party donee beneficiary: person who receives the benefit of a contract in order to receive a gift from the promisee.

Time of the essence clause: contractual clause in which a specified time for performance is made a key element of the contract.

Token chose: item of symbolic, rather than monetary, significance.

Undisclosed principal: a person, represented by an agent, who is party to a contract but has not revealed his or her identity to the other party.

Undue influence: mental duress by a person in a close and particular relationship to the innocent party.

Unenforceable contract: a contract that is otherwise valid but for breach of which there is no remedy at law.

Uniform Commercial Code (UCC):   statutory enactment codifying certain areas of contract law, specifically with respect to sales contracts and security agreements.

Unilateral contract: a promise for an act.

Unilateral mistake: misconception of the subject matter of a contract by only one party to the contract.

Usury: rate of interest higher than the rate allowed by law.

Valid contract: an agreement that meets all six contractual requirements.

Vested: having a legally enforceable right.

Void contract: a situation in which the parties have attempted to create a contract, but because one or more of the requisite elements are missing no contract exists.

Voidable contract: a contract that one party may avoid at his option without being in breach of contract.

Voir dire: process used to challenge the authentication of a document proffered into evidence.

Voluntary disablement: volitional act by a promisor making her obligation virtually incapable of being performed.

Waiver: forgiveness of a contractual obligation.

Warranty: guarantee made by the manufacturer or seller with respect to the quality, quantity, and type of good being sold.

Warranty of fitness for a particular use: guarantee that goods can be used for a specified purpose.

Warranty of merchantability: guarantee that goods can be used in their current condition.

Warranty of title: guarantee that seller has a title sufficient to transfer the goods to the buyer.

Index

Acceptance, 3, 59
  bilateral contract, 64
  defined, 59
  mailbox rule, 65
  silence, 62
  termination of ability to accept, 68
  undisclosed principal, 63-64
  Uniform Commercial Code, 171
  unilateral contract, 67, 70
  varying terms of offer, 60
  who may accept, 63
Accord and satisfaction, 92
  discharge of obligations, 237
Age
  contractual capacity, 114
Agent, 64
Alcohol
  contractual capacity, 116
Ambiguity, 312
  latent, 312
  patent, 312
Antenuptial agreement, 149
Arbitration, 275
  drafting simple contracts, 307
Assignment, 220
  assignee, 221
  assignor, 221
  consent of the promisor, 222
  creating, 220
  defined, 220
  drafting simple contracts, 303
  effect of, 223
  estoppel, 225
  irrevocable, 224
  multiple assignees, 235

  novation, 235
  performance, 225
  token chose, 224
  writing, 224
Auction with reserve, 69
Auction without reserve, 69
Authentication, 309

Battle of the forms, 180
Benefit conferred, 84
Best evidence rule, 309
Bilateral contract
  acceptance, 64
  mutuality of consideration, 84
  rejection, 66
  revocation, 69
Bilateral obligation, 6
Breach of contract, 243
  discharge of obligations, 237

Charitable subscription, 93
Choice of law
  drafting simple contracts, 307
Compensatory damages, 265
Condition
  concurrent, 155
  constructive, 156
  defined, 153
  express, 156
  implied-in-fact, 156
  implied-in-law, 156
  precedent, 154
  subsequent, 154
Conditional contracts
  risk of loss, 183

Consequential damages, 267
Consideration, 4, 83
    accord and satisfaction, 92
    benefit conferred, 84
    charitable subscription, 93
    conditional promises, 90
    debtor's promises, 94
    defined, 84
    determining what is not
        consideration, 86
    detriment incurred, 85
    formal contract, 95
    gift, 87
    guarantee, 94
    illusory promises, 87
    moral consideration, 86
    mutuality, 84
    nominal, 90
    past consideration, 86
    preexisting duty rule, 88
    promissory estoppel, 91
    sham, 90
    subject matter, 36
    sufficiency, 89
Constructive condition, 156
Contract
    acceptance, 3
    bilateral, 3
    consideration, 4, 83
    contractual capacity, 114
    contractual intent, 127
    defined, 2
    enforceability, 11
    executed, 11
    executory, 11
    express, 8
    formal, 10
    implied, 8
    implied-in-fact, 8
    implied-in-law, 8
    informal, 10
    legality of subject matter, 4
    offer, 2
    proving the terms, 308
    quasi-contracts, 8
    requirements, 2
    timing, 10
    unenforceable, 12
    unilateral, 6
    valid, 11
Contracts not to be performed within
    one year, 149

Contractual capacity, 5, 114
    age, 114
    alcohol, 116
    drugs, 116
    mental capacity, 116
Contractual fraud elements, 129
Contractual intent, 5
    defined, 128
    duress, 130
    economic duress, 131
    fraud, 129
    mental duress, 131
    misrepresentation, 129
    mistake, 133
    physical duress, 130
Counteroffer, 61
Covenant
    defined, 152

Damages
    compensatory, 265
    consequential, 267
    limitation of, 268
    liquidated, 268
    punitive, 266
    speculative, 267
Death of parties, 248
    discharge of obligations, 237
Debtor's promises, 94
Delegation, 226
    drafting simple contracts, 303
Destination contracts
    risk of loss, 185
Detriment incurred, 85
Discharge of obligations, 237
    accord and satisfaction, 246
    agreement of parties, 245
    anticipatory breach, 241
    breach of contract, 243
    death of parties, 248
    destruction of subject matter, 248
    excuse of conditions, 239
    frustration of purpose, 249
    impossibility of performance, 247
    insolvency, 241
    substituted agreement, 246
    supervening illegality, 248
    voluntary disablement, 240
Drafting simple contracts, 295
    arbitration, 307
    assignments, 303
    checklist of clauses, 297

choice of law, 307
delegation, 303
description of
    consideration, 298
description of parties, 297
duration, 305
notice, 306
remedies, 306
risk of loss, 302
security agreement, 300
signatures, 308
special provisions, 304
submission to jurisdiction, 308
termination, 305
terminology, 303
title to property, 301
waivers, 302
warranties, 301
Drugs
contractual capacity, 116
Duration
drafting simple contracts, 305
Duress, 130
    contract of adhesion, 132
    economic, 131
    mental, 131
    physical, 130

Economic duress, 131
Enforceability of contract, 11
Equitable remedies, 270
    injunction, 270
    quasi-contractual remedies, 273
    reformation, 272
    rescission and restitution, 271
    specific performance, 271
Executed contract, 10
Executor's promise to pay decedent's
    debts, 151
Executory contract, 10
Express condition, 155

Formal contract, 10
Fraud, 129
Frustration of purpose
    discharge of obligations, 249

Gambling, 113
Guarantee, 94, 151

Hearsay, 309
    business record exception, 311

Implied contract, 8
Implied warranties, 182
Implied-in-fact condition, 156
Implied-in-fact contract, 8
Implied-in-law condition, 156
Implied-in-law contract, 8
Impossibility of performance
    discharge of obligations, 247
Informal contract, 10
Injunction, 270
Intent, 127

Jurisdiction
    drafting simple contracts, 308

Leases, 179
Legality of subject matter, 110
    gambling, 113
    licensing statutes, 113
    malum in se, 110
    malum prohibitum, 111
    Statute of Frauds, 111
Licensing statutes, 112
Liquidated damages, 268

Mailbox rule, 65
    rejection, 66
Malum in se, 110
Malum prohibitum, 111
Marriage, 148
Mental capacity
    contractual capacity, 116
Mental duress, 130
Mirror image rule, 61
Misrepresentation, 129
Mistake
    mutual mistake, 133, 313
    unilateral mistake, 133, 313
Mutual mistake, 133

Novation
    assignment, 225
    discharge of obligations, 247

Offer, 3, 29
    acceptance. *See* Acceptance
    alternate offers, 37
    ambiguity, 36
    certainty, 33
    communication to offeree, 32
    defined, 30
    definiteness, 33

essential terms, 34
parties, 38
price, 34
subject matter, 36
termination, 68
time of performance, 39
varying terms of offer, 60
Operation of law, 71
Output contract, 37

Palimony, 149
Parol evidence rule, 158
Parties
offer, 38
Perfect tender, 187
Physical duress, 130
Preexisting duty rule, 88
Prenuptial agreement, 149
Price, 34
Principal
defined, 64
Principal-agent relationship, 64
Promissory estoppel, 91
Proving the terms of a contract, 308
Punitive damages, 266

Quantum meruit, 273
Quantum valebant, 273
Quasi-contract, 8
Quasi-contractual remedies, 273
arbitration, 275
available to buyer, 187
available to seller, 186
drafting simple contracts, 295
equitable. *See* Equitable remedies
legal remedies. *See* Damages

Requirements contract, 38
Rescission and restitution, 271
Risk of loss, 183
conditional contracts, 183
destination contracts, 185
drafting simple contracts, 302
shipment contracts, 184
Rules of construction, 157

Sale of goods, 177
background, 177
battle of the forms, 180
between merchants, 179
express warranties, 181
goods defined, 177
implied warranties, 182

leases, 179, 189
remedies, 185
risk of loss, 183
warranties, 181
warranty of title, 182
written assurances, 188
Secured transactions
defined, 190
priorities, 195
Security agreement, 192
Security interest, 192
attachment, 192
perfection, 193
requirements to create, 191
Shipment contracts
risk of loss, 184
Signatures
drafting simple contracts, 308
Specific performance, 271
Speculative damages, 267
Statute of Frauds, 146
antenuptial agreement, 149
contracts not to be performed
within one year, 149
executor's promise to pay, 151
legality of. *See* Legality of subject
matter
Stipulation, 310
Supervening illegality, 248
discharge of obligations, 237

Termination
drafting simple contracts, 305
Terminology, 303
Third party contracts, 211
assignment. *See* Assignment
beneficiary contracts, 212
creditor beneficiary contracts, 215
delegation, 226
donee beneficiary
contracts, 218
incidental beneficiaries, 215
intended beneficiaries, 213
promisee, 214
promisor, 214
real party in interest, 215
vested, 215
Time of the essence clauses, 40
Time of performance, 39
Title
Article IX, secured transactions. *See*
Secured transactions
drafting simple contracts, 301

Unilateral contract
  acceptance, 67
  mutuality of consideration, 84
  revocation, 70
Unilateral mistake, 133
Unilateral obligation, 6
Usury, 112

Valid contract, 11
Vested, 215
Void contract, 11
Voidable contract, 11, 115

fraud, 129
  misrepresentation, 129
Voir dire, 310

Waiver, 274
  drafting simple contracts, 302
Warranties
  drafting simple
    contracts, 301
  express, 181
  implied, 182
  title, 182